FULKE'S

ANSWERS TO

STAPLETON, MARTIALL, AND SANDERS.

STAPLETON'S FORTRESS OVERTHROWN.

A REJOINDER TO MARTIALL'S REPLY.

A DISCOVERY OF THE DANGEROUS ROCK OF THE POPISH CHURCH COMMENDED BY SANDERS.

BY

WILLIAM FULKE, D.D.,

MASTER OF PEMBROKE HALL, CAMBRIDGE.

EDITED FOR

The Parker Society,

BY THE

REV. RICHARD GIBBINGS, M.A.,

RECTOR OF RAYMUNTERDONEY, IN THE DIOCESE OF RAPHOE.

WIPF & STOCK · Eugene, Oregon

"HECTOR ROMULIDUM CECIDIT SUB ACHILLE JUELLO.
RHEMENSI HANNIBALI SCIPIO FULCUS ERAT."

Wipf and Stock Publishers
199 W 8th Ave, Suite 3
Eugene, OR 97401

Stapleton's Fortress Overthrown. A Rejoinder to Martiall's Reply.
A Discovery of the Dangerous Rock of the Popish Church
Commended by Sanders.
By Fulke, William
ISBN 13: 978-1-60608-425-0
Publication date 3/02/2009
Previously published by Cambridge University Press, 1848

CONTENTS.

PAGE

ADVERTISEMENT vii

Stapleton's Fortress overthrown 1

A Rejoinder to Martiall's Reply against the Answer of Master Calfhill to the blasphemous Treatise of the Cross . . . 125

A Discovery of the dangerous Rock of the popish Church commended by Sanders 213

ADVERTISEMENT.

The editor has not considered it necessary to cancel the note in page 45, in which, though he correctly attributed *The Defence of the truth* to Bishop Jewel, yet he erred in identifying it with the *Apology*. For his first acquaintance with the tract in question he is indebted to the Rev. Dr. Jelf, whose valuable edition of Bp. Jewel's works was published since this note was written. (See vol. iv. p. 201: v. 62.) The volume sought for is marked in the Bodleian "8°. C. 322. Linc.", and the title-page of the former portion is as follows: "An Apologie of private Masse, spred abroade in writing without name of Authour: as it seemeth, against the offer and protestacion made in certayne Sermons by the reverent father Bisshop of Salsburie: with an answer to the same Apologie, set foorth for the maintenance and defence of the trueth. Perused and allowed by the Reverent father in God, Edmond, Bishop of London, accordyng to the order appointed by the Queenes maiestie."—The title-page of the work in reply, as far as it can now be read, is, "An Answere in defence of the truth. Againste the Apologie of" * * * *. Fulke has given the passage in a compressed form; but Stapleton had cited it at length, and it is thus in the original: "There lacked not gods promisses amonge the Iewes. There lacked not succession of bishops and pristes. There lacked not opinion of great holinesse and austeritie of life. There lacked not great skil and knowledge of the law of god: And yet it is moste evident that they erred; that they refused the trueth; that, under the name and gay shewe of the church, in very deede they persecuted the church. Why shal we not thinke that the like may bee in this time?"

With the foregoing transcript the editor has been favoured by his kind friend the Rev. Dr. Jacobson, Regius Professor of Divinity, Oxford; and the Rev. Joseph Mendham, of Sutton Coldfield, has supplied him with information relative to the *Harborowe* of Bishop Aylmer: p. 37.

Erase the comma after "princely," page 16, l. 33; the crotchets and letter *a*, p. 132, and the second l in "Jewell," note, p. 296.

Page 371, line 6, after "refused," insert [usurped,].

The mistake in Fox, spoken of in p. 98, note 3, has, as the editor understands, been corrected in the recent 8vo. edition.

Sept. 19, 1848.

FULKE'S CONFUTATION

OF

STAPLETON AND MARTIALL.

T. STAPLETON *and Martiall (two Popish* Heretikes) confuted, and of their particular heresies detected.

By. D. Fulke, Master of Pembrooke hall in Cambridge.

Done and directed to all those that loue the truth, and hate superstitious vanities.

Seene and allowed.

AT LONDON,
Printed by Henrie Middleton
for George Bishop.

ANNO. 1580.

A CATALOGUE

OF ALL SUCH POPISH BOOKS, EITHER ANSWERED OR TO BE ANSWERED, WHICH HAVE BEEN WRITTEN IN THE ENGLISH TONGUE FROM BEYOND THE SEAS, OR SECRETLY DISPERSED HERE IN ENGLAND HAVE COME TO OUR HANDS, SINCE THE BEGINNING OF THE QUEEN'S MAJESTY'S REIGN.

---

1. HARDING against the Apology of the English Church, answered by M. Jewel, Bishop of Sarum.

2. Harding against M. Jewel's Challenge, answered by M. Jewel.

3. Harding's Rejoinder to M. Jewel, answered by M. Edward Deering.

4. Cole's quarrels against M. Jewel, answered by M. Jewel.

5. Rastel's Return of untruths[1], answered by M. Jewel.

6. Rastel against M. Jewel's Challenge, answered by William Fulke.

7. Dorman against M. Jewel, answered by M. Nowel.

8. Dorman's Disproof of M. Nowel's Reproof, answered by M. Nowel.

9. The man of Chester[2], answered by M. Pilkington, Bishop of Duresme.

10. Sanders on the Sacrament, in part answered by M. Nowel.

11. Fecknam's Scruples, answered by M. Horne, Bishop of Winchester.

12. Fecknam's Apology, answered by W. Fulke.

13. Fecknam's Objections against M. Gough's Sermon, answered by M. Gough, and M. Lawrence Tomson.

14. Stapleton's Counterblast, answered by M. Bridges.

15. Martiall his Defence of the Cross, answered by M. Caulfehill.

16. Fowler's Psalter, answered by M. Sampson.

17. An infamous libel or letter (*incerto authore*) against the teachers of God's divine Providence and Predestination, answered by Master Robert Crowley.

18. Allen's Defence of Purgatory, answered by W. Fulke.

19. Heskins' Parliament, repealed by W. Fulke.

20. Riston's Challenge, answered by W. Fulke and Oliver Carter.

[1] [Stapleton, and not Rastell, was the author of *A Returne of untruthes upon M. Jewelles Reply*. 4to. Antwerp, 1566.]

[2] [Bp. Pilkington's *Works*, p. 481. ed. Parker Soc.]

21. Hosius Of God's express word, translated into English, answered by W. Fulke.

22. Sander's Rock of the Church, undermined by W. Fulke.

23. Sander's Defence of Images, answered by W. Fulke.

24. Shaclocke's Pearl, answered by M. Hartwell.

25. The Hatchet of Heresies[1], answered by M. Bartlet.

26. Master Evans, answered by himself.

27. A Defence of the private Mass, answered (by conjecture) by M. Cooper, Bishop of Lincoln.

28. Certain assertions tending to maintain the Church of Rome to be the true and Catholic Church, confuted by John Knewstub.

29. Sander upon the Lord's Supper, fully answered by D. Fulke.

30. Bristowe's Motives and Demands, answered by D. Fulke.

31. Stapleton's Differences, and Fortresse of the Faith, answered by D. Fulke.

32. Allen's Defence of Priests' authority to remit sins, and of the popish Church's meaning concerning Indulgences, answered by D. Fulke.

33. Martiall's Reply to M. Calfehill, answered by D. Fulke.

34. Frarin's railing declamation, answered by D. Fulke.

These popish treatises ensuing are in answering. If the Papists know any not here reckoned, let them be brought to light, and they shall be examined.

1. Stapleton's Return of untruths.
2. Rastel's Reply.
3. Vaux his Catechism.
4. Canisius his Catechism translated.

[1] [This was the title given by Shacklock to his translation of a treatise by Cardinal Hosius, *De Hæresibus nostri temporis.* 8vo. Ant. 1565.]

AN OVERTHROW,

BY W. FULKE,

DOCTOR OF DIVINITY, AND MASTER OF PEMBROKE HALL IN CAMBRIDGE,

TO THE FEEBLE FORTRESS OF POPISH FAITH[2], RECEIVED FROM ROME, AND LATELY ADVANCED BY THOMAS STAPLETON, STUDENT IN DIVINITY.

THOMAS STAPLETON, student in divinity, translated the five books of Bede's History of the English Church into the English tongue[3]; before which History it pleased him to set a table of forty-five Differences between the primitive faith of England, continued almost a thousand years, and the late pretended faith of the Protestants: all which we will consider in order.

First are five apostolical marks, found in their preachers, and wanting (as he saith) in ours.

1. Augustin (whom he calleth their Apostle) shewed the token of his Apostleship in all patience, signs and wonders. Beda, Lib. i. C. xxx. & xxxi. L. ii. C. ii. Miracles, in confirmation of their doctrine, Protestants have yet wrought none.

I answer, Peter, Paul, Matthew, James, John, &c. are Apostles to us, sent not from Gregory of Rome, but by Christ Himself out of Jewry; the sign of whose Apostleship being shewed "in all patience, signs and wonders[4]," and our doctrine being the same which we have received of their writings, needeth no other confirmation of miracles to be wrought by us. If Augustin, sent from Gregory a man, have planted any human traditions, and confirmed them by lying signs and miracles, as a forerunner of Antichrist, which was even immediately after his time to be openly shewed; or if by

[2] [The name, "*A Fortresse of the Faith,*" was probably derived from the *Fortalitium Fidei* of Alphonsus de Spina. Vid. Moshemii *Instt. Hist. Eccles.* Sæc. xv. Par. ii. p. 634. Helmst. 1755.]

[3] [Antwerp, 1565. A copy is in the Lambeth library.]

[4] [2 Cor. xii. 12.]

subtle practice miracles have been feigned to have been done by him, and reported by a credulous man Bede, it hurteth not our cause; seeing other writers[1] report him to have been both a proud and a cruel man. And yet we receive all that doctrine which he taught, agreeable to the doctrine of the Apostles of Christ: whatsoever he taught beside, we are not to receive it of an Angel from heaven, much less of Augustin from Rome.

2. Their Apostles tendered unity, labouring to reduce the Britons to the unity of Christ's Church. Nothing is more notorious in Protestants than their infamous dissension.

Augustin indeed laboured to bring the Britons in subjection to himself and to the Church of Rome; which argueth no desire of christian unity, but savoureth of antichristian ambition and tyranny, as his cruel threatening executed upon them did shew sufficiently[2].

The dissension of the Protestants is not in articles of faith; nor such but that they are all brethren, that unfeignedly profess the doctrine of salvation; although they dissent in the matter of the Sacrament, in orders, rites and ceremonies.

3. Their Apostles were sent by an ordinary vocation. Protestants have preached without vocation or sending at all, such as the Church of Christ requireth.

They were sent by Pope Gregory, who had none ordinary authority to send Apostles or preachers into foreign countries. Wherefore, if they had any sending, it was extraordinary; of charity, and not of office. The Protestants that first preached in these last days had likewise extraordinary calling. But if the calling of the Papists may be counted a lawful calling, they were called of the popish Church to be preachers and teachers, before they knew or preached the truth of the Gospel.

4. Their preaching was of God by Gamaliel's reason[3], because their doctrine continued nine hundred years; whereas the Protes-

[1] Gal. Mon. [Geoffrey of Monmouth, "whose Welsh blood was up, as concerned in the cause of his countrymen." (Fuller's *Church Hist. of Britain*, Cent. vii. p. 63. Lond. 1655.)]

[2] [Bede distinctly states that Augustin died long before the massacre of the Monks of Bangor. See Calfhill, p. 306. ed. Parker Soc.]

[3] [Acts v. 39.]

tants' faith is already changed from Lutheran to Sacramentary in less than twenty years.

This reason of Gamaliel would prove Mahomet's enterprise to be of God, because it hath likewise continued nine hundred years: and yet it is false that the popish faith hath had so long continuance. For the Papists are departed, as from many other points of doctrine, so even from that of the Lord's Supper, which Augustin planted among the Saxons, unto carnal presence and Transubstantiation; the contrary of which were taught by Augustin, as appeareth by the public Saxon Homily, lately[4] translated into English and imprinted. The diversity of opinions concerning the Sacrament maketh no alteration of faith in them that agree in all other necessary articles. Besides that, it is most false which he saith, that Luther of the Protestants is counted a very Papist.

5. Their Apostles taught such a faith as putteth things, by the belief and practice whereof we may be saved. The faith of the Protestants is a denial of popish faith, and hath no affirmative doctrine but that which Papists had before.

The Protestants' faith affirmeth, that a man is justified by it only; that the sacrifice of Christ's death is our only propitiatory sacrifice; that Christ is our only Mediator of redemption and intercession, &c. Generally, it affirmeth whatsoever the Scripture teacheth, and denieth the contrary.

Then follow thirty-nine Differences in doctrine.

6. Their Apostles said Mass, which the Protestants abhor.

The popish Mass was not then all made; therefore they could not say it. They ministered the Communion, which Bede and other writers called *Missa:* they said no private Mass, such as the Papists now defend.

7. In the Mass is an external sacrifice offered to God the Father, the blessed body and blood of Christ Himself. Lib. v. Cap. xxii., this

[4] [Viz. in 1567, under the patronage of Archbishop Parker. The original volume is without date, but the year of its publication can be discovered by the names of the Prelates who attested the genuineness of the work. L'Isle's second edition of the Homily appeared in 1623; and in 1638 the first two leaves of this impression were changed, and a fictitious reprint was issued with the title, "Divers ancient Monuments," &c.]

doctrine is expressly reported. This seemeth blasphemy to the Protestants.

The words of Bede, according to M. Stapleton's own translation, are these, out of the Epistle of Ceolfride to Naitan King of the Picts: "All Christian Churches throughout the whole world (which all joined together make but one Catholic Church) should prepare bread and wine for the mystery of the flesh and precious blood of that immaculate Lamb, which took away the sins of the world; and when all lessons, prayers, rites and ceremonies used in the solemn feast of Easter were done, should offer the same to God the Father, in hope of their redemption to come." Here is no sacrifice of the body and blood of Christ, but of bread and wine for the mystery thereof; no sacrifice propitiatory for sins, but of thanksgiving, and remembrance of the propitiation made by the Lamb Himself, in hope of eternal redemption; no oblation by the Priest only, but by the whole Church and every member thereof, as was the oblation of the paschal lamb, whereunto he compareth this sacrifice, interpreting those words of Exod. xii.: "Every man shall take a lamb according to their families and households, and offer him in sacrifice at the evening." That is to say, (saith Ceolfride,) All Christian Churches, &c. as before. By which words it is manifest, that the Papists now-a-days are departed even from that faith of the Sacrament and sacrifice thereof that Augustin brought from Rome.

8. This sacrifice is taught to be propitiatory, Lib. iv. C. xxii.; which Protestants abhor.

There is no mention of propitiatory sacrifice in that chapter, but there is told a tale of a prisoner, that was loosed from his bonds so oft as his brother, which was a Priest, said Mass for his soul, supposing he had been slain in battle; by which many were persuaded, that the wholesome blessed sacrifice was effectuous to the everlasting redemption and ransoming both of soul and body. So were they worthy to be deceived, that would build a doctrine, without the word of God, upon the uncertain report of men; who either devised this tale as being false, or else, if it were so, could not discern the illusions of Satan, seeking to maintain an error contrary to the glory of Christ.

9. Confession of sins made to the Priest, Lib. iv. Cap. xxv. & xxvii. This Sacrament of the Protestants is abolished.

In neither of these chapters is mentioned the popish Auricular Confession, as a Sacrament necessary to salvation. In the twenty-fifth mention is made of one, which, being troubled with conscience of an heinous sin, came to a learned Priest to ask counsel of remedy, and shewed what his offence was. In the twenty-seventh chapter it is expressly said, that all the people did openly declare unto S. Cuthbert in Confession the things that they had done. Such Confession as either of both these were, the Protestants have not abolished, although they number not Confession among the Sacraments.

10. Satisfaction and Penance for sin enjoined appeareth, Lib. iv. Cap. xxv.; which the Protestants' court admitteth not.

There is no word of Satisfaction for his sins, but of fasting and prayers, as fruits of repentance, whereunto he was first exhorted by the Priest, according to his power and ability; but he, not content herewith, urged the Priest to appoint him a certain time of fasting for a whole week together: to whose infirmity the Priest somewhat yielding, willed him to fast two or three days in a week, until he returned to give him farther advice. Every man may see a broad difference betwixt this counsel and popish Satisfaction and Penance.

11. Merit of good works in this story is eftsoones[1] justified, Lib. iv. Cap. xiv. & xv.; which the Protestants count prejudicial to God's glory.

In the fourteenth chapter there is no mention of the merit of good works, but that after the brethren had fasted and prayed, God delivered them of the pestilence. We never denied but that God regardeth our prayer and fasting, though not as meritorious, but as our obedience which He requireth of us, and saveth us only for His mercy sake. The fifteenth chapter scarce toucheth any matter of religion; and therefore I know not what he meaneth to quote it, except it be an error of the printer[2].

[1] [often, ever and anon.]

[2] ["Not presuming to alter any of Stapleton's words, take it with all the printer's faults, done probably by an outlandish press." (Fuller, Cent. v. p. 29.) However, it is certain that the MSS. vary in the numbers prefixed to some of the chapters.]

12. Intercession of Saints Protestants abhor; the practice whereof appeareth, Lib. i. Cap. xx. & Lib. iv. Cap. xiv.

In the former place Beda supposeth, that God gave the Britons victory at the intercession of S. Alban; but where learned he this kind of intercession out of the holy Scriptures?

In the latter place a boy being sick of the plague reporteth, that God would cease the plague at the intercession of S. Oswald, as the Apostles Peter and Paul declared to him in a vision. But seeing the Apostles have taught no such doctrine in their writings, they have admonished us to beware of such fantastical visions. Gal. i.; 2 Thessa. ii.

13. The Clergy of their primitive Church, after holy orders taken, do not marry, Lib. i. Cap. xxvii. Now, after holy orders and vow to the contrary, Priests do marry.

The counsel of Gregory to Augustin is this: "If there be any among the Clergy out of holy orders which cannot live chaste, they shall take wives." These words command some of the Clergy to take wives; they forbid not the rest to marry. For what shall they that are in holy orders do, if they cannot live chaste? Again, the histories are plentiful, that Priests were married in England three or four hundred years after Augustin.

14. In their primitive Church the vow of chastity was thought godly and practised. Now they are counted damnable and broken.

Such vows as were made without consideration of men's ability to perform them are justly accounted rash and presumptuous. Such is the vow of virginity in a great many, which our Saviour Christ affirmeth to be a rare gift, not in every man's power. As for the vow of chastity, if any were made by popish Priests, it was oftener broken before the restoring of true knowledge than since; whose incontinency hath infected the world with whoredom and uncleanness.

15. Such Monks and Virgins lived in cloisters, in obedience and poverty; which are overthrown of Protestants as a damnable estate.

The horrible abuse of cloisteral life hath caused the subversion of them, beside their errors, superstition and idolatry.

16. Prayer for the dead, *Dirige* over night, and *Requiem* Mass in the morning, was an accustomed manner, Lib. iii. Cap. ii. Lib. iv. Cap. xxi.; which the Protestants count to be abomination.

Prayer for the dead is an older error than popish Religion. But *Dirige* and *Requiem* Mass had another meaning, Lib. iii. Cap. ii., than the Papists have now; for there it is said: "In the self-same place the religious men of Hagustalden[1] church have now of long time been accustomed to come every year, the eve and the day that the same King Oswald was afterward slain, to keep *Diriges* there for his soul; and in the morning, after Psalms being said solemnly, to offer for him the sacrifice of holy oblation." You must understand, that this Oswald was of them that so did taken for an holy Martyr; and therefore these psalmodies and sacrifices were of thanksgiving for the rest of his soul, not of propitiation for his sins, as the Papists account them. Lib. iv. Cap. xxi., there is nothing to the matter in hand; but in the next chapter following is the tale of him that was loosed from his fetters by saying of Mass; by the relation whereof, and not by the word of God, many began to think the sacrifice of the Mass profitable for the dead.

17. Reservation of the Sacrament thought no superstition, Lib. iv. Cap. xxiv. Now counted profanation of the Sacrament.

Reservation was an older error than Popery; yet contrary to the commandment of Christ, "Take ye, and eat ye."

18. Houseling[2] before death used as necessary for all true Christians, Lib. iv. Cap. iii. & xxiv. Protestants, under pretence of a Communion, do now wickedly bereave Christian folk of it.

These chapters shew that it was used, but not that it was used as necessary. The Communion of the sick is also used of us. Neither can M. Stapleton prove, that it was then ministered to the sick person alone, as is used among them. But in the twenty-fourth chapter of the fourth book it may be gathered, that as many as were present with the party received with him, because there was a mutual demand of his being in charity with them, and they with him.

19. Consecrating of Monks and Nuns by the hands of the Bishop

[1] [Hexham.]

[2] [Receiving the Sacrament of the Lord's Supper.]

a practised solemnity in their primitive Church, Lib. iv. Cap. xix. & xxiii.; which Protestants, by the liberty of their Gospel, laugh and scorn at.

Chap. xix., it is said, that Wilfride gave to Ethelrede the vail and habit of a Nun; and Cap. xxiii., that one Hein [Heiu] took the vow and habit of a Nun, being blessed and consecrated by Bishop Aidan. In those elder times no virgin was suffered to profess virginity but by the judgment of the Bishop; who was not only a minister of the ceremony of profession, but also a judge of the expedience and lawfulness of the vow; so that the vow of virginity was moderated, and kept within more tolerable bounds than is used of the Papists.

20. Commemoration of Saints at Mass time, Lib. iv. Cap. xiv. & xviii. Such commemorations in the Protestants' Communion are excluded as superstitious and unlawful.

Chap. xiv., it is said, upon the report of a boy's vision, "And therefore let them say Masses, and give thanks that their prayer is heard, and also for the memory of the same King Oswald, which sometime governed their nation." Admitting this vision to be true, here is but Mass and memory of thanksgiving. In the eighteenth chapter is nothing to any such purpose. In the Communion of our Church is a thanksgiving with Angels, Archangels, and all the glorious company of heaven, although we make no special mention of any one Saint by name.

21. Pilgrimage to holy places, especially to Rome, a much weighty matter of all estates, Lib. iv. Cap. iii. & xxiii. & Lib. v. Cap. vii. Nothing soundeth more profane and barbarous in the ears of Protestants.

In the first of these places there is mention of pilgrimage into Ireland, not for the holiness of the place, but for the wholesome instruction that then was there. For it seemeth by the story in many places, that Ireland (although not subject to the see of Rome) was then replenished with godly learned men, of whom men sought out of Britain to be informed in Religion. Peregrination to Rome was used of superstition, and opinion of great learning to be had from thence. Yet was there no pilgrimage to Images, nor to Rome, so filthy a sink of all abominations as it hath been since those days.

22. Of the Reliques of holy men, of reverence used towards them, and miracles wrought by them, the history is full. Nothing is more vile in the sight of Protestants than such devotion of Christians.

Such superstition and credulity of the former age is justly misliked of us; but the idolatry and forging of Reliques, which is too common among the Papists, is rightly detested of us.

23. Blessing with the sign of the Cross, accounted no superstition, Lib. iv. Cap. xxiv. & Lib. v. Cap. ii., in the devotion of the Protestants is esteemed magic.

Signing with the sign of the Cross, which sometime against the Gentiles was an indifferent ceremony, used of the Papists for an ordinary form of blessing is both superstitious and idolatrous.

24. Solemnity of burial Protestants despise; whereas it was the devotion of their primitive Church to be buried in monasteries, churches and chapels.

Honourable burial of the Saints' bodies, which were the temples of the Holy Ghost, and are laid up in hope of a glorious resurrection, Protestants despise not. Yet were the first Archbishops of Canterbury buried in a porch beside the church, Lib. ii. Cap. iii. There was no burial-place appointed in the monastery of Berking until by a light it was revealed, as the history saith, Lib. iv. Cap. vii.; but with time superstition of burial grew; yet nothing comparable in that age to the superstition of Papists of these latter times. There was no burial in S. Francis' cowl, nor after the popish solemnity.

25. Benediction of the Bishop, as superior to the people, was used; which Protestants scorn at. Lib. iv. Cap. xi.

The Protestants allow benediction of the Bishop in the name of God, as the superior, although they justly deride the popish manner of blessing by cutting the air with Crosses; neither is there any such blessing spoken of in the chapter by him cited.

26. The service of the Church was, at the first planting of their faith, in the Latin and learned tongue, Lib. i. Cap. xxix. Lib. iv. Cap. xviii.; which the Protestants have altered.

There is no such thing to be proved in the first place, nor any thing sounding that way but only this, that Gregory sent into England to Augustin many books, of which it is a popish consequence to gather, that they were books of Latin service. In the latter it is declared, that John the Chanter of Rome brought from thence the order of singing and reading; and put many things in writing which pertained to the celebration of high feasts and holydays for the whole compass of the year. But this being almost an hundreth years after the coming of Augustin, it appeareth the Church of England had no such Latin service before. For Gregory willed Augustin to gather out of every Church what ceremonies he thought expedient for the English Church, and bound him not to the orders or service of the Church of Rome. And it may be gathered, that long after there was no certain form of administration of the Sacraments put in writing and generally received; but that the Priests, which then were learned, ordered the same according to their discretion; for their chief labour was in preaching and instructing. For Beda reporteth, upon the credit of one which lived in his time, and was Abbot of Wye, Herebald by name, that he being in great extremity and danger of death, by falling from an horse, S. John of Beverley, the Bishop that was his master, asked him whether he knew without all scruple or doubt that he was baptized or no. To whom he answered, that he certainly knew that he was baptized, and told the Priest's name that baptized him. To whom the Bishop replied, saying, "If you were baptized of him, doubtless you were not well baptized; for I know him well, and am right well assured, that when he was made Priest he could not, for his dull-headed wit, learn neither to instruct nor to baptize. And for that cause I have straitly charged him, not to presume to that ministry which he could not do accordingly." By this it may be gathered, that the form of Baptism was not set down in writing, which every dull-headed dogbolt Priest can read; but that it was referred to the learning of the Minister, which did instruct them that were of age, and came to receive Baptism. But this ignorant Priest, whom S. John of Beverley deprived of his ministry, could neither catechise nor baptize: for which cause the young man being catechised again, and after he recovered of his fall, was baptized anew, as one that was not rightly baptized before. Moreover, Lib. iv. Cap. xxiv., Beda sheweth of one Cednom, in the abbey of Hilda, to whom was given miraculously the gift of singing and making hymns for religion in his mother tongue, of the creation of the world, and all histories of the Old Testament, of the incarnation, passion, resurrection, and ascension of Christ, &c., which by all likelihood were used in the churches. And when Latin service was first used, it is not incredible but that the people did meetly well understand it; for the Latin tongue was in those days understood in most places of the western Church: and Beda noteth some especially, which understood no language but the Saxon. The interpreters which Augustin brought out of France do confirm this conjecture. For the rude Latin tongue spoken in France was better understood of the vulgar people than that was spoken at Rome and in Italy: for which cause there was a Canon made in the third Council at Tours[1], that the Homilies should be turned *in rusticam Romanam linguam*, "into the rude Latin tongue," that they might more easily be understood of all men. Again, the Britons and Picts, which converted the greatest part of the Saxons, how could they have been understood preaching in Welsh, but that the vulgar Latin tongue was a common language to them both? Finally, the manifold uses of divers churches, as Sarum, York, &c., declare, that the Latin service was but lately in comparison set down, when knowledge decayed both in the Priests and the people.

27. Protestants have plucked down altars, which they had of old time.

They had altars, but standing in the midst of the church, as the tables stood in the primitive Church.

28. Altar-cloths and vestments, used of them, Protestants admit not.

A sorry ceremony, in which no part of Christianity consisteth. The like I say of the 29, holy vessels, 30, holy water, and 31, ecclesiastical censure, about which there was no small ado.

32. Their primitive Church was governed by Synods of the Clergy only, in determining controversies of religion, which Protestants have called from thence unto the lay court only.

[1] [Cap. xvii. apud Crabbe *Concill.* Tom. ii. p. 620. Colon. Agripp. 1551.]

The latter part is a slander upon the Protestants, the former part a lie upon the ancient Saxons; for at the Synod holden at Strenshalch [Strenaeshalch] not only the Kings Oswine and Alfride were present, but also King Oswine did order the Synod, and in the end concluded the matter in controversy. Lib. iii. Cap. xxv.

Viz. Whitby in Yorkshire.

33. The spiritual rulers of the primitive Church were Bishops and Pastors duly consecrated. Protestants have no consecration, no true Bishop at all.

This is another lewd slander against the Protestants; for they have true Bishops, though not consecrated after the popish manner. Laurence, the second Archbishop of Canterbury, acknowledgeth the Ministers of the Scots and Britons for Bishops, although they were not subject to the Church and see of Rome. Lib. ii. Cap. iv. Aidanus, Finanus, Colmanus are judged of Beda for true Bishops, although they were divided from the Church of Rome: and so are such Bishops as were ordained by them; for they converted the greatest part of the Saxons unto Christian faith, as Northumbrians, Mercians, and East Saxons.

34. Protestants have brought the supreme government of the Church to the lay authority. In the primitive faith of our country the lay was subject to the Bishop in spiritual causes.

And so are they now in such causes as they were subject then. But that the supreme authority was in the civil Magistrate at that time, it may appear by these reasons. First, Pope Gregory himself calleth the Emperor Mauritius his sovereign lord, Lib. i. Cap. xxiii. & xxviii. & xxix. & xxx.; and after him Pope Honorius called Heraclius his sovereign lord, Lib. ii. xviii. King Sonwalch preferred Agilbert and Wini to be Bishops: afterward he deposed Wini, which for money bought of Wulfher King of Mercia the see of London. Lib. iii. Cap. vii.

Earcombert King of Kent, of his princely, authority, purged his realm of idolatry, and commanded that the fast of forty days should be kept. Lib. iii. Cap. viii.

King Oswine ordered the Synod at Strenshalch. Lib. iii. Cap. xxv. Oswine and Egbert, Kings, deliberate touching the peaceable government of the Church; and, by the choice and consent of the Clergy, did nominate Wighard Archbishop of Canterbury. Lib. iii. Cap. xxix.

King Ecgfride deposed Bishop Wilfride. Li. iv. Ca. xii. Ostfor, [*al.* Oftfor,] at the commandment of King Edilred, was consecrated by Wilfrid, Bishop of the Victians. Li. iv. Ca. xxiii. These places of the history shew, that Kings had chief authority both over persons and causes ecclesiastical, such as we now acknowledge our Princes to have.

35. The final determination of spiritual causes rested in the see Apostolic of Rome, which is now detested of Protestants.

Although the see of Rome usurped much in those days, yet was not the authority thereof acknowledged by the Churches of the Britons, Irish and Scots. The Britons before Augustin's time sent not to Rome, but unto France, for aid against the Pelagian heretics. At Augustin's coming, and long after, they refused to yield obedience to the see of Rome: yea, among the Saxons themselves, Wilfrid, deposed by the King, and absolved by the Pope, could not be restored but by a Synod of his own country. Li. v. C. xx.

36. Their faith and Apostles came from the see of Rome. The Protestant departeth therefro.

The Protestants are returned to the ancient faith, which was in this land before Augustin came from Rome; which did not so much good in planting faith where it was not, as in corrupting the sincerity of faith where it was before he came.

37. Their faith was first preached with Cross[1] and procession. Heresies first raged by throwing down the Cross, and altering the procession therewith.

The popish faith began with superstition, which the Christian Catholics have justly abolished.

38. Their first Apostles were Monks. The first preachers of the Protestants have been apostataes, as Luther, Œcolampadius, Martyr, &c.

Nay, they have returned from apostasy to the true faith and religion of Christ. Augustin and the rest of the Monks of that time differed much from the popish Monks of the latter days. For they were learned preachers, Lib. iii.

[1] ["'Tis very true indeed, that there is not the least intimation in Bede that they worshipped it." (Manning's *England's Conversion and Reformation compared*, p. 122. Antw. 1725.)]

Cap. xxvi; these idle loiterers: they laboured with their hands, Lib. v. Cap. xix; these lived of the sweat of other men's brows. They made no such vow, but they might serve the Commonwealth if they were called thereto: Sigbard [Sighard] of a Monk was made King, Lib. iv. Cap. xi.: these professed themselves dead to all honest travail, either in the Church or Commonwealth.

39. The first imps[1] of their faith, and scholars of the Apostles, were holy men. Luther confesseth his scholars to be worse than they were under the Pope[2].

There were hypocrites in those days; also there were incontinent Nuns. Lib. iv. Cap. xxv. And Beda confesseth, that Aidane (which was no slave of the Romish see) was more holy than the Clergy of his time, whose devotion was key cold. If Luther flattered not his scholars, he is more to be commended; yet cannot Stapleton prove, that he speaketh so of all, but of some carnal professors only.

40. Their first preacher lived Apostolically in voluntary poverty. This Apostolical perfection Protestants, that bear themselves for the Apostles of England, neither practise themselves, nor can abide in other.

First, it is a slander, that any Protestants bear themselves for Apostles of England. Secondly, let the world judge whether the preachers of the Gospel come nearer to the poverty of the Apostles than the Pope, their great Apostle of the Romish Church, with the rest of the pillars of the same, the Cardinals, &c.

[1] [The word "imp" was formerly taken in a good sense, and signified offspring.]

[2] [Staphylus, from whom, as there is abundant reason for believing, Stapleton derived this accusation against Luther's followers, refers for his authority to the "Postilla magna" upon the Gospel for the first Sunday in Advent. (*Apologia*, edit. Lat. 2. *De vero Scripturæ sacræ intellectu*, fol. 47. Colon. 1562.) The *Kirchen-Postilla*, or *Postilla Ecclesiastica*, was valued by Luther above most of his other writings, and must not be confounded with his *Hus-Postilla*, or *Postilla Domestica*, a work of inferior moment. (Cf. Jo. Alb. Fabricii *Centifolium Lutheranum*, pp. 297, 299. Hamb. 1728. & Joan. Fabric. *Hist. Bibl. Fabr.* Par. ii. pp. 232—3. Wolfenb. 1718.) Of the first part of the former treatise the editor has before him copies of the earliest editions, Argentor. et Basil. 1521; and in neither of these can the acknowledgment in question be discovered.]

41. Their faith builded up monasteries and churches. Protestants have thrown down many, erected none.

The first monasteries were colleges of learned preachers, and builded for that end. King Edilwald builded a monastery, wherein he and his people might resort to hear the word of God, to pray, and to bury their dead. Lib. iii. Cap. xxiii. The like practice was in the abbey of Hilda. Lib. iv. Ca. xxiii. From which use seeing they were of late degenerated into idleness and filthy lusts, they were lawfully suppressed. And as for building of churches where they lack, Protestants have and do employ their endeavour.

42. By the first Christians of their faith God was served day and night. Protestants have abolished all service of God by night, and done to the Devil a most acceptable sacrifice.

Protestants have abolished no service of God by night, but such as was either impious or superstitious; for they also serve God both day and night, even with public prayer, and exercise of hearing the word of God preached.

43. By the devotion of the people first embracing their faith much voluntary oblations were made to the Church. By the reckless religion of the Protestants due oblations are denied to the Church.

Of them that be true professors of the Gospel both due oblations are paid, and much voluntary oblations also, for the maintenance of the preachers, for relief of the poor, the strangers and captives, &c.

44. Princes endued the Church with possessions and revenues. The lewd looseness of the Protestants hath stirred Princes to take from the Church's possessions so given.

Nay, the pride, covetousness, and luxuriousness of popish Clergy have moved them to do that is done in that behalf.

45. Last of all, their faith reduced the Scottish men living in schism to the unity of the Catholic Church. This late alteration hath moved them from unity to schism.

Nay, their superstition at length corrupted the sincerity of faith in the Britons and Scots; and from the unity of the Catholic Church of Christ, brought them under the schismatical faction of the see of Rome; from which they are now again returned with us, God be thanked, to the unity of Christ's true Catholic and Apostolic Church.

These Differences, which he hath either falsely observed, or else craftily collected out of the dross and dregs of that time, he promiseth to prove to concur with the belief and practice of the first six hundred years in the second part of his feeble Fortress; which is easily blown over with one word. Although some of these corruptions have been received within the first six hundred years, yet is he not able to prove that they have been from the beginning, and so continued all that time. Wherefore his Fortress will do them small pleasure, to establish them for Christian truths, which have had a later beginning than our Saviour Christ and His Apostles.

But forasmuch as he hath gathered Differences of the first Church of the Saxons from ours, I have also gathered Differences of the same from theirs at this time; and let the readers judge of both indifferently.

1. The Church of English Saxons, for three hundred years after Augustin, did believe bread and wine to remain in the Sacrament after consecration, which the Papists deny: proved by a Sermon extant in the Saxon tongue, translated out of Latin[1] by Ælfrike, Archbishop of Canterbury, or Abbot of S. Albone's[2], appointed to be read unto the people at Easter before they received the Communion; also by two Epistles of the same Ælfrike[3].

2. The Church of English Saxons believed the Sacrament to be the body and blood of Christ, not carnally, but spiritually; expressly denying as well the carnal presence as Transubstantiation, which the Papists hold. Ælf. Serm. Pasc. & Ep.

3. The Church of English Saxons did give the Communion under both kinds unto the people, which the Papists do not. Ælf. Serm. Pasc. & Beda, Lib. i. Cap. xxvii. & Lib. v. Cap. xxii.

[1] [Very many passages were directly translated from the famous book of Ratramn. See Ussher's *Answer to a Challenge*, pp. 54—56. Lond. 1686. The parallelism has been still more accurately shewn by Hopkins, in the Dissertation prefixed to his English version of Ratramnus, pp. 40—51. Lond. 1688.]

[2] [Vid. Whartoni Dissert. de duobus Ælfricis: *Anglia Sacra*, Tom. i. pag. 125, seqq. Archbishop Nicolson's *Correspondence*, Vol. i. p. 19. Soames's *Anglo-Saxon Church*, pp. 219—22, 237—8. Lond. 1838.]

[3] [Published, so far as concerns "the sacramentall bread & wyne," by Archbishop Parker, with the Saxon Homily.]

4. The Priests of that time said no private Mass on working-days, but only on holy-days, which therefore were called Mass-days. Ælfr. Ser. Pasc. Popish Priests every day.

5. The people did then communicate with the Priest. Beda, Lib. ii. Cap. v. The popish Priest eateth and drinketh all alone.

6. The English Saxon Church did celebrate Easter with the old Jews in one faith, although they differ from them in the kind of external Sacraments: whereby they affirmed the substance of the Sacraments of both the Testaments to be all one, which the Papists deny. Ælfr. Serm. Pasc. & Epist. Bed. Lib. v. Ca. xxii.

7. The Sacrament of the Lord's Supper was not then hanged up to be worshipped, nor carried in procession, because they had not the opinion of carnal presence which the Papists have, &c.

8. The English Saxons' Church denied that wicked men received the body and blood of Christ. Ælfr. Serm. Pasc. The Papists hold, that not only wicked men, but also brute beasts eat the body of Christ, if they eat the external Sacrament thereof[4].

[4] ["Si corpus Domini a muribus vel araneis consumptum ad nihilum devenerit, sive multum corrosum fuerit, si integre vermis in eo inventus fuerit, comburatur. Si sine horrore residuum prædicto modo corrosum sumi poterit, tutius est ut sumatur." (*Cautele Misse,* in *Missal. ad sacros. Rom. eccles. vsum,* fol. cxii. Paris. 1529.) In the instructions "De defectibus in celeb. Missarum occurrentibus," prefixed to the Roman Missal published by the command of Pope Pius V., there is a remarkable section, "Si Hostia," which provides for the disappearance of the consecrated Host, in the event of it having been taken "a mure vel alio animali:" but in the modern Missals, sanctioned by Popes Clement VIII. and Urban VIII., all mention of the mouse, and of its capture, death and burning, is omitted.—"Quid ergo sumit mus, vel quid manducat?" asks Peter Lombard; (*Sententt.* Lib. iv. Dist. xiii.) and he answers, "Deus novit hoc." However, the Master of the Sentences is condemned for having taught, "quod brutum *non* sumit verum corpus Christi, etsi videatur;" (See his "Errores" annexed to the Paris edition, 1553. fol. 418.) and Pope Gregory XI. excommunicated those who should maintain the same opinion. Vid. Eymerici *Directorium Inquisitorum,* pp. 33, 197. Romæ, 1578. Cosin's *Hist. of Transub.* pp. 102, 152. Lond. 1676. Jewel's *Reply to Harding's Answer,* Art. xxiii. Innocent. Pap. III. *De sacro Altaris myster.* Lib.

9. The English Saxons allowed the Scriptures to be read of the people in the Saxon tongue; whereof Canutus made a law, that all Christian men should diligently search the law of God[1]. The Papists deny the search of God's law to all Christian men, that are not of the Clergy, or learned in the Latin tongue.

10. The English Saxons decreed in Synod, after Latin service prevailed, and the knowledge of Latin decayed, that the Priests should say unto the people on Sundays and holy-days the interpretation of that Gospel in English; Ælfr. Lib. Can.[2]; which the Papists neither do nor will suffer to be done.

11. The English Saxons commanded, that all men should be instructed by the Priests to say the Lord's Prayer, the Creed, and the Ten Commandments in the English tongue; Will. Mal. Li. i. de part. [Pont[3].] Ælfr. in Lib. Can. Canut. in Leg.; which the Papists have taught to be heretical.

12. The English Saxons decreed in Synod, and King Canutus made a law, that the Priests should instruct the people in the understanding of the Lord's Prayer, the Creed, &c. *ubi supra;* which the Papists altogether neglect, affirming ignorance to be the mother of devotion[4].

iv. Cap. xi. fol. 58. Lipsiæ, 1534. Waldens. *Doct. ant. Fid.* Tom. ii. C. 46. f. 80. Venet. 1571. Gab. Biel *Sac. Can. Miss. Exposit.* Lect. lxxxviii. fol. 266. Basil. 1510. *Canones Penitent.* Casus quadrages. Lips. 1516. Boxhornius, *De Harmon. Euchar.* p. 214. Lugd. Bat. 1595. Gavanti *Thesaur. sac. Rit.* T. ii. p. 8. Venet. 1823. Wilkins, i. 139. Gage's *Survey of the West Indies*, pp. 446—9. edit. 4. Lond. 8vo.]

1 [See the laws of Canute in Lambard's Ἀρχαιονομία, p. 105. ed. Wheloc. Cantab. 1644.]

2 [The decree is to be found in the twenty-third Canon of Ælfric to Wulfinus, annexed by Whelock to Lambard's book. Ussher, when using this testimony, and referring to this sentence in Fulke, has three times adduced a single passage, in consequence of his not having been aware that Ælfric's "Epistola ad Clericos," "Epistola Anglo-Saxonica," and "Liber Canonum" are one and the same work. (*De Scripturis et Sacris vernaculis*, pp. 128—9. Conf. Whartoni *Auctarium*, p. 377. Lond. 1690.)]

3 [Guil. Malmesburiensis, Lib. i. *De gestis Pontiff. Angl.* p. 112. edit. Savil. Lond. 1596. cit. Usser. in *Hist. Dogmat.* p. 197.]

4 [See Bp. Jewel's *Works*, Part i. p. 57. ed. Parker Soc.; the xxviith Article of his *Reply to Harding's Answer;* and the *Zurich Letters*, first series, p. 15. Cambr. 1842.]

13. The worshipping of Images, and the second Council of Nice that decreed the same, was accursed of the Church of God in England and France, and written against by Alcuinus[5] in the name of the Church of England and France. Math. West[6]. Symeon Dunel[7]. Rog. Houed[8]. &c. The Papists defend both that idolatrous Council, and their wicked Decree.

14. The Priests in the primitive Saxon Church were married for three or four hundred years; witness all histories of England; which the Papists do not allow.

15. The vow of chastity was not exacted of them that were made Priests, for the space of more than four hundred years after the arrival of Augustin into Kent; which Decree was made by Lanfrancus in a Synod at Winchester, anno 1076[9].

16. Notwithstanding this Decree and many other, both Priests refused to make that vow, and kept their wives by the King's leave. Gerard. Ebor. Ep. ad Anselm.[10] Histor. Petroburg[11]. Papists permit neither of both.

17. Lanfrancus decreed, that such Priests as had wives should not be compelled to put them away. The Papists enforce Priests to put away their wives.

18. The Popes that were founders of the English Saxon Church acknowledged the Emperors to be their sovereign lords. Bed. Li. i. Cap. xxiii. Lib. ii. Cap. xviii.

5 [Who is supposed to have written the Caroline Books, A.D. 790. These were published by Du Tillet in 1549.]

6 [*Flores Histor.* p. 146. Francof. 1601.]

7 [*De Regibus Anglorum*, apud Twysdenum, *S. R. A.* p. 111. Lond. 1652.]

8 [*Annall.* P. i. *Rer. Angl. Scriptt.* p. 405. Francof. 1601. See Soames's *Bampton Lectures*, pp. 170—1. Oxford, 1830.]

9 ["Nullus Canonicus uxorem habeat. Sacerdotum vero in castellis vel in vicis habitantium, habentes uxores non cogantur ut dimittant; non habentes interdicantur ut habeant." (*Concill.* x. 351. ed. Labb. et Coss.) It was natural that Labbe should say of this Synod, "plerisque suspecta est." (*Concill. Histor. Synops.* pag. 158. Lut. Paris. 1661.]

10 [See the extract from the letter of Gerard, Abp. of York, in Fox. ii. 403. Lond. 1684.]

11 [The testimony of the author of the Saxon History of Peterborough may be found in Sir Henry Spelman's *Councils*, Tom. ii. p. 36. Compare Wharton's *Treatise of the Celibacy of the Clergy*, p. 160. Lond. 1688.]

19. Pope Honorius took order, that the Archbishop of Canterbury might be consecrated in England, without travelling to Rome. Bed. L. ii. Ca. xviii. The latter Popes denied this.

20. Pope Gregory exhorteth King Ethelbert to set forth the faith of Christ to his subjects, to forbid the worship of Idols, &c. Bed. Lib. i. Cap. xxxii. The Papists would not have the civil Magistrate govern in ecclesiastical causes.

21. And lest you should say, (as M. Sander doth,) that the King was herein the Bishop's Commissary, Earcombert, King of Kent, of his princely authority purged his realm of idolatry, and commanded the fast of forty days to be kept. Bed. Lib. iii. Cap. viii. The Papists deny that a King may do such things of his princely authority.

22. Kings in those times preferred men to bishoprics; Bed. Lib. iii. Cap. vii.; which the Papists affirm to be unlawful.

23. Kings in those days deposed Bishops, as Senwalch did Wini; Bed. Li. iii. Cap. vii. Ecgfrid deposed Wilfride, Lib. iv. Ca. xii.; which the Papists do not admit.

24. King Ecgfride would not receive Wilfrid, being restored by the Pope. Bed. Lib. iv. Cap. xiii. & Lib. v. Cap. xx. The Papists count it blasphemy not to obey the Pope's decree.

25. The same Wilfride, being again deprived by means of King Aldfride, and being the second time absolved by the Pope, could not be restored to his bishopric but by a Synod of his own Clergy. Bed. Lib. v. Cap. xx. By which it appeareth, the Clergy were not then in perfect slavery to the Pope.

26. Kings in those days were present at Synods, and ordered them, and concluded in them, as Oswine did at Strenshalch. Lib. iii. Cap. xxv.

27. Archbishops were commanded by Kings to consecrate Bishops; as Wilfride was to consecrate Ostfor [*al.* Oftfor,] at the commandment of King Edilred. Bed. Li. iv. Cap. xxiii. Papists deny Kings to have sovereign authority in ecclesiastical causes.

28. Privileges of monasteries sought at Rome had first the consent of the King unto them. Bed. Lib. iv. Cap. xviii. Papists of later times seek privileges against the King's will.

29. Monks in that time were called to serve the Commonwealth; as Sighard, a Monk, was made King of the East Saxons. Lib. iv. Ca. xi. Papists call such apostataes.

30. Monasteries were then colleges of learned men, to furnish the Church with Ministers and Bishops. Li. iv. Ca. xxiii. Among Papists they be stalls to feed idle bellies, that serve neither the Church nor the Commonwealth.

31. Study of the Scriptures and hand labour was the exercise of Monks in those first and better times. Bed. Lib. iv. Cap. iii. Idleness and vain ceremonies is the exercise of popish Monks.

32. Monasteries were founded, that men might in them hear the word of God, and pray. Bed. Li. iii. Ca. xxiii. Popish monasteries in latter times were builded only to pray for men's souls, and to say Masses in them, &c.

33. Upon Sundays the people used ordinarily to flock to churches and monasteries, to hear the word of God. Bed. Lib. iii. Cap. xxvi. In popish monasteries there neither was nor is any ordinary resort to hear the word of God, nor any ordinary preaching.

34. The Monks of that time were all learned preachers. Bed. Lib. iii. Cap. xxvi. The popish Monks are most unlearned, and few preachers out of their dens.

35. In those days every Priest and Clerk was a preacher; so that when any came to any town, the people would resort to them to be taught of them. Bed. Lib. iv. Cap. xxvi. The greatest number of popish Priests, in these latter days, are most ignorant asses, and void of all spiritual understanding.

36. Unlearned Priests were forbidden to serve in the church; Bed. Lib. v. Cap. vi.; insomuch that S. John of Beverley baptized again a young man which was baptized of an unlearned Priest. The Papists allow unlearned Priests to baptize and say Mass, that cannot catechise and instruct their hearers.

37. Songs and hymns out of the holy Scriptures were made meet for religion in the mother tongue. Bed. Lib. iv. Cap. xxiv. Papists can abide no songs of Scripture in the English tongue.

38. Anchorets of that time laboured with their hands. Bed. Lib. iv. Cap. xxviii. Popish Anchorets live idly, and labour not with their hands.

39. *Dirige* and Mass was said for Saint Oswald's soul: by which it is manifest, that they esteemed the Mass to be a sacrifice of thanksgiving. Lib. iii. Cap. ii.

40. Bega, a Nun, after she saw the soul of the Abbess Hilda carried into heaven, exhorted her sisters to be occupied in prayers and psalms for her soul. Whereby it appeareth, that the doctrine of Purgatory was not yet confirmed among them. Lib. iv. Ca. xxiii. Nothing is so certainly defended among Papists as Purgatory.

41. Holy men fasted then with eating of milk, as Egbert. Bed. Lib. iii. Ca. xxvii. And Cedda fasted Lent with eggs and milk. Lib. iii. Ca. xxiii. Papists of later times have utterly forbidden all white meats in Lent and fasting-days.

42. There was a Church of Christ in Britain before the coming of Augustin, not subject to the see of Rome, which continued long after his coming. Lib. ii. Cap. iv. The Papists account none Christians, but such as be bondslaves to the see of Rome.

43. Laurence, the second Archbishop of Canterbury, accounteth the Bishops of the Scots and Britons for Bishops, although they were not subject to the see nor Church of Rome. Bed. Lib. ii. Cap. iv. The Papists take none for Bishops that be not under the see of Rome.

44. The churches of the Britons were builded after another form than the churches of the Romish obedience. Bed. Lib. iii. Cap. iv. The Papists affirm there were no churches ever builded, but in fashion and use of Popery.

45. The Scottish Church, instructed from Ireland, observed all such works of devotion as they could find in the Prophets, Gospels, and Apostles' writings; and therefore of Bede and the English Church were acknowledged for Christians, although they would not become members of the Church of Rome. Bed. Li. iii. Ca. iv. The Papists hold that there is no salvation out of the Church of Rome; which is a new Church in England, in comparison of the elder that was before Augustin's time.

46. Aidanus, a preaching Bishop, having no possessions, labouring to fulfil all that was written in the holy Scriptures, the Prophets and Apostles, shining in miracles both in his life-time and after his death, was never subject to the Church of Rome; yet accounted a Saint of the Church in those days. Bed. Lib. iii. Cap. xvi. The Papists allow no Saints but canonized by their Pope.

47. The exercise of Aidanus' company, both shorn and laymen, was reading of the Scriptures, and learning of the Psalms. Bed. Lib. iii. Cap. v. The exercise of popish Bishops' servants is nothing less.

48. The greatest part of the English Saxons were converted to Christianity by the Britons and Scots, that were no members of the Church of Rome. As, all the kingdom of Northumberland, both Bernicians and Deires, were converted by Aidanus; except a few persons whom Paulinus, the Roman, in long time had gained. The whole kingdom of Mercia, which was the greatest part of England, received the faith and baptism of Finanus the Scot, the successor of Aidanus. Bed. Lib. iii. Cap. xxi. The East Saxons by Cedda, that was also of the Scottish ordering. Lib. iii. Cap. xxii. The Papists affirm that all our religion came from Rome.

49. Ceadda was consecrated by Wini, Bishop of the West Saxons, assisted by two Briton Bishops that were not subject to the see of Rome; and was nevertheless accounted for a lawful Bishop. Bed. Lib. iii. xxviii.

50. Beda accounted Gregory for the Apostle of the Englishmen. Lib. ii. Cap. i. The Papists now take Augustin for their Apostle.

I omit many other opinions and ordinances of that age: as, Augustin would have none forced to religion; that Wednesday should be fasting-day; the Bishop of London should have a pall as well as York, &c., wherein the Papists differ from them; that brag of nothing but antiquity, universality, and consent.

AN OVERTHROW

OF

STAPLETON'S FORTRESS,

OR, AS HE CALLETH IT HIMSELF,

THE PILLAR OF PAPISTRY.

THE FIRST BOOK.

CHAPTER I.

STAPLETON. *Stapleton.* AN introduction, declaring the necessity of the matter to be treated upon, and the order which the author will take in treating thereof.

FULKE. *Fulke.* Omitting the necessity of the matter, his order which he promiseth to keep is this. First, he will prove, if he can, that Papistry is the only true Christianity. This proposition he will follow by two principal parts. In the former, he will prove by authority of Scriptures, and answering of the adversaries' objections, that the Church cannot possibly err. Secondly, that this Church must be a known Church; that no malignant Church can prevail against it; that Papistry can be no schism nor heresy. In the latter part, after a few reasonable demands, that Protestants must not refuse to answer, putting the case that the known Church of nine hundred years is a kind of Papistry, he will prove that the faith of Protestants is differing from that was first planted among Englishmen in more than forty points; and that in all those points of difference he will shew they agree with the first six hundred years, which he saith (but falsely) that Protestants offer to be tried by. For although the Bishop of Sarum made challenge of many articles now holden of the Papists, not to be found within the compass of the first six hundred years, and therefore to be new and false doctrines; yet neither he, nor any Protestant living or dead, did ever agree to receive what doctrine soever was taught within the first six hundred years. But this I dare avow, that what article of doctrine soever we do affirm, the same hath been affirmed of the godly Fathers of the primitive Church; whatsoever we deny, the same cannot be proved to have been universally affirmed and received of all the godly Fathers, by the space of the six hundred years together.

CHAPTER II.

Stapleton. That Protestants do condemn the universal Church of Christ, of these many hundred years; and the reason of the whole disputation following grounded thereupon. STAPLETON.

Fulke. To prove that the Protestants condemn the universal Church of Christ these many hundred years, he allegeth the sayings of some Protestants, miserably wrested from their meaning: that Latimer was our Apostle; that Luther begat truth; that the Gospel doth arise; in the first appearing of the Gospel, &c.: or as though by these sayings, and such like, they should deny that ever there had been any Church in the world before these times; whereas every child may understand, they speak of the restitution of the truth of the Gospel into the open sight of the world in these latter days. Likewise, where some have written, that the Pope hath blinded the world these many hundred years; some say a thousand years, some twelve hundred, some nine hundred, some five hundred, &c.; and the Apology affirmeth, that Christ hath said the Church should err, he cavilleth that all the Church for so many years is condemned of all error: whereas it is evident to them that will understand, that although some erroneous opinions have prevailed, and in process of time have increased in the greatest part of the Church, for many hundred years; yet so long as the only foundation of salvation was retained, the universal Church of Christ so many hundred years is not condemned. But when Antichrist (the mystery of whose iniquity wrought in the Apostles' time, 2 Thess. ii.) was openly shewed, and that apostasy which the Apostle foresheweth was fulfilled, then and from that time, whensoever it was, not the universal Church of Christ is condemned, but the general apopasy [apostasy] of Antichrist is detected. FULKE.

THE ARGUMENT,

WHEREUPON THIS FIRST PART OF THE VAWMURE[1] OF THIS FORTRESS IS BUILDED, IS THUS FRAMED BY THE BUILDER HIMSELF.

STAPLETON. *Stapleton.* THE known Church of Christ doth continue, and shall continue always without interruption, in the true and upright faith:

But Papistry was the only known Church of Christ all these nine hundred years:

Ergo, Papistry all these nine hundred years hath continued, and shall continue always, even to the world's end without interruption, in the true and upright faith.

FULKE. *Fulke.* This argument hath never a leg to stand upon: for understanding (as he doth) the known Church to be that which is known to the world, to continue without interruption so known to the world, the *major*, is false. For although the Church shall continue always without interruption, yet it shall not continue always so known; but, as in the days of Elias, be hid from the outward view of men.

Again, the *minor*, that Papistry was the only known Church, understanding (as he doth) that it was only reputed, taken, and acknowledged so to be, it is utterly false. For the Greek and oriental Church, which is not the popish Church, hath been reputed, taken, and acknowledged to be the Church of Christ by as great a number of professors of Christianity as have acknowledged the popish Church. So that where he thinketh and saith all his labour remaineth to prove the *major*, you see that if he could prove it, yet all his labour is lost. But, to follow him in his *major*, he divideth it into two parts: the one, that the Church doth always continue in a right faith: the other, that this is a known Church. Both these he promiseth to prove by Scripture. And the first truly he shall not need: but yet it followeth not, but that the Church may err in some particular points, not necessary to salvation; although it continue in a right faith, concerning all principal and necessary articles.

[1] [Vawmure: outwork.]

CHAPTER III.

Stapleton. Evident proofs and clear demonstrations out of the Psalms, that the Church of Christ must continue for ever without interruption sound and upright. STAPLETON.

Fulke. He is plentiful in proving that which needeth no proof, that the Church of Christ shall continue always: and first out of the lxxxviii.[2] Psalm, which he rehearseth, and interpreteth of the Church out of Augustin, lest he should trust his own judgment, as he fantasieth that our preachers do, altogether refusing to read interpreters. We affirm, that the Church of Christ hath and shall continue to the world's end: but we deny that the popish Church is that; which could not be before there was a Pope, before their heresies were brought out of the bottomless pit, which were not breathed up all in six hundred years after Christ, no not in a thousand years after Christ, and some not almost in fourteen hundred years after Christ; I mean the sacrilegious taking away of the Communion of the blood of Christ from the people in the Council of Constance[3]. What impudency is it of Papists, to urge the perpetual continuance of Christ's Church without interruption, and then to begin at six hundred years after Christ; and not to be able to shew a perpetual course of all their doctrine from Christ, His Apostles, and the primitive Church! FULKE.

But, to prove that the Church of Christ cannot possibly (as Protestants wickedly do fable) have failed and perished these many hundred years, he citeth the lxi. Psalm, with Augustin's exposition thereupon. But what Protestant so fableth, M. Stapleton? You had need to make men of paper, to fight against the paper walls of your fantastical Fortress. The Papists, when they cannot confute that we say, they will beat down that we say not. "How say the Protestants, that these nine hundred years and upward the Church hath perished; it hath been overwhelmed with idolatry and superstition?" The Protestants never said so, M. Stapleton. The Church hath not perished, though the greatest part of the world hath been overwhelmed with idolatry and superstition. God can provide for His chosen, that they shall not be

[2] [Engl. lxxxix.—Stapleton's *Fortresse*, p. 30. S. Omers, 1625.]

[3] [Sess. xiii. an. 1415.]

drowned, when all the world beside is overwhelmed. Another testimony to the like effect, and with the like conclusion, he bringeth out of the Psalm civ., and thereupon a pithy syllogism. "We prove the Catholic Church by the continuance of Christianity: The continuance of Christianity only in Papistry is clear: Ergo, Papistry is only the true Church of Christ." *Nego tibi minorem*, M. Stapleton. When will you prove the continuance of Christianity only in Papistry, when Papistry began since Christ and His Apostles? and if you mean Christianity for the external profession of Christ's religion, then will you prove the oriental Churches to be Papistry, which defy the authority of your Pope.

Last of all, out of the Psalm ci., and Augustin's application of the same against the Donatists, which said that the Church was perished out of all the world except Africa where they were, he would compare the Protestants to them, whereas indeed the Papists are more like to them. For they, holding that there is no Church of Christ but the Romish Church, affirm in effect as the Donatists, that the Church of Christ for many hundred years hath perished out of all parts of the world beside Europa, where only, and yet not in all parts thereof, they have borne the sway. Whatsoever, therefore, Augustin writeth against the Donatists, for shutting up the Church of Christ only in Africa, may be rightly applied to the Papists, for restraining it only to a part of Europa. But, contrary to the Papists and Donatists, we affirm, that the Catholic Church of Christ is and hath been, even in the most dark times of Antichrist's kingdom, dispersed throughout the whole world; nothing doubting but God, which preserved seven thousand in one corner of Israel, not much greater than some shire of England, hath preserved seven thousand thousand in all parts of the wide world, which never bowed their knees to the Romish Baal, nor kissed him with their mouth.

CHAPTER IV.

STAPLETON. *Stapleton.* Proofs and testimonies out of the prophet Esay, that the Church of the Messias continueth for ever unto the world's end, assisted always by God Himself.

FULKE. *Fulke.* The testimonies of the perpetuity of the Church out of the Prophet Esay, with the exposition of Hieronym upon them, maketh nothing against us, which willingly acknowledge the same, but deny that they pertain to the popish Church, which had her beginning long after Christ and His Apostles, and her full tyranny confirmed more than a thousand years after Christ. The same Hierom disputeth against the custom of the particular Church of Rome, and appealeth to the Church of all the world: *Si auctoritas quæritur, orbis major est urbe,* &c.: "If authority be sought, the world is greater than a city." And again: *Quid mihi profers unius urbis consuetudinem?* "What bringest thou forth to me the custom of one city?" *Evagr.*[1] We stand for the Catholic Church of Christ dispersed over all the world, against the particular, schismatical, heretical, and antichristian Church of Rome; which, though she have invaded by tyranny over a great part of Europe, yet never did she prevail over the whole Church throughout the world, nor yet over all Europe.

CHAPTER V.

Stapleton. The doctrine of Calvin touching the Church is examined to the touchstone of the holy Scriptures alleged. Wherein also is treated and disputed by what marks the Church may be known. STAPLETON.

Fulke. First he confesseth that Calvin[2] hath learnedly, largely, and truly treated of the unity, authority, and obedience of the Church. He affirmeth also, that he acknowledgeth a visible Church in the world; whose communion we ought to keep, and of her to receive the spiritual food of doctrine and Sacraments; which ought not to be forsaken for the evil life of the members thereof. All this he commendeth and alloweth. But herein he sheweth his malicious cavilling stomach, that he supposeth Calvin to affirm, that the universal FULKE.

1 [S. Hieron. *Ep. ad Evagrium;* (or rather *ad Evangelum.*) Opp. ii. 329. Basil. 1565. This remarkable Epistle was published, with a preface by Luther, Vitebergæ, 1538. Almost the entire of it is included in the Canon Law; (*Dist.* xciii. Cap. xxiv.) and Christfrid Wæchtler has examined its contents. (*Acta Eruditor.* an. 1717. pp. 484, 524, seqq. Lips.) Latterly, in Germany, the authenticity of the Letter has been questioned. See Gieseler, i. 65.]

2 [*Institut.* Lib. iv. Cap. i.]

Church of Christ is visible, where he speaketh but of particular congregations, members of the whole, which are visible, not to the world always, but to the members of the same.

The marks of the Church, which Calvin sayeth to be true preaching of the word of God, and due administration of the Sacraments, although he confesseth them to be in the Church, yet he denieth them to be the marks of the Church. For the mark must be better known than the thing whereof it is a mark: But the Church is more evident than those marks: *Ergo* they be no true marks. The *minor* he proveth by that which Calvin teacheth, that we must learn of the Church the true meaning of the Scripture. But hereof it followeth not, that the Church is better known than these marks. For there is a farther trial, which ought to be better known, by which both are to be known: namely, the word of God; whereunto we must have recourse, to try whether those things that are preached are even so indeed; as the Thessalonians [Bereans] did by the preaching of Paul and Barnabas. [Silas.] Act. xvii. ver. 11. The unmoveable truth is to be sought in the Scriptures: what preaching or Church agreeth with that truth is to be received, and none other. And whereas he sayeth that heretics challenge these marks as well as Catholics, I grant they do so: but no more do they challenge these marks than they challenge the Church to be on their side; for there was never heresy, but they bragged as much of the Church as of the truth. Therefore the Church is not more clear than these marks; but these marks, tried by the word of God, are more clear than the Church, which is therefore the Church because it maintaineth true doctrine. The doctrine is not true because the Church maintaineth it. The cause is better known than the effect; for knowledge is to understand by causes.

But M. Stapleton hath two better marks than Calvin describeth: to wit, the universality and communion of all nations; the continuance and ever-remaining thereof among Christians. These marks by no logic can be causes of the Church, but adjuncts unto it; and therefore the worst arguments that can be to know it by: even such as the foolish man's argument was, that knew his horse by the bridle. But admit these to be proper adjuncts of the Church, yet shall not the popish Church be able to prove those to be her marks.

For Popery neither doth, neither ever did, possess all the world, except a piece of Europe be all the world. The Church of Christ is Catholic, although there were but three or four persons in all the world that maintained true doctrine: as there was not many when Christ and His Apostles, and a few other, were the only Church in all the world, and the Catholic Church before they were dispersed into many nations. For the Church is called Catholic or universal, not because all men or most men do pertain unto it; but because all that be members of Christ, how many or how few soever they be, and wheresoever they be, are members of that Church. But M. Stapleton saith, "The universality of the Church is a matter evident to the eye; and therefore the Catholic Church is always visible." To this I answer, that if the Catholic Church, or the universality thereof, were always visible, or at any time visible, or the universality thereof evident to the eye, it should be no article of faith: for faith is of such things as are not seen with the eye, but believed with the heart. Heb. xi. ver. 1. We agree with Augustin against the Donatists, that no heresy was in all countries and in all ages. For Papistry, which is the greatest heresy and apostasy, was never in all countries and all ages. But if an heresy were in all countries and ages, yet proveth it not itself to be a Catholic truth. Idolatry hath been in all countries and ages; yet is it not thereby proved to be a Catholic truth. The Church of Christ, whereof we are members, hath been in all parts of the world and in all ages; though not always nor ever received of the greatest part of men. And if this be a "most clear and evident mark," (as he saith,) "that no heretic can pretend to be joined in communion with all Christian countries," the popish Church hath not this mark; which is not joined in communion with the Greeks, Armenians, Chaldeans, Ethiopians, and so many nations as at this day, and since the Apostles' times, have been christened countries.

But now we come to the second mark of the Church, the continuance thereof from the beginning to the end of the world; which is indeed a proper adjunct of the Church of Christ, not to be found in any heresy, nor in Papistry, the greatest of all heresies. But M. Stapleton, which cannot prove that Papistry hath continued always, will argue upon that it hath continued a certain time. "The Church" (saith he) "hath continued a certain hundred years in that faith and doctrine only which Papists do teach: But in those very hundred years the Church neither could lack, neither could have a wrong faith, or be seduced with damnable doctrine: Therefore Papists had all that time the true faith; and their faith and doctrine is true, sound and upright." The *major* of this argument he affirmeth to be our confession, which is nothing else but an impudent lie of his own confiction. For which of the Protestants ever confessed that the Church hath continued so many hundred years in that faith and doctrine only which the Papists teach? If he have the wit to draw such confessions from us, he may prove what he list against us. But he promiseth to prove abundantly the continuance of popish doctrine from the beginning, which we so stoutly deny. In the meantime he returneth to Calvin, whom he chargeth to have learned his opinion and doctrine of the Donatists, concerning the marks of the Church; taking to witness the *Ep.* xlviii.[1] of Augustin *ad Vincentium,* where the Donatists answered the argument of universality, that the Church was called Catholic, "not because it did communicate with the whole world, but because it observed all God's commandments, and all His Sacraments." But what a vain quarrel this is, he himself doth sufficiently declare, when he bringeth in Augustin immediately, confessing the Church to be called Catholic because it holdeth that verity wholly and throughly, whereof every heresy holdeth a part or piece only; and addeth thereunto the communication with all nations, *videlicet,* that hold that verity wholly and throughly. And lest this might seem to be borrowed of the Donatists only, Augustin himself affirmeth as much, *De Genesi ad literam, imperfect.* Cap. i.[2]: *Constitutam ab Eo* [*Illo*] *matrem Ecclesiam; quæ Catholica dicitur ex eo quia universaliter perfecta est, et in nullo claudicat, et per totum orbem diffusa est:* "That by Him the Church is appointed our mother; which is called Catholic for that it is universally perfect, and halteth in nothing, and is dispersed throughout the whole world." Whereas Augustin requireth universal perfection in all true doctrine and administration of the Sacraments with universality, the Papists

[1] [al. xciii. §. 23. *Opp.* ii. 182. ed. Ben. Antw. (Amstel.) 1700.]

[2] [§. 4. *Opp.* Tom. iii. P. i. col. 71.]

take universality alone, which Augustin never said nor taught to be a sufficient note of the Church.

After this he chargeth Calvin to deny the perpetual continuance of the Church, because he said, that the pure preaching of the word hath vanished away in certain ages past: by which he meaneth not, (as this foolish caviller taketh him, or rather mistaketh him,) that true preaching had utterly perished out of the whole world, but out of the popish Synagogue; which in Europe boasted itself to be the only Church of Christ, when in the chief articles of Christianity it derogated from the glory of Christ, and was subject to the doctrine of the Man of sin, the adversary and enemy of Christ. And if malice had not blinded him, he would have so understood Calvin; alleging his saying immediately after, wherein he confesseth, that the Church of Christ never failed out of the world. Whereupon he demandeth, whether the Church of the Protestants is that which hath never failed? If we say it is, he demandeth further, where those marks of preaching and ministering of the Sacraments have been these many hundred years? which question he hopeth some disciple of Calvin will assoil him. I answer, those marks were to be seen in such places, where the Churches were gathered, that had separated themselves from the Church of Rome. If he urge me further to shew him the particular places, let him resort to the book of Acts and Monuments, which it seemeth he hath read over. If that will not satisfy him, by example of our Saviour Christ I will refel his vain question with another question: Where did those seven thousand, that God preserved in the days of Elias, assemble for prayers, preaching and sacrifice? If he cannot tell, no more am I bound to shew him in what particular places they preached and ministered the Sacraments. And therefore neither need the Apology to recant, nor the Harborough[3] be revoked, nor M. Foxe call in his book, nor M.

[3] [*Fortresse*, page 74.—This "Harbourough", "which saieth that Luther begott truth," was previously quoted by Stapleton in p. 20. The reference is to Bp. Aylmer's work against John Knox, entitled: *An Harborowe for faithfull and trewe subjects, against the late blowne Blaste, concerning the government of Women;* Strasburg, 1559. See Strype's *Life of Aylmer*, last edit. page 147; or the article added to Bayle's *Dict.* ii. 514. Lond. 1735. Fuller, Book ix. p. 223. Lond. 1655. Martin Mar-Prelate's *Epistle*, p. 3. new ed. Petheram, Lond. Neal's

Nowell his Reproof. It will not suffice a wrangling caviller an hundred times to affirm, that the Church hath always continued, even when Papistry most prevailed, and even under the tyranny and persecution of Papistry; like as the Church was among the idolatrous Baalites in the days of Elias, or among the wicked Jews that persecuted the Prophets. But hereto he replieth, that though the assemblies of the Jews were no Churches, yet their temple, sacrifices, ceremonies, law and doctrine was good. I answer, so much of these as they retained according to God's law was good; and so I confess of the doctrine and Sacraments of the Papists: as Baptism, concerning the substance of the Sacrament; the historical faith of the Trinity, of the Incarnation, Passion, Resurrection of Christ, &c. But if these and many more pieces of truth might be sufficient to make them the Church of Christ, many heretics might challenge the Church; which have confessed and practised a great number of truths more than they; which err but in one article, as the Arrians, Pelagians, &c.; whereas the Papists err in many; yea, in the whole doctrine of Justification by faith, and the worship of God. And therefore Papistry is not only a schism, error or heresy; but, as Calvin, out of Daniel ix. and Paul, 2 Thessal. ii. rightly concludeth, an apostasy, defection, and antichristianity; not abolishing, but retaining the names of Christ, of the Gospel, and of the Church; but the true virtue, power, and strength of the same utterly forsaking, denying, and persecuting.

CHAPTER VI.

STAPLETON. *Stapleton.* Other prophecies alleged and discussed, for the continuance of Christ's Church in a sound and upright faith.

FULKE. *Fulke.* Divers texts of Scripture are cited, some rightly, some strangely applied, to prove that we deny not; namely, the perpetual continuance of the Church of Christ in a sound and right faith, in all matters necessary to salvation: upon

History of the Puritans, Vol. i. p. 276. Lond. 1822.—Aylmer is spoken of in Becon's *Jewel of Joy*: Catech. &c., p. 424. ed. Parker Soc.]

every one of which he inferreth, how could Christ forsake His Church these nine hundred years? as though we said that Christ hath had no Church in the space of nine hundred years; which we never doubted of.

CHAPTER VII.

Stapleton. Proofs out of the Gospel, for the continuance of Christ's Church in pure and unspotted doctrine. STAPLETON.

Fulke. When M. Stapleton cometh to prove that which we deny, his proofs will be neither so plentiful nor so sufficient. His counterfeit painted Fort must have puppets made to assail it. The Church of Christ, concerning the substance of doctrine necessary to salvation, shall continue pure and unspotted, although in other matters she may be deceived; even as every one of God's elect, for whom our Saviour Christ prayeth, John xvii.; which text M. Stapleton citeth to prove the continuance of the Church. We will never say, that hell-gates have prevailed against the universal Church of Christ, though they have prevailed against the see of Rome. Yet must we say, as the Scripture teacheth us, that Antichrist shall prevail in the world. 2 Thessal. ii. One Scripture is never contrary to another. We are challenged to read you out of the Scriptures the breach, interruption, and failing of the Church of Christ so many hundred years. As you understand the breach and failing for an utter abolishing of the Church of Christ out of the world; such breach and failing, as we do not read it, so we do not affirm it. But that we affirm we read, that in the latter days some shall depart from the faith, attending to spirits of error in hypocrisy, &c.; whose marks are, to forbid marriage, and to abstain from meats, which God hath created, &c. 1 Tim. iv. We read, that before the coming of Christ shall be an apostasy; and the Man of sin shall be openly shewed, which shall deceive a great part of the world. 2 Thess. ii. We read, that the whore of Babylon, which all ancient writers expound to be Rome, shall with her sorcery enchant and make drunk all nations, &c. Apoc. This and much more we read, to shew what your universality is, and to take away the ob- FULKE.

jection of our paucity, and not appearing to the greatest part of the world, at such time as it pleased God, for the unthankfulness of men, to send them the efficacy of error, to be deceived, because they would not receive the truth.

CHAPTER VIII.

STAPLETON. *Stapleton.* To deny the continuance of the Church in a sound and upright faith is to defect the mystery of Christ's incarnation.

FULKE. *Fulke.* This man hath great leisure, with store of ink and paper, that filleth so many chapters with proof of that which none of his adversaries will deny; who all with one mouth confess, and cry out against him so loud, that if he were not either deaf or dead he might hear; that as Christ the head continueth for ever, so doth the Church His body: but that the popish Church at this time, and many hundred years before this time, is the body of Christ, the spouse of Christ, the flock of Christ's sheep, which is divided from Christ, which is an adulteress from Christ, which heareth not the voice of Christ; this we all deny, and this you shall never be able to prove while the world standeth, babble and scribble as long as you will.

CHAPTER IX.

STAPLETON. *Stapleton.* That Protestants do condemn the practice and belief of the first six hundred years in many things, no less than of this latter age.

FULKE. *Fulke.* If Papists do allow the practice and belief of the first six hundred years in all things, they may justly reprove us for refusing the same in some things. But if they refuse the practice and belief of that age in many things, because their Church, their judge, doth now practise and hold the contrary; why should they require us to be bound to the practice and opinion of those times in all things, when by Scriptures, the only rule of truth with us, we find that they have erred in some things? But, to leave his impudent railing and lying, that we or any of us did ever offer to justify whatsoever was done or held by godly men of the first six hundred years, let us see what practice and belief he chargeth us to condemn.

First, (saith he,) they not only reprove certain Fathers for certain errors, but in many points they condemn all the Fathers for common errors; as Invocation of Saints, and Prayer for the dead. And do not you Papists reprove the practice of all the Fathers, and Pope Innocent[1] with them, not only for ministering the Communion to infants, but also for holding that they be damned, except they receive the Communion? *Augustin. Cont. duas Ep. Pelag. ad Bonifac.* Lib. ii. Cap. iv.[2] Do you not reprove the practice and opinion of all the Fathers, for allowing marriage in the Ministers of the Church, which you utterly condemn? What shall I say of the Communion in both kinds, given to the lay-people by consent of all antiquity; of communicating with the Priest; and many such-like things, the practice and belief whereof you utterly refuse?

But, to return to the examples of Invocation of Saints, which Stapleton saith are clear by all writers of the first six hundred years; railing like a saucy merchant at M. Jewell and M. Grindall, men whose learning and godliness he may envy, but will never attain unto. What a bold bayard is this, to affirm that Invocation of Saints is clear by all writers of the first six hundred years, when no writer of three hundred years after Christ hath any one jot either of practice or belief to allow it! Epiphanius among the heresies of the Caianes counteth Invocation of Angels. Tom. iii. Hær. iii.[3] The other error of Pray-

1 [Exstat Rescriptum Innocentii Papæ I. inter S. August. *Oper.* Tom. ii. col. 487. ed. Ben.—"Hinc constat" (says Binius, *Concill.* i. i. 624. Colon. Agripp. 1618.) "Innocentii I. sententia, (quæ sexcentos circiter annos viguit in Ecclesia, quamque S. Augustinus sectatus est,) Eucharistiam etiam infantibus necessariam fuisse." It is remarkable that the Council of Trent has not spared a Pope any more than others; for its decision is: "Si quis dixerit, parvulis, antequam ad annos discretionis pervenerint, necessariam esse Eucharistiæ Communionem, anathema sit." (Sess. xxi. Can. iv. Compare Whitby's *Idolatry of the Church of Rome*, pp. 246—8. Lond. 1674.)]

2 [§. 7. *Opp.* x. 288.]

3 [*Adv. Hœr.* Lib. i. Tom. iii. Hær. xxxviii. *Opp.* i. 277. Paris. 1622.—S. Epiphanius (Hæres. lx.) also speaks of the extinct heresy of the Angelici, but confesses his ignorance as to the origin of their name. S. Isidore of Seville, however, declares: "Angelici vocati quia

ing for the dead is more ancient: but yet it sprang first from the heresy of Montanus; neither is there any writer ancienter than Tertullian a Montanist, in whom any steps of Prayer for the dead are to be found. To these he adjoineth a slander of Calvin, whom he affirmeth to teach, that God is the cause and author of evil; which how impudent a lie it is, all they that have read Calvin of Predestination can testify. The reservation of the Sacrament of the Lord's Supper Calvin confesseth to have been an erroneous practice of the ancient Church. And what say you Papists? Was it not erroneous to reserve that which Christ commanded to be eaten and drunken? But you make no bones of Christ's commandment. If it were not erroneous, why was it forbidden in divers Councils?

If you care not for that, yet think not to mock the world with the ancient practice of reservation, which you yourselves condemn. Will you suffer men and women to carry home the Sacrament, and lock it in their chests; to hang it about their necks; to receive it in their houses when they list? If you allow not these things, which was the reservation of ancient times, you are twice impudent to charge us for reproving that practice, which you yourselves do not admit to be lawful. But yet again, he chargeth Calvin to condemn the whole primitive Church of Jewish superstition, for saying the Fathers followed rather the Jewish manner of sacrificing, than the ordinance of Christ in the Gospel. What a shameless beast is this, to slander Calvin to condemn the whole primitive Church; when he speaketh only of the later and

Angelos colunt"; (*Origg.* Lib. viii. Cap. v.) and the Canon Law contains this statement. (Gratiani *Decret.* ii. Par. Caus. xxiv. Qu. iii. Cap. Quidam autem.) S. Augustin has given similar evidence: "Angelici, in Angelorum cultu inclinati." (*De Hœress.* Cap. xxxix.) Photius adds, that the famous thirty-fifth Canon of the Laodicean Council was made concerning the Angelites. (*Nomocanon*, Tit. xii. Cap. ix.) The shameless corruption of this Canon by Merlin, Crabbe, Carranza and others, who have changed "Angelos" into "Angulos", is well known: and Hen. Agylæus, in his Latin translation of the *Nomocanon*, annexed to the first Greek edition published by Chr. Justellus, Lut. Paris. 1615, has avoided all reference to the same Decree. It requires some attention in a reader to enable him to perceive that Canon λέ, the rendering of which number is omitted in the Latin, is the one which has passed sentence περὶ Ἀγγελιτῶν.]

more corrupt times, in which he sheweth their error, but condemneth not the Church!

But now he will prove, that Protestants hold six heresies condemned within the first five hundred years. The first is Justification by faith only, condemned in Aerius [Aetius] and Eunomius, *August. Hær.* liv. *Epiph. Hær.* lxxvi.: which is a very shameless slander, for there is no such Justification by faith only condemned in them as we hold; which no man of the ancient Fathers more copiously defendeth than Augustin himself. The second is also a most impudent lie; that to condemn free will in man to work well, as we mean it, is an heresy of the Manichees and Marcionists: for both which opinions, as we hold them, Augustin himself shall speak, *Ep.* cv.[1], *Sixto: Restat igitur ut ipsam fidem, unde omnis justitia sumit initium, propter quod dicitur ad Ecclesiam in Cantico Canticorum, Venies et pertransies ab initio fidei, non humano, quo isti extolluntur,* [al. *quod isti extollunt,*] *tribuamus arbitrio; nec ullis præcedentibus meritis, quoniam inde incipiunt bona quæcunque sunt merita; sed gratuitum donum Dei esse fateamur, si gratiam veram, id est, sine meritis cogitemus:* "Therefore it remaineth, that we ascribe not faith itself (from whence all righteousness taketh beginning, for which it is said unto the Church in the Ballad of Ballads, Thou shalt come and pass through from the beginning of faith,) unto man's free will, whereof they are proud; nor to any merits going before, for all good merits whatsoever they are begin from thence; but that we confess it to be the freely given gift of God, if we think of true grace, which is without merits." Thus writeth Augustin against the Pelagians, which maintained free will to do well, and were counted heretics therefore; the contrary whereof Stapleton doth now count to be heresy in us. The third heresy imputed to Aerius was the denial of Prayer for the dead; which neither Augustin nor Epiphanius, that count it for an error, can by the word of God convince to be so. The fourth is Jovinian's opinion, making marriage equal with virginity; which we do not hold, but that in some respect virginity is preferred, as the Apostle teacheth, 1 Cor. vii. But that we exhort them to marry, which cannot keep their vow of continence, which rashly and presumptuously they

[1] [alias cxciv.]

made, we are warranted by Epiphanius, *Contra Apostolicos, Hær.* lxi.[1]; Hieronym. *Ad Demetriadem*[2]. The fifth, that is, the contempt of fasting-days appointed by the Church, we hold not with Aerius and Eustachius, but contrariwise that they are to be observed; although we make none account of the fasting-days appointed and superstitiously kept by the popish Church. The sixth, the superstition of Christians used at the tombs of Martyrs, we condemn with Vigilantius and Augustin, *De moribus Ecclesiæ Catholicæ,* Lib. i. Cap. xxxiv.[3] Neither is Vigilantius condemned of any man in his time, but by the private judgment of Hieronym only[4].

Now in how many heresies the Papists communicate with the old heretics, I have shewed before in other treatises, which it were needless here to repeat.

CHAPTER X.

STAPLETON. *Stapleton.* Objections of Protestants to prove the Church may err, by the example and similitude of the old law, answered and confuted.

1 [§. vii. *Opp.* i. 512. ed. Petav.]

2 [This Epistle to Demetrias, which commences with the words "Inter omnes materias", (S. Hier. *Opp.* i. 62. Basil. 1565.) is altogether different from that ("Si summo ingenio", Tom. iv. p. 12.) which Erasmus has placed among "Pseudepigrapha docta", and which S. Augustin attributes to Pelagius. See Bp. Taylor's *Lib. of Proph.* Sect. viii. *Polem. Disc.* p. 1010. Lond. 1674. In the genuine Epistle the metaphorical expression "a sancta Christi synoride" is employed by S. Jerom with reference to Proba and Juliana, the grandmother and mother of Demetrias. S. Chrysostom (*De Lazaro* Concio iv. *Opp.* i. 752. Conf. ii. 578. ed. Ben.) likewise has made mention "τῆς ξυνωρίδος" of Martyrs; and in this case a most extraordinary circumstance occurred: for Petrus Galesinius and Cardinal Baronius, having found the word "Synoridis" in some old Latin version, and being extremely ignorant of Greek, transformed S. Chrysostom's "ξυνωρὶς", "biga", or *pair* of Martyrs, viz. Juventinus and Maximinus, into a previously unheard of female Saint, whom they styled *Synoris* of Antioch! Vid. Bar. *Martyrol. Rom.* edit. i. ad diem 24 Jan. Ottii *Exam. in Annall. Baron.* Cent. iii. p. 125. Tiguri, 1676. Dallæum, *De vero usu Patrum,* pp. 97—8. Genev. 1656. Ant. Reiseri *Launoii Anti-Bellarmin.* p. 862. Amst. 1685. Theod. *Hist. Ecc.* iii. xv.]

3 [*Opp.* i. 531. ed. Ben.]

4 [Christiani Kortholti *Disquiss. Anti-Baron.* p. 346. Lips. 1708.]

Fulke. The objection is only this, out of the Defence of the truth[5], fol. 94, as he saith: The Church of the Jews lacked not God's promises, succession of Bishops and Priests, opinion of holiness and austerity of life, knowledge of the law of God; and yet they erred: why may we not think the like may be in this our time[6]? Both *major* and *minor* of this argument, he saith, is false; for first, they had not such promises as the Church of Christ hath, of perpetual continuance in the truth, because they were not appointed to continue always: wherein he bewrayeth his gross and beastly ignorance, that cannot discern between the nation of the Jews, and the Church of God among the Jews, which hath even the same promises of everlasting continuance that the Church of the Gentiles hath; which is not another Church from the Church of the Jews, but an accession and an addition unto it. How many promises of eternal continuance be made in the Prophets to Israel, to Zion, to Jerusalem! Read Esa. ca. lx. lxii. & lxiii., among a number. The accomplishment whereof, although it be seen in the Church gathered of the Gentiles, yet who would be so impudent to deny that they pertain principally to the Church of Israel, as to the elder brother? But what strive we further, when the Apostle to the Romans, cap. ix. vers. 3. [4.] expressly affirmeth, that the promises pertain to Israel; even as the adoption, the glory, the covenants, the giving of the law, &c.? Yet M. Stapleton thinketh himself a sharp FULKE.

5 [At first it appeared not very easy to trace either the author of this book, or the work itself; but after some examination it became manifest that Bp. Jewel's *Apology* is here referred to, and that the substance of several passages is cited rather than any exact words. See Chap. iv. pages 66, 68, 70, 71. Chap. vi. 133—4. Lond. 1685. Compare *Def. of Apol.* p. 121. Lond. 1609. Harding (p. 496.) styled his opponent "Sir Defender"; and the title of the English Apology, as given by Strype (*Annals*, Vol. i.) and by Bp. Jewel himself, (*Def. of Ap.* p. 1.) is this: "An Apologie, or *Answer*, in *defence* of the Church of England; with a briefe and plaine Declaration of the *true* Religion professed and used in the same." This excellent work, as is well known, was first published in the year 1562; and in 1565 John Rastell put forth his "Reply against an *Answer*, (falsly entit.) *A Defence of the truth*"; copies of which are in the Bodleian and Lambeth libraries. Stapleton's Bede and Fortresse were printed in the last named year; and he has evidently quoted from Rastell.]

6 [. . . "and is the Church of Rome the only Church that can neither fall nor err?" (*Apol.* p. 72.)]

disputer, when he objecteth out of the Epistle to the Hebrews, Heb. viii., that the testament of Messias is established in more excellent promises, because of the new covenant out of Jeremy xxxi.; as though both the testaments did not pertain to the Catholic Church of Christ, as well that of the Jews as this of the Gentiles. The new testament and promises are better than that was made in Sinai; but the new testament of Messias pertaineth as much to the Church of the Jews as to the Church of the Gentiles: or else the Apostle had laboured in vain, writing to the Jews, to draw them from the ceremonies of the old testament to the covenant of Messias, established only in mercy and forgiveness of their sins. Christ was the Lamb slain from the beginning of the world; whose redemption pertained as much unto the fathers that lived before His incarnation, as unto them that are born since: therefore the promise of the eternity of the Church beginneth not at the nativity of Christ, but at the beginning of the world. So that for continuance and perpetuity of God's Spirit with His Church, without the which it cannot be the Church of God, the promises from the beginning have been the same that are now; although, according to God's most wise dispensation, they have been more clearly revealed in the latter times, and most clearly of all by Christ Himself and His Apostles.

Now remaineth the *minor* to be proved; that the Church of the Jews hath erred. Which he denieth[1], because the High Priests answered truly of the nativity of Christ, and because Caiphas prophesied unwittingly of the virtue of Christ's death; than the which nothing can be more blockish. They erred not in one article; *ergo* they erred not at all. One of them spake the truth against his will in one point; *ergo* the Synagogue of the Jews never erred. Again he saith, the whole Synagogue, before the law of Christ took place, in necessary knowledge of the law of Moses did never err. For proof whereof, more like a block than a man, he bringeth such places of Scripture, as either shew what the Priests' duty should be, but not affirm what their knowledge was; or else prophesy a reformation of the corrupt state of the Clergy from ignorance to knowledge. As Ez. xliv.[2]:

[1] [*Fortresse*, p. 112. Compare Jewel's *Apol.* Chap. vi. p. 111.]

[2] [Ezek. xliv. 15, 23.]

"The Priests and Levites shall teach my people." And Mal. ii.: "The lips of the Priest should keep knowledge, and men should require the law of his mouth." Agg. ii.: "Ask the Priest the law[3]." But what drunken Fleming of Douay would reason thus: the Scribes and the Pharisees sat in Moses' chair; therefore the Synagogue did either never or not then err? Our Saviour Christ willed them to be heard, while they spake out of Moses' chair; not while they taught to worship God in vain, preferring their traditions before the commandment of God. But who would spend any more time in reasoning against such a one, as defendeth that the Scribes and the Pharisees did not err; whose false doctrine concerning adultery, murder, swearing, the worship of God, not only the Person, but also the quality of Messias and His kingdom, our Saviour Christ Himself so often and so sharply doth reprove? But the whole Synagogue (saith he) in necessary knowledge of the law of Moses did never err. If he understand the whole Synagogue for every man, we confess the same; and so we say that the whole Church, that is, all the elect, neither in the first six hundred, nor in the latter nine hundred years, did never err in necessary knowledge of the Gospel. But if you take the whole Synagogue for the whole multitude that had the ordinary authority, and did bear the outward face and countenance of the Church, they have erred before the coming of Christ. Example in the whole Synagogue, in the days of Josias, when the very book of the law was unknown unto the Priests, until it was found, by occasion of taking out of money out of the temple, by Hilchiah the Priest. So that from the beginning of the reign of Manasse until the eighteenth year of the reign of Josias, which was almost eighty years, idolatry openly prevailed in the temple of God; the whole Synagogue, that is, all in authority and countenance, embracing the same, except a few poor Prophets, that were slain for crying out against it. 2 King. xxii. & 2 Chro. xxxiv. And such was the state of the Church in the most corrupt times; continuing as then, but yet in persecution, adversity, and being unknown unto the world, except now and then God stirred up some witness to testify His truth, which was slain of the beast. Apoc. xi. Now concerning the childish sophism, that although it was not possible

3 [Haggai ii. 11.]

that the Church could err, yet it is not proved that it hath erred, what should I speak, when the Defender directly oppugneth that paradox which the Papists hold; namely, that the Church cannot err? To conclude, while he walketh under a cloud of the Church sanctified and assisted by the Holy Ghost, defended by the presence of Christ, &c., he playeth bo-peep under a coverlet. For whatsoever promises are made to the faithful spouse of Christ pertain nothing at all to the popish Church of Antichrist; which is departed from the faith, carrying the brand-marks of hypocrisy, in prohibition of marriage and meats, so evident that all the water in the sea cannot wash them out.

CHAPTER XI.

STAPLETON. *Stapleton.* Objections out of the New Testament moved and assoiled[1].

FULKE. *Fulke.* The first objection is, the abomination of desolation standing in the holy place, that is, the Church. Matth. xxiv. He asketh where the Defender[2] hath learned to expound this holy place of the Church? Forsooth, where M. Stapleton learned, that it may be understood of the temple at Jerusalem, where Pilate placed Cæsar's image, or of the image of Adrian: namely, in Hierom, upon this text, Matth. xxiv.; which understandeth the abomination of desolation to be Antichrist, of whom Saint Paul speaketh, whom he denieth not but that he shall sit in the Church. His words are these[3]: *De hoc et Apostolus loquitur, quod Homo iniquitatis et adversarius elevandus sit contra omne quod dicitur Deus et colitur; ita ut audeat stare in templo Dei, et ostendere quod ipse sit Deus: cujus adventus secundum operationem Satanæ destruat eos, et ad Dei solitudinem redigat, qui se susceperint. Potest autem simpliciter aut de Antichristo accipi, aut de imagine Cæsaris,* &c.: "Of this abomination of desolation the Apostle also speaketh, that the Man of sin and the adversary shall be lifted up against all that is called God or worshipped; so that he dare stand in the temple of

[1] [solved.] [2] [Jewel's *Apology*, Chap. iv. pp. 66, 72.]
[3] [*Opp.* Tom. ix. p. 71. Basil. 1565.]

God, and shew himself as God: whose coming according to the working of Satan may destroy them, and bring them to solitariness from God, which shall receive him. And it may either be taken simply of Antichrist, or of the image of Cæsar," &c.

Let him now reason with Hieronym, how the sacrifice should cease after the end of sixty-two weeks: although, for my part, I think the pollution of the temple, which was a token of the desolation imminent, was a figure of the corruption of the Church by Antichrist.

The second objection. S. Paul witnesseth that Antichrist should sit in the temple of God, that is, in the Church. What of this? (saith he;) will it follow that he hath sitten there these nine hundred years? as though the Defender were to prove how long Antichrist should sit, and not rather that the visible and outward multitude of the Church should err.

Like madness, (shall I say?) or impudence, he sheweth where he saith, the Protestants commonly name S. Gregory to be that Antichrist[4]; which I am sure he never read nor heard any Protestant affirm[5]. But the Pope cannot be Antichrist, (saith he,) because Antichrist should then labour to extirp the faith of Christ; for the Pope hath called people from infidelity to Christianity. That letteth not but that he is Antichrist; for the Pope calleth none but unto the name of Christianity, under colour of which he exerciseth tyranny: otherwise he laboureth to extirp the faith of Christ, and to prefer himself before Christ; whose redemption he teacheth to take away only the guilt of sin, whereas his pardon taketh away both the pain and the guilt of sin.

The third objection is out of S. Peter[6]; that in the Church should be many masters and teachers of lies. But these (saith he) shall not tarry nine hundred years, for their destruction sleepeth not. A wise shift; as though the Apostle

4 [On the contrary, Pope Gregory the Great is frequently appealed to as one who utterly condemned the assumption of the title of Universal Bishop. Vid. *Epistt.* Lib. iv. Capp. lxxvi, lxxviii, lxxx, lxxxii, lxxxiii. & L. vi. C. cxciv. *Opp.* Tom. ii. Antv. 1572. Compare Bp. Jewel's *Apol.* Chap. iv. p. 73; and Ch. vi. p. 137.]

5 [Brereley's *Apologie of the Romane Church*, pp. 2, 3. an. 1604. Morton's *Catholike Appeale for Protestants*, pp. 60, 61. Lond. 1610.]

6 [2 Pet. ii. 1—3.]

gave not a general admonition for the Church in all ages, even in that wherein he lived himself.

The last is out of 1 Tim. iv.; that in the latter days such should come, which shall give ear to the doctrine of Devils, forbidding to marry, and eat such meats as God hath created to be received with thanksgiving. In this matter he professeth to be short; as he hath no lust to tarry being in that, wherein his cauterized conscience is so galled. But he answereth briefly, it was fulfilled in the Manichees. What then? Doth it follow that it is not fulfilled in the Papists? Doth the Spirit speak evidently of the Manichees, an obscure heresy; and not rather of the apostasy of Antichrist, whose hypocrisy should be cloaked by feigned chastity and fasting[1]? No, no, Master Stapleton, your conscience, although marked with a hot iron, yet cannot but inwardly confess, that this prophecy pertaineth especially to Papistry, the greatest heresy that ever was.

CHAPTER XII.

STAPLETON. *Stapleton.* Other common objections of Protestants, taken out of the Law, discussed and assoiled.

FULKE. *Fulke.* The objections are these: where was the outward face of the Church in the time of Noe, in the time of the departing of the ten tribes, in the days of Elias? He answereth out of Augustin, *De unitate Ecclesiæ*, against the Donatists, Cap. xii.[2], which made the same objections; that as these examples of fewness of the Church are read in the Scriptures, so the Church to be dispersed over all the world is read in the same Scriptures, and therefore it cannot be restrained to the communion of Donatus in Africa.

The like say we, (howsoever it pleaseth his malice to slander us;) that the Church is and was these fifteen hundred years dispersed over the whole world, and therefore cannot be restrained to the faction or communion of the Pope in a part of Europe.

Concerning the apostasy of the ten tribes he answereth, that the Clergy, *videlicet* the Priests and Levites, re-

1 [Conf. *Can. Apostol.* li, & liii. Bevereg. *Pand.* i. 34, 35.]

2 [*Opp.* ix. 244. ed. Ben. a Cler.]

mained in sound religion, and many of the people: so God hath His Church always; which we deny not. Yet, in the days of Manasse, where can he shew me any Clergy of the Jews that continued in sound religion? And yet I doubt not, but there were some particular persons; for God had His Church among them even then: but the outward face of the Church was all turned into idolatry and false worshipping of God. Where he saith, except the Church had remained in Europe these nine hundred years, Protestants should not have had from whence to depart, I answer; Protestants are not departed out of the Church of Christ, but out of Babylon. And yet I acknowledge, that there were members of Christ's Church dispersed, yea, and Churches gathered also in the time of deepest ignorance, in most regions of Europe, though not regarded, or condemned for heretics; in Calabria, in France, in England, in Bohemia. Finally, whereas he would seem to repair the Pope's loss in Europe with the recovery of large countries in the East, wise men may easily see, and fools also may laugh at it, how vain a brag it is, to boast of matters so far off as none can bear witness of but himself, and such as he is.

CHAPTER XIII.

Stapleton. That the true Church of Christ, which continueth for ever, is a visible and known Church; no privy or secret congregation. STAPLETON.

Fulke. His name is Thomas, forsooth; and therefore he saith, he will never believe that there was any other Church but the Church of Rome, except he may so see it that he may point to it with his finger. But, gentle Thomas, our Saviour Christ saith, Blessed are they that believe, and see not. If the Catholic Church of Christ might be seen at any time, it should be no article of our faith, which is an evidence of things that are not seen. Heb. xi. The members thereof, as several congregations, are seen, sometimes of many of all sorts of men; sometimes of them only that are true members of them: but Jerusalem which is above, and is the mother of all the faithful, is not seen but with the eyes of faith. Therefore, Thomas, if you will never believe the Catholic Church, except you see it with your bodily eyes, you can never be any member thereof. FULKE.

You allege out of Esay ii., "The hill of the house of the Lord shall be prepared in the top of all hills," &c. This is fulfilled in the calling of the Gentiles, which have not ceased to walk in the light of our God since they were first called; though not always in like numbers, not always in favour with the powers of the world, nor always in sight of the blind
Is. xlix. worldlings. And Christ is the "light of the Gentiles," unto the uttermost parts of the earth: therefore not unto one part of Europe only, as you popish Donatists do affirm. And the
Matth. v. Apostles were "the light of the world," to carry the light of
Is. lxi. salvation unto the furthermost parts of the earth. "And their seed shall be known among the Gentiles, and their buds among the people. All that see them shall know them, that they are the seed which the Lord hath blessed." The Church of the Gentiles confesseth the seed of Abraham, which sometimes was obscure and known to few, to be the blessed seed; and rejoiceth that by faith she is engraffed into the stock of Abraham, to be partaker of the same blessing.

All this proveth no light, sight, or knowledge of a Church to be pointed at with unfaithful Thomas his finger; but heavenly, spiritual, and to be discerned by faith.

Is. lii. Again, when Esay sayeth, God "hath prepared His arm in the eyes of all nations, and all the ends of the earth shall see the salvation of our God," he meaneth to the elect and chosen of all nations, to the predestinate people. "Not only so, Sir Protestant." Why so, Sir Papist? "The Prophet sayeth further: *Quibus non est narratum viderunt; et qui non audiverunt contemplati sunt:* 'Such as the Messias hath not been preached unto, yet they have seen; and such as have not heard have yet beholden.'" *Ergo,* not the elect only.

What then, Sir Papist, tag and rag, all the reprobate of all times, is this your interpretation? But, Thomas, I pray you give us leave to believe the interpretation of S. Paul before you, who expoundeth it clean contrary to you; Romans xv. ver. 20: "Yea, I enforced myself to preach the Gospel, not where Christ was named, lest I should have built on another man's foundation: but, as it is written,
Is. lii. To whom he was not spoken of, they shall see; and they that heard not shall understand." Lo, Thomas, Saint Paul expoundeth this text of them which had seen Christ and known the Gospel first by his preaching; and not of "such

as the Messias hath not been preached to." Therefore, be no more unfaithful, but believe the Catholic Church, though it cannot be seen.

Yet will he not leave the matter so; for Esay prophesieth, that "the Lord would be a perpetual light and glory Is. lx. of His Church; that the sun of the Church shall not go down any more, nor the moon vade, because the Lord shall be her everlasting light." "Nations shall walk in their [her] light, and Kings in the brightness of her arising."

Verily, Thomas, though our bodily eyes cannot see this, yet do we most constantly believe, that it is fulfilled in the Church as it was promised. But that the external brightness of the Church is not promised to be in all ages alike, we may clearly see by this that he saith: "Kings shall walk in the brightness of thy rising up:" for every age of the Church hath not had Kings to walk in the brightness of her light. Let Thomas, which will not believe the continuance of our Church, except it be so shewed that he may point at it with his finger[1]; let him, I say, point out with his finger what Kings in every age, for the space of the first three hundred years, did walk in the brightness of the Church's arising. It will not serve him to name Algarus [Abgarus] of Edessa, or Lucius of Britain: but he must shew a continual succession of Kings for all that time; or if he cannot, let him confess, that the external glory and brightness of the Church is not in all ages to be seen, as the spiritual magnificence and light thereof is everlasting.

His next reason is of the continuance of pastors and teachers in the Church, which he imagineth to have failed in our Church for nine hundred years; but he is altogether deceived. For when the state of the Romish Church was grown to be such a confuse Babylon, that it was necessary for God's people to go out of it, Apoc. chap. xviii. verse 4; which came not to the full ripeness of iniquity until a thousand years after Christ; God sent pastors and teachers to His Church so departed out of Babylon, in these parts of Europe; which continued by succession even until God restored His Gospel into open light of the world again.

[1] ["Yes, Sir, my name is Thomas: and vnlesse you shew me who they are; when and where they taught as you teache, that I may point vnto them with my finger; I will neuer beleeue there were any such." (*Fortresse*, pp. 137—8.)]

Beside that, a great number of Eastern Churches have continued even from the Apostles' time unto this day, though not in soundness of all opinions, yet in open profession of Christianity; among whom doubtless some retained the foundation always, which were never obedient to the see of Rome, neither partakers of a great number of her horrible heresies: so that if it were granted that the Church must always be visible, yet the Papists are never the near [nearer] to prove their faction to be the Church; because the Greek Church, for outward shew of a Church, hath been always as notorious in the East as the Latin Church in the West.

Finally, where Augustin sayeth[1], (although upon a text wrongly interpreted[2],) that the Church is placed in the sun, that is, a manifest place of the world; not in a corner, like the conventicles of heretics; he meaneth not that the Church is always seen of all men, but that it seeketh no corners or coverture of darkness, as heretics do, to shroud their falsehood in; although in the time of persecution it be driven into straits, and is content to be hidden from the adversaries thereof; except in some cases, where the glory of Christ requireth an open confession.

The same Augustin would have the Church to be known only by the Scriptures. *De unitate Ecclesiæ*, Cap. xvi.[3]: *Sed utrum ipsi Ecclesiam teneant, non nisi [de] divinarum Scripturarum canonicis libris ostendunt [ostendant]:* "But whether they hold the Church, let them shew by none other ways but by the canonical books of the holy Scriptures." If the Papists were able to prove their doctrine by the Scriptures, they would not labour so much for the title of the Church; which of necessity would follow them if they taught nothing but that, and all that, which the holy Scriptures do teach.

1 [*Enarrat. in Psal.* xviii. fol. 16, b. Lugd. 1519.—"Dominus autem, ut adversus regna temporalium errorum belligeraret; non pacem sed gladium missurus in terram; in tempore, vel in manifestatione posuit tanquam militare habitaculum Suum; hoc est, dispensationem incarnationis Suæ." S. Augustin's second exposition of the verse is this: "In manifestatione Ecclesiam Suam: non in occulto; non quæ lateat; non velut operta; ne forte fiat sicut operta super greges hæreticorum."]

2 [Psal. xviii. Lat. xix. Engl. 4.]

3 [*Contra Donat. Ep.* Cap. xix. §. 50. *Opp.* ix. 253.]

CHAPTER XIV.

Stapleton. Three reasons why the Church of Christ ought of necessity always to be a clear, evident, visible, and known Church. In the second of which reasons a sensible disputation is made, to try whether our country among other might possibly have attained to the right faith, without the help of a known Church, in all this pretensed time of Papistry. STAPLETON.

Fulke. The first reason is, that except the Church and true pastors thereof might be openly known, the infidel seeking for Christianity shall come from paganism to heresy, &c.; the grace and gift of Christ should be unprofitable as a rich treasure fast locked up, &c.; which were inconvenient in many respects, &c.: therefore the Church must be openly known and evident, &c. I answer; this reason savoureth of Pelagianism, which is enemy to the grace of God; presupposing that infidels of their own good motion, without the grace of God, may seek Christianity. But if we remember what our Saviour Christ saith, "No man cometh unto Me, except My Father draw him," Joan. vi. ver. 44, we must acknowledge, that as it is the only grace of God that moveth in infidels a desire to seek Christ; so the same grace, and no outward appearance to be judged by carnal reason, shall direct them, whom He hath chosen to eternal life, among so many sects in the world to find, see, and acknowledge the only true Church and pillar of truth, out of which there is no salvation. Wherefore this reason hath no ground but upon a supposition of Pelagianism; that God hath only revealed His truth unto men of the world, and left men to their own reason to find it out by external notes, such as infidels, not lightened by God's grace, by the light of natural reason may discern. FULKE.

The second reason is, "that it hath pleased God, that because faith leaneth upon authority, and authority is strong in a multitude; although in the primitive Church, by miracles, and evident gifts of the Holy Ghost, the authority of a few drew whole countries to the faith; yet, miracles ceasing, to keep the Church always in a known multitude, whose authority might draw the simple, persuade the learned, and keep out the heretics." If this carnal reason were good, there were small or no use of the Scriptures at all. The authority of the Church, and that always known, might suffice for all matters. But Augustin, (saith he,) in his book *De utilitate credendi, ad Honoratum*, Cap. xiv.[1], useth this reason to bring Honoratus from the Manichees to the Catholics; out of whom he citeth a long discourse to this effect: that as the common multitude and fame moveth a man to believe that there was such a one as Christ, and that His writings and Scriptures are to be credited; so of the head rulers of that multitude, and not of any privy and new sect, such as the Manichees was, he must learn the understanding of this book and Scriptures. This he taketh upon him to exemplify by the state of our country, at the first conversion thereof by Augustin. Although this carnal reason might have some shew with Honoratus, a stranger from the Church, and one not lightened with the Spirit of God; yet how vain it is, being applied to the Papists, you may easily see by this; that since the Church of Rome hath been the Church of Antichrist, as great a multitude, which might and hath moved many infidels to receive the profession of Christianity, hath been separated from it as hath cleaved to it. Put the case, then, of an infidel in the East, which, moved by the fame and consent of many nations, hath thought well of Christ, hath given credit to the Scriptures; to what head rulers should he resort for instruction in the Scriptures? To the rulers of that multitude, by which he was first moved to believe? Then should he never become a Papist; for all the Patriarchs of the East Church have been and are still at utter defiance with the Pope of Rome. You see, therefore, by plain demonstration, that this reason holdeth no further than Augustin's authority extendeth; who in other places appealeth only to the Scriptures; and even against the Manichees confesseth, that the plain demonstration of the truth (which is to be found in the holy Scriptures) is to be preferred before the consent of nations, authority of miracles, succession of Bishops, universality, consent, name of the Catholic Church, and whatsoever can be taught beside. *Contra Epist. Manich. quam vocant Fundamenti*, Cap. iv.[2]

The third reason why the Church must always be a known multitude is, for keeping out of wolves and heretics;

1 [Tom. viii. col. 48. ed. Ben.]
2 [*Opp.* viii. 110.]

which must be, that they which are tried may be made manifest; which cannot be in a secret congregation. Yes, M. Stapleton, very well. The Church was never so secret but it was known to the members of it; which might use the authority thereof for trying, avoiding, and excommunicating of heretics, according to the holy Scriptures. But evermore you do wilfully deceive yourself when you affirm, that there was no Christians known in the world, by the space of nine hundred years, but Papists. You cannot deny but Brittany, Scotland, and Ireland had Christians at and since the coming of Augustin; which were no Papists, as by the History of Beda is manifest. What should I here name so many nations of Europe, Asia, and Africa; which yet to this day continue in profession of Christianity, and never were subject to the tyranny of the Romish Bishop; and from whom the Romish Bishop, with his sect of Papists, hath clearly departed many hundred years ago? Wherefore, according to Augustin's sentence[3], the Catholic Church is not a particular sect in Europe, but an universal gathering of the dispersed over all the world, where God hath His elect in all places. Or, if you understand the Church for a visible multitude professing Christ, there is no reason why the Churches of the East, so many, so large, so ancient, should be excluded; and the multitude of Papists, holding of one city in Italy only, to be received.

CHAPTER XV.

Stapleton. A number of shameless shifts and silly surmises, which Protestants have invented to establish their variable doctrine, and to confound the authority of the Church. STAPLETON.

Fulke. Indeed, a number of these, which he rehearseth as shameless shifts, are shameless lies and impudent slanders, devised by the Devil to bring the truth in disdain; but yet so openly proved to be false, that they need no confutation. First he sayeth, that Luther condemned all Councils and Fathers[4], yea, all learning of philosophy[5] and humanity; so FULKE.

3 Cont. Faust. Li. xiii. Ca. xiii. [col. 185. *Opp.* Tom. viii.]

4 [Cf. Coccii *Thesaur. Cathol.* Tom. i. p. 1118, seqq. Colon. 1619. Brereley's *Apologie*, p. 134. A.D. 1604.]

5 [It is true, that Luther called Aristotle "sceleratus nebulo."

that books were burned, and common schools ceased for certain years in Germany, with other like monstrous lies; alleging for his author that beastly apostata Staphylus[1]. This slander deserveth no answer, being raised by one shameless liar against an hundred thousand witnesses.

The second shift is, that Luther did afterward receive philosophy and books of humanity, yea, and Divines of five or six hundred years, and some Councils also; with this perilous condition, so far as they repugned not to holy Scripture. This seemeth an unreasonable condition to Stapleton; who belike would have all Gentility[2] and many heresies absolutely received.

The third: "The Fathers should not be admitted, when they taught anything beside the express Scripture[3]; as worshipping of Images, praying to Saints, &c., which they had by tradition." If such things came from the Apostles, why were they not written by them as well as such Fathers of later time? yea, why did the Apostles write that which is contrary to such traditions?

The fourth: "The first six hundred years they did admit, because they knew there was little in them against them clear and open; because few books were written in that time, and many lost that were written." And yet there remain more written in that time than a man can well read over in seven years. "Again, cities being stuffed with heathen, Jews, and heretics, every mystery was not opened in pulpit, nor committed to writing." These belike were greater mysteries than the Apostles and Evangelists have committed to writing. But I marvel how they were taught, if neither in pulpit nor in writing. Belike in secret confession: but our Saviour Christ would have His mysteries preached in the housetops. "Last of all, for that many controversies now in hand were never heard of in those days." Therefore M. Jewell made his Challenge of the first six hundred years; which Stapleton thinketh he was not able to abide by, and that M. Nowell suspected no less, because he accounted it a very large scope. But how

(*Lucubrat. in Psal.* xxi. [xxii.] "In tomo operationum nuper excuso obmiss." sig. I iv. Basil. 1522.)]

1 [De Germanica Bibliorum versione, in *Apolog.* fol. 124, sqq. Colon. 1562.]

2 [Heathenism.]

3 [Calvini *Instit.* Lib. iv. Cap. viii.]

he hath abiden by it is sufficiently proved, to the glory of the truth, and the confusion of Papistry.

The fifth: "They reject the latter nine hundred years, because painims yielding to the faith, and heretics to the Church, the mysteries of our faith were more openly published in pulpits and writings." It appeareth, and that in records of the latter nine hundred years, that many old heretics still remained in the cities, beside the Jews remaining until this day; of which he made the Fathers of the first six hundred years so much afraid, for uttering the mysteries, as of painims and heretics.

The sixth: "Some hold, that all the Church might err for a time." None ever held, that all the Church might err so far as that they fell away from Christ.

The seventh: "Other said, there was a Church all this nine hundred years, but oppressed by the miscreants, being privy and unknown." This, he saith, is "vain and blasphemous, being against holy Scripture and good reason, as he hath proved." What he hath proved you have seen; and how the Scripture must be fulfilled, which prophesieth of the coming of Antichrist, and the apostasy of men from the faith: which cannot be, if the Church should always flourish in multitude, and external appearing of visible glory.

The eighth: "That Protestants' books have been lost."

The ninth: "Books of holy Fathers have been corrupted."

The tenth: "False writings have been devised, and fathered upon the first Popes of Rome." All these he counteth to be but suspicions and surmises; which are yet so manifest truths that even Thomas, the unbelieving Apostle, without the judgment of his senses, might feel them with both his hands and be satisfied; although Thomas, the apostata from God, and traitor to his Prince and country, will neither see nor handle them. But all these surmises he will overthrow with supposing one case. If a man have continued in possession, and could bring records of his right from William the Conqueror, and all his neighbours to say for his quiet possession, without check or nay, as the Papists can deduct the possession of their religion from eight hundred years, &c.; were it a good plea against such a man to say, his records are false, his evidences forged, his possession injurious, &c., without bringing in any affirmative proofs, records, evidence or witness, &c.? I answer, it were no good plea. But first I deny that you Papists can bring such records, witness, and possession of nine hundred years; and secondly I affirm, that we can bring good records, evidences, and witness to the contrary. Wherefore this case helpeth you nothing at all; as it is false that the religion now called Papistry hath been professed these nine hundred years: which I have proved by more than forty Differences, gathered out of the History of Bede, and other monuments of antiquity.

CHAPTER XVI.

STAPLETON. *Stapleton.* A note of countries and provinces brought to the faith of Christ from paganism, within the compass of those latter nine hundred years.

FULKE. *Fulke.* He beginneth with the conversion of the English Saxons and Brittany, and so proceedeth to the conversion of divers small nations in Germany and other parts: last of all, he cometh to the conversion of many thousands in the isle of Goa, testified by letters of the Jesuits; all which he maketh to be converted into one faith and religion of Papistry. But that is false; for I have proved by many Differences, that although the first beginning of these nine hundred years was corrupt in many things, yet was it not so corrupt as Papistry, nor agreeing with Papists in many of their chief heresies for three or four hundred years after. Now touching such as have been converted to plain Popery since that time, or by the Jesuits in this time, if their monstrous reports be credible, it proveth not that they are of an Apostolic spirit[1]. The Scribes and Pharisees were zealous to make proselytes to Judaism. The great and mighty nations of the Goths, Vandals, Huns, &c., that overran the greatest part of the Roman Empire, were converted from Gentility by the Arrians; whose heresy a long time they held, as all histories do record. The Nestorians converted great nations that yet continued in their heresy. Photius the heretic converted the Bulgarians. Finally, the Greek Church hath converted as many nations unto their

[1] [See a remarkable statement, with regard to the formation of Romish converts in China, in the *Church Missionary Record* for Nov. 1847, p. 259.]

profession of Christianity as the Romans have done to their Papistry. Wherefore this argument of conversion of nations doth no more prove Papistry to be true Christianity than it doth justify Judaism, Arrianism, Nestorianism, Grecism, which the Papists count to be an heresy as well as the other.

CHAPTER XVII.

Stapleton. Whether at any time the religion of Protestants have converted any infidels to the faith. STAPLETON.

Fulke. The religion which we hold, whom he calleth Protestants, being the same which was delivered by Christ Himself and His Apostles, hath converted all nations of the world, that ever were converted, from infidelity to the true faith and religion of Christ. Wherefore it is a foolish fantasy, that he requireth us to shew one country, city or man, converted within these nine hundred years. If Protestants could brag as well as the Jesuits, they might boast of many thousands converted by them in the new-found lands of Gallia Antarctica[2] and India, beside many Jews that are known to be turned to the Christian faith in this part of the world. If in the time of persecution, when they had much ado to save their own faith from deceiving, and their lives from cruelty, they had no leisure to travel into heathen countries to seek the conversion of infidels, no wise man will marvel. The slanderous reports of Villegagnon[3] and the Jesuits are of as good credit as their persons are of honesty and soundness of religion. FULKE.

CHAPTER XVIII.

Stapleton. The argument of continuance of the known Church is fortified out of the most ancient and learned Fathers. STAPLETON.

Fulke. The ancient and learned Fathers never allowed any continuance of the Catholic Church and faith but such as had their beginning at Christ and His Apostles; and not such as began five or six hundred years after Christ, as all FULKE.

2 [Brazil.]

3 [Fox, ii. 129. ed. 1684. *Catal. des livres* de Van de Velde, i. 445. Gand, 1831.]

the testimonies which he citeth do plainly prove unto us. First, Augustin, *Ep.* clxvi.[1], reproveth the Donatists, for that they would not acknowledge the Church which Christ Himself had planted, and which had continued even until that time. But it pleaseth this man greatly which Augustin writeth, *Cont. Ep. Parm.* Lib. iii. Cap. v.[2]; that "there is no security of unity, except the Church be declared out of the promises of God; which, as it is said, being set upon an hill cannot be hid, and therefore it is necessary that it be known to all parts of the earth." The known Church that Augustin speaketh of is not the peculiar Church of Rome, but the universal Church of Christ dispersed over all the world; which is in such sort known and seen, as the mountain whereon it is builded is known and seen. But that mountain is Christ, spoken of in Daniel, which is not known or seen but by faith: no more is the universal Church of Christ known or seen but by faith. And thus he writeth against the Donatists, which challenged the society of the just to be only in Africa; whereon, as also that the mountain in the which the Church is set is Christ, Augustin writeth in the same chapter: *Qui ergo non vult sedere in concilio vanitatis, non evanescat typho superbiæ, quærens conventicula justorum [a] totius orbis unitate separata; quæ non potest invenire. Justi autem sunt per universam civitatem, quæ abscondi non potest, quia supra montem constituta est: montem illum dico Danielis; in quo lapis ille, præcisus sine manibus, crevit, et implevit universam terram. Per totam igitur istam civitatem, toto orbe diffusam, justi gemunt et mœrent ob iniquitates quæ sunt [fiunt] in medio eorum:* "He therefore that will not sit in the council of vanity, let him not vanish away in swelling of pride, seeking the conventicles of the just separated from the unity of all the world; which he cannot find. Now the just are throughout the whole city, which cannot be hid, because it is set upon an hill: I mean that hill of Daniel; in which that stone, being cut off without hands, increased, and filled the whole earth. Therefore in all this city, dispersed over all the world, the just do groan and mourn for the iniquities which are in the midst of them."

Thus Augustin, being rightly understood, maketh alto-

[1] [al. cv. §. 17. *Opp.* ii. 230.]

[2] [col. 50. §. 28. *Opp.* Tom. ix.]

gether against the schismatical Church of Rome; which is not set upon that mountain which is invisible to the eye of the flesh; but seeketh the utter ruin of that city, which, being builded on Christ, is known in all parts of the world by faith.

But Hieronym saith much for the matter, *Contra Luciferianos*[3]*:* "I could dry up all the streams of thy propositions with the fame [flame] of the Church." And who doubteth, but where the Church is acknowledged to be, the clear doctrine thereof may stop the mouth of any heretic which acknowledgeth it for the Church? The same Hieronym, *Ad Dammach.* [*Pammach.*] *et Oceanum, de error. Orig.*[4] *Cur post,* &c., writeth thus: "Why, after four hundred years, labourest thou to teach us which we knew not before? Why dost thou bring forth that which Peter and Paul would never teach? Even until this day the Christian world was without this doctrine. I will hold that faith an old man, in which I was born a child." A worthy saying of Hierom, which may be rightly applied against the Papists; which teach such doctrine as neither Peter nor Paul would ever teach, nor the Christian world knew for six hundred years after Christ; yea, for almost a thousand years after Christ in many points. The like force is in the saying of Gregory Nazianzen against the Arrian, *Ep.* ii. *ad Clidon.*[5] *Si ante hos triginta,* &c.: "If our faith began but thirty years ago, when there are almost four hundred years since Christ was shewed, and [then] the Gospel hath for so long space been in vain, our faith also hath been in vain; and they which have given witness thereto have testified in vain; so many and so worthy Prelates in vain have governed the people." This saying is verified of Christian faith, which had continued in the world six, seven, or eight hundred years before Papistry in many points began. Christ hath been preached, and yet Papistry never heard of: yea, whatsoever doctrine had a later beginning than Christ and His Apostles this Father condemneth of error. Even as the same man writeth in the other place by M. Stapleton cited, *De Theod.* Li. ii.[6] *Ut hæc præsidia omittam,* &c.: "To omit these helps, yet it

[3] ["Poteram . . . omnes propositionum rivulos uno Ecclesiæ *sole* siccare." (*Opp.* ii. 147. Basil. 1565.)]

[4] [*Opp.* Tom. ii. p. 192.]

[5] [Ad Cledonium: *Opp.* i. 748. Lut. Paris. 1609.]

[6] [Oratio ii. *de Theologia.* Orat. xxxiv. *Opp.* Tom. i. pp. 541—2.]

should satisfy us, that none of those which have been inspired with the Spirit of God hath hitherto either pronounced this sentence, or allowed it being uttered by any other; and the doctrine of our Church doth abhor it." He braggeth not upon the present opinion of the Church, but as the same hath always been allowed of all the Apostles and their successors, and the contrary never received. Therefore, whereas Theodoret[1] reporteth, that that confession of the faith was admitted (in the Council of Nice,) which prevailed and was published throughout the world, he meaneth not that the Fathers followed either the multitude, or the common opinion of men, which were reputed for the Church in that time; but because the same confession had always, even from the beginning, been received and continued in the Church, as consonant and agreeable to the word of God, by which the Church must be tried to be the true Church; and whereas articles of faith are not proved true, because they be held by them that are commonly taken to be of the Church. To conclude, the prescription of Tertullian[2] against Hermogenes we do willingly admit, and offer to be tried thereby; that whether of our religion or theirs is the more ancient, that undoubtedly must be truth. But then the prescription of nine hundred years, whereof Stapleton so often and so much doth cackle, will not serve the Papists; as they cannot prescribe scarce half so long for many of their opinions. For except we be able to prove our religion as ancient as the time of Christ and His Apostles, we refuse not to be accounted heretics. If we teach nothing but that we can justify by manifest demonstration out of the holy Scriptures; the same also in the most principal points being confirmed with the testimony of the ancient Fathers of the primitive Church; the Papists, which accuse us of heresy, shall be found not only to be heretics, but blasphemers of God, and slanderers of His Saints.

1 [The reference seems to be to a sentence in his *Eccles. Hist.* Lib. i. Cap. vii.; which may be found also in the *Historia Tripartita,* Lib. ii. Cap. v., and may be taken in connexion with a passage in the *Theophiles* or *Religiosa Historia,* in the Life of S. James, Bishop of Nisibis, inaccurately cited by Stapleton, p. 208.]

2 [*Adv. Hermog.* Cap. i. Opp. 233. Lut. Paris. 1675.—Dr. Burton remarks that this edition is the same as that published in 1664, except that the title-page was changed. (*Test. of Ante-Nicene Fathers:* List of edit. Oxford, 1826.)]

CHAPTER XIX.

Stapleton. It is proved, by three reasons or arguments, deducted out of holy Scripture, that all the time of Papistry can be no schism or heresy, and therefore was true Christianity. STAPLETON.

Fulke. The first reason is this: No heresy or schism is universal: The faith of England these nine hundred years was universal: *Ergo*, it was no schism or heresy. The *minor*, which is false, he would prove by this reason: The faith of England was the faith of France, Spain, Italy, Germany, and of all other Christian countries: therefore it was universal. This antecedent is false; for beside that in England, France, Spain, Italy, &c., since the Church of Rome ceased to be the Church of Christ, there were always true Christians which yielded not to Papistry, as many regions as he hath named of the East country held not the faith which was then openly received in England, in many principal articles; and namely in that which they make to be the chief of all, the article of the Pope's supremacy, and subjection to the Church of Rome: therefore all christened countries were not of the same faith of Papistry these nine hundred years. He laboureth like a wise man to prove that no sect is universal: but that Popery was universal, it is sufficient for Papists to say, because they are never able to prove it. FULKE.

The second reason is, that No heresy is of long continuance to prevail over true believers, to oppress the truth, &c.: Papistry hath continued these nine hundred years: Therefore Papistry is no heresy. Although the *minor* be not simply true, yet the *major* is utterly false. But he would prove the *major* out of S. Paul, 2 Tim. iii., saying of such as should withstand the truth, like Jannes and Jambres, that they should "not further prevail; for their foolishness shall be made known to all men, even as theirs was." Admit that this were spoken of those which should forbid marriage and meats, which he would have to be the Manichees, 1 Tim. iv., as it is spoken of hypocrites, which shall be in the Church to the end of the world; yet here is no shortness of time prescribed for the continuance of their error; for he said before, 2 Tim. ii. vers. 16, that "they shall increase unto more ungodliness, and their word shall fret as a canker." He meaneth therefore, that they shall not long continue unknown, not to all men, but to all faithful and godly men; as the folly of Jannes and Jambres was not made manifest to all the Egyptians, but unto the Israelites. Likewise, whereas Peter saith, 2 Peter ii., that the destruction of false Prophets "sleepeth not," he meaneth not but that they may have by succession a long continuance in the world: for he himself admonisheth us, that we may not count the Lord's delaying of judgment to be slackness, as Stapleton doth, if it should be deferred nine hundred years; "for one day with the Lord is as a thousand years, and a thousand years as one day." Heretics therefore shall have a quick judgment, and heresy shall shortly have an end; for that neither of both shall continue alway uncondemned. But that his *major* proposition is utterly false, which is, "No heresy is of long continuance," I shew by these instances. The heresy of them that joined Circumcision with the Gospel is more than fifteen hundred years old; and yet it continueth in Africa among Ethiopians, as witnesseth Munster and other writers of geography: as also the heresy of the Nestorians, which is twelve hundred years old, and yet continueth among the Georgians. Finally, so ancient as the full tyranny of the Pope is, so ancient is the departure of the Greek and Eastern Churches from him; which they count to be a schism and heresy.

The third reason: No heresy can continue, and overgrow the true Church: Papistry hath continued: *Ergo,* Papistry is no heresy. The *minor* of this syllogism is false; for Papistry hath not continued from the time of Christ, but hath had her beginning long since; and was not grown to a ripeness of all her heresies in more than a thousand years after Christ, as I have shewed in the table of Differences. Therefore, whatsoever he saith to prove the *major* is to no purpose, when the *minor* is manifestly false.

CHAPTER XX.

Stapleton. The third reason of the former chapter is fortified out of the ancient and learned Fathers. STAPLETON.

Fulke. Now he taketh in hand a goodly piece of fortification; and, like a worthy surveyor of the Pope's buildings, he bestoweth great cost out of Hilarius[1], Chrysostom[2], and Clemens Alexandrinus[3], for defence of such a point as none of his adversaries would ever offer to assail: namely, the continuance of the Church and true religion; which cannot be overcome, nor kept down by any tyranny or heresy; but the more it is persecuted and oppressed, the more it will flourish and increase. And for this cause the true Church and faith of Christ, although it have been long trodden down and afflicted by the tyranny of Antichrist, even to such time as God had appointed that Antichrist should rage in the world, for the sins thereof, and especially for the contempt of the truth, 2 Thess. ii.; yet hath it in the end prevailed, increased, and flourished, and by no craft or cruelty of Antichrist could any longer be suppressed or kept under. Let not Papists therefore brag that they have prevailed so long; but let them now behold their overthrow by the increase of God's Church, and look for their final destruction at the glorious appearing of our Saviour Christ. We doubt not therefore, but determine with Augustin, *De utilitate credendi,* to rest in the bosom of that Church, which, from the seat of the Apostle, by consent of mankind, hath continued by succession of Bishops, and hath obtained the height of authority: all heretics barking about it; which, partly by the judgment of the people, partly by the gravity of Councils, partly by the majesty of miracles, have been condemned. But we utterly deny the popish Church to be this Church: which hath had no continuance of succession from the Apostles' seat in faith and doctrine; though it claim never so much the succession of persons and places. With the Donatists, Simon Magus, Marcion, Eunomius, and other heretics, we have nothing to do. If truth in Aerius and Vigilantius was FULKE.

1 [*De Trinitate,* Lib. vii. Opp. col. 917. ed. Ben. Paris. 1693.]

2 [*De Pentecoste,* Hom. i. §. i. Opp. Tom. ii. 457. ed. Bened.]

3 [*Stromat.* Lib. vi. Opp. pp. 697—8. Lut. Paris. 1641.]

condemned for error, not by the Scriptures, but by the tradition of men; such condemnation can be no prejudice to them or their opinion, when, being called again into judgment, they are found by sentence of God's word, and the judgment of the more ancient Fathers, to have been wrongfully condemned. To conclude, Papistry hath not prevailed against the Church of God; which, having sought by all means so long time to root her out of the earth, yet was never able to bring to pass her wicked device, but that the Church of Christ, and the true religion thereof, hath at last, in the sight of all men, gotten the upper hand, in despite of the Pope and Papistry, and all Papists.

THE SECOND PART OF THE FORTRESS.

CHAPTER I.

Stapleton. CERTAIN demands to Protestants; putting the case that Papists these many hundred years have lived in a wrong faith: all which (the case so put) they ought of necessity to satisfy. STAPLETON.

Fulke. Whatsoever the Protestants can say for themselves, (as their credit is not great with him,) except they can prove one of his two demands, he thinketh no godly or wise man will regard any thing they can say. FULKE.

The first demand is: Where, or under what Pope or Emperor Papistry began? I answer: Papistry being Antichristianity, the mystery of that iniquity began even in the time of the Apostles, 2 Thess. ii., Claudius being Emperor of Rome; and so continued increasing in apostasy until the time of Sigismund the Emperor, who procured the Council of Constance, in which the lay-people were robbed of the cup of the Lord's blood. Stapleton must bear with me, if I cannot name the Pope, because at that time there were no less than three Popes at once; and no man then living, but as he was affectionate to one of those three, could determine which of them was Pope. This Stapleton, though he have a brasen face, will not deny. He requireth us further to shew the complaint of other Churches against Papistry. First, for the beginning of the mystery of iniquity, S. Paul complaineth, 2 Thess. ii.: and for the proceeding of that which was the chief point thereof, namely, the tyranny of the Bishop of Rome, always, as it shewed itself, some there were which complained of it. Victor is the first Bishop of Rome which discovered the hid mystery of iniquity, in usurping against his fellow Bishops, in the time of the Emperor Severus: against whom complained, and sharply reproved him, Irenæus, Bishop of Lyons, Polycrates, and many other. Euseb. Lib. v. Cap. xxv.[1] Afterward, in the days of Theodosius, Honorius and Arcadius, the Emperors, when the Bishops of

[1] [Cap. xxiv. in edit. Vales. See Beaven's *Account of S. Irenæus*, pp. 44—53. Lond. 1841.]

Rome, Innocentius, Bonifacius, Zosimus, Anastasius, and Celestinus usurped more openly; insomuch that they forged among them a Decree of the Council of Nice[1], whereby they claimed their authority; they were complained of by the Bishops and

[1] [The history of this matter is involved in much obscurity; and there is scarcely any end to the contradictions and falsehoods exhibited in the statements of those who assert, that an appellate jurisdiction was granted to the Bishops of Rome by the Council of Sardica in the year 347. (Vid. Morton's *Grand Imposture*, pp. 141—156. Lond. 1628. Sergeant's *Anti-Mortonus*, Chap. xxvii. pp. 419—50. an. 1640. Geddes, *Essay on Can. of Sard.* Tracts, ii. 415. Lond. 1730. Comber's *Roman Forgeries*, ii. 107—11. Ib. 1689. Brereley's *Prot. Apol.* pp. 47—8. Butler's *Lives of the Saints*, ii. 145. Dubl. 1833. Marc. Ant. Cappellus, *De Appellatt. Eccles. Afric.* Cap. v. 178. Romæ, 1722.) With respect to the "forgery" in question, it is to be observed, that Apiarius, an excommunicated African Priest, having taken refuge in Rome, Pope Zosimus directed that he should be at once restored; and founded his own title to obtain obedience upon a pretended Nicene (but really upon a doubtful Sardican) Decree, which appeared to recognise the Pontiff's claim. (Ittigii *Hist. Conc. Nic.* p. 68. Lips. 1712. Jewel's *Replie*, Art. iv. p. 356. ed. Parker Soc. Ballerin. *De ant. coll. Can.* ii. i. §. iii. Gallandii *Sylloge*, p. 125. Venet. 1778.) Two hundred and seventeen Bishops, amongst whom was S. Augustin, being assembled at the sixth Council of Carthage, denied that they could discover any Greek or Latin Canon, sanctioned at Nicæa or elsewhere, which could be alleged in vindication of appeals to Rome: "nulla invenimus Patrum Synodo constitutum." (Binii *Concilia*, i. i. 757. Colon. Agripp. 1618. Rob. Burhillus, *Contra Eudæmon-Joannem*, p. 110. Oxon. 1613.) It would seem to be utterly incredible, that Zosimus could have been ignorant of the nature and number of the Nicene Decrees; and equally impossible that he could have innocently confounded Nicæa with Sardica; a great Œcumenical Council with a Synod of western Bishops held twenty-two years afterward. (Edm. Richerii *Hist. Concill. Gen.* i. 70. Colon. 1683. Ussher's *Letters*, p. 19. Lond. 1686. Cave's *Discourse of anc. Church-Govern.* pp. 236—7. Ib. 1683.) The African Prelates knew not any thing of the since celebrated Sardican Ordinance: (Coci *Censura*, p. 230. Lond. 1614. Thorndicius, *De ratione ac jure fin. Controv. Eccles.* p. 432. Lond. 1677. Fulke's *Reioynder to Bristow's Replie*, p. 198. Ib. 1581. Tillemont, *Mémoires*, viii. 50. A Brux. 1732. Lupi *Synod. Decret.* i. 214—15. Lovan. 1665.) and after having sent to Constantinople, Alexandria and Antioch, and having received from the Patriarchs "most faithful copies" of the "entire Canons" framed at Nicæa, and finding therein no allusion to the assumed papal privilege, but rather the reverse; remembering also the decision of the second Council of Milevis, peremptorily refused to submit to usurpation, the offspring of secular

Church of Africa in open Council, the forgery detected, and Decrees made, that none in Africa should appeal to any Bishop over the sea; and that the Bishop of the first see should not be called Prince of Priests, nor by any such name of pride, but only Bishop of the first see. *Conc. Milevit.* C. xxii.[2] *Conc. Carth.* vi. Cap. iv. *Conc. African.* C. xcii. & *Ep. Concil. ad Bonifac. & Cœlestinum.*

arrogance and fraud: "ne fumosum typhum seculi" (they said) "in Ecclesiam Christi videamur inducere."

Some other reflections naturally present themselves. The first is, that the papal claim to monarchy by divine right was manifestly renounced by Zosimus, Boniface and Cœlestin, when they rested solely upon human authority, viz. the alleged Decree. (Du Pin, *De antiq. Eccl. Discip.* p. 109. Col. Agr. 1691. Reiseri *Launoii Anti-Bellarm.* p. 133. Amstel. 1685.) Secondly, even if the genuineness of the Canon were allowed, the Synod granted to the Roman Pontiff nothing further than the power to appoint a new trial, in the case and country of a Bishop oppressed and injured like S. Athanasius. (De Marca, *De concord. Sac. & Imp.* vii. iii. 311. Paris. 1669. Pasch. Quesnelli *Append. ad Opp. S. Leonis M.* pp. 256—7. Lugd. 1700.) Besides, let Baronius (*Martyrol.* die 16 Octob.) and those who have followed him reason as they may, there appears to be sufficient reason for believing, that there was a most remarkable conclusion to the entire dispute. The Churches of Africa remained for a century at variance with the Church of Rome; but were restored to "peace" when Eulalius, Archbishop of Carthage, condemned and anathematized those who, "through the instigation of the Devil," as he declared, had resisted the encroachments of the Roman see. (Binii *Concill.* ii. i. 644, 645.) This last circumstance proves irresistibly, that though Brereley and others may boast of "S. Austin's Religion," as if it were in unison with theirs, yet the eminent Saint and Father, whom they profess to delight to honour, actually died out of communion with the Church of Rome. (Laud's *Conference with Fisher*, pp. 172—5. Lond. 1639. Morton's *Catholike Appeale for Protestants*, pp. 448—50. Ib. 1610. Du Moulin, *Nouveauté du Papisme*, p. 405. A Genève, 1633.)]

2 [The twenty-second Canon of the second Synod of Milevis, an. 416, ends with these words: "Ad transmarina autem qui putaverit appellandum, a nullo intra Africam in communionem suscipiatur." (Binius, i. i. 705.) Gratian has shamelessly annexed this absurd exception: "nisi forte Romanam sedem appellaverint." (*Decret.* ii. Par. Caus. ii. Qu. vi. Cap. xxxv. Placuit.) "Sed hæc exceptio non videtur quadrare." (Bellarmin. *De Rom. Pont.* Lib. ii. Cap. xxiv.) Gratian may have borrowed his appendix from a sentence in the second spurious Epistle of Pope Cornelius. Vid. Blondelli *Pseudo-Isidor. & Turrian. vapulant.* p. 316. Genevæ, 1628.]

Afterward, in the days of the Emperor Mauritius, when John of Constantinople usurped the title of Universal Bishop, as the forerunner of Antichrist, Gregory himself, Bishop of Rome, complained of him, and pronounced that he was the forerunner of Antichrist. Wherefore Stapleton lieth shamefully, when he saith we make him the first Antichrist: for, as I have testified before, although there was in him a superstitious affection unto ceremonies, and that he was infected with certain old errors that had prevailed before his time; yet because he held the foundation of salvation by Christ only, and detested the usurpation of that antichristian title, we account him for a member of the true Church of Christ. But after him, when, in the days of Phocas, Bonifacius by pride and simony had usurped the same antichristian authority, and procured that the Church of Rome should be counted head of all Churches, he was complained of by the Church of Ravenna in Italy; which would not acknowledge that antichristian title, neither would submit herself unto the whore of Babylon before the time of Donus the Pope, which was almost seventy years after. That Master Stapleton misnameth Martianus instead of Mauritius, I will impute it to no ignorance; although, if such a fault escape any of us, we are by and by cried out upon to be ignorant in all antiquity, &c. Thus have I answered Master Stapleton's demand, concerning the principal foundation and rock of Papistry; although no necessity such as he supposeth doth move me. For albeit the precise time of the entering of any heresy cannot be named, yet it followeth not that the same heresy is a truth therefore.

The second demand is: When and by whom Luther was called, when he begun to preach the Gospel? I answer; if calling of the popish Church be lawful, as the Papists will not deny, Luther had such ordinary calling as the Church where he lived did allow: for he was called to be a public teacher before the Pope's pardoner came into Saxony; against whose most impudent blasphemies and shameless errors he first inveighed in his public sermons. Wherefore, concerning his vocation, the mouths of Papists ought to be stopped. But Stapleton will not be so satisfied; for he sayeth, that the popish Church would never call him to preach against herself. That is not material. The popish Church gave him such authority as she had to preach; which he used first to seek her reformation, if she had been reformable: but when he saw her oppose herself against the manifest truth, he had just cause to depart from her unto the Catholic Church of Christ.

It sufficeth not Stapleton, that he learned by the Scriptures that the Church erred, because all heretics abuse the Scriptures: as though there were no certainty of truth to be found in the Scriptures: which blasphemy derogateth all authority from the holy Scriptures inspired of God; which the Apostle sayeth to be able to reprove all errors, "that the man of God may be perfect, prepared to all good works." 2 Tim. iii. ver. 16, [17.] Again, where he affirmeth, that he had the interpretation of the Scriptures from heaven, Stapleton urgeth, that then he must shew some miracle: as if the ordinary inspiration of God's Spirit, without the which no man can understand any of God's mysteries, of necessity requireth confirmation of miracles. But Luther himself (he sayeth) requireth miracles of Muncer, which boasted of revelation; and so ought we to do of Luther. No, Sir; Muncer boasted of an extraordinary revelation, and taught a doctrine directly contrary to the word of God written; and therefore the case is nothing like. After this he telleth a slanderous fable, out of that runagate Baldwin[1], of the Conference at Poissy; that Beza and Martyr could not agree whether their calling was ordinary or extraordinary: the conclusion whereof was this, that Beza was ordained of Calvin, and Calvin, as Beza said, of none. Which how impudent and shameless a lie it is that Beza should report of Calvin, it is manifest to all men that know the story of that Church and city of Geneva; that Calvin was called and ordained by the Church there, when he was altogether unwilling to remain in that city, but in a manner compelled by the earnest obtestation of Farellus. Cal. *in Præfa. in Psalm.* Beza, *in Vita Calvini.*

And yet more monstrous is that lie, that Beza should grant the rebellion that followed to be a sign of his vocation; when the world knoweth, that the beginning of these civil wars came altogether from the Papists; the Duke of Guise giving the occasion by the devilish slaughter and butchery

[1] [Franciscus Balduinus, in *Responsione ad Calvinum.*]

of Vassie[1]. But to the principal matter in question: that Luther and some other, having an extraordinary calling from God to teach and reform the Church, need not to confirm their calling by miracles, when they teach nothing but that is confirmed by manifest authority of holy Scriptures, in the consciences of all men that wilfully oppose not themselves against the truth, either that they will not know it, or that they will not obey it, it is evident by so many Prophets as God stirred up in the old time; which had no extraordinary [ordinary] calling of the Church, being not of the tribe of Levi; yet, being only interpreters of the law, needed no signs or miracle to confirm their calling.

Our Saviour Christ Himself confirmeth the extraordinary calling of the Scribes and Pharisees, when he willeth them to be heard sitting in Moses' chair: of which yet a great number, and almost all, were no Levites nor Priests; therefore had no ordinary calling.

Yet Gregory himself, in the History of Bede, at the first planting of the particular Church in England, alloweth extraordinary ordaining of Bishops. Lib. i. Cap. xxvii.

Wherefore, if Luther's calling were altogether extraordinary, (as Papists cannot say, except they deny the calling of their own Church,) he is not bound to approve his calling by miracles; when his doctrine, and all things in which he departeth from the Church of Rome, is proved true, and agreeable to the word of God.

The third demand is, that we must shew a succession from the Apostles; as the Scripture witnesseth the Church to have, and the ancient Fathers exacted of heretics.

The Scripture requireth no succession of names, persons[2], or places, but of faith and doctrine: and that we prove, when we approve our faith and doctrine by the doctrine of the Apostles. Neither had the Fathers any other meaning, in calling upon new upstart heresies for their succession, but of

1 [See Moreri's *Dict.* art. Guise, (François de Lorraine, Duc de) ed. Amst. 1740. Bulkley's addition to Fox, Vol. iii. p. 862. Lond. 1684.]

2 [While the words of the promise "Lo, I am with *you* alway," &c., imply a succession of *persons* bearing a distinctive character, the injunction "Teaching them to observe all things whatsoever I have commanded you" keeps before the view of the Church the obligation of transmitting the hereditary *faith*.]

a succession of doctrine as well as of persons. Which is manifest by Tertullian, *De præscript.*[3]: *Ita per successiones*, &c.: "So coming down by successions from the beginning, that their first Bishop have for his authors and antecessors one of the Apostles or Apostolic men, but yet such a one as hath continued with the Apostles." These words of Tertullian are manifest, that succession of Bishops even to the Apostles helpeth not, except there be a continuance in the doctrine of the Apostles: which when the Papists can shew, we will gladly yield unto them. In the meantime, it is not the continual succession of persons in any place, which teach contrary to their antecessors which have taught in that place, that can carry away the credit of the whole doctrine and religion of Christ.

CHAPTER II.

Stapleton. An Introduction to the proofs which follow in the second part of this Fortress. STAPLETON.

Fulke. Repeating what he fantasieth he hath fortified before (which how weak it is, I have sufficiently discovered), in this chapter, he promiseth first to declare, by divers sure and necessary tokens which Protestants do lack, that the faith then planted was a right faith; which, in many principal points, we do not deny but that it was a right faith. FULKE.

Secondly, repeating the difference in doctrine, government, ceremonies, course and consequence of both the religions, he will prove all that they had differing from us, partly by Scripture, and partly by the faith of the first six hundred years. To which I reply; first, that whatsoever was then taught, contrary to that we teach for matter of faith, cannot be proved by Scripture: secondly, that although some errors, which then were taught, may be proved to have been held within the six hundred years, yet they cannot be proved to have been held always, especially in the oldest

3 [*De præscript. Hæreticor.* Cap. xxxii.—"Edant ergo origines Ecclesiarum suarum: evolvant ordinem Episcoporum suorum, ita per successiones ab initio decurrentem, ut primus ille Episcopus aliquem ex Apostolis, vel Apostolicis viris, qui tamen cum Apostolis perseveraverit, habuerit auctorem et antecessorem."]

times; and therefore can make no prejudice against our cause, which take not upon us to allow all things that were held in six hundred years, no more than the Papists themselves do. Finally, I have shewed as many Differences of that time from the Papists as he is able to shew of us from them; and yet some of his Differences are impudent forgeries.

CHAPTER III.

STAPLETON. *Stapleton.* Five Apostolical marks found in our Apostles, and wanting in Protestants; who must be our Apostles, if the other were not.

FULKE. *Fulke.* The Protestants take not upon them to be Apostles, but professors and teachers of the Apostolic doctrine. And therefore they boast of no miracles, which is with him the first note of Augustin's Apostleship: which miracles, if they were testified to us by an Evangelist, we might well believe them; but seeing they are written by a credulous man, that recordeth every fable that was told him, we have small cause to credit them. Bede's History is no Gospel. Beside that, the British Histories utterly deny those supposed miracles; reporting Augustin to be a minister of Satan rather than of God.

But admit that he did some of those things as are reported of him; it might please God in respect of Christian faith, which he planted among the English nation, to work some miracles by him, and yet not to allow all things that he taught. Shall not the very workers of iniquity say in that day, "Lord, we have wrought miracles in Thy name?" Matth. vii. vers. 22. As for the miracle supposed to be done by Master Lane of Westchester[1], which he scorneth at, I see not but it is as good as the best done by Augustin: and yet, for mine own part, I think it was no miracle, but a natural work; the maid perhaps being affected with the mother, or some suchlike disease.

The lies he telleth[2] of Luther and Calvin, out of that ungodly rascal Staphylus, I think not worthy to be spoken of:

[1] [See some particulars respecting the exorcism in one of Mr. Maitland's pamphlets on Fox's Martyrology: *Puritan Thaumaturgy*, pp. 121—124. Lond. 1842.]

[2] [*Fortresse*, pp. 256—7. Stapleton refers to fol. 404 of his English

although he make himself witness of the one; and the other is a monstrous invention of Satan, which, being reported to be done in a noble city, and before so many witnesses, can find none that had the brasen face like Staphylus to say he saw it. Which making and loving of lies sheweth Papists to be the right-begotten children of the Devil, the father of lies.

The miracles reported by Master Fox, the shameless beast, when he cannot deny, being testified by witnesses above all exception he can make, affirmeth "to be esteemed of his own fellows but as civil things, and such as may happen by course of reason." I say not this as though I would have our doctrine the rather to be credited one jot more for any such miracle; but to shew the shameless dogged stomach of this popish slanderer; which, when he had none other answer to make as concerning such miracles, forgeth that we ourselves deny all such to have been miracles: which he is not able to prove, although he would burst for malice against the truth.

The second mark and Difference is, that there was "one heart" of the believers[3]: Augustin and his company never disagreed. The Protestants are at great variance among themselves; not for learning's sake, as the Concurrents in Italy[4]; nor upon quirks and subtilties in matters indifferent, as the Schoolmen that hold positions; but upon the weightiest articles of our belief, as heretics are wont to hold opinions.

I answer: Among them that have departed from the Church of Rome unto the Church of Christ, there hath been some variance about the Lord's Supper; but yet in no greater matters than hath been between two godly Martyrs of the primitive Church, Cornelius of Rome, and Cyprian of Carthage, about Baptism; although not handled with like modesty on the one part as was then of both: yea, no greater than as yet remaineth undecided among the Papists, touching the authority of the Pope and the popish General Council; although they all, like Pilate and Herod[5], the Pharisees and

translation of the "absolut Apologie" of Staphylus. The editor has not discovered the passage in the Latin version by Laurentius Surius, Colon. 1562.]

[3] [Acts iv. 32.]

[4] [Stapleton, p. 260.]

[5] [S. Jerom anciently used this similitude, when speaking of the

Sadducees, can agree together to put Christ to death, and to persecute the truth. Finally, if in the first restoring of the truth, some matters to some men were not so apparent, what marvel; when your Augustin, and ours also, as far as he was Christ's, was doubtful and ignorant, even in very small and trifling matters; which argued some dissension of opinion in him and his Monks, or else those questions might have been determined without sending to Rome? Li. i. Cap. xxvii., &c.

The third mark is an ordinary vocation, which Luther lacked. I deny that Augustin had an ordinary vocation to preach in England; or that the Bishop of Rome hath any ordinary authority to send Apostles into the countries of any infidels: which if he had, they should be the Bishop of Rome's Apostles, and not the Apostles of Christ; for they be his Apostles which hath authority to send them. But if Augustin had ordinary vocation by the Bishop of Rome, why had not Luther ordinary vocation of that Church which authorised him to preach? If you say, he could have no ordinary vocation because he was an heretic, I answer; it followeth not: for even heretics have had ordinary vocation; namely, so many Bishops and Priests of Rome, Alexandria, and other places, as after their calling have fallen into heresies. Wherefore leave his vocation, which against you is good enough, and try his doctrine. If his doctrine be found true, and agreeable to the word of God, who hath stirred him up to discover openly the heresies of Antichrist, let not his doctrine be refused for his extraordinary calling. The slanders and unlearned conclusions against Luther I omit, as unworthy any answer; being either false lies of Staphylus, or inconsequent collections of Stapleton.

The fourth Apostolical mark is the continuance of nine hundred years; whereas the Protestants' doctrine hath continued but thirty years[1], or, as the blockheaded Papist scorneth at M. Haddon, thirty years except six; with Gamaliel's counsel upon the matter, which with this popish Priest is good divinity: "If this counsel or work be of men, it will

enemies of the Church: "nulli dubium est, ut qui inter se discrepant in Ecclesiæ oppugnatione consentiant; juxta illud, quod Herodes et Pilatus, inter se discordantes, in Domini passione amicitia fœderantur." (*Super Esaiam*, Lib. iii. Cap. vii. sig. C ii. Venet. 1497.)]

1 [Stapleton, pp. 265—6. Cf. Staphyli *Apolog.* fol. 95, b.]

come to nought," &c.: whose antecedent being true, the conclusion is stark naught. To this I answer: I have shewed by many Differences, that the religion brought in by Augustin hath not continued without alteration in many points these nine hundred years. And albeit it had, yet it is not thereby proved true; because divers heresies have continued much longer time, which are not thereby justified; as of the Circumcisers, Nestorians, &c.: yea, Mahometism hath continued nine hundred years; begun with feigned miracles; commended by Sergius, a Monk, which had ordinary vocation to teach; continued with great consent these nine hundred years; which are four of Stapleton's Apostolic marks; and also teacheth many things that before were unknown, which is the fifth mark. Whereas Protestants have added nothing to the faith of Christ, but taken many things away from it, I answer; if Augustin with him brought in all truth, and besides that some errors, which have increased in process of time thick and threefold, Protestants were worthy of thanks for removing the errors, though they brought in no new matters of faith; as he is thanksworthy which weedeth a garden or field, although he sow no new seeds therein. But it is most untrue that Papists had all truth before we discovered their errors: for the doctrine of Justification, of the worship of God, of the use of good works, and of the Sacraments, was either almost or altogether lacking in Popery; which by the doctrine of the Gospel is restored.

But now let us see what Protestants have taken away. Forsooth, "From the quick, from the dead, from faith, from the Church, from Saints, from God. From the quick, free will, state of perfection, and all merit of good works." Yea, Sir Pelagian, the Scripture sayeth, "No quick man shall be justified in the sight of God;" Psalm cxliii. v. 2; which taketh away all that you haven given him. "From the dead, all prayer and intercession for them." When you can allow the dead these things out of the Scripture, we will not deny it to them. "From the faith, an article of Christ's descension into hell." A lewd lie of a slanderous Papist. "From the Church, as it is the whole body, five Sacraments." Three more than Christ instituted. "The continual assistance of God's Holy Spirit, promised by our Saviour." A shameful lie. "And the visible sight in this world, assured unto us by holy Scripture." That Scripture is yet to shew, whereby the Church should be promised always to be in open sight of the greatest part of the world. "From the Church, as the spiritual part, they have taken supreme government in matters ecclesiastical." None other than such as is against the Scripture, "Let every soul submit itself to the higher powers." Rom. xiii. ver. 1. "Authority of making that which Christ bade them to make in His last Supper." If you say you make the body of Christ, in such sense as you affirm the Sacrament to be the body of Christ, God's curse light on you. The doing of all that Christ commanded to be done in remembrance of Him we take not away. "The power of binding and loosing, with most of the authority due unto that estate and vocation." A very slander. "From the Church they take Altars, Crosses, Images," &c. Because the temple of God hath nothing to do with Images. 2 Cor. vi. ver. 16. "From God Himself, an external sacrifice; the true proper service due to God only and continually, as S. Augustin proveth at large, *De Civitate Dei*[1]." A slander of Augustin, which, Lib. x. Cap. xx., calleth the Lord's Supper a Sacrament of the oblation of Christ, the only singular sacrifice[2]: so that now there remaineth no more sacrifice for sin; "for by one sacrifice once offered He hath made perfect for ever those that are sanctified." Heb. x. ver. 14. By which only sacrifice there was forgiveness of our sins; and "where there is forgiveness of sins, there is no more sacrifice for sin." Heb. x. 18.

You see what sure and stedfast Apostolic marks these are, which are found in Mahomet as much as in Augustin: so that if Augustin had not the word of God, to warrant the principal parts of the faith which he preached in England, by these five marks he might neither be proved to be an Apostle, nor yet a true preacher.

1 [Stapleton had the boldness to refer to the fourth and fifth chapters, though in the latter may be found these words: "Illud, quod ab hominibus appellatur sacrificium, signum est veri sacrificii." Cf. Crompton's *Saint Austin's Summes*, p. 119. Lond. 1625.]

2 ["Per hoc et Sacerdos est, Ipse offerens, et Ipse oblatio. Cujus rei Sacramentum quotidianum esse voluit Ecclesiæ sacrificium."]

CHAPTER IV.

Stapleton. Differences in doctrine between the primitive faith of England and the heresy of Protestants. And first of Mass; of the propitiation thereof; of intercession of Saints; of their commemoration at Mass-time; of Confession of sins; and of merit of good works. STAPLETON.

Fulke. Concerning the Differences I have written already, in answer to his table of Differences. Now must we see how he proveth them by testimony of the first six hundred years. The first in this chapter and sixth in number is the Mass; whose name he may indeed find within the compass of six hundred years, although otherwise taken than it is of Papists: but yet from Christ until four hundred years be complete[3], the name of *Missa* is not found in any ancient authentical writer[4]. And therefore he beginneth with Ambrose, in his Epistle, *E.* xxxiii. [al. xiv.] which place you shall find discussed in mine answer to Heskins, Lib. iii. Cap. xxxii.; letting you to understand by the way, that he citeth the words otherwise than they be, and so doth M. Heskins; and yet neither of them both as they be in Ambrose: by which it appeareth, that neither of them both read them in Ambrose. Stapleton citeth them thus: *Missam facere cœpi: dum of-* FULKE.

[3] [Strictly speaking, this statement is inaccurate; for S. Ambrose died in the year 396, according to Mabillon, and at all events not later than 398, which is the period fixed upon by Papebroch. Vid. *Acta Sanctt.* Tom. i. April. Fabricii *Biblioth. Eccles.* pp. 213—14. Hamb. 1718.]

[4] [S. Ambrose was the first who used this well-known word to designate the Eucharistic office. (*Epist.* xiv. Lib. ii. *Opp.* v. 205. Lut. Paris. 1661.) Gieseler (i. 294.) erroneously appeals for its introduction to the third Canon of the second Council of Carthage, A. D. 390. Compare Johnson's note on the sixth Canon of the African Code. (*Vade-mecum,* ii. 173.) It is strange that Mr. Newman should have adduced, except as a matter of curiosity, the third spurious Epistle of Pope Pius I. A. D. 161. (Fleury, i. 15. Oxf. 1842.) He or Mr. Christie might have added the evidence of the equally fictitious letter of Pope Cornelius to Lupicinus, dated, as Baronius asserts, anno 255. (Vid. Blondelli *Pseudo-Isidor. & Turr. vap.* pp. 199, 320.) The expressions "inter Missarum solemnia" are contained in an Epistle professedly more ancient than either; namely, in the first of those falsely attributed to Pope Alexander I., and assigned to the year 115. (Blondellus, p. 165.) Moreover Ivo (Par. iii. Cap. lxii.) and Gratian (*De Consec.* Dist. i. C. xiv.) quote the phrase "Missas celebrare" from the third decretal letter of the Pseudo-Clement, circiter A. D. 68.]

ferrem, nunciatum est, &c.: "I began to say Mass: while I offered, word was brought to me," &c. Ambrose saith somewhat otherwise. The next testimonies he citeth are out of Augustin, *Ser.* ccli. & ccxxxvii. *de Tempore,* which all learned men know to be none of Augustin's[1]; but if they were, they be after four hundred years beforesaid.

The next is Leo, *Ep.* lxxxi. Cap. ii.[2], which in mine answer to Heskins, before quoted, you shall find handled at large. After this follow the Canons of seven or eight Councils Provincial, in which the name of *Missa* is found: but all kept above four hundred years after Christ; and therefore prove not a perpetual continuance of that name from Christ until the first six hundred years ended. Besides that, the Masses so named were neither in form nor matter that which the popish Mass is[3]. For, concerning the form, it was patched together in many parts long after the first six hundred years; as their own Pontifical and other histories witness. Concerning the matter, it was not the popish Mass, for that there was in it a Communion; and the natural body of Christ was not offered therein, which within the first six hundred years was not believed to be really and corporally in the Sacrament.

1 [The former Sermon is rejected by the Benedictines, and is placed by them in the Appendix to the fifth volume, where it is ranked as *Sermo* cclxxx. *de Diversis.* coll. 330—31. It does not appear that there is any ground for doubting the authenticity of the latter document; (*De Scripturis, Serm.* xlix. *Opp.* v. 189.) but it would be difficult to construe the words alleged by Stapleton from the eighth chapter, viz. "Ecce post Sermonem fit missa" [Catechumenis,] into anything favourable to Romanism. It is particularly observable that he has omitted the term "Catechumenis," which decides the meaning of the passage: and instead of the expressions signifying, as he renders them, "After Sermon Masse is saied," they would seem merely to imply, "After the Sermon the Catechumens *are dismissed*"; and then, as S. Augustin proceeds to say, "manebunt fideles," &c., "the communicants will remain" in church, and go to the place of prayer.]

2 [al. *Ep.* xi. p. 221. in edit. Quesnell.—Bp. Jewel, in his Sermon at Paul's Cross, (p. 17. ed. Parker S.) quoted this authority for administering the Communion more than once upon a single day. Gratian (*De Consec.* Dist. i. Cap. li.) has falsified the conclusion of the Epistle by changing "Apostolicæ autoritatis" into "Apostolicæ *sedis* autoritas."]

3 [Bingham's *Antiquities,* Book xiii. Chap. i. Sect. iv. Morton, *Of the Masse,* B. i. C. i. Lond. 1631.]

The seventh Difference is, "that the Mass is a propitiatory sacrifice; and was so believed in the first six hundred years." Whereof he reporteth him to Cyprian, *Ser.* v. *de lapsis*[4], who saith, "The conscience of sinners is purged with the sacrifice of the Priest." But Cyprian's words are not so. He speaketh of them, which, being fallen in time of persecution, made haste to the Communion without due repentance and public satisfaction to the Church, and prayer of the Priests made for their sins: *Ante exomologesin factam criminis; ante purgatam conscientiam sacrificio et manu Sacerdotis:* "Before confession of their offence being made; before their conscience be purged by sacrifice and hand of the Priest," &c. These words do shew, that he meaneth none other purging of their conscience by sacrifice than by imposition of the Priest's hands; which can be no propitiatory sacrifice, but the sacrifice of prayer of the Priest for them. As for the sacrifice of the Mass, there is no mention of it.

Again, he reporteth him to Hierom, To. i. *in Jovinianum*[5], saying, "The Priest to offer daily for his own sins, and the people." Neither are Hierom's words as he citeth them, but thus: *Sacerdoti, cui semper pro populo offerenda sunt sacrificia, semper orandum est:* "The Priest, which must always offer sacrifice for the people, must always pray." Where is here the sacrifice propitiatory of the Mass, when Hieronym expoundeth his sacrifice for prayer in the second part of the same work[6]; saying that Christ *in typo sanguinis Sui non obtulit aquam sed vinum,* "in the figure or type of His blood offered not water but wine;" both denieth Transubstantiation and the carnal presence, and also expresseth what manner of oblation he meaneth, when he useth the name of sacrifice, offering, oblation; namely, a sacrifice of thanksgiving in remembrance of Christ's death?

Thirdly, he reporteth himself to Ambrose, Lib. i. *Offic.* Cap. xlviii.[7], who affirmeth "Christ to be yet offered in the Church for the remission of our sins." But the report of Ambrose is clean against him: *Ante agnus offerebatur; offerebatur vitulus.*

4 [*Opera*, p. 128. Oxon. 1682.]
5 [*Opp.* Tom. ii. p. 40. Basil. 1565.]
6 [ut sup. pag. 73.]
7 [fol. 47. Colon. 1520.]

Nunc Christus offertur: sed offertur quasi homo, quasi recipiens passionem; et offert Se Ipse quasi Sacerdos, ut peccata nostra remittat: [al. *dimittat:*] *hic in imagine, ibi in veritate; ubi apud Patrem pro nobis quasi Advocatus intervenit:* "Before a lamb was offered; a calf was offered. Now Christ is offered: but He is offered as a man, as suffering His passion; and He offereth Himself as a Priest, that He may forgive our sins: here in an image, there in truth; where He maketh intercession for us as an Advocate with the Father." What can be more evident against the sacrifice of the Mass than that he sayeth, Christ is offered here in an image, not in truth: He is offered by Himself, not by a popish Priest: He is offered as a man suffering His passion; therefore not in an unbloody sacrifice, but in an image of His bloody sacrifice?

Fourthly, he reporteth himself to Gregory Nazianzen, *Orat.* i. *in Julianum*[1], who sayeth, that "by the oblation of this sacrifice we are made partakers of the passion of Christ." He speaketh not of the Mass, but thus he saith: *Mox incruenti sacrificii oblatione manus commaculat; per quod nos Christo unimur, necnon passionis ac divinitatis Ejus participes reddimur:* "Anon he defileth his hands with the offering of the unbloody sacrifice; by which we are united to Christ, and are made partakers of His passion and divinity." He calleth the ministration of the Communion the oblation of the unbloody sacrifice, as the Fathers of that time did speak unproperly. But elsewhere he sheweth expressly, that the only sacrifice of Christ's death is a propitiatory sacrifice, and such as cannot be repeated: *In sanct. Pasc. Or.* iv.[2]: *Magnum illud et insacrificabile* (*ut ita dicam*) *sacrificium, quod in prima natura legalibus intermixtum est hostiis, non pro parva orbis parte, neque pro paucis, sed toto mundo purgationem obtulit æviternam:* "That great and unsacrificeable sacrifice, (as I may call it,) which in the first age was set forth by the sacrifices of the law, He offered to be an eternal purgation; not for a small part of the world, nor for a few, but for the whole world."

His fifth report, out of the counterfeit Epistle of Alexander, Bishop of Rome[3], I will not vouchsafe to answer.

[1] [*Opp.* Lat. Tom. i. p. 204. Paris. 1583.]

[2] [*Orat.* xlii. sec. in Pasch. Tom. i. pag. 921.]

[3] [*Epist.* i. Alex. Papæ I. apud Blondell. p. 166.]

His sixth reporter is Origen, *Hom.* xiii. *in Leviticum*[4]; who writeth of the commemoration, that Christ commanded in His last Supper to be done, that *Ista est commemoratio sola quæ propitium facit hominibus Deum:* "This is the only commemoration which purchaseth propitiation and mercy of God to men." Although here be never a word of the sacrifice of the Mass, yet how shamefully he applieth only to the commemoration of the last Supper that which Origen speaketh not of that only, but of the propitiation by faith in His blood, you shall easily see by Origen's whole sentence, out of which he hath gelded this patch. *Sed parva satis et tenuis est hujusmodi intercessio. Quantum enim profecit ad repropitiandum, ubi uniuscujusque tribus per panem fructus, per fructus opera consideranda sunt? Sed si referantur hæc ad mysterii magnitudinem, invenies commemorationem istam habere ingentis repropitiationis effectum. Si redeas ad illum panem qui de cœlo descendit, et dat huic mundo vitam; illum panem propositionis, quem præposuit Deus propitiationem per fidem in sanguine Ejus; et si respicias ad illam commemorationem de qua dicit Dominus, Hoc facite in Meam commemorationem, invenies quod ista est commemoratio sola quæ propitium faciat hominibus Deum.* Speaking of the shewbread of the law, he sayeth: "But small and little worth is such intercession. For how much hath it profited unto propitiation, where the fruit of every tribe by bread, and by their fruit their works are to be considered? But if these things be referred to the greatness of the mystery, thou shalt find this commemoration to have effect of great propitiation. If thou return to that bread which came down from heaven, and giveth life to the world; that bread of proposition, which God hath set forth to be a propitiation by faith in His blood; and if thou look unto that commemoration, of which the Lord sayeth, Do this in remembrance of Me, thou shalt find that this is the only commemoration which maketh God merciful to men." Thus you see that Origen taketh not the Sacrament alone, but Christ, and faith in His blood, whereof the Sacrament is a commemoration, to be the only propitiation for our sins, figured in the shewbread.

His last man is Augustin, *De Civitate Dei,* Li. xxii.

[4] [The perverted sentence from this Homily has been cited by Coccius also. (*Thesaur. Cathol.* Tom. ii. p. 657. Colon. 1620.)]

Ca. viii.[1]: *Vir tribunitus* [*tribunitius*] *Hesperius*, &c.: "Hesperius, a worshipful man who is with us, hath in his territory of Fussala a piece of ground called Cuber. [Zubedi.] In the which place, understanding his house to be vexed with evil Spirits, to the great affliction of his cattle and servants, required in my absence our Priests, that some of them would go thither, by whose prayers they might depart. One went thither: he offered there the sacrifice of the body of Christ; praying as much as he was able, that the same vexation might cease. Incontinently, through the mercy of God, it ceased." Here is nothing but the name of sacrifice, which the Fathers then used unproperly for the celebration of the Communion. But that by merit of that sacrifice God was pacified to cast out those devils Augustin sayeth not, but Stapleton absurdly gathereth: for Augustin calleth the death of Christ the singular and only true sacrifice. *Cont. advers. Leg. et Proph.* Lib. i. Cap. xviii.[2] Therefore the Communion was unproperly a sacrifice, but of thanksgiving, as the same Augustin writeth. *De fide, ad Pet.* Cap. xix.[3] & *Cont. advers. Leg. et Proph.* Lib. i. Cap. xx.[4] Wherefore, his popish brag notwithstanding, here is never an ancient Father, within the six hundred years, that acknowledgeth the propitiatory sacrifice of the Mass[5].

The eighth Difference is intercession of Saints, which Protestants abhor. There is no man denieth, but that this error prevailed within the time of the first six hundred years, and namely in the latter three hundred years; for in the first three hundred there is nothing to be found, whereby it may be gathered. Epiphanius accounteth Invocation of Angels an heresy of the Caiani. Tom. iii. H. xxxviii.[6] And although some shew of Invocation of Saints in the latter time may be

[1] [col. 1344. Basil. 1570. Vid. Waterland's *Review of the doctrine of the Eucharist*, pp. 528—31. Lond. 1737. *Discussion* between Rev. Messrs Pope and Maguire, pp. 246—7. Dublin, 1827.]

[2] ["unum verum et singulare sacrificium." (*Opp.* viii. 403.)]

[3] ["gratiarum actio." (Tom. vi. Append. 510.) This work was doubtless written by S. Fulgentius Ruspensis. Exstat in Raynaudi *Heptade Præsulum*, p. 485, seqq. Paris. 1671. Conf. *Erotemata de malis ac bonis libris*, p. 128. Lugd. 1653.]

[4] ["Sacrificium laudis." (viii. 404.)]

[5] [Bp. Morton, *Of the Masse*, Book vi.]

[6] [See before, page 41.]

excused by rhetorical exornation, as M. Grindall[7] truly said; and some Prayers for the dead, as that of Ambrose for Theodosius; whom both he calleth a perfect servant of God, and yet prayeth for his rest[8], which agreeth not with popish prayers for them in Purgatory; yet it is confessed that this was one of the spots of that time; which, being not proved by Scripture, can be nothing else but a superstition of men. What said I? can it not be proved by Scripture? Behold the learned Clerk, M. Stapleton, proveth it out of S. Peter, Ep. ii. Ca. i.: "I think it right, as long as I am in this tabernacle, to stir you up and admonish you; being certain that I shall shortly leave this tabernacle, according as our Lord Jesus Christ hath signified unto me. But I will endeavour also to have you often after my death, that you may remember these things." Here is a strange kind of translation of these words of his own Latin text: *Dabo autem operam et frequenter habere vos post obitum meum, ut horum memoriam faciatis*: "But I will endeavour also that you may have, after my departure, whereby to make remembrance of these things." For I will neither trouble him with the Greek text, which perhaps he regardeth not, nor with Erasmus' translation, which are without all ambiguity. But I appeal to grammarians, whether *habere vos*, in this place, may be reasonably construed "to have you," or else be resolved by *ut habeatis vos*, "that you may have." His collection is more monstrous than his construction; for thus he addeth immediately after his translation: "I ask here, How will S. Peter, after his death, endeavour and procure that the people may remember his sayings? They will not, I dare say, say that he will come in a vision or by revelation unto them. What remaineth then, but that he will further them with his good prayers? And so do the ancient Greek scholies expound this place." And I ask here, How prove you that S. Peter, after his death, will endeavour and procure for them? O shameless corruption! S. Peter saith, that, because he hath not long to live, he will not only put them in remembrance living; but

7 [*Remains*, p. 26. ed. Parker Soc. Compare Stapleton's *Fortresse*, pp. 105, 277.]

8 ["Da requiem perfectam [al. perfecto] servo Tuo Theodosio." (*Concio de obitu Theod. Imp*. Opp. v. 122. See Ussher's *Answer to a Challenge*, p. 200. Lond. 1631.)]

also leave his Epistle, that it may be a perpetual admonition of them, even after he is dead. But the ancient Greek scholies[1] (as he saith) do so expound it. Why are not those scholies set down; and their antiquity shewed to be within the compass of the first six hundred years? Indeed Œcumenius, which lived about five hundred years last past, reporteth that some did wrest that text unto such a sense: but they, which did "simply handle" the words of S. Peter, did expound it as I have done before.

The ninth Difference is commemoration of Saints at Mass-time. If you mean commemoration only, as I have shewed before, we make it in our Communion; and therefore this is no Difference, but a lie of Master Stapleton; for we say, "Therefore with Angels and Archangels, and all the holy company of heaven, we laud and magnify," &c. Likewise in the Collects mention is made of the Apostles, whose memory our Church doth keep. Indeed we use no Invocation of Saints, which was used within the latter three hundred years, but not to be proved in the first three hundred years. Neither do we think the honour of Saints to be a dishonour to God, but such honour as robbeth God of His glory, which He will not communicate with any creature. But Augustin[2] sheweth the memory of Martyrs to be kept of the Christian people, *Ad excitandam imitationem; et ut meritis eorum consocietur, atque orationibus adjuvetur:* "To stir up imitation; and that they may be joined in fellowship of their merits, and helped with their prayers." The fellowship of their merits he meaneth to be, made like them in good works: for he acknowledged no desert of our good works, but only the mercy of God. It is pity that Julian the Apostata had so great occasion to charge the Christians with superstition of sepulchres, whereof they had no ground in the Scriptures:

1 [These "auncient Scholies" are probably the *Enarrationes vetustissimorum Theologorum*, published by Joannes Hentenius, Paris. 1545. The comment is merely this: "Nonnulli per hyperbaton intelligunt hoc modo: Dabo autem operam, et post meum exitum, vos habere semper, sive indies et continue, horum memoriam: volentes ex hoc ostendere, quod etiam post mortem Sancti eorum meminerunt quæ hic pro viventibus perfecerunt. Alii vero, simpliciter tractantes illud dictum," &c. (foll. 138—9. Cf. Œcumenii *Opp.* Tom. ii. p. 534. Lut. Paris. 1631.)]

2 [*Opp.* viii. 246. *Contra Faustum*, Lib. xx. Cap. xxi.]

although Cyrillus defendeth no superstition, but only a reverent estimation of the tombs of the Martyrs for their virtues' sake, after the example of the heathen. Again he saith, that the reliques of the dead were not seen bare, and negligently cast upon the earth; but well laid up, and hidden in the bosom of their mother in the depth of the earth: wherein they differed not a little from the usage of Papists about their reliques. Cyrill. *Contr. Julian.* Lib. x.[3] The pride of Eustachius in contemning the public churches, ministering in corners, we condemn with the Council of Gangra[4]. Concerning the reading of the passions of Martyrs in the church, which he cavilleth that Master Jewell left out in his reply to Doctor Harding [Cole[5],] out of the seven and forty Canon of the Council of Carthage iii., Bartholomew Garizon [Carranza[6]] confesseth that it is an addition; and without all such addition the same that M. Jewell requireth, that nothing be read in the church but the canonical books; as the fifty-ninth Canon of the Council of Laodicea.

The tenth Difference is of Confession and Penance; in which he maketh two kinds, open Confession and private. For the open Confession, used in the primitive Church, he bringeth many proofs out of Acts xix., Augustin, Tertullian, Cyprian, the Council of Nice: which need not; for we grant that it was used, and we ourselves, according to such discipline as our Church of England hath, do use it; that public and notorious offenders make public Confession of their faults, for satisfaction

3 [pag. 335. edit. Ezech. Spanhem. Lips. 1696.]

4 [Videatur Synodi Gangrensis Præfatio, in *Cod. Can. vet.* p. 44. Lut. Paris. 1609.]

5 [*Works,* Part i. p. 70. Comp. pp. 265, 269. ed. Parker S. *Def. of Ap.* v. iii. 10.]

6 [*Summa Conciliorum,* p. 137. Salmant. 1551. The word "Additio" is in the margin near the end of the Canon in this volume; but it has disappeared from the edition Lugduni, 1601. It was restored in the reprint adorned with the improvements of Sylvius and Janssens, Lovan. 1668; but in this twelfth edition the reference to the Council of Laodicea was suppressed. It would seem that there was sufficient reason for Carranza's insertion of the word "Additio," inasmuch as the third Council of Carthage is said to have been held in the year 397, while the Boniface mentioned in the latter part of the forty-seventh Canon was not Bishop of Rome for more than twenty years afterward. See Bp. Cosin's *Scholastical History,* p. 112. Lond. 1672.]

of the congregation. But when this public Confession was abused, he saith, that this practice of the Church, and the counsel of S. James, willing Christians to confess one before another, was restrained to the auricular Confession of the Priest only. But neither he sheweth when, nor by what authority, the counsel of the Apostle, and practice of the Church was thus altered. He citeth an Epistle of Innocentius *ad Decentium*, Cap. vii.[1] to prove, "that particular Confession was not first instituted in the Council of Lateran[2], as Calvin babbleth; but that if a man were diseased, he should not tarry for the time of Easter, but *Mox confiteri*, be shriven[3] out of hand; which was not done in the face of the Church, but privately in the chamber:" whereas this *Mox confiteri*, for all his shameless and ignorant babbling, is not at all in that chapter; which is this: *De pœnitentibus vero, qui sive ex gravioribus commissis sive ex levioribus Pœnitentiam gerunt, si nulla interveniat ægritudo, quinta feria ante Pascha eis remittendum, Romanæ Ecclesiæ consuetudo demonstrat. Cæterum de pondere æstimando delictorum, Sacerdotis est judicare; ut attendat ad Confessionem pœnitentis, et ad fletus atque lacrymas corrigentis; ac tum jubere dimitti, cum viderit congruam satisfactionem. Sane, si quis in ægritudinem inciderit, atque usque ad desperationem devenerit, ei est ante tempus Paschæ relaxandum; ne de sæculo absque Communione discedat:* "Now concerning penitents, which either for greater or smaller offences do Penance, if no sickness come between, the custom of the Church of Rome sheweth, that they must be released the fifth day before Easter. But as for esteeming their offences, it is the Priest's part to judge; that he may give heed to the Confession of him that repenteth, and to the tears and weeping of him that amendeth; and then to bid him be dismissed,

1 [Jac. Merlini *Concill.* Tom. i. fol. clxxi. Colon. 1530. This Epistle is considered counterfeit. Vid. Coci *Censur. quorund. scriptt.* p. 105. Joan. Denisonus, *De Confess. Auricular. vanitate*, p. 65. Oxon. 1621.]

2 [Conc. Lat. iv. sub Innoc. III. hab. an. 1215. Cap. xxi. Vid. Sirmondi *Concill. Gen.* Tom. iv. p. 50. Romæ, 1612. A commentary on this celebrated Decree is entitled, *Perutilis repetitio famigerati. c. Omnis utriusque sexus*, &c. Lips. 1517.]

3 [Shriven: heard at Confession.]

when he shall see convenient satisfaction. But truly, if any man fall into sickness, and that he be come even to desperation, he must be released before the time of Easter; that he depart not out of the world without the Communion." Here is no word of shriving; for the Confession was made publicly before Penance enjoined: and if, in this case, of necessity there were Confession in the chamber, it is not proved to be auricular, nor common to all men without the case of necessity. That which he citeth afterward out of Hierom, *in Eccles.* Cap. x.[4], is meant of asking counsel of an afflicted conscience; for Innocentius, that was after Hieronym, testifieth of the public Confession of the Church. The rest also that he citeth out of Augustin and Cyprian is plain of open Confession: and never a word of auricular Confession, enjoined by Papists under pain of damnation, he can bring within the first six hundred years. Wherefore I will help him. Sozomenus, Lib. vii. Cap. xvi.[5] sheweth, that in the Church of Constantinople a Priest was appointed, which should hear Confessions of them that came to him; and, enjoining Penance, should absolve them: but by Nestorius this order of Confession was taken away, because a certain noble woman was corrupted in the church by a Deacon. Where also he sheweth, that the custom of Rome was to do open Penance, and not private. This writer testifieth of private Confession, used and abolished within the six hundred years; but with infinite inconveniences instituted afresh in the later Romish Council of Lateran.

The eleventh Difference is of the merit of good works; which he will prove by Scripture, first out of Ecclesiasticus xvi.: "All mercy shall make place to every man, according to the merit of his works:" which is neither canonical Scripture, nor rightly translated; for according to the truth of the Greek it is thus: "He will give place to all good deeds; and every one shall find according to his works[6]." The second text is 1 Pet. iv.: "Charity covereth the multitude of sins:" by which the Apostle meaneth, (as Salomon, out of whose Proverbs[7] he

4 [Denisonus, ut sup. p. 64.]

5 [*Eccles. Hist. Autores*, p. 680. Basil. 1549.]

6 [The verse is thus given in a Latin Bible, Paris. 1523: "Omnis misericordia faciet locum unicuique, secundum meritum operum suorum." It is the same in the Vulgate, or Clementine, version.]

7 [x. 12.]

citeth it,) that even as hatred causeth brawling, and discovering of men's infirmities, so charity covereth and concealeth the multitude of our brother's offences. This is nothing for merit. The third place, 2 Pet. i., "when he biddeth us to 'labour to make sure our vocation and election' by good works:" by which words the Apostle willeth us to confirm unto ourselves the certainty of our calling and election, which is most certain to God, by the necessary effects and fruits of our election and calling; which are good works, not the cause, but the effect and end of our election. "He hath chosen us that we might be holy," Ephe. i., not because we were holy. His fourth text is, 2 Cor. viii.: "Let your abundance supply their lack, that their abundance may supply your lack also:" which I agree with him and Theodoret to be the communion of Saints; but I deny that the communion of Saints is of merits, but of graces and benefits of God.

The last text is Col. i.: "S. Paul performed in his flesh such as lacked of the passions of Christ; that is, the effects and fruits thereof; which was, to suffer with Christ for His body, which is the Church: meaning that the Church, and not he only, should have merit thereby." This blasphemy was far from S. Paul's meaning; who saith not, that he should merit any thing which Christ had not merited; but that he as a member should suffer that which Christ had not suffered, who suffered as the Head for our eternal redemption: and Paul as a member suffered to be made conformable to the Head; not to redeem the Church, but to give testimony to the Gospel of salvation, for the edifying of the Church. Wherefore I will conclude with Ambrose, *ad Virgin. Exhor.*[1]*: Unde mihi tantum meriti est, cui indulgentia pro corona est?* "Whence should I have so great merit, when mercy is my crown?" and with Augustin, *in Psal.* xliii.[2]: *Quid dicturi sumus? merita nostra fecisse ut nobis illa salus perpetua mitteretur a Domino? Absit. Si merita nostra aliquid facerent, ad damnationem nostram veniret:* "What shall we say? that our merits have caused that this perpetual salvation should be sent to us from the Lord? God forbid. If our merits did any thing, it should come to our damnation."

1 [*De hortat. ad Virg. Tract.* Opp. iv. col. 444. Lut. Paris. 1661.]
2 [fol. 69. Lugd. 1519.]

CHAPTER V.

Stapleton. Of the single life in the Clergy; of the state of virginity in Nuns; of Monks and Friars; of the vowed profession of both. STAPLETON.

Fulke. The twelfth Difference is the single life of the Clergy. He saith, "We read expressly, Lib. i. Cap. xxvii., in Bede's History, that none of the Clergy had wives that were within holy orders." How expressly we read, you shall hear the very words of his own translation: "And if there be any among the Clergy out of holy orders which cannot live chaste, they shall take wives, and have their stipend allowed them without." Here is no express words, that none of the Clergy that were within holy orders had wives; but a particular order for Augustin, and in respect that he was a Monk, not to have his portion of the oblations severed from his Clergy; and if any of his Clergy were married, so that he was not to live in the College among unmarried men, that he should have his stipend allowed abroad. For the manner of the see Apostolic was then, (as Gregory saith,) which the Papists now observe not, to give commandment to such as be made Bishops, that all manner of oblations that are given be divided into four portions; and the one thereof given to the Bishop toward his hospitality, the other to the Clergy, the third to the poor, the fourth to the reparation of the churches. So that there is no rule for the Clergy of other Bishops, that were no Monks, but that they might marry, if they could not live chaste, as well within holy orders as without: and so was the practice of the Church of England more than four hundred years after, until the Decree of Lanfrancus, anno 1076[3]; who yet was more favourable to them that had wives than Stapleton, which would have them put away. *Decretum est, ut nullus Canonicus uxorem habeat: Sacerdotum vero in castellis vel in vicis habitantium habentes uxores non cogantur ut dimittant; non habentes interdicantur ut habeant. Et deinceps caveant Episcopi, ut Sacerdotes vel Diaconos non præsumant ordinare, nisi prius profiteantur ut uxores non habeant:* "It is decreed, that no Canon may have a wife: but of Priests dwelling in towns and villages, FULKE.

[3] [Fox, ii. 403. Vid. ante, p. 23.]

such as have wives, let them not be compelled to put them away; but such as have not, let them be forbidden to have. And from henceforth let Bishops take heed, that they presume not to ordain Priests or Deacons, except they do first profess to have no wives."

This Decree proveth, that before this time not only married men were ordained Priests, but also that Priests after they were ordained did take wives. The same is proved by the words of the Epistle of Gerardus, which was afterward Archbishop of York, unto Anselm, Archbishop of Canterbury[1]: *Cum ad ordines aliquos invito, dura cervice renituntur, ne in ordinando castitatem profiteantur*: "When I call any to orders, they resist with a stiff neck, that in taking order they do not profess chastity." But now when this jolly fortifier should prove the single life of all the Clergy in the first six hundred years, he can bring nothing but certain Decrees, that such as were promoted to Priesthood unmarried should not after marry: yet he confesseth that there were many married men taken unto the order of Priesthood; but seldom, he saith, in the Latin Church. Yet let us see his authorities. First Augustin, Lib. ii. Cap. ult. *De adulter. in conjugis*[2], saith, that they were wont to bring example of the continency of Clerks, to persuade men to abstain from adulterous marriages. *Solemus eis proponere etiam continentiam Clericorum, qui plerumque ad eandem sarcinam subeundam capiuntur inviti; eamque susceptam usque ad debitum finem Domino juvante producunt:* [*adjuvante perducunt:*] "We are wont to set before them the continency of Clerks, which are oftentimes taken against their wills to bear the same burthen; and when they have taken it upon them, do bring it to the due end, the Lord assisting them." Of this he gathereth, that the Clergy in Saint Augustin's days refrained from wives all the days of their life: which, as it is true of some, so it is utterly false of all. Again, the compulsion which he speaketh of was not unto continency, but unto the ministry; and in the ministry not of necessity of greater estimation; as the words immediately following do declare. *Dicimus ergo eis, Quid si et vos ad hoc subeundum populorum violentia caperemini, nonne susceptum caste custodiretis officium;*

[1] [See page 23.]

[2] [*De Conjugiis adulterinis:* Opp. Tom. vi. col. 306.]

repente conversi ad impetrandas vires a Domino, de quibus nunquam antea cogitastis? Sed illos, inquiunt, honor [plurimum] consolatur. Respondemus, Et vobis amplius timor [timor multo amplius] moderetur. Si enim hoc multi Dei ministri repente atque inopinate impositum susceperunt, sperantes se illustrius in Christi hæreditate fulgere; quanto magis vos adulteria cavendo vivere [continenter] debetis; metuentes non in regno Dei minus lucere, sed in Gehennæ ignibus [Gehenna ignis] ardere? "We say therefore unto them, What if you also were taken by the violence of the people to bear the same, would you not keep chastely the office taken upon you; being suddenly turned to obtain of the Lord such strength as before you never thought of? But the honour (say they) doth comfort them. We answer, And fear should more restrain you. For if many ministers of God have taken upon them this thing, being laid upon them suddenly and unlooked for, hoping that they shall shine more notably in the inheritance of Christ; how much more ought you to live so as you beware of adultery, fearing not to shine less in the kingdom of God, but to burn in the fires of hell?"

Next he citeth a Canon ascribed to the Apostles[3] out of Justinian[4], confirmed in the sixth General Council of Constantinople in Trullo[5]: *Ex conjugatis,* &c.: "Of such as come to the Clergy unmarried, and after will marry, we permit that only to the Readers and Singers." Nevertheless he confesseth that Zonaras[6] expoundeth this so, that if any refuse to live chaste, being asked at his orders taken, he is permitted first to marry, and then admitted to the ministry. And the Council of Constantinople, in the same sixth Canon: *Si quis autem eorum qui in Clerum accedunt velit lege matrimonii mulieri conjungi, antequam Hypodiaconus vel Diaconus vel*

3 [Can. xxvi. in vol. cum Zonaræ Comment. prim. ed. cura Joan. Quintini, Paris. 1558.]

4 [*Constit. Novell.* vi. p. 15. Greg. Haloandro interp. Noremb. 1531. This Constitution was made in the year of the Consulate of Belisarius, viz. 535.]

5 [Or rather in the sixth Canon of the Quinisext Council, held A. D. 692. The Decrees of this Synod are not now received by the Western Church.]

6 [Vid. Joan. Zonaræ *Commentar.* p. 135. Lut. Paris. 1618.]

Presbyter ordinetur hoc faciat : "But if any of them which come into the Clergy will be joined to a woman by the law of matrimony, let him do it before he be ordained Subdeacon, Deacon, or Priest." Where is now the necessity of single life in the Clergy?

After this he citeth the Council of Ancyra[1], Can. x.; which is clean contrary to his purpose[2], if he had recited it whole, as he only taketh the tail. The Canon is this: *Diaconi quicunque cum ordinantur, si in ipsa ordinatione protestati sunt dicentes, velle se habere uxores, nec posse se continere; hi postea, si ad nuptias venerint, maneant in ministerio, propterea quod his Episcopus licentiam dederit. Quicunque sane tacuerunt, et susceperunt manus impositionem, professi continentiam, si postea ad nuptias venerint, a ministerio cessare debebunt :* "Whosoever when they are ordained Deacons, if in the very time of their ordaining they make protestation and say, that they will have wives, and that they cannot contain; if these afterward come to be married, let them remain in the ministry, because the Bishop hath given them licence. But truly whosoever hath held their peace, and received imposition of hands, professing continence, if after they marry, ought to cease from the ministry." This Canon sheweth, that it was lawful for the Clergy being in holy orders to marry, if they professed not continence; to which profession none was bound, as they are in Popery. Again, if after profession they married, they were not divorced, as Papists used in Queen Mary's time; but commanded to abstain from the ministry.

The last authority he citeth is out of the Synod of Neocæsaria[3]: *Presbyter,* &c.: "A Priest, if he marry a wife, ought to be deposed from his order." It followeth in the same Canon: "But if he commit fornication or adultery, he must be moreover cast out of the Church, and driven to do Penance

[1] [A. D. 314. Joverii *Sanctiones Ecclesiasticæ,* Class. ii. fol. 1. Par. 1555.]

[2] [Gratian confesses that, tempore Neocæsariensis et Ancyranæ Synodi, "nondum erat introducta continentia ministrorum altaris." (*Dist.* xxviii. Cap. xiii.)]

[3] [hab. an. 314, vel 315. Can. 1.—The last two authorities have probably been borrowed from the Canon Law. (*Dist.* xxviii. Capp. viii, ix.)]

among laymen[4]." This was a Decree of seventeen Bishops in the province of Paulus Polemoniaca, [Pontus Polemoniacus;] and is to be understood of such a Priest as professed continency[5]: whose marriage yet was not made void, but he put out of his office; whereas he that had committed fornication was put both out of the ministry and of the Church. Which seeing the Papists observe not in their lecherous Priests, they have small right to use this Canon; which yet bindeth none but that province that made it.

Now where he saith it was a rare thing for the Clergy of the Latin Church to be married, Hierom, no friend to marriage, shall testify the contrary; who speaketh of it as an ordinary matter. *Eliguntur mariti in Sacerdotium, non nego, quia non sunt tanti virgines quanti necessarii sunt Sacerdotes*[6]*:* "Married men are chosen unto the Priesthood, I deny not, because there are not so many virgins as it is necessary there should be Priests." And *Oceano*[7] he confesseth, that by the doctrine of the Apostles Priests might have wives; complaining that in his time all other qualities of a Minister described by the Apostle were neglected, only the liberty of marriage looked unto. *Qui dixit unius uxoris virum,* &c.: "He that said 'the husband of one wife,' even he commanded that he should be unreproveable, sober, wise, comely, harbourous, a teacher, modest, not given to wine, no fighter, no quarreller, not covetous, no young novice in the faith." *Ad hæc omnia claudimus oculos; solas videmus*

[4] [There is not any mention of laymen in the Greek, nor in the Latin version by Dionysius Exiguus.]

[5] [The Canon does not prevent a married Deacon from obtaining Priest's Orders, but forbids a Presbyter to marry after his ordination.]

[6] [This declaration is made in the first book against Jovinian. *Opp.* Tom. ii. p. 40. Basil. 1565.]

[7] [*Epistt.* Par. i. Tract. iii. Ep. l. sig. u vi. Lugd. 1508: vel *Opp.* Tom. ii. p. 324. edit. Erasm. sup. cit.—The Epistle here quoted commences with the words "Nunquam fili," and must not be mistaken for the supposititious letter to Oceanus, *De vita Clericorum.* Baronius is surprised that the latter document should have been condemned as spurious; (*Martyrol. Rom.* die Sept. 23. p. 406. Antverp. 1613.) but Erasmus, in his Censure prefixed to it, expresses his conviction, that "Quisquis hunc sermonis characterem non potest ab Hieronymiano secernere, is nec asinum ab equo distinguet." (S. Hier. *Opp.* iv. 317. Cf. not. in Gratiani *Decret.* Dist. xxxii. Cap. xvii. ed. Pith. Paris. 1687.)]

uxores: "At all these things we shut our eyes; we see nothing but their wives."

Likewise, *in Aggeum,* Cap. i.[1], he inveigheth against the rulers of the Church, which, building their carnal house, providing for their children and possessions, neglected the building of the temple of God. Again, *in Epi. ad Eph.* Li. iii. Ca. vi.[2], he inveigheth against Bishops and Priests of his time, that brought up their children in secular and profane learning, peradventure at the charges of the Church. Yea, divers Popes have been married men[3]: for Pope Silverius was son of Pope Hormisda, as the very Pontifical[4] witness-

[1] [*Opp.* vi. 230. "Hæc autem universa quæ dixi possunt de Ecclesiæ rectoribus intelligi; qui ædificantes carnalem domum, liberisque suis et possessionibus providentes, non curant vel in seipsis exstruere templum Dei, vel ecclesiam Domini quæ infecta et diruta est instaurare."]

[2] [*Opp.* Tom. ix. p. 237. "Legant Episcopi atque Presbyteri, qui filios suos sæcularibus literis erudiunt, et faciunt Comœdias legere, et mimorum turpia scripta cantare, de ecclesiasticis forsitan sumptibus eruditos."]

[3] [It would be easier to prove from the Pontifical that divers Popes have been the sons of Priests. Fox, quoting from Wicelius, has mentioned several names, but with excessive inaccuracy. (Vol. ii. p. 391. ed. 1684.) It is a singular fact that the father of Pope Theodorus was a Bishop; and that Boniface I., Felix III., Agapetus I., and John XV. are spoken of as having been the sons of Presbyters. A Subdeacon was the father of S. Deusdedit; and Adrian II. was the son of Talarus, who was afterwards raised to the episcopate.]

[4] [The authority of the *Liber Pontificalis,* which is called by Gibbon "a curious and authentic record of the times," (*Decline and Fall,* Vol. iv. p. 474. ed. Milman, Lond. 1846.) will not be denied by papal advocates. It is needless to enter here upon any minute discussion with respect to the author or the character of the work, concerning which many particulars may be seen in Spanheim (*Miscell. sac. Antiq.* Lib. v. Cap. viii. *Opp.* ii. 647. Lugd. Bat. 1703.) and Oudin. (*Comm. de Scriptt. Eccl.* ii. 258—307. Lips. 1722.) Bishop Pearson maintains that the book was composed by an anonymous and uncertain writer in the sixth century: (*De success. prim. Rom. Episc.* p. 129. Lond. 1687.) while Romanists at first boldly ascribed it to Pope Damasus; and when this supposition was found to be untenable, the compilation was attributed to Anastasius Bibliothecarius, who lived in the ninth age, and who at all events wrote not any more of the Lives of the Pontiffs than those few which extend from Gregory IV. to Nicholas I. The entire work bears the name of Anastasius in the first edition published by the Jesuit Joannes Busæus, 4to, Mogunt. 1602, and in the finely

eth[5]; and Beda sheweth, Lib. ii. Cap. i., that Pope Felix was great grandfather to Pope Gregory[6].

I will spend no more time in so clear a matter. Wherefore the single life, required of necessity in the Clergy, is not proved within the six hundred years so often named.

The thirteenth Difference is "of the state of virginity in men and women. Such state Protestants acknowledge not; but rather abhor it, and persecute it." It is a mere slander: for we honour virginity that is not counterfeit in them that had made themselves chaste for the kingdom of heaven. But when Master Stapleton will make virginity impossible to no man, he is directly contrary to our Saviour Christ; *Non omnes,* &c.: "All men cannot receive this saying, but they to whom it is given," Mat. xix.; and to Saint Paul, 1 Cor. vii.; *Qui non continet:* "He that cannot contain, let him marry." I confess also, that within the six hundred years there were some Colleges of virgins; which differed as much from popish Nuns as many popish Nuns from honest women. They lived not idly, as popish Nuns, of their lands and revenues; but with spinning and making of cloth they maintained themselves. August. *De moribus Eccl. Catholicæ,* Cap. xxxi.[7] They lived continently, or else they married: popish Nuns, though they live never so incontinently, yet will they never

printed folio volume edited by Fabrotus, Paris. e Typog. Reg. 1649; and we learn from Lucas Holstenius that the Pontifical has been assigned to Luitprandus also. (*Collect. Rom.* Par. ii. p. 121. Romæ, 1662.) It is quite certain, however, that Joannes Rainoldus, (*Prælect.* clxxx. *de libris Apocr.* Tom. ii. col. 817. Oppenheim. 1611.) Cocus (*Censura,* pag. 138.) and Ger. Joan. Vossius (*De Histor. Lat.* Lib. ii. Cap. viii. p. 64. Amst. 1697.) were misled by the idea that all the Lives are to be referred to the authorship of a single writer. Vid. Joan. Ciampini *Examen Lib. Pontif.* Romæ, 1688.]

5 ["Silverius, natione Campanus, ex patre Hormisda, Episcopo Romano." (p. 53. Mog. 1602.) Platina thought it advisable to omit the word "Romano;" (*De vit. Pontiff.* fol. xxxvi. Venet. 1518.) but the sentence is given correctly in the Catalogue of Daniel Papebrochius. Vid. Bolland. *Præfationes, Tractatus,* &c., Tom. ii. p. 164. Antuerp. 1749.]

6 [Beda states that Pope Felix, probably the third, whose death took place A. D. 492, was "atavus" to Pope Gregory the Great, who died in the year 604; but this word cannot be taken literally.]

7 [*Opp.* Tom. i. col. 529. ed. Ben. Ant.]

marry. Epiph. Lib. ii. Tom. i. *Hær.* lxi.[1]: Popish Nuns are for the most part like those Monks and Nuns of the heretics Origeniani Turpes: *Non student castitati, sed simulatæ castitati, et nomen saltem habenti:* "They study not for chastity, but such as is feigned chastity, and hath only a name of chastity:" *volentes esse in honore propter putatam apud ipsos castitatis exercitationem:* "willing to be in honour for the supposed exercise of chastity among them," when there is nothing less than chastity.

Concerning the rule of Augustin, *Ep.* cix.[2], prescribed to the virgins that tumultuously and seditiously would have changed their governess; if we do admit it to be written by Saint Augustin, yet it is not sufficient to authorise the superstitious orders of popish Nuns: among whom their habit is not the least part of their superstition; which Augustin in his virgins forbiddeth to be notable, or differing from other women. *Non sit notabilis habitus vester; nec affectetis vestibus placere, sed moribus:* "Let not your apparel be such as may be noted or marked; neither desire ye to please with garments, but with manners." The like writeth Hierom concerning the apparel of virgins of his time. Again, S. Augustin's virgins were not bound to their cloister; but might depart, if they liked not the severity of their rule, or else were expulsed from thence. *Convicta secundum præpositæ vel Presbyteri arbitrium debet emendatoriam sustinere vindictam: quam si forte* [al. *ferre*] *recusaverit, et si* [al. *etsi*] *ipsa non abscesserit, de vestra societate projiciatur:* "She that is convicted (but of wanton looks,) according to the decree of the governess or Priest, ought to sustain a punishment for her amendment: which if she refuse to bear, and if she herself depart not away, let her be cast clean out of your society." If this rule were observed, few popish Nuns should be left in their cloisters. Moreover, Saint Augustin's virgins were commanded to understand what they did pray or sing: not one among forty of popish Nuns understand their popish service which they sing. *Psalmis et hymnis cum oratis Deum, hoc versetur in corde quod profertur in voce:* "When you

[1] [*Hæres.* lxiii. p. 170. Basil. 1578. Fulke has used the Latin version by Cornarius.]

[2] [alias ccxi. *Opp.* ii. 597.]

pray to God with psalms and hymns, let that be in your heart which is pronounced in your voice."

These and many other Differences may be observed; which are sufficient to confute Stapleton, which would make his popish Nuns all one with the virgins of the ancient and purer Church. But Eusebius out of Philo sheweth, that even in the Apostles' time there were σεμνεῖα καὶ μοναστήρια, "oratories and monasteries" of men and women. Lib. ii. Cap. xvi.[3] It is true that Eusebius so judgeth: but whoso readeth Philo his own writing shall plainly see, that he speaketh rather of a sect of Jews at Alexandria, given to contemplation, and not of Christians[4]. Beside this, the monasteries which he speaketh of were not abbeys wherein they lived, but only solitary places of study for a time: for in them they had neither meat nor drink; as Philo expressly affirmeth. To conclude, seeing that in the Scripture we have no commandment for virgins, we commend them that have the gift, and exhort them so to continue. But seeing the gift is rare in our days, and the examples of them that have professed virginity, and lived abominably, are too many; we think it neither needful nor expedient to set up Colleges of virgins, nor to exact any vow of them; but to leave them to their conscience and liberty, which the Holy Ghost hath given them.

The fourteenth Difference is "of Monks and religious men,"

[3] [*Hist. Eccles.* Cap. xvii. in edit. Vales.]

[4] [There cannot be any doubt that Eusebius hastily formed an erroneous judgment relative to this matter: and the idea that the Therapeutæ, described by Philo, give countenance to modern asceticism is perfectly absurd; for they were neither Monks nor Christians. Basnage (*Histoire des Juifs*, Liv. ii.) appears to have proved that Philo's treatise was written in the time of Augustus: (Compare Gibbon, i. 515.) and though Scaliger, Mosheim and others have pleaded for the identity of the Essenes and Therapeutæ, it would seem that there was not any necessary connexion between the Jewish sect and the Egyptian mystics. Conf. Jos. Scalig. *De emend. Temp.* vi. 538. & *in Chronolog. Euseb.* p. 14. Amst. 1658. Moshem. *De rebus Christ. ante Const.* pp. 54—7. Helm. 1753. Neander's *Hist.* Vol. i. p. 53. Lond. 1842. Burton's *Bampton Lectures,* pp. 74—5, 350—1. Oxf. 1829. *Lect. on Eccles. Hist.* Vol. i. pp. 22, 300. Ib. 1833. Valesii not. in loc. Euseb. Bruckeri *Hist. Philos.* ii. 759. Photii *Biblioth.* Cod. civ. Fabricii *Vita,* p. 243. Hamb. 1737. *Bibl. Græc.* Vol. iv. pp. 738—9. ed. Harles. R. P. Tassin, *Hist. Lit. de la Congrégation de S. Maur,* pp. 597—8. A Brux. 1770.]

as though none were religious but Monks. I confess they had within the six hundred years men that lived a solitary life, called Monachi, Anachoreti,[æ,] Eremitæ, &c.; but no more like our popish boars, living in their franks, than Angels are like to Devils. Their Differences I have shewed, even out of Bede, in the Table of Differences. But Stapleton saith, that the faults of a few ought not to have caused subversion of the whole orders. I answer; they were so few that offended that they were almost all naught. And what be the Monks of Flanders, where he dwelleth at this day? be they much reformed? Is not idleness, drunkenness, brawling, their greatest exercise, when they be free from idolatry and superstition? How many learned men be in those cloisters that are diligent preachers, even in the popish Church? What their chastity is, God knoweth: but the country speaketh evil of them. In his title of the chapter he speaketh of Friars; whereof I had great marvel to see his impudency, that would promise to prove them to have been within the first six hundred years, that sprung not up more than twelve hundred years after Christ; but in this section of the chapter there is no word of them: neither could the popish Monks themselves abide them, ever since their arising.

The fifteenth Difference is vows of virginity, both in men and women; and here he bringeth in Friars, in the Devil's name, to be as ancient as S. Augustin, whose words he thus translateth, *in* 1 *Tim.*[1] v.: *Nemo ergo positus in monasterio Frater dicat, Recedo de monasterio:* "Therefore let no Friar placed in a monastery say, I will depart out of the monastery," &c. "This testimony of Saint Augustin" (he saith) "may suffice to shew, that in the Church of the first six hundred years both Friars and Nuns vowed virginity," &c. Surely my lungs will not serve me to cry loud enough against the impudency of this shameless creature; that, to abuse the ignorant, translateth *Frater* in S. Augustin by the popish French-English name of Friar; to make them believe that the Augustin Friars were instituted by Saint Augustin, which are not yet two hundred year old. For, about the year of our Lord one thousand four hundred and six, this order of Friars, under

[1] [S. Augustin was expounding 1 Tim. v. 12, but the passage quoted is contained in his comment upon the seventy-fifth Psalm. fol. 61, b. Lugd. 1519.]

the name of Saint Augustin, was first erected by one Redus, Comes Montis Granelli, and one Gualterus Marsus his coadjutor, at Fesula, a city of Etruria; confirmed by Gregory XII., one of the two Popes that then ruled the roast both together, the one in Italy, the other in France. *Cronic. Cronicorum Herm. Sched.*[2]

Now touching the vow of virginity made in those ancient times, that it was not free to return to the world, as both Erasmus[3] and Polydore[4] affirm, whom he chargeth "very fondly and ignorantly so to write;" how far it did bind you shall hear, first out of Epiphanius, and then out of Hierom.

Epiphanius, *Contra Apost. Hær.* lxi. Lib. ii. To. i.[5], thus writeth: *Melius est itaque unum peccatum habere, et non plura. Melius est lapsum a cursu palam sibi uxorem sumere secundum legem, et a virginitate multo tempore pœnitentiam agere; et sic rursus ad Ecclesiam induci, velut qui mala operatus est, velut lapsum et fractum, et obligatione opus habentem; et non quotidie occultis jaculis sauciari ab improbitate, quæ a Diabolo ipsi infertur. Sic novit Ecclesia prædicare: hæc sunt sanationis medicamenta:* "Therefore it is better to have one sin, and not many. It is better for him which is fallen from his course openly to take him a

[2] [The reference is to the *Chronicon mundi*, or *Chronicon Chronicorum*, commonly called the Nuremberg Chronicle, the author of which was Hartmann Schedel. It was first published Norimb. 1493. (Vid. Placcii *Theatrum Anon.* p. 272. Hamb. 1708. Fabricii *Bibl. med. & inf. Latin.* Lib. viii. 568. Ib. 1735.) Bergomensis, from whom the writer borrowed much, was evidently the source of this entire statement; (*Supplem. Chronic.* Lib. xiv. fol. 316. Brixie, 1485.) but the Monks he speaks of are those Mendicants bearing the name of S. Jerom, and under the rule of S. Augustin. Cf. Hospin. *De origine Monachat.* fol. 287, b. Tiguri, 1588. Ant. Dadin. Alteserræ *Ascetic.* p. 47. Paris. 1674.]

[3] [D. Hieronymi *Vita*, sig. BB. This is the very passage to which the following reference was erased by order of Cardinal Quiroga, in his Expurgatory Index: "Votorum nulla vincula apud veteres Monachos." (fol. 134. Madriti, 1584.)]

[4] [Polydorus Vergilius, *De rerum inventoribus*, Lib. vii. Cap. i. p. 440. Basil. 1550. Eleven lines in this place have been sentenced to extinction by the Inquisitor General, Cardinal Zapata. (*Ind. lib. prohib. & expurg.* p. 825. Hispali, 1632.)]

[5] [pag. 167. Jano Cornar. interp.]

wife, according to the law, and to repent long time from his virginity; and so to be brought again unto the Church, as one that hath wrought evil, as one that is fallen and broken, and having need of binding up; and not to be daily wounded with secret darts, which of the Devil are cast against him. So knoweth the Church to preach: those be the medicines of healing."

Saint Hierom, *ad Demetriadem*[1], writeth thus: *Sanctum virginum propositum, et cœlestis Angelorumque familiæ gloriam, quarundam* [al. *quorundam*] *non bene se agentium nomen infamat. Quibus aperte dicendum est, ut aut nubant, si se non possunt continere; aut contineant, si nolunt nubere:* "The report of some that behave not themselves well slandereth the holy purpose of virgins, and the glory of the heavenly and angelical family. To whom it must be said openly, that either they should marry, if they cannot contain; or else they should contain, if they will not marry." Wherefore, by these two Doctors' judgment, our doctrine differeth not from the doctrine of the primitive Church within the six hundred years after Christ.

CHAPTER VI.

STAPLETON. *Stapleton.* Of Prayer for the dead; of solemnity in Christian burials; of Houseling before death; of reservation of the Sacrament; of the sign of the Cross; of benediction of Bishops.

FULKE. *Fulke.* The sixteenth Difference is Prayer for the dead, with *Dirige* and Mass in the morning. The fortification thereof he leaveth, because it is done sufficiently by another; he meaneth Master Allen of Purgatory: and for the assault and battery of that piece, I also refer the reader to my overthrow of the same Defence.

The seventeenth Difference is solemnity of Christian burial; which is used and allowed of us so far as it is without superstition. He allegeth that Paulinus did write to Saint Augustin, from the sea-coasts of Italy to the sea-coasts of Africa, to be fully instructed, whether the holiness of the place any thing availed the burial of the body, &c. But why did not he send nearer home, to the Apostolic see of

[1] [ad fin. *Opp.* i. pag. 71.]

Rome, the Pope whereof (or else you lie) cannot err? For Augustin was not able to resolve him; who, although he suppose this benefit there may be, that the friends of the body buried near a Martyr's tomb may be occasioned thereby, in remembering the place of his burial, to commend his soul to that Martyr, yet he cannot tell how the Saints departed should know the requests of them that live. Cap. xvi. Lib. *De cura pro mortuis*[2]. And except this occasion of praying for their souls, he knoweth not what the holiness of the place can help them[3]: wherein he differeth from Papists, that think it a great matter of itself to be buried in a holy place; which of them for that purpose is exorcised and hallowed.

The eighteenth Difference is "Houseling before death; which the Sacramentaries make to be of no necessity, because they bind the sinner to a number of other communicants." If it be a matter of necessity, how is it with all infants; how with many that die suddenly, &c.? are all such damned? But he sayeth, the practice of the primitive Church proveth it to be necessary; as in the example of Serapion, Euseb. Lib. vi. Cap. xliv.[4], and of Satyrus, Saint Ambrose's brother, *In obitum Satyri*[5], &c. And is it even so? Doth the example of one man that was excommunicated, and could not be quiet until he had received the Communion; and of another that never received it, nor was baptized, prove it necessary for all men? "Yea," (saith Stapleton,) "who will read only but one Canon of the Nicene Council shall find therein not only a general commandment for all Christendom, but also the ancient practice of the Church before that time." And I say, whoso will read not only the whole Canon, but the very title thereof, shall find, that it was a remission only for excommunicated persons. Cano. xii. *De excommunicatis a sæculo exeuntibus*[6]: "Of excommunicated persons departing

[2] [*Opp.* Tom. vi. col. 385. Cf. Ussher's *Answer to a Challenge*, p. 435. Lond. 1631.]

[3] Cap. ii.

[4] [pag. 246. ed. Vales.]

[5] [*Opp.* iv. 315.]

[6] [Both the title of the Canon and the Decree itself are given by Fulke according to the old version in Isidore's collection, published by Merlin. (*Concill.* i. lix, lx. Colon. 1530.) The same translation has been adopted in the Canon Law. (*Caus.* xxvi. Qu. vi. Cap. ix.)]

this world." *De his vero qui recedunt ex corpore, antiquæ legis regula observabitur etiam nunc: ita ut si forte quis recedat ex corpore, necessario vitæ suæ viatico non defraudetur. Quod si desperatus aliquis recepta Communione supervixerit, sit inter eos qui sola oratione communicant. De omnibus tamen his, qui a corpore recedunt in tradendo eis Communionem, et cura et probatio sit Episcopi:* "But concerning them which depart out of this body, the rule of the ancient law[1] shall be observed even now also: so that if perhaps any depart out of the body, he may not be defrauded of the necessary provision of his life. But if any being at the point of death after he have received the Communion do recover and live, let him be among them that communicate in prayer only. Nevertheless, concerning all those men that depart out of the body in delivering to them the Communion, let both the charge and the trial be in the Bishop's discretion."

This Canon was not made for all Christian men, that at times of public administration of the Sacraments might freely be partakers; but only of such as were excommunicated, and appointed a time of penance for their trial, before they should be admitted to the Lord's Supper: before which time, if they were at the point of death, and the Bishop allowed of their repentance, this Canon provideth, that they might be received to the Communion for their comfort; but yet so, that if any did recover and live, they should accomplish their time among the penitents that was before enjoined them. This thing being so apparent, what shall we say of these English Louvainists; that either they never read the books out of which they cite their authorities, or else without all shame they wrest them against their own conscience?

The nineteenth Difference is the reservation of the Sacrament; wherein as I confess in some erroneous kind of reservation we differ from some of the primitive Church, so they differed from Christ, which commanded it to be eaten and drunken: and it is manifest, that their reservation differed from the popish reservation, both in the manner and in the end. But concerning reservation, I refer the reader to mine answer to D. Heskins' first book, Cap. xxiv., xxv., xxvi., &

[1] [The "ancient and canonical law" here alluded to seems to be the injunction contained in the fifty-second Apostolic Canon, with regard to the reception of penitent sinners.]

xxvii.; where you shall find all his authorities discussed, except the fourteenth Canon of the Council of Nice; out of which he allegeth[2], that the Deacons might, *absente Episcopo et Presbytero, proferre Communionem et comedere,* "in the absence of the Bishop and Priest, take out the Communion and receive it:" "whereby," he sayeth, "it is evident, that it was reserved in the churches, where the Deacons might come to receive it." But I must admonish the reader, that these words which he citeth are an addition of Gratian[3] and the popish Church[4]; and are not in the true copies in Greek of that Council; nor in the right Latin translation[5], as even Peter Crabb the Papist confesseth[6]; nor yet in the edition of Ruffinus[7]. But such draff and dregs of falsifications, additions, detractions, mutations, &c., are good enough for popish swine.

The twentieth Difference is blessing with the sign of the Cross: for fortification of which piece he referreth the reader to Martiall's Treatise of the Cross[8]; and I to M. Calfhill's Answer[9], and my Rejoinder.

The twenty-first Difference is benediction of the Bishop, which he sayeth is mocked at and reviled by Protestants. But he sayeth untruly: for although we may justly deride the

[2] [*Fortresse*, p. 333.]

[3] [This is a mistake. The truth is, that Gratian's chapter (*Dist.* xciii. Cap. xiv.) is free from the interpolation; and that as far as the word "amputentur" he used the Isidorian version of the fourteenth Nicene Canon, while the remainder is taken from the eighteenth Canon as translated by Dionysius Exiguus, who is followed by Ivo (*Decret.* ii. Cap. xxxvi. Lovan. 1561.) and the *Codex* printed at Mentz in 1525.]

[4] [Jac. Merlini *Concilia*, i. lx.—From Isidorus Mercator Stapleton may have derived this spurious passage: "Quod si non fuerit in præsenti vel Episcopus vel Presbyter, tunc ipsi proferant et edant."]

[5] [By Dionysius Exiguus, whose version accompanies the Greek in Binius. (i. i. 278.)]

[6] [*Concill.* Tom. i. pp. 255, 256. Colon. Agr. 1551.]

[7] [Another error is apparent here; for in Rufin's abridgment of the Canon we find this strange decision inserted: "Si vero Presbyter nullus sit in præsenti, tunc demum etiam ipsis licere dividere." (*Hist. Eccles.* Lib. i. C. vi. Basil. 1549.) Fulke's inaccuracy may be detected by consulting the Centuriators. (*Cent.* iv. Cap. vii. col. 491. & Cap. ix. c. 658. Basil. 1562.)]

[8] [Art. v.]

[9] [p. 250, seqq.]

vain ceremonial casting of Crosses in the air of their bite-sheeps rather than Bishops with their two fingers, which is nothing else but a ridiculous superstition; yet we contemn not the godly benediction of a Christian Bishop and pastor, which useth the same according to the word of God. Therefore the examples of Nectarius, which desired the benediction of his Bishop Diodorus at his departure; and Aurelius, which blessed Augustin and his company, after he had visited them, shew no Difference of them from us. And if Eudoxia the Empress desired Chrysostom to bless her son Theodosius his godson, what did Chrysostom but pray for him, and wish him well in the name of the Lord? And how did Diodorus bless Nectarius, and Aurelius bless Augustin and the rest, but by godly prayer made to God for them? not with vain, dumb, and idle ceremonies after the popish manner: so that the manner of blessing of the ancient times doth rather prove a Difference of Papists from them, than of us from them. And moreover you may consider how, to make up a number of Differences, what small matters he is fain to fly unto; and even such as he hath no shew of hold at all in the writers of the ancient Church of six hundred years after Christ for them; but only to set a face of the matter, as though there were nothing new amongst them: when not only their ceremonies, but also many of the principal articles of their doctrine, wherein they differ from us, were either not heard of in those ages, or else were openly impugned by writers of those times. Only the dregs and refuse of the former age they retain; as Prayer for the dead, Invocation of Saints, and a few other such matters.

CHAPTER VII.

STAPLETON. *Stapleton.* Of Pilgrimage and Reliques; of church service; of Altars; of church ornaments, and holy vessels; of the Ecclesiastical Tonsure; and of Holy Water.

FULKE. *Fulke.* The twenty-second Difference is pilgrimage to holy places, especially to Rome. Indeed we find that peregrination to Jerusalem was esteemed of many, and great resort to Rome of the wiser sort; not for the holiness of the places, but for the frequence of godly and learned men then living in those places. Otherwise, for the holiness of the place, S. Hierom, *ad Paulinum*[1], whither M. Stapleton sendeth us, doth sufficiently declare what was to be esteemed of it. *Non Hierosolymis fuisse, sed Hierosolymis bene vixisse laudandum est:* "It is no praise to have been at Hierusalem, but to have lived well at Hierusalem." And speaking even of our own country, he addeth: *Et de Hierosolymis et de Britannia æqualiter patet aula cœlestis:* "The court of heaven is open equally from Jerusalem and from Britain." Again: *Beatus Hilarion, cum Palæstinus esset, et in Palæstina viveret, uno tantum die vidit Hierosolymam; ut nec contemnere loca sancta propter vicinitatem, [viciniam,] nec rursus Dominum loco claudere videretur:* "Blessed Hilarion, when he was a Palestine born, and lived in Palestine, saw Jerusalem but one day only; that neither he might seem to contemn the holy places because of nearness, nor again to shut up the Lord in a place." And because Master Stapleton maketh pilgrimage a matter of faith, he saith further, after he hath shewed how many excellent men never came at Jerusalem, &c.: *Quorsum, inquies, hæc tam longo repetita principio? Videlicet, ne quicquam fidei tuæ deesse putes, quia Hierosolymam non vidisti:* "Thou wilt say, To what end are these things fetched from so long a beginning? Verily, that thou shouldest not think any thing to be wanting to thy faith, because thou hast not seen Jerusalem." Thus Hierom, albeit it was much used, yet judged peregrination unto Jerusalem to be a matter of small importance[2].

1 [*Opp.* Tom. i. 102. Conf. Pet. Molin. *De Peregrinationibus superstitiosis*, p. 36. Hanov. 1607.]

2 [The most remarkable ancient treatise, discommending pilgrimages to Jerusalem, is probably the Oration or Epistle of S. Gregory Nyssen, *De iis qui adeunt Hierosolyma.* As it might have been expected, Bellarmin devotes a folio column to the endeavour to "dilute" its strength. (*De cultu Sanctorum*, iii. viii. 1087. *Disp.* T. ii. Ingol. 1601.) He commences with saying, "forte non esse Nysseni illam Orationem"; and, to give weight to his suspicion, he adds, "forte etiam Græce non invenitur." It happens, however, that the genuineness of the document has been fully demonstrated; and that, a considerable time before he wrote, this tract had been published both in Latin and Greek, 8vo. Paris. apud Guil. Morelium, 1551. In the year 1562, on account of its rarity, the Centuriators reprinted the anonymous Latin version; (*Cent.* iv. Cap. x. coll. 936—8.) and Peter Du Moulin's edition appeared at Paris in 1606, and again Hanov. 1607. Oudin (*De Scriptt.*

But Chrysostom sayeth, *Hom.* v. *de beato Job*[1], that if strength of body did serve, and that he were not letted with the charge of his Church, he would have travelled to Rome, to see the chains wherewith Saint Paul was bound: and this Stapleton will warrant to have been done without superstition. I would fain know how he will discharge this saying of his, in the same Homily, either of superstition or of an excessive commendation: *Si quis me cœlo condonet omni, vel ea qua Pauli manus vinciebatur catena, illam ego honore præponerem*: "If any man could give me all heaven, or else that chain wherewith Saint Paul's hand was bound, I would prefer that chain in honour[2]." Excuse this if you can, so it be not with a rhetorical exornation; for that you cannot abide. Nevertheless, the same Chrysostom sheweth, that it was not needful for obtaining remission of sins to take in hand any pilgrimage. *In Epist. ad Phil. Hom.*[3]: *Non opus est in longinqua peregrinando transire, nec ad remotissimas ire nationes; non pericula, non labores tolerare, sed velle tantummodo*: "There is no need to go a pilgrimage

Eccles. i. 608.) has charged Claud Morell with having been prevailed upon by the Jesuit Fronto Ducæus to suppress a treatise which had been issued by his father; but it is comprised amongst the collected works of S. Gregory, Tom. ii. pp. 1084—7. Paris. 1615, and is followed by the intemperate notes of the malevolent Gretser. Conf. Fabricii *Bibl. Græc.* ix. 120. ed. Harles. Montfaucon, *Diarium Italicum*, Cap. xxi. p. 309. Paris. 1702.]

[1] [These five Homilies, set forth in Latin by Lælius Tiphernas, are utterly fictitious, (Cf. ed. Ben. vi. 579.) though Sixtus Senensis assigns them to S. Chrysostom "sine ulla controversia." (*Biblioth.* iv. 277. Franc. 1575.)]

[2] [See some striking language toward the end of the thirty-second Homily on the Epistle to the Romans.—A spurious Sermon, *In adorationem venerabilium Catenarum*, &c., is frequently attributed to S. Chrysostom; but Baronius rejects it, because "nondum Petri Catenæ innotuissent, nec Constantinopolim delatæ essent." (*Annall.* Tom. v. ad an. 439. n. v. Conf. not. in *Martyrol.* die Aug. 1. Crakanthorp, *Contra Archiep. Spalatens.* p. 414. Lond. 1625. Coci *Censur.* p. 166.) The words "membra mihi optabilia, *ipsaque cœlesti gloria longe meliora*," in reference to S. Peter's martyrdom, occur in the counterfeit "Oratio encomiastica in principes Apostolorum Petrum et Paulum." (*Opp.* T. viii. Par. ii. p. 10. ed. Bened.)]

[3] [Fulke has used the Latin version of S. Chrysostom's first Homily on the Epistle to Philemon, by Ambrosius Camaldulensis. Vid. pag. 1738. ed. Commelin. 1596.]

into far countries, nor to go to the furthest nations, nor to suffer perils nor travels, but only to be willing." Now let the wisdom of the Papists take heed, as he admonisheth the wisdom of the Protestants, that they charge not Chrysostom with the heresy of *sola fides,* or licentious liberty, more than we check him for superstition. The like of remission of sins, without pilgrimage, he sayeth, *Hom. de Anima,* [*Anna,*] *et educatione Samuelis*[4]; which is as contrary to the draff of popish pilgrimage as the peregrination used in this day is out of use with us. For Papists were wont to make pilgrimage a meritorious work; and many had it in penance, persuaded by their ghostly father they could not otherwise have remission of their sins, except perhaps by a Pope's pardon, with a commutation of penance.

Concerning the place of Augustin which he citeth, *Ep.* cxxxvii.[5], it proveth no ordinary pilgrimage then in use; but only sheweth Augustin's device in a case of such doubt, as he could not find out the truth between one that was accused and his accuser; that it was not amiss they should both travel to some such place, where miracles are said to be wrought, if happily [haply] there in such place the truth might be revealed by miracle. And yet I confess, not urged by any thing Stapleton saith, that Augustin elsewhere speaketh of peregrination to Rome. *In Psal.* lxxxv.[6]: *Quales isti Principes venerunt de Babylone? Principes credentes de sæculo. Principes venerunt ad urbem Romam, quasi caput Babylonis: non ierunt ad templum Imperatoris, sed ad memoriam piscatoris:* "What are these Princes that came from Babylon? Princes of the world, that believe. The Princes came to Rome, as to the head of Babylon: they went not to the temple of the Emperor, but to the memory of a fisher."

To conclude, as there was used peregrination to Jerusalem and other places, to the memories of Martyrs, so was there never any pilgrimage to Images, which is the greatest pilgrimage of Papists, within the six hundred years mentioned: wherein Papists differ as much from their practice as we, and more also.

The twenty-third Difference is the reverence of Reliques,

4 [The Homily cited is the third Sermon on Hannah, translated by Erasmus. Vid. Tom. iv. p. 723. ed. Bened.]

5 [al. lxxviii. *Opp.* ii. coll. 138—9.]

6 [lxxxvi. (Engl. lxxxvii.) fol. 83, b. Lugd. 1519.]

used within the six hundred years, as witnesseth Basil, Chrysostom, and other. The Reliques or bodies of the Saints we reverence, so far as we have any warrant out of the holy Scriptures. Neither did those ancient Fathers (although immoderate in that kind of reverence) yet make idols of them; nor set them bare to be seen or handled, and worshipped, but laid up in the earth; as I have before shewed[1] out of Cyrillus, Lib. x. *Contra Julianum.* But what inconvenience grew by that excessive esteeming of the dead bodies of the Saints Sozomenus sheweth, Li. vii. Ca. x.[2]: *Pauli Constantinopolitani Episcopi corpus in ecclesia repositum est. Id quod et multos veritatis ignaros, præsertim mulieres ac plures e plebe, in eam opinionem induxit, ut Apostolum Paulum ibi conditum esse putent:* "The body of Paul, Bishop of Constantinople, was buried in the church. Which thing brought many ignorant of the truth, especially women and many of the common people, into this opinion, that they think the Apostle Paul to be buried there." But whereas in the end he would have us restore so many holy Reliques of abbeys and churches as have been spoiled and profaned, it is needless, seeing the Papists can make as many when they list; even by the same cunning that they make some of the Apostles to have two or three bodies apiece, beside heads, arms, ribs, and other parts in infinite places: whereof he that will hear more, let him read Calvin's book of Reliques; and credit him but as a reporter of that which all the world is able to reprove him of, if he should wilfully feign any thing.

The twenty-fourth Difference is Altars; for proof whereof he bringeth Chrysostom and Augustin, which speak of Altars, whom also he confesseth to call the same tables: but that neither in matter nor form they were like popish Altars, but tables indeed made of boards, and removable, and standing in the midst of the church, I have shewed sufficiently in mine answer to Doctor Heskins, Lib. iii. Cap. xxxi.; by which it is proved that the Papists, and not we, differ from the primitive Church in this point.

The twenty-fifth Difference is Latin service; which he would prove out of Bede by the books "that Gregory sent to Augustin; which could be none other but Latin." But

[1] [p. 89.]

[2] [The extract commencing at "Id quod" is taken from the Latin version by Musculus.]

how prove you that those books were service-books[3]? or that, if they were service-books, they were not translated into the vulgar tongue? As for the fortification of this piece by the elder times, he referreth us to Doctor Harding's proof against Master Jewell's Challenge: and to the same Bishop's learned Reply do I refer the reader for overthrow of the same feeble fortress of Harding.

The twenty-sixth Difference is of altar-cloths, church-vestments, &c. Such altar-cloths and such vestments as Christ used in the celebration of the holy Sacrament we think not only to be sufficient, but also most convenient, for the administration of the same. Nevertheless, if any other vestments, without superstition, be appointed by lawful authority, we think no strife or contention is to be raised for so small matters.

But let us see of what antiquity he will make the holy vestments. First, Tertullian, *Lib. de Monogam.*[4], maketh mention of *infulas*, the upper garment of the Priest. But he might understand Tertullian (if he were disposed) to use that term but in derision of them, that, when they would be proud against the Clergy, they alleged that we are all Priests, &c.; but when we are called (said he) to the same severity of discipline with the Clergy, *deponimus infulas, et pares sumus*[5], "we put off our rochets, and we be private men." This *infula* was the apparel of the heathen Priests; to which he alludeth, when he scoffeth at them that in dignity would be Priests, but in discipline laymen. The alb which is spoken of, *Con. Carthag.* iv. Can. xli.[6], was nothing like your popish alb; but a white garment, which was used in sign of dignity, and was forbidden of the Deacons to be worn, but only in time of the oblation and reading. Saint John's *petalum*[7], if he

3 [Bede merely mentions "codices plurimos." (Lib. i. Cap. xxix.)]

4 [Cap. xii. Tertullian was a Montanist when he composed this treatise.]

5 [Rigaltius correctly reads "impares sumus."]

6 ["Ut Diaconus tempore oblationis tantum, vel lectionis, alba induatur." (Joverii *Sanctiones Eccles.* Class. ii. fol. 21. Paris. 1555.)]

7 [Eusebius (*Hist. Ecc.* iii. xxxi.) quotes an Epistle of Polycrates, in which he states that S. John wore "τὸ πέταλον," a golden plate, (called also "the plate of the holy crown,") such as that which adorned the forehead of the High Priest. See Exod. xxviii. 36: xxxix. 30. Lightfoot's *Temple Service*, Chap. iii. p. 21.]

could tell what to make of it, he would not call it generally "a pontifical vestment." Saint John was a poor *Pontifex* to go *in pontificalibus*. The rich garment which Constantine gave to the church of Jerusalem, if it had been a cope, (as he saith,) it had been an unhandsome garment to dance in; as the story saith it came into the hands of one that danced in it[1]. The admonition that he giveth[2] to such as sleep in Church goods, meaning belike such as have their beds garnished with old copes, were more meet to be made to some of his benefactors that sleep in abbeys, and yet will not awake out of them.

To conclude, although there is some mention of garments, applied specially for the use of divine service, yet the popish tragical trumpery of this time differeth as much from them in form and use as they do in time and age.

The twenty-seventh Difference is of holy vessels. Such vessels as are comely and decent for the ministration of the Sacraments we have without superstition; which, beginning to grow in the ancient times, the Fathers did rather reprove than foster.

Gregory Nazianzen, whom he citeth in his Oration *Advers. Arrianos, et de seipso*[3], speaking of the ministering vessels that might not be touched of many, meaneth allegorically of profaning the mysteries of Christian religion; alluding to the profanation of the vessels of the Jewish temple by Nabuzardan and Balthasar[4], as his words do plainly shew: Ποῖα λειτουργικὰ σκεύη, τοῖς πολλοῖς ἄψαυστα, χερσὶν ἀνόμων ἐξέδωκα,

1 [and fell down dead. Vid. *Histor. Tripartit.* Lib. v. Cap. xxxvii. August. 1472.]

2 [Stapleton's excellent admonition is this: "Let such as sleepe in church gooddes awake at this example. Let them remember that by their impenitent hart they heape vnto themselves wrath in the day of iudgement. Let them not be carelesse, though now they sit soft; but rather feare, that the longer the blow is a fetching, the sorer it shall strike when it falleth downe." (*Fortresse*, p. 352.) The Epistle to the reader, prefixed to Sir Henry Spelman's tract *De non temerandis Ecclesiis*, Oxf. 1646, contains sufficient proof, that there is nothing unfounded in the fear, that those who are guilty of sacrilege will not "be visited after the visitation of all men." Many are the judgments which may be traced to the commission of this sin, in the United Kingdom as well as on the Continent.]

3 [*Opp.* Tom. i. p. 433. Lut. Paris. 1609.]

4 [2 Kings xxv. Dan. v.]

ἢ Ναβουζαρδάν; &c.: "What ministering vessels, not to be touched of many, have I delivered to the hands of the wicked; either to Nabuzardan, or to Balthasar, which rioted wickedly in holy things, and suffered punishment worthy of his madness?"

Chrysostom reproved the preposterous superstition of the people, which durst not touch the holy vessels, but yet feared not to defile themselves with sin. *In Ep. ad Eph. H.* xiv.[5]: *Non vides,* &c.: "Dost thou not see those holy vessels? Be they not always used to one purpose? Dare any man use them to any other purpose? Now art thou thyself more holy than these vessels, and that by much. Why then dost thou pollute and defile thyself?" He hath forgotten Exuperius, Bishop of Tholosse[6], which carried the Lord's body in a wicker basket, and His blood in a glass, when he maketh so much ado about holy vessels. Hier. *Ad Rusticum*[7]. Acacius, Bishop of Amida, is commended for melting the vessels of the Church of gold and silver, to redeem prisoners from the Persians[8].

The twenty-eighth Difference is the shaven crown of Priests; for antiquity whereof he citeth Eusebius *in Panegyric.*[9]*: Vos amici Dei Sacerdotes, longa talari veste et corona insignes;* "Ye friends of God, ye Priests, seemly by your long side-garment and crown." Verily he is worthy to be shorn on his poll with a number of crowns, that understandeth this of a shaven crown. If nothing else could have driven him from this dream, at least he should have remembered the solemn disputation, whereof he spake immediately before, in Beda, Li. v. Ca. xxii.[10]; by which it appeareth, that the Greeks

[5] [p. 1127. ed. Commelin. 1596.]

[6] [Toulouse.]

[7] ["Nihil illo ditius, qui corpus Domini canistro vimineo, sanguinem portat in vitro." (*Opp.* i. 48. Conf. Le Faucheur, *De la Cene du Seigneur,* p. 380. A Genève, 1635.)]

[8] [Socratis *Hist. Eccles.* Lib. vii. Cap. xxi. Musculo interp. Basil. 1549.]

[9] [This insufficient reference is not to the *Oratio de laudibus Constantini,* but to what is called in the English version "A Panegyrick concerning the splendid posture of our affairs." (*Eccl. Hist.* x. iv. Lond. 1709. Cf. Nicephor. Lib. vii. Cap. xl. Paris. 1562.) Baronius relies upon the same perverted testimony which was adduced by Stapleton. (*Annales,* ad an. 58. sect. cxxxiv.)]

[10] [al. xxi. Conf. Prosper. Stellartium, *De Coronis et Tonsuris,* p. 169.

were shorn square, and not round; and therefore Eusebius, speaking to Greek Priests, would never have called their square tonsure a crown. But the words of Eusebius put all out of doubt: Ὦ φίλοι Θεοῦ καὶ Ἱερεῖς, οἱ τὸν ἅγιον ποδήρη, καὶ τὸν οὐράνιον τῆς δόξης στέφανον, τό τε χρίσμα τὸ ἔνθεον, καὶ τὴν ἱερατικὴν τοῦ Ἁγίου Πνεύματος στολὴν περιβεβλημένοι, &c.: "O ye friends and Priests of God, which are clothed with the holy long garment, and the heavenly crown of glory, and with the divine unction, and the priestly robe of the Holy Ghost," &c. Is there any block so senseless to think that he called a shaven head the heavenly crown of glory? Who seeth not, that in commendation of the spiritual dignity of the Ministers of the Church, he alludeth to the Aaronical attire of the Priests of the Law?

The next testimony is out of the Tripartite History[1]; that Julian the Apostata, to counterfeit religion, shore himself to the hard ears: therefore religious men were then shorn. There is no doubt but the Clergy, and such as professed sobriety and modesty, used to poll their heads; whereas the licentious multitude delighted in long hairs: which shearing or polling after grew to a ceremony, and from a ceremony to a superstition; but small mention of the ceremony there is within the six hundred years, and that toward the latter end of them. But where he compareth the scoffing, that the Turk might make at the blessed passion of Christ, with such pleasant railing as Protestants use against their Friars' cowls and shaven crowns, he sheweth in what blasphemous estimation he hath such vile dung of men's invention, to compare it with the only price of our salvation.

The twenty-ninth Difference is Holy Water; for antiquity whereof he allegeth two miracles: the one out of Bede, Li. i. Cap. xvii., of Germanus, which, with casting a few sprinkles of water into the sea, in the name of the Trinity, assuaged a tempest; the other of Marcellus, Bishop of Apamea[2], which, when the temple of Jupiter could not be burned with fire, after prayers made, commanded water signed with the Cross to be sprinkled on the altar: which done, the Devils departed,

Duaci, 1625. Usserii *Britann. Eccles. Antiqq.* Cap. xvii. p. 478. Lond. 1687.]

[1] [Lib. vi. Cap. i. Conf. Socratis *E. H.* L. iii. C. i.]

[2] [*Histor. Tripart.* ix. xxxiv.]

and the temple was set on fire, and burned. But these miracles wrought by water prove not an ordinary use of Holy Water in the Church in those times. As for the counterfeit Decree of Alexander, the fifth[3] Bishop of Rome, is a worthy witness of such a worshipful ceremony[4].

In the end of this chapter he inveigheth against a new trick, which he saith the preachers have, to make their audience cry Amen; comparing it with the applause and clapping of hands used in the old time, but misliked of godly Fathers, Chrysostom and Hierom[5]. So that for the preacher to pray to God, and to give God thanks, whereto the people answereth Amen, it is counted of Stapleton a new trick; and yet it is as ancient as S. Paul. 1 Cor. xiv. vers. 16. But to make such a loud lie, that Satan himself, the father of lies, (I suppose,) for his credit's sake, would be ashamed to make in his own person; videlicet, that "to tears, to lamenting, or to bewailing of their sins, no Protestant yet moveth his audience;" it is an old trick of a cankered-stomached Papist.

CHAPTER VIII.

Stapleton. Differences between the former faith of Catholics and the late news of Protestants, concerning the government and rulers of the Church. STAPLETON.

Fulke. The thirtieth Difference is Synods of the Clergy; which is a lewd and impudent slander, for we allow them, and use them, as all the world knoweth. But (saith he) no conclusion is made in them, but such as pleaseth the Parliament. This is a false lie; for although no Constitution made in the Convocation hath the force of a law except it be confirmed by Parliament, yet many Constitutions and Canons have been made, that were never confirmed by Parliament. FULKE.

The thirty-first Difference is Imposition of hands; which is a mere slander, for that ceremony is used of us in ordaining of Ministers. Likewise where he saith, that when all the popish Bishops were deposed, there was none to lay hands on the Bishops that should be newly consecrated, it is utterly

3 [or seventh.]
4 [Calfhill's *Answer to Martiall*, p. 16. ed. Parker Soc.]
5 [See Bingham's *Antiquities*, xiv. iv. xxvii.]

false: for there was one of the popish Bishops that continued in his place[1]; there were also divers that were consecrated Bishops in King Edward's time[2]: and although there had been but one in that time of reformation, it had been sufficient by his own Gregory's resolution. Bed. Lib. i. Cap. xxvii.[3] Another example is Lib. iii. Cap. xxviii., of Ceadda, Archbishop of York, consecrated by Wini, Bishop of the West Saxons, assisted by two Briton Bishops, that were not subject to the see of Rome: because at that time there was never a Bishop of the Romish faction in England but this Wini; who was also a simoniac, and bought the bishopric of London for money. I speak not this, as though in planting of the Church where it hath been long time exiled, an extraordinary form of ordaining were not sufficient; but to shew that the Papists do pick quarrels, contrary to their own pretended records of antiquity, and Catholic religion.

Where he inveigheth against the unsufficiency of a number of our Ministers, which are come out of the shop into the Clergy, without gifts sufficient for that calling; as I cannot excuse them nor their ordainers, so I dare be bold to affirm, they are no worse, either in knowledge or conversation, than the huge rabble of hedge Priests of Popery.

The thirty-second Difference; that such Bishops as were created by the Archbishops of Canterbury and York were created by the appointment of the Pope. This is a shameless lie; for which he can bring no colour, either out of the first six hundred years, or out of Bede's History. Where he saith, "If it can be shewed by any history, that at any time by

[1] ["The only See in England, which did not undergo any change at that time, was Llandaffe: the Bishop whereof (Anthony Kitchin) had such dexterity as to stand his ground in all Revolutions; and to continue *semper idem*, which way soever the wind blew, in all those four seasons, which were variously influenced by King Henry and Edward, Queen Mary and Elizabeth!" (Lindsay's *Preface* to Mason's *Works*, p. xxvii. Lond. 1734.)]

[2] [Palmer's *Jurisdiction of British Episcopacy vindicated*, pp. 166—7. Lond. 1840.]

[3] ["Respondit Gregorius: Et quidem in Anglorum Ecclesia, in qua adhuc solus tu Episcopus inveniris, ordinare Episcopum non aliter nisi sine Episcopis potes." The Benedictine editors of S. Gregory's works observe, that the erroneous reading "nisi *cum* Episcopis" is found in some MSS.]

the mere temporal authority ever any Catholic Bishops were created, he dare yield and grant that ours are lawful Bishops;" for answer, that Catholic Bishops of old by as mere temporal authority were created as any are created among us, I refer him to Bede, Lib. iii. Cap. vii. & xxix. Lib. iv. Cap. xxiii., of Agilbert and Wini, by authority of Sonwalch, [Coinualch;] Wighard nominated by authority of Oswine [Osuiu] and Egbert; Ostfor [Oftfor] consecrated at the commandment of King Edilred: beside Wini made Bishop of London for money by Wulfher, King of Mercia; which authority he could not have abused, except it had been in him lawfully to use.

The thirty-third Difference is, that Princes had not the supreme government in ecclesiastical causes. For proof whereof he allegeth Gregory Nazianzen and Saint Ambrose; both which speak not of chief authority, but of knowledge of spiritual matters; which is not to be sought ordinarily in Princes, but in the Clergy. Secondly, he citeth Calvin and Illyricus, which do write against such civil Magistrates as think by their supremacy they have absolute authority to decree what they will in the Church: whereas we in England[4] never attribute so much to the Prince's authority, but that we always acknowledge it to be subject to God and His word. The Papists right well understand this distinction; but it pleaseth them to use this ambiguity of supreme authority, to abuse the ignorance of the simple.

The thirty-fourth Difference is, that the Bishops and godly men in matters of doubt counselled with the Pope of Rome. So did the Pope of Rome with them, while there was any modesty in him: so did Pope Sergius ask counsel of poor Beda. Math. West.[5] Nay, but Saint Hierom, so well learned,

[4] [Art. xxxvii.]

[5] [Matthew of Westminster, in his *Flores Historiarum*, published by Abp. Parker in 1567 and 1570, has only repeated a misstatement which can be traced to William of Malmesbury. The latter writer informs us, that Pope Sergius wished for the advice of Beda about certain matters, and that he accordingly addressed a letter to Ceolfrith, Abbot of Jarrow, requesting that the historian might be sent to Rome. Baronius (ad an. 701. sect. ii. Tom. viii. 641. Antverp. 1611.) has given this Epistle interpolated by Malmesbury, who hesitated not to corrupt the document by the introduction of Beda's name, and by assigning to him the rank of Presbyter, to which he had not then attained. The whole difficulty respecting Beda's pretended journey

consulted with Pope Damasus, which entered his see with the slaughter of sixty persons. I might answer, that Damasus also asked counsel of Saint Hierom[1]: so that in him which is consulted there is rather opinion of knowledge than of authority. But Hierom confesseth that he will not separate himself from the Church of Rome, &c. *Ep. ad Dam.*[2] ii. So long as the Church of Rome was the Church of Christ, there was great cause he should join with it. But now is it ceased to be the spouse of Christ, and is become an adulteress, as the Prophet saith of Jerusalem: yea, it is become Babylon, the mother of all abominations; and therefore that heavenly voice commandeth all Christians to depart out of her. But concerning the Pope's authority, I have answered at large to D. Sander's Rock of the popish Church.

The thirty-fifth Difference (but I know not how it differeth) is the Pope's authority abolished; by whom Christianity was first in this land received. It is well known, that there was Christianity before Gregory sent Augustin, not of Pope-like authority, but of godly zeal, as it seemeth, to win the English nation to Christ. After followeth a large complaint for abolishing the Pope's authority; a canon invective against dissensions among us; and slight fortification of the Pope's authority, for unity's sake, out of Hierom, *Cont. Jovinian.*, and Cyprian, *De simpl. Prœl.*, answered at large in the Discovery of D. Sander's Rock.

The thirty-sixth Difference: Augustin came first in presence of the King with a Cross of silver, and an Image of Christ painted in a table: the Protestants began with taking away the Cross, and altering the Litany. But this part is left unfortified, except it be with a marginal note, that Chrysostom used in Litanies Crosses of silver and burning tapers. Indeed I read Chrysostom had certain candlesticks or cressets of silver, made in form of a Cross, to carry lights upon them,

to Rome was for the first time removed by Mr. Stevenson, the excellent editor for the English Historical Society. (Ven. Bed. *H. Ecc.* Introduct. pp. x—xiii. Lond. 1838.)]

[1] [*Opp.* Tom. ii. p. 131. Basil. 1565. A spurious correspondence between S. Jerom and Pope Damasus exists in the fourth volume, pp. 319—20. Erasmus humorously declares, that the author of these letters was certainly not free from fever.]

[2] [loc. sup. cit.]

in the night-season; but not of any tapers burning by day, and carried before the Crucifix, after the popish manner: Socr. Li. vi. Ca. viii.: but hereof ye may see more in mine Answer to Martiall's Reply, Articl. vii.[3]

The thirty-seventh Difference: "Augustin and his company, to the number of forty, were Monks: the first preachers of this no faith were runagate Monks and apostate Friars." Their learning, godliness, and just cause of departing out of those cloisters of unclean birds, is sufficiently testified to the world.

The thirty-eighth Difference: "The preachers which were traded up by them were of a virtuous, lowly, simple, poor, and meek conversation." Then were they very unlike your popish Prelates. But Luther complaineth that his scholars were more wicked than under the Pope[4]. If some were so, it followeth not that all are so. Again, "Beza sold his benefice to two men." If he had not confessed it himself, Stapleton might never have known of it. Afterward he raised rebellion for a sign of his vocation, and persuaded Poltrot[5] to murder the Duke of Guise, or else Stapleton belieth him. What Mallot and Pieroreli were, I know not[6]: I doubt not but they were honester than many Popes have been. "Knokes was a galley-slave three years." The more wicked those Papists which betrayed him into the galley; the master whereof was glad to be rid of him, because he never had good success so long as he kept that holy man in slavery: whom also, in danger of tempest, though an errant Papist, he would desire to commend him and his galley to God in his prayers. The ejection of the nobles from Zuicherland is as truly imputed to the Zuinglians by your author Staphylus as all the rest of his slanders and monstrous lies are to be credited; which was done by the Papists in that country, almost two hundred years before Zuinglius was born. Christerne, King of Denmark, was expelled his realm

[3] [Calfhill, pp. 298—301. ed. Parker Soc.]

[4] [See before, p. 18.]

[5] [Stapleton (or the printer) wrongly calls him "Poultron."]

[6] ["Mallot, an other famous preacher of Fraunce, had bene for his good deedes marked in the shoulders, as such offenders in England are burned in the hand. Pierroceli, the third chiefe ghospeller of hugenots, was a rennegat frier of the Franciscanes." (*Fortresse*, p. 402.)]

for his tyranny by all the states, before they received the Gospel. How dutiful the doing of the Protestants in France hath been, let the King's own Acts of Pacification testify; which always dischargeth them of rebellion, and acknowledgeth all that they have done to have been done in his service.

The thirty-ninth Difference: "Voluntary poverty in Augustin not found in the first planters of this new trim tram." A matter worthy to be answered with a whim wham. It were easy to shew how many have forsaken great dignities and livings among the Papists, to become poor preachers of the Gospel.

CHAPTER IX.

STAPLETON. *Stapleton.* Differences concerning the consequences and effects of the first faith planted among us, and of the pretended faith of Protestants.

FULKE. *Fulke.* The fortieth Difference: "They that were converted builded churches and monasteries: Protestants pull down monasteries, churches, chapels, hospitals, and almshouses." In the table of Differences I have shewed how much those monasteries then builded differed from popish abbeys: and where he chargeth Protestants with pulling down all monasteries, he forgetteth that Cardinal Wolsee, by the Pope's authority, pulled down the first in our time that were suppressed; and that the popish Clergy consented to the act of suppression; which were the Devil rather than Protestants. For hospitals and almshouses, it is a slander, except some private person of covetousness hath overthrown any. As for churches and chapels builded by us, so many as are necessary, it is apparent to the world. Almshouses and hospitals by us are erected, such as are none in Popery. The Universities also are augmented, both in buildings and revenues, since the pulling down of abbeys[1].

The forty-first Difference: "In monasteries God was

[1] [A curious and interesting "Catalogue of good workes done since the times of the Gospell," viz. within sixty years during the reigns of Edward, Elizabeth, and James I., is contained in Willet's *Synopsis Papismi*, pp. 1220—43. Lond. 1634.]

served day and night with external prayer at midnight." Although rising at midnight ordinarily be an inconvenient hour in many respects, and therefore we have no ordinary prayer at that time, yet have we early in the morning before it be day, in many places, exercise of prayer and preaching. Neither was it at midnight that the Nuns of Berking sung their lauds and hymns, Lib. iv. Cap. vii.: for it was after Matutines, which could not be but in the morning, although early and before day.

The forty-second: "The devotion of those Christians brought in voluntary oblations; which are now ceased, and due tithes grudged at." The voluntary oblations of the godly are not now wanting, where need is.

The forty-third: "The Princes and higher power[s] endued the bishoprics with lands: now they take them away." It was necessary when they had none before, but were newly erected. If any be now taken away, and sufficient left, it is not the matter we regard, but good proceeding of the Gospel. If covetousness of any man procure from the Church where it wanteth, they shall answer it, and not we.

The forty-fourth: "Ethelbert established Christianity by laws; making special statutes and decrees for the indemnity and quiet possession of the Church goods, and of the Clergy. Now no state is more open to the oppression than the Clergy." If Ethelbert established Christianity by laws, he did more than Papists would have Princes to do now. But if the Clergy be now oppressed, it is not for want of good laws, or good will in the Prince and higher powers to defend it; but by occasion of a number of dissembling Papists, to whom execution of justice in some places is committed.

The forty-fifth Difference is, "Unity then where is dissension now." God be praised, we consent in all articles necessary to eternal salvation: and if the Scots, by our example, are come to the same unity of faith with us, it is the Lord's work; for whom we give Him hearty thanks.

The conclusion of this fantastical Fortress is an exhortation to Papists not to dissemble their Papistry, nor to communicate with us; dissuading them by many examples of such as yielded not to the persecution of the Arrian heretics. But seeing by the word of God we cannot be convinced of heresy, those examples make nothing against us. And yet I wish the Papists (if it be not God's will to open their eyes, that they may see the truth,) yet to give over their dissembling, and openly to shew themselves as they are. For whether their religion be good or bad, dissembling and counterfeiting cannot be but evil.

God be praised.

A REJOINDER

TO

JOHN MARTIALL'S REPLY AGAINST THE ANSWER OF MASTER CALFHILL

TO THE BLASPHEMOUS TREATISE OF THE CROSS.

BY W. FULKE,

DOCTOR IN DIVINITY.

TO THE READER.

Of all the treatises sent over within these twenty years from the Papists, there is none in which appeareth less learning and modesty, nor greater arrogance and impudency, than in this one book of Martiall. Who, as he termeth himself a Bachelor of Law, so, more like a wrangling petty-fogger in the Law than a sober student in Divinity, doth in a manner nothing else but cavil, quarrel, and scold. Which as it were an easy matter to wipe away with a sharp answer, for him that would bestow his time therein, so I think it for my part neither needful nor profitable. The memory of that godly learned man Master Doctor Calfhill, whom he abuseth, is written in the book of the righteous, and shall not be afraid of any slanderer's report. Omitting therefore all frivolous quarrels, I will only endeavour to answer that which hath in it any shew of reason or argument to defend the idolatry of the Papists. In which matter also, as many things are the same which are already satisfied in my confutation of Doctor Sander's book of Images, so I will refer the reader to those chapters of that treatise where he shall find that which I hope shall suffice for the overthrow of idolatry.

This Reply, as the first Treatise, is divided into ten Articles; all which in order I will set down, with such titles as he giveth unto them. But first I must say a few words concerning his request made to the Bishop of London, and the rest of the superintendents of the new Church, as it pleaseth him to call them, and his Preface to the reader. His request is, that the Bishops should certify him by some pamphlet in print, whether sixty-one Articles, which he hath gathered out of Master Calfhill's book, be the received and approved doctrine of the new Church of England; able to be justified by the word of God, and the Fathers and Councils within six hundred years after Christ. How wise a man he is in making this request, I leave to reasonable men to judge.

And touching the Articles themselves, I answer, that some of them be such as the Church of England doth hold and openly profess; as that Latin service, monkish vows, the Communion in one kind, &c., are contrary to God's word: the other be particular affirmations of Master Calfhill, which in such sense as he uttered them may be justified for true, and yet pertain not to the whole Church to maintain and defend: as whether Helena were superstitious in seeking the Cross at Jerusalem; whether Dionyse and Fabian were the one suspected, the other infamed, &c. Beside that a great number of them be so rent from the whole sentences whereof they were parts, that they retain not the meaning of the author, but serve to shew the impudency of the caviller: as that the counsels of Christ in His Gospel be ordinances of the Devil; the prayers of Christians a sacrifice of the Devil; the Council of Elibeus [Eliberis[1]] was a General Council, &c. Wherefore I will leave this fond request, with all the railing that followeth thereupon, and come to the Preface to the reader.

First, he findeth himself greatly grieved, that not only ancient Fathers are by M. Calfhill discredited, but also the holy Cross is likened to a gallows, &c.; which moved him to follow Salomon's counsel, and to answer a fool according to his folly. After this he taketh upon him to confute M. Calfhill's Preface, in which he proveth, that no Images should be in churches to any use of religion, because God forbiddeth them, Exo. xx. and Levit. xix., in the first table of religion. His reply standeth only upon those common foolish distinctions of Idols and Images, of *Latria* and *Doulia*, which are handled more at large and with greater shew of learning by D. Sander in his book of Images, Cap. v., vi., vii., viii.; whither I refer the reader for answer. Likewise, that discourse which he maketh, to prove that an Image of Christ is not a

[1] [Calfhill, pp. 154, 302.]

lying Image, is answered in the same book, Cap. vii. The authority of Epiphanius he deferreth to answer unto the fifth Article. To Irenæus he answereth, that he only reporteth that the Gnostic heretics had the Image of Jesus, but reproveth not that fact; but he reproved them only because they placed the Image of Christ with the Images of Plato, Pythagoras, &c., and used them as the Gentiles do. This were indeed a pretty exception for a brabbling lawyer to take: but a student in Divinity should understand, that Irenæus in that book and chapter, Li. i. Ca. xxiv., declareth no fact of the heretics that was good, but his declaration is a reproof. And so it is throughout that whole book, containing thirty-five chapters.

But he chargeth M. Calfhill for falsifying Augustin in saying, that he alloweth M. Varro affirming "that religion is most pure without Images;" first quarrelling at the quotation, which by error of the printer is *De Civitate Dei*, Lib. iv. Cap. iii., where it should be Cap. xxxi.[2]; a meet quarrel for such a lawyer: secondly, shewing that the Latin is *Castius observari sine Simulachris religionem*: "That religion would have been more purely kept without Idols, or feigned Images;" as though there be any Images but feigned: and the word *Imago*, even in their own Latin translation of the Bible, is indifferently taken for *Idolum* and *Simulachrum*, and that in many places. Deut. iv. ver. 16; 4 Reg. xi. ver. 18; Sapient. Cap. xiii. & xiv.; Esai. xl. ver. 18, & xliv. ver. 13; Ezec. vii. vers. 20, where *Imagines* and *Simulachra* are both placed together; Ezech. xvi. Ca. [ver.] 17; Amos v. ver. 23, [26,] where he sayeth, *Imaginem Idolorum*, "the Image of your Idols," and many other places declare, that this counterfeit distinction was not observed, no not of the Latin interpreter. As for his other logical quiddity, wherein he pleaseth himself not a little, that *religio non suscipit magis et minus*, sheweth that either his law is better than his logic, or else both are not worth a straw.

Further he chargeth M. Calfhill for adding words which are not found in Augustin[3], "where Images are placed in temples, in honourable sublimity," &c. These words are found in the *Ep.* xlix. *ad Deogratias: Cum hiis locantur*

[2] [Calfhill, p. 43.]
[3] [See Calfhill, page 43.]

sedibus, honorabili sublimitate, ut a precantibus atque immolantibus attendantur: "When they are placed in these seats, in honourable sublimity, that they are looked upon by them that pray and offer," &c.: but Martiall looked only to the quotation, Ps. xxxvi. & cxiii. Yet doth not M. Calfhill rehearse the words, but the judgment of Augustin; from which he doth nothing vary, except Martiall will cavil at the words "Images in temples," where Augustin sayeth *Idola hiis sedibus,* "Idols in these seats," speaking of temples in which Images were placed. But he speaketh (saith Martiall,) in [on] the Psalms, against the Images of the heathen, and not of the Christians. Then read what he writeth, *De moribus Ecclesiæ Catholicæ*, Lib. i. Cap. xxxiv. & *De consensu Evangelist.* Lib. i. Cap. x., where you shall find his judgment of such Images as were made of Christians, to be all one with those of the Gentiles. The judgment of other Doctors, whom he nameth, you shall find answered in the fourteenth or thirteenth chapter of Master Sander's book of Images.

That the Jews had no Images in their temple, he saith it is a Jewish and Turkish reason to prove that we should have none: much like the Priest that would not believe in Christ, if he knew that he were a Jew. So wise he is, to compare the superstition of the wicked Turks with the observation of the law by the godly Jews. Nay, he is yet more eloquent, and sheweth that the Protestants are like the Turks, in condemning of Images, in allowing marriage after divorce, &c.: as though we might not acknowledge one God, lest we should be like the Turks and Jews; nor honour virtue, nor dispraise vice, because they do so; nor obey Magistrates, nor eat and drink, because the Turks and Jews do so. O deep learning of a lawyer Divine!

That Images do not teach, he sayeth it is a position more boldly advouched than wisely proved; and then quoteth Gregory, *Ep.* ix. Lib. ix., &c.: but he is deceived if he think we hold that Images teach not; for we affirm with the Prophet Abacuc, that they teach lies, Cap. ii. ver. 18; and vanity. Jer. x. ver. 8.

As for the story of Amadis the Goldsmith, and the Epistle of Eleutherius fetched out of the Guildhall in London[1], as

[1] [Calfhill, pp. 52, 53. Compare Mason's *Works* by Lindsay, pp. 66—68. Lond. 1734.]

M. Calfhill maketh no great account of them, so I pass them over; although Martiall would have men think they be the strongest arguments the Protestants have against the superstition of the Cross, and the usurped tyranny of the Pope.

Finally, the excuse he maketh of his railing by M. Calfhill's example, how honest it is, I refer to wise men to consider. If M. Calfhill had passed the bounds of modesty, it were small praise in Martiall to follow him, yea, to pass him. But if M. Calfhill (as indifferent men may think) hath not greatly exceeded in terms of heat against Martiall's person, whatsoever he hath spoken against his heresies, the continual scorning both of M. Calfhill's name and his person, used so often in every leaf of his Reply, in the judgment of all reasonable persons will cause Martiall to be taken for a lawless wrangler, rather than a sober and Christian lawyer.

THE FIRST ARTICLE.

Fulke. This Article hath no title, and in effect it hath no matter: for thirteen leaves are spent about a needless and impertinent controversy, of the authority of the holy Scriptures and of the Church of God; whereof the one is the rule of faith, the other is the thing ruled and directed thereby. Now whether ought to be the judge, the rule, or the thing ruled, is the question: the rule, say we, as the law: the Church, sayeth he, as the justicier. And then we are at as great controversy, what or where the Church is. In effect, the controversy cometh to this issue; whether he be a justicier, or an injusticier, which pronounceth sentence contrary to the law. I would think that common reason might decide these questions: that he which giveth sentence against the law may have the name and occupy the place of a justicier, but a true justicier he cannot be indeed. Right so the popish Church, which condemneth the truth for heresy, hath usurped as the judge, but indeed is a cruel tyrant. But the controversy is not of the word, but of the meaning: and where shall that be found but in the mouth of the Judge? (sayeth he.) If this were true, I would never be a Bachelor of Law, if I were as Martiall; nor yet a Doctor thereof, except it were to deceive poor clients for their money, if there were not a sense FULKE.

or meaning of the law, which other men might understand as well as he that occupieth the place of the Judge, that I might appeal when I saw he gave wrong sentence. But let us briefly run over his Achillean arguments.

The Eunomians, Arrians, Eutychians, and Maximus the heretic rejected the testimonies of the Fathers, and the authority of the Church, and appealed to the Scriptures. So doth many a wrangling lawyer, to continue his fee from his client, appeal when he hath no cause, but received right sentence according to the law: *ergo* no appeal is to be admitted. This is Martiall's law, or logic, I know not whether. But what was this Maximus you name so often, Master Martiall, that S. Augustin writ against? Could you read your note-book no better? Against Maximinus the Arrian he writeth, that neither of them both was to be holden by the authority of Councils, the Nicene or the Ariminense, but by the authorities of the Scripture. Lib. iii. Cap. iv.[1]

But Tertullian would have heretics convinced by the authority of the Church, and not of the Scriptures. Yea, verily, but such heretics as denied certain Scriptures, and perverteth the rest by their false interpretations. Such are the Protestants, sayeth Martiall: for Luther denieth the Epistle to the Hebrews, the Apocalypse, the Epistle of S. James, and S. Jude. But Luther is not all Protestants; neither did Luther always or altogether deny them. Neither do the Protestants affirm any thing in matters of controversy in their interpretations, but the same is affirmed by writers of the most ancient and pure Church. Martiall objecteth, that Christ sent not His disciples always to the Scriptures; "but sometimes to the fig-tree, to the flowers of the field, to the fowls of the air, &c.: Paul allegeth the heathen Poet; also custom and tradition." And we also use similitudes of God's creatures, and allege custom and condition [tradition:] but so that the Scripture be the only rule of truth; whereto whatsoever in the world agreeth is true, whatsoever disagreeth from it is false. The traditions of the
2 Thess. ii. Apostles, which by their writings we know to be theirs, we reverently receive, not as men's traditions, but as the doctrine
Luke x. 1 John iv. Matt. xviii. of God; for we hear them even as God. Also we hear the voice of the Church admonishing us, if we give offence.

Exod. x. Joel i. Eph. iv. Finally, the Patriarchs, Prophets, Apostles, Evangelists,

[1] [Calfhill, pp. 10, 129.]

Pastors, and Doctors, we all reverence and hear, as the messengers of God; but so that they approve unto us their sayings out of the word of God and doctrine of Christ. Likewise we admit the writings of the Fathers so far as they agree with the writings of God; and further to be credited they themselves required not. The sayings of the Doctors that Martiall citeth, for the credit of old writers, you shall find satisfied in mine Answer to Heskins, almost in order as they be here set down: for one Papist borroweth of another; and few of them have any thing of their own reading. The saying of Clemens is answered, Lib. i. Cap. viii.; Eusebius concerning Basil and Gregory, and Hieronym, Cap. vii. The sayings of Irenæus and Athanasius, that we ought to have recourse to the Apostolic Churches, which retain the doctrine of the Apostles, against new heresies, as also of Tertullian to the like effect, we acknowledge to be true: but seeing the Church of Rome retaineth not the Apostolic doctrine at this day, we deny it to be an Apostolic Church. Therefore as many as build upon it, or upon any ancient writer's words, which hath not the holy Scriptures for his warrant, as M. Calfhill said, buildeth upon an evil ground; for "if an Angel from heaven teach otherwise than the Apostles have preached unto us, he be accursed." Here the quarrelling lawyer findeth fault with his translation, because *evangelizavimus* may be referred as well to the disciples as to the Apostles: so that the disciples' preachings are to be credited as well as the Apostles'. No doubt, if they preach the doctrine of the Apostles; of which the controversy is, and not of the persons that preach it. But these quarrels, Sir Bachelor, are more meet for the bum courts, where perhaps you are a prating Proctor, than for the schools of Divinity. We are gone out, you say; and that we confess in our Apology. Yea, we are gone out of Babylon; but not out of the Church of God, but abide in the doctrine of Christ: and you are gone out of the Church of God, which remain in the sink of Rome, that is departed from that which was heard from the beginning, and was *sacrosanctum apud Apostolorum Ecclesias*[2], "most holy in the Apostles' Churches."

You cannot abide to be charged with the saying of Christ, "They worship Me in vain, that teach the doctrine and pre- Matt. xv.
cepts of men." First you say "the Apostles were men whose

[2] Tert. Li. iv. cont. Marc. [Cap. v.]

traditions the Church must receive." Yea, Sir, but they delivered no doctrine of their own. Secondly, "Christ speaketh of the Scribes and Pharisees, and their fond traditions; and not of the Church, and her Catholic traditions and customs." And they be Scribes and Pharisees, which even in the Church teach a false worshipping of God, according to the doctrines and traditions of men, disannulling the commandments of God; as the popish teachers in their doctrine of Images, Communion in one kind, private Mass, &c.

That Augustin, framing a perfect preacher, willeth him to confer the places of Scripture together; you say it is a profound conclusion to infer, that he sendeth him not to Doctors' distinctions, censure of the Church, canons of the Popes, nor traditions of the Fathers, "but only to quiet and content himself with the word of God." And these last words, you say, are not found in Augustin, *De Doct. Chr.* Cap. ix. *et sequentibus;* as though Master Calfhill[1] recited the words, and not the sense, for which he referreth you not only to that chapter, but to the rest following, in all which there is no mention of Doctors' distinctions, Popes' canons, &c. "But this is an argument *ab authoritate negative.*[*a.*]" Make as much and as little as you will of Augustin's authority, Master Calfhill hath rightly inferred upon Augustin's judgment, that if conference of Scriptures will make a perfect preacher, which you grant, he needeth neither Doctors' distinctions, nor Church censures, &c., but may quiet and content himself with the only word of God.

But it would make an horse to break his halter, to see how Martiall proveth out of Augustin, that God teacheth us by men, and not by Angels, and that knowledge of the tongues and instructions of men is profitable for a preacher; yea, the consent of most of the Catholic Churches, and the interpretations of learned men: as though all those were not to be referred to the due conference of Scriptures, where only resteth the substance of doctrine and the authority of faith, and not in Doctors' distinctions, Church censures, Popes' canons, &c., which have no ground in the Scriptures, or else be contrary to them. Where Master Calfhill sheweth, that as before the New Testament was written all things were examined according to the words and sermons of the Apostles, so after

1 [page 57.]

the New Testament was written all things ought to be examined according to their writings, because there is none other testimony of credit extant of their sermons and writings; Martiall replieth out of Saint Augustin, that we have many things by tradition which are not written, which, being universally observed, it were madness to break. *Ep.* cxviii.[2] But Augustin speaketh not of doctrine, but of ceremonies or observations. Out of Hierom, *ad Pam.*[3], he objecteth, that our Creed is not written in the Scriptures: which is utterly false, although the form of the Symbol be not set down as we rehearse it.

Thirdly, out of Epiphanius, *Contra Apostolic.* Lib. ii. *Hæres.* lxi.[4], "that we must use tradition, because all things cannot be taken out of the holy Scriptures. Therefore the holy Apostles delivered certain things in writing, and certain things in tradition," &c. But they delivered nothing in tradition contrary to their writings; neither omitted they to write any thing that was necessary for our salvation. The matter whereof Epiphanius speaketh is, that it is a tradition of the Apostles that it is sin to marry after virginity decreed: and yet he holdeth, that it is better to marry after virginity decreed than to burn; contrary to the doctrine of the Papists. But Martiall frankly granteth, that no Doctor is to be credited against the Scripture, and the consent of the whole Church; yet where Master Calfhill said, that no man in any age was so perfect that a certain truth was to be builded on him, bringing examples of Aaron and Peter, the one the High Priest of the Jews, the other affirmed by the Papists to be the same of the Christians, he quarrelleth at his induction, because he sayeth not *et sic de singulis;* whereas his argument followeth not of the form of induction, but of the place *a majore ad minus.*

After this, (as he doeth nothing but cavil,) he chargeth Master Calfhill for corrupting Saint Augustin, saying, "Trust

[2] [al. liv. *Opp.* Tom. ii. 93—4. ed. Ben. Amst.]

[3] [It would appear that the reference is to the following passage in the letter against the errors of John of Jerusalem: (*Opp.* ii. 173.) "In Symbolo fidei et spei nostræ, quod, ab Apostolis traditum, non scribitur in charta et atramento, sed in tabulis cordis carnalibus," &c.—S. Jerom evidently alluded to 2 Cor. iii. 3.]

[4] [p. 511. ed. Petav. Paris. 1622.]

me not, nor credit my writings," &c.; *Proœm.* Lib. iii. *de Trinit.;* for Saint Augustin sayeth not "Trust me not[1]:" but he confesseth that he sayeth, "Do not addict thyself to my writings, as to the canonical Scriptures." See what a corruption here is, when Master Calfhill rendereth not the words, but the meaning of Augustin.

Again, Saint Basil (he sayeth) is vilely abused, because Master Calfhill sayeth, Saint "Basil setteth forth by a proper similitude with what judgment the Fathers of the Church should be read;" *Conc. ad Adol.*[2]*;* whereas Basil speaketh of profane writers: as though Basil's similitude may not serve to shew how both should be read, because he speaketh but of one sort.

Likewise he crieth out that Saint Hierom is not truly alleged, because the printer in the English translation of Hierom's words hath omitted this word "not," which he hath set down in the Latin. The four pretty persons he putteth upon Master Calfhill, as foolish and childish I omit; only the slanderers' persons I will touch. In saying that "the Fathers declined all from the simplicity of the Gospel in ceremonies," he chargeth M. Calfhill to be a slanderer; because God hath not suffered all the Fathers to decline, lest hell-gates should have prevailed against His Church: although M. Calfhill spake of those Fathers only whose writings are extant, yet the gates of hell in idle ceremonies did but assault, they did not prevail against the Church. And these Fathers departed not from the Gospel, but declined from the simplicity thereof: but you Papists have departed from the Gospel and doctrine of salvation, in setting up a new sacrifice, in seeking justification by works, in overthrowing the true and spiritual worship of God.

As for the two judges, the word and the Spirit, he denieth them, finding many "defects in the word; as that it is senseless, dumb, deaf, not able to prove itself to be the word of God; having no more power to be a judge and decide controversies than the book of statutes to put on my Lord Chief Justice's robes, and to come to the King's Bench and give sentence." I think there is no Christian man but ab-

[1] ["Noli meis literis, quasi Scripturis canonicis, inservire." But the word "crede" occurs in the same sentence.]

[2] [Calfhill, p. 59.]

horreth to read these blasphemies. But let us see whether the book of statutes (although it put on no robes) is not judge, even over my Lord Chief Justice himself; who is a minister serving to pronounce the law, not a King to alter the law; for he himself must be obedient to the law. Now in all controversies that be *de jure*, either the law is plain to be understood, or it is obscure. If it be plain, as that a felon must be hanged, or the son must inherit his father, &c., the Judge, pronouncing the law with authority, and execution following his sentence, bridleth the obstinate person that will not obey the law, which he knoweth as well as the Judge. If the law be hard to be understood, the Judge must seek the interpretation thereof according to the mind of the law-maker, and not according to his own fantasy. So that in all cases the Judge hath no authority over the law, but under the law: so that if he give wrong sentence, both he and his sentence are to be judged by law. Or else why do you, Martiall, in your civil law courts so often cry out, *Sit liber judex*, "Let the book be judge," if you will not allow the book of God's law to be judge, even over them which have authority, as Justices have in the common law, to pronounce it, and to declare it?

The Spirit he refuseth to be judge, "because It is invisible, secret, unknown, unable to be gone to, but in the Church:" therefore the Church is the judge, and neither the word nor the Spirit. But the Spirit, by His own substance incomprehensible, is by His effects in the holy Scriptures visible, revealed, known, and able to be gone unto: therefore a sufficient judge, taking witness of the Scriptures, and bearing witness unto them. For that majesty of truth, that power of working, that uniform consent, which is in all the Scriptures inspired of God, maketh a wonderful difference of them from all writings of men of all sorts.

But let us see Martiall's arguments against the Spirit of God to be judge of the interpretation of the Scriptures. Paul and Barnabas in the controversy of circumcision, went not to the word and Spirit, but to the Apostles and Elders at Jerusalem. O blockhead and shameless ass! Paul and Barnabas doubted not of the question, but sought the general quiet of the whole Church by consent of a Council. But whither went the Apostles and Elders for decision of the question but to the word and Spirit? Read Act. xv.

Again, he citeth Deuteronom. xvii., that the people in controversies should resort to the Priests for judgment: but where should they fetch their judgment but of the law of God, as it is in the same place?

Again, Christ hath appointed Apostles, Evangelists, &c.: therefore it is not a general precept for all men to try, all men to judge what doctrine they receive; because all be not Apostles, Evangelists, &c. Then in vain said Christ to all men, "Search the Scriptures;" in vain the Apostles, "Try the spirits:" neither did the Bœrheans well, that "daily sought the Scriptures, to see if those things were so" as the Apostles taught.

James v. [John v. 39.] I John iv. Acts xvii.

Martiall is to be pitied, if he know no difference between authority of public teaching, and the trial and examination of doctrine; whereof this pertaineth to all men, the other to such only as are called thereto. But Martiall proceedeth to shew, that as God appointed one High Priest to the Jews, to avoid schisms, so he appointed Peter among the Christians: and for this purpose he citeth divers sentences of the ancient Fathers, which all in order almost the reader shall find cited and satisfied in mine Answer to Doctor Sander's book of the Rock of the Church, Cap. v.; except one place of Tertullian, *De pudicitia*[1], which I marvel this popish lawyer would allege, being so contrary to his purpose, but that the poor man understood it not. *Qualis es*, &c.[2]: "What art thou overthrowing and changing the intention of our Lord, giving this personally to Peter? Upon thee (said He) I will build My Church." If it were personally said to Peter, (Sir Bachelor,) counsel with Baldus and Bertholdus whether it go by succession to the Pope or no, which Tertullian denieth to pertain to every Elder of the Church, because it was spoken personally to Peter.

And now at the length beginneth he to come to the argument of his book, the sign of the Cross; which he said was the fourth signification of the word "Cross" in Scripture, and calleth it "the material and mystical sign of the Cross;" which Master Calfhill denieth to be once mentioned in Scripture in that sense that Martiall taketh it. Martiall repeateth that which he had said before, that Esay, cap. xlix., saith, "I

1 [Written after he had become a Montanist.]

2 [Cap. xxi. *Opp.* p. 574.—"In ipso Ecclesia exstructa est; id est, per ipsum."]

will set out Mine sign on high to the people;" which Hierom upon that place expoundeth to be "the standard of the Cross; that it may be fulfilled which is written, 'The earth is full of His praise;'" *et iterum*, &c., "and again, 'In all the earth His name is wonderful.'" Which words following immediately Martiall craftily suppresseth; and falleth into a brabbling matter, that preaching, which Master Calfhill said was this standard, is not the only standard or sign lifted up by God for conversion of the Gentiles, but miracles and good examples of life, &c.: whereas the question is, whether the popish sign of the Cross be the sign spoken by Esay and Hierom. And the exposition added by Hierom sheweth plainly, that he meaneth not a red or blue Cross banner, but the preaching of Christ crucified[3]; whereby the earth is filled with the praise of God, and His name is wonderful in all the earth. But Martiall in the end concludeth, that "it hath pleased the ancient Fathers to appoint and ordain the sign of the Cross to be one mean among many, by which the praise of God is set forth;" where he should have proved, that the sign of the Cross (as he taketh it) is mentioned in the Scriptures. Other cavils and slanders, not more false than foolish, I will clearly omit, as I purposed in the beginning; and follow only such matter as is proper to the question in controversy, namely the sign of the Cross.

The second text, to prove that the sign of the Cross is mentioned in the Scripture, he citeth out of Jere. iv., "Lift up a sign in Sion;" which Hierom likewise expoundeth, "Lift up the standard of the Cross in an high tower, that is, in the height of the church." Concerning this interpretation of Hierom, how apt it is for the place, I will spend no time with Master Martiall: only this is sufficient for the purpose, that Saint Hierom meaneth not the Cross on the top of the steeple, but the passion of Christ; whereto he exhorteth the people to run for aid, as to a standard of comfort, against the enemy that was coming upon them.

The third text is Matth. xxiv.: "The sign of the Son of man shall appear in the clouds:" which divers of the old writers expound to be the sign of the Cross: some to be Christ Himself; as Chrysostom, *in Matt.* xxiv. *Hom.* xlix.: some to be the Cross itself on which He died; as Chrysost. *in Matt. Hom.*

3 [Calfhill, page 94.]

lxxvii., and Theophylact, *in* xxiv. *Matth.*: some other the passion, or sign of the Cross; as Hierom upon that place: so that the Doctors being in divers opinions, and speaking doubtfully, there is no certainty of the matter. That the sign of the Son of man is Christ Himself, as Chrysostom rehearseth some to have thought in his time, is the most probable opinion; because both Mark cap. xiii. and Luke xxi. do seem so to expound that sign of the Son of man in Matthew. But Martiall is such a perilous logician, that he will admit nothing but necessary consequences; which we must be bold to urge and require of him for the mention of the sign of the Cross, in such variety of Doctors' opinions, and a matter so obscure.

The fourth text is Ezechiel ix., the sign *Thau* set on the foreheads of them that should be preserved from destruction. But what argument or authority hath he to prove that this mark was the sign of the Cross? None at all: only he quarrelleth after his manner against M. Calfhill's reasons, which shew it was not the sign of the Cross, but an inward spiritual mark. And lest he should flee to the figure of the Samaritan letter *Thau*[1], which Hierom saith in his time was somewhat like a Cross, Hierom himself sheweth that the Septuagintes, Aquila, and Symmachus translate *Thau* a mark, as the word signifieth: only Theodotion left the Hebrew word untranslated; which, because it is the name of the last Hebrew letter, divers thought to signify *Thorah,* "the law," whereof they were observers that were so marked. Cyprian also taketh it for a mark, without naming the letter *Thau. Contra Demetrianum*[2]. Wherefore, seeing here is nothing whereby the fashion of the mark may be gathered, fondly doth Martiall gather that it was the sign of the Cross.

The fifth text is the mark commanded to be set upon all God's servants in the Apoc. vii., which Martiall out of Thomas Aquinas concludeth to be the sign of the Cross. But that is disproved by M. Calfhill's three reasons; which Martiall, like an impudent wrangler, will understand only of the place of Ezechiel. 1. The Spirit of life and faith is not given with the sign of the Cross: 2. which is not sufficient to discern the good from the bad: 3. but is received of all sorts. Therefore the seal spoken of in those places is not the sign of the Cross.

[1] [Calfhill, p. 107.]
[2] [*Ad Demetr.* Opp. p. 194. ed. Episc. Fell.]

Martiall's Cross, not being found in the holy Scriptures, hath yet often remembrance among the ancient Fathers; whom M. Calfhill doth justly reprove in this behalf, so highly to extol that sign, which hath no ground in the word of God, either in contention against the Gentiles that disdained it, or in emulation of the heretics that first used it. For if all records of ecclesiastical antiquity be sought, that are authentical, and not manifestly counterfeited, there shall no mention be found of Martiall's Cross in the fourth signification before the superstition of the Valentinian heretics, which called the Cross *Horon, confirmativam Crucem;* which Irenæus, Lib. i. Ca. i.[3], doth speak of: so doth Epiphanius. *Contra Valent. Hær.* xxxi.[4] But against this reproof of the old writers Martiall hath a plausible common-place to sport himself: in which, notwithstanding, every wise man can see how fondly he behaveth himself, to be patron to them which either need not his defence where they write well, or cannot be justified by him where they write amiss. I will therefore pass over all such fruitless controversies, and keep me only to the argument.

That Chrysostom was immoderate sometimes in extolling the sign of the Cross, and such-like matters, either Martiall must confess, or else excuse it by a rhetorical hyperbole: as where he saith of Saint Paul's chain, *Si quis me cœlo condonet omni, vel ea qua Pauli manus vinciebatur catena, illam ego honore præponerem:* "If any man could reward me with all heaven, or else with that chain wherewith Paul's hands were bound, I would prefer that chain in honour[5]." Such are many excessive speeches in Chrysostom, both of the sign of the Cross, of the Lord's Supper, of Baptism, and other things. In Tertullian's time the sign of the Cross was used among Christians, to shew themselves to be Christians, against the Gentiles; if it were not a piece of Montanus' superstition.

But whereas Martiall citeth Constantinus for the commendation of his Cross, he sheweth himself an egregious ignorant person both in antiquity and in the history. For the sign which Constantine commended to be a healthful

[3] [*Adv. Hæres.* p. 7. Paris. 1575.]

[4] [p. 59. Cornar. interp. Basil. 1578.]

[5] [S. Chrysostom has already been released from responsibility for these expressions. See page 110.]

sign, and true token of virtue, by which he delivered the city from tyrants, was not the sign of the Cross, but the character of the name of Christ, which was shewed to him from heaven with this inscription, ἐν τούτῳ νίκα, "In this God," not in this sign, thou shalt "overcome[1]."

And lest Martiall should cavil at the sign of the Cross named by Eusebius, *De Vit. Const.* Lib. i.[2], you shall understand, that he describeth the standard of Constantine to have been a long spear, in the top whereof a bar went overthwart like a Cross, to hang the banner upon; which even the heathen Emperors used. But in the banner was set forth in gold and precious stones that sign which Constantine did see; which was the Greek letter P, with the letter X in the midst thereof, after this manner: ☧ which is to be seen in many hundreds of ancient coins, both of Constantine and other Christian Emperors; which is the character of the name of Christ; agreeing with the words of Eusebius, χιαζομένου τοῦ Ρ κατὰ τὸ μεσαίτατον. By which you may see how ridiculously Martiall and the Papists look only to the cross staff upon which the banner hanged; and see not the very wholesome sign indeed, which was described in the banner; namely, in the name of Christ, by whom Constantine had so glorious victories.

But Martiall, omitting to speak of the Cross used among the heathen Priests of Serapis, will discuss Master Calfhill's two rules: the one, that whatsoever is brought in under the cloke of good intent is not straightway allowable. To this he sayeth, that some things are brought in by private men, without authority of the Pope; and for private men he counteth the Bishops of Spain and France, in their Provincial Councils. These bind not generally, except the Pope allow them. Some things are received by tradition and custom, generally received unaltered: such is the Cross. Some are brought in by tradition and custom, but not generally received; as that infants should receive the Communion, &c.: such the Cross is not. But seeing he hath not concluded the contradiction of Master Calfhill's sixte [fixed, or first] rule, it standeth still unmoveable; that some things are brought in of a good intent, which are not allowable.

The second rule is, Whatsoever hath been upon good

[1] [Calfhill, p. 111.] [2] [Cap. xxxi.]

occasion received once must not necessarily be retained still; but, by advice of Stephanus, Bishop of Rome, if it be turned to superstition, be altered by them that come after. These after-comers, saith Martiall, are none other but the Bishops of Rome his successors; who, as they made the law, so they must repeal it. But Stephanus sayeth[3], *Si nonnulli ex prædecessoribus et majoribus nostris fecerunt aliqua;* naming not only his predecessors, but also his elders: wherefore he meaneth that not only his successors, but also his after-comers in every particular Church, as well as his successors in the Church of Rome, ought to abolish with good authority such abused customs. But Martiall will not acknowledge that crossing hath bred such inconveniences, that the inward faith hath been untaught, and that the virtue hath been given to the sign, which only proceedeth from Him which is signified; for crossing was not the cause, but the negligence of the Clergy: as though there may not be many causes of one thing; and if crossing were but an occasion of such inconveniences, there were good cause to take it away. Also he denieth that they attribute the virtue of [to] the sign, without relation to the merits of Christ's passion: whereas M. Calfhill speaketh not of such shifts as crafty lawyers can make for their excuses, but of the opinion of the ignorant people, who have thought, without any further relation, that the sign of the Cross was an holy, blessed, and wholesome thing. And what do they that use the example of Julian, who, crossing himself of custom, and not with any relation to Christ whom he despised, prove what virtue the sign of the Cross hath, when the Devils immediately avoided? Do they not manifestly ascribe virtue to the sign, without relation of the maker? Yea, saith Martiall, but Christ gave such virtue to that sign by His death and passion. Shew that out of the Scriptures, and the controversy is at an end.

But Martiall the lawyer, for the virtue of the Cross, citeth Martiall the Apostle; for so he will be called, and was, as his cousin Martiall the lawyer affirmeth, one of the seventy-two Disciples of Christ. But seeing he and his Epistles have slept seven or eight hundred years in a corner, that they were never heard of by Eusebius, Hierom, Gennadius, nor any other of those times, he cometh too late now to challenge the

[3] [Gratiani *Decret.* Dist. lxiii. Cap. xxviii.]

name of an Apostle or Disciple of Christ, whose name or writings in so many hundred years no man hath registered. But this argument is of authority negative, quod [quoth] Martiall. But what argument have you so good to prove him authentical, as this is probable to prove him counterfeit? Nay, if we believe Martiall, Master Calfhill hath falsified the Scripture, in saying that no man dare come near nor resist Leviathan and Behemoth the Devils: for beside the quotation is false, Cap. xl. for xli.[1], the popish translation hath not so; and Christ His Apostles and faithful do resist the Devil. Yea, Sir, but not with sword nor spear, whereof he speaketh, nor with your Cross, but with spiritual armour. As for the error of the quotation and your translation, every child may see how fond a quarrel it is.

The excuse that Master Calfhill maketh for Damascen, seeing Martiall doth not allow, let him make a better himself: for some of Damascen's errors were such as Martiall himself and the Papists will not allow.

"But Lactantius maketh the blood of the paschal lamb sprinkled on the door-post a figure of the Cross on men's foreheads." That is false in your sense, Master Martiall: for he speaketh allegorically of the spiritual impression of the blood of Christ by faith; and that his words declare, where he saith[2], that Christ is salvation "to all which have written the sign of blood, that is, the sign of the Cross upon which He shed His blood, on their foreheads." But Christ is not salvation to all that have your sign of the Cross on their bodily foreheads. But whereas Lactantius in the next chapter saith, that Devils are chased away both by the name of Christ, and by the sign of His passion[3]; if it pleased God, in those times, by such outward signs to confound His adversaries, what is that to defend the superstitious and erroneous abuse of those signs at this time?

And here Martiall falleth into another brabble[4]: for, mistaking his argument, which is not worth a straw, the end is, the Cross is like a Sacrament, although that it be not as good as a Sacrament. But wherein is it like? It hath neither institution, nor element, nor promise, nor effect of a Sacrament: then it is as like as an apple is like an oyster. You say it is

1 [Calfhill, p. 70.]
2 Lib. iv. Cap. xxvi. De vera Sap.
3 [Calfhill, p. 83.]
4 [Brabble: brawl.]

instituted by tradition. Prove that tradition to have come from Christ and His Apostles. I have shewed it came from heretics. Again, God said to Constantine, *In hoc signo vince.* I have shewed that God spake neither of a Cross nor of a sign: and yet if He had, it was but a particular vision, authorising no general observation. You say, it may be a Sacrament as well as bread and wine, which hath no promise. You lie like an arrogant hypocrite: for bread and wine in the use of the Lord's Supper hath as good promise as water in Baptism. Concerning the effect of the Sacraments, and how they be causes of grace, not as principal efficients, but as instrumental means by which God useth to work in the faithful, it were to begin a new matter to stand in argument with you, which do nothing but wrangle, scoff, and rail in this argument, as you do in all the rest.

Wherefore, to return to the Cross, Master Calfhill saith, that if there were such necessity in the Cross to fight against Satan, the Apostles dealt not wisely to omit such a necessary weapon. Martiall answereth, that neither he nor the Fathers defend it as necessary. Well then, we have gained thus much, that the Cross is a needless weapon against the Devil. But if it had been necessary, he saith, it had been none oversight in the Apostles, which have in some Epistles omitted more needful matters; as though they were bound to speak of all matters in every Epistle. But of the use of the Cross they never speak: no, not where they instruct a Christian man to fight against the Devil; against whom it is needful to use all weapons that be of any force. The quarrel of altering Saint Peter's words I omit, as childish: Master Calfhill rehearseth his meaning, and not his words. The other argument that followeth, of heretics resembling Antichrist in denying, you shall find answered in my Confutation of D. Sander's Rock, Cap. xviii., in the eleventh mark of an Antichristian.

But Martiall is not content that his error in citing the thirty-ninth Question for the thirty-eighth of Athanasius *ad Antiochum* should be noted[5]. Indeed, the error of number is a small matter: but when a man will follow wilfully a corruption for a truth, it cannot be excused. That Devils fly when they see the Cross is Question fifteen in the best reformed prints, whatsoever Martiall doth follow. But to the

[5] [See Calfhill, pp. 73—4.]

purpose, except Martiall can declare unto us with what eyes the Devils behold the Cross, he shall have much ado to persuade us that this author speaketh of his sign of the Cross in this place. Otherwise I doubt not, but when Devils consider the conquest of Christ upon the Cross, they tremble and flee away, and are miserably tormented, as Athanasius saith: but not whensoever they see the Cross borne in procession, or set up in the market-place, or pointed in the air, either by a superstitious Papist, or by a devilish conjurer. Saint Anthony's counsel, as great and as good as you make him, may well be suspected, seeing it hath no ground in the holy Scriptures.

That Chrysostom alloweth signing with the Cross in the body is confessed; but that he accounteth it an idle ceremony, where faith in The crucified is not, Martiall cannot deny: nor yet, that faith in the death of Christ is sufficient, without the sign of the Cross in the body. Yet will he not grant it to be superfluous; but resembleth it to the incarnation and passion of Christ, without which we might be saved by the absolute power of God, to the use of Ministers, good works, &c.: whereas we ought to say, that all these things are necessary, because God hath so ordained them; but the crossing of the body is no ordinance of God, but of men.

That Origen, *in Cap.* vi. *ad Rom.* Li. vi., speaketh not of Martiall's Cross, but of the passion of Christ, the whole context of his words proveth, as M. Calfhill sheweth[1]. But Martiall replieth that he saith, "So great is the virtue of the Cross of Christ, that if it be set before our eyes, and faithfully retained in our mind, so that we look still upon the death of Christ with the eyes of our mind, no concupiscence, &c., can overcome us." These words (saith he) prove two Crosses; one before the eyes, the other before the mind. But if he would shore[2] up his eyes, he might see that Origen speaketh not of the eyes of the body, but of the eyes of the mind. As for the tautology that he would avoid, it may please his wisdom to understand, that the explaining of a metaphor is no tautology, or vain repetition.

That Cassiodorus[3] and Lactantius speak of the sign of the Cross, it is granted. But because they speak of it beside the book of God, Master Calfhill doth well to disprove their

[1] [p. 79.] [2] [Shore: lift.]

[3] [*Expos. in Psal.* iv. Opp. ii. 19. ed. Ben.]

reasons: as where Cassiodore compareth that sign of the Cross upon the faithful to the Prince's stamp on the coin, the comparison is naught. For the sign of the Cross which is upon hypocrites sheweth them not to be Christ's servants: neither did Christ give any such outward sign, by which they should be known that would profess to be His servants, but Baptism. How good Christians the Friars, that are the greatest crossers, be, I will not stand to discuss: their hypocrisy is too well known in the world.

Again, where Lactantius joineth the sign of the Cross with the name of Christ to be of force to drive away Devils, he doth as if a man should join a straw with a spear to run at tilt withal. For the name of Christ is sufficient, and needeth none assistance of the sign of the Cross, to cast out Devils, where Christ hath given that power and faith. Yet Martiall objecteth, that the name of Christ was not sufficient to cast out some kind of Devils, as in example of the man's son, Matt. xvii. But it was not for want of the sign of the Cross, but for want of faith, which must be obtained at the hands of God by prayer and fasting. He would have Scripture whereby the sign of the Cross is forbidden to be used; as though every indifferent thing that may be abused is expressed by name. To make a sign or figure of the Cross is an indifferent thing: to make it for a defence against Devils is a superstitious thing; and forbidden by all such texts of Scripture [as] forbid superstition, and confidence reposed in any thing saving in God only, by such means as He hath appointed.

That young novices in the faith were crossed before they were baptized in Augustin's time, it need to be no question: and yet it followeth not, that those words of Augustin which Martiall citeth, *De Symb. ad Catech.* Lib. ii. Cap. i.[4], were spoken of the signing, but of that which was signified by the sign, as Master Calfhill answereth.

The rest of this Article is spent in frivolous quarrels; in which is no argument to uphold the superstitious use of the Cross, but that Devils are afraid of it; as in the story of Julian, and a Jew, in which God declared what force it had *ex opere operato,* of the work wrought, even without faith; but this he maketh extraordinary. A simple force, that the

[4] [See Calfhill, p. 84.]

Devil should seem to fly from them in whose hearts he dwelled still. But Martiall would know how Master Calfhill is assured that the Devil did counterfeit fear, and was not afraid indeed. Verily, I think there need to be no better reason given, than that in outward appearance he pretended to fly from their bodily presence, from whose hearts he departed not at all, or rather for their wicked conjuring entered with greater force. How little the Devil is afraid of the sign of the Cross where faith is not, the story of the seven sons of Sceva declareth, Act. xix.; where the Devil, being conjured by the name of Jesus whom Paul preached, fell upon the conjurers and tormented them: unless Martiall think it was because they lacked the sign of the Cross; which would have made them fly away, when the name of Jesus and Paul prevailed not against them.

To conclude, it cannot be denied but divers of the ancient Fathers affirm more of the sign of the Cross than they can justify by the holy Scripture: and yet they are abused oftentimes by Martiall and such as he is, as though they spake of the sign, when they had respect only to the death and passion of Christ; as before is shewed, and more remaineth afterward to be shewed.

THE SECOND ARTICLE.

MARTIALL. *Martiall.* That the Cross of Christ was prefigured in the law of nature, foreshewn by the figures of Moses' law, denounced by the Prophets, and shewed from heaven in the time of grace.

FULKE. *Fulke.* Master Calfhill said, that the sign of the Cross was neither prefigured in the law of nature, nor foreshewed by the figures of Moses' law, nor denounced by the Prophets, nor shewed from heaven in the time of grace; but the passion of Christ, and manner of His death. Against whom cometh forth Martiall, and offereth to prove, that the Cross whereon Christ died was prefigured, &c.; which is no contradiction of M. Calfhill's assertion: although the Fathers rather dally in trifling allegories than soundly to prove that the Cross was prefigured in those places which he allegeth. As August. *Contra Faust.* Lib. xii. Cap. xxxiv.[1]; that the two sticks which the widow of Sarepta gathered did prefigure the Cross

[1] [*Opp.* Tom. viii. col. 174.]

whereon Christ died, not only by the name of wood, but by the number of the sticks: *et De* v. *Hæres. ad QuodvultDe.* Cap. ii.[2]; that Moses, lifting up his hands to heaven, did prefigure the Cross whereby Christ should redeem the world: so saith Tertullian and Augustin in divers places. All which prove not that the Image or sign of the Cross, but that the Cross itself, whereon Christ died, was prefigured: whereof we make no question but it might be, seeing it was in God's determination that Christ should die on the Cross; although we would wish sounder proofs than these for such prefiguration. Here would Martiall excuse his ridiculous argument, because it is not in mode and figure: but indeed it faileth both in form and matter; for his *minor* is false, that the sign of the Cross was prefigured by the hands of Moses: as though there were no difference between the Cross on which Christ suffered, and a superstitious sign of the Cross that a Papist maketh.

Concerning the sign *Thau* in Ezechiel, cap. ix., I have spoken sufficiently in the first Article, that it was not the figure of any letter like a Cross, but a mark unnamed or described, as Apo. vii. And whereas Hierom saith that the Samaritans had a letter somewhat like a Cross, it is not to be thought that the Samaritans had the true form of letters, and the Jews lost it. Chrysostom[3] draweth it to the Greek letter, and trifleth of the number which the letter *Tau* signifieth. Tertullian[4] is indifferent between the Latin letter and the Greek; and setteth this T for the mark of his forehead, differing somewhat from our popish ✠: for which cause Martiall calleth the character of the Latin letter *Tau*, saying, "Our *Tau* is a sign of the Cross." But of this mark more, Art. i., and in my Answer to D. Sander's book of Images, Cap. xiii. or xii.

Concerning the figure of the Cross that was in the old

[2] [The *Tractatus contra quinque Hæreses* (in Append. T. viii.) is fictitious, though defended by the Louvainists and Bellarmin. It is here confounded with the genuine *Liber de Hæresibus*, ad Quodvult-Deum.]

[3] In Mark H. 14. [The fourteen Homilies on the Gospel by S. Mark are spurious, and "Monachi alicujus satis inficeti opus." (Cave, *Hist. Lit.* i. 317. Oxon. 1740.)]

[4] Adver. Mar. Li. 30. [Lib. iii. Cap. xxii.—Calfhill, p. 106.]

time in the idol Serapis, whereunto he thinketh scorn to be sent for the antiquity of that sign, he answereth out of Socrates, that it was there set by the providence of God, as the inscription of the altar in Athens; and among the hieroglyphical letters of the Egyptian Priests signified life to come. But this proveth no more the superstitious use thereof than the altar in Athens proveth that we should set up such altars, and dedicate them to the unknown God.

Next followeth the brawl about the story of Constantine's Cross, which should be the figure of the Cross shewed from heaven in the time of grace; wherein Martiall noteth no less than six contradictions and four lies in M. Calfhill: but of them let the reader judge. The sign shewed I have proved before not to have been Martiall's Cross, but the character of the name of Christ: and so doth Constantinus himself call it, speaking to Christ; *τόν Σου χαρακτῆρα ἐφαλλόμηνος*, &c.[1]: "Holding forth Thy character, I have overcome," &c.; meaning the standard in which that character was embroidered. But of this I have spoken sufficient, Art. i., and against D. Sander's book of Images, Cap. xiii. Ar. or [xii.] after the error of his print.

After much wrangling and brabbling about M. Calfhill's principles, wherein it were easy to display Martiall's folly, but that I have professed to omit such by-matters, he cometh to the sign of the Cross shewed to Julian, and marked in his soldiers' apparel: which if it were true, as Sozomenus reporteth it, yet proveth it not that the sign of the Cross was shewed from heaven that it should be used of Christians; and the less, because it was shewed to none but Jews, and forsakers of Christian religion, as Master Calfhill noteth[2]: which might probably be thought to be the mark of persecutors rather than of Christians. But seeing the sign of the Cross hath very oftentimes appeared not only in clouds, but also on men's apparel, with divers other sights, as Conradus Lycosthenes in his book *De Prodigiis* observeth; whether the cause of those apparitions be natural or supernatural, or sometime perhaps artificial, the appearing of that sign from heaven doth no more argue an allowance of the popish ceremony of cross-

[1] ["*Τὴν Σὴν σφραγῖδα πανταχοῦ προβαλλόμενος, καλλινίκου ἡγησάμην στρατοῦ.*" (Euseb. *De vita Const.* Lib. ii. Cap. lv.)]

[2] [page 120.]

ing in religion than the appearing of other shapes and sights in heaven do teach us to frame ceremonies of armour, of horsemen, of beasts, of trees, of pillars, of circles, and suchlike, because the figures of them have been shewed from heaven. So that hitherto the sign of the Cross hath not been proved to have been prefigured in the law of nature, nor of Moses, neither denounced by the Prophets, nor used by the Apostles, nor shewed from heaven to be a pattern of the allowance of superstitious crossing among the Papists.

THE THIRD ARTICLE.

Martiall. That every church, chapel and oratory, erected to the honour and service of God, should have the sign of the Cross. MARTIALL.

Fulke. First, it is to be remembered, that for this position he hath no shew of the authority of the holy Scriptures; nor yet the testimony of any ancient writer, that any church, chapel, or oratory should have any Cross graven or painted within it or upon it, for five hundred years after Christ. Eusebius, describing divers churches builded in his time, sheweth no such necessary furniture of a Christian church; although he set forth even the fashion of the stalls or stools where the Ministers should sit. Lib. x. Cap. iv. FULKE.

But Martiall, to have shew of antiquity, beginneth with a new-found old Doctor, called Abdias: whose authority seeing Master Calfhill rejecteth as a mere counterfeit, Martiall spendeth certain leaves in quarrelling at some of his reasons; and the rest he passeth over, because he can say nothing against them. But touching the credit of this Abdias, if any man be not satisfied with M. Calfhill's reasons, I refer him further to the Bishop of Sarum's book against Harding. Art. i. Div. v. p. 8[3].

To speak of the vow of virginity supposed to be made by the Virgin Mary, it is impertinent to the cause. It cometh somewhat nearer, that he defendeth building of churches in the honour of Saints, because some churches of old have had the name of Saints. But Augustin saith of the Saints: *Quare honoramus eos charitate, non servitute. Nec eis templa construimus. Nolunt enim se sic honorari a nobis; quia nos ipsos, cum boni simus, [sumus,] templa summi Dei*

3 [Bp. Jewel, pp. 112—13. ed. Parker Soc. Calfhill, pp. 126—35.]

esse noverunt: "Wherefore we honour them with love, not with service. Neither do we build churches to them. For they will not be so honoured of us; because they know that we ourselves, when we are good, are the temples of the highest God." *De vera Religion.* Ca. lv.[1] Also, *Ep.* clxxiv. *Pascentio*[2], he proveth the Holy Ghost to be God, because He hath a temple. Also. *Ench. ad Laurent.* Cap. lvi.[3] The like judgment he hath *De Civit. Dei,* Li. viii. Cap. xxvii. & Li. xxii. Ca. x.; shewing that it is a divine honour proper to God to have temples erected to His honour; and declaring that the Martyrs' churches were places set up in their memory, not temples in their honour.

But Martiall, finding nothing for the space of five hundred years after Christ for his purpose, at length stumbleth upon a Canon of the Provincial Council of Orleans in France; that "No man should build a church before the Bishop came and set up a Cross." This Canon made in those days sheweth, that churches before the making thereof were builded without a Cross: neither bindeth it any but such as build churches within the province of Orleans: beside that it may be doubted of the antiquity of the Canon, seeing it is not found in the records of that Council, but taken out of the Pope's Canon Law, where is most counterfeit stuff[4]: beside that it is not observed among the Papists themselves, that before any church, chapel, or oratory be builded, the Bishop of the diocese should come and make a Cross there.

The next Canon he citeth out of the Council of Tours the second: *Ut corpus Domini in altari, non in armario, sed sub Crucis titulo componatur:* "That the Lord's body be laid on the altar, not in a chest or almery, but under the title of the Cross." But Martiall doth English it thus: "That the body of our Lord, consecrated upon the altar, be not reposed and set in the revestry, but under the Rood." He braggeth, that when he was usher of Winchester school, he taught his scholars the true signification of the Latin words. But beside that he translateth *armarium,* "a revestry," which Tully useth for a place wherein money was kept[5], which could not well be an open house, and also maketh a manifest difference between

Pro Clu. Pro Cel. In Ant.

1 [*Opp.* Tom. i. col. 588.] 2 [alias ccxxxviii. *Opp.* ii. 651.]
3 [*Opp.* vi. 159.] 4 [Calfhill, p. 135.]
5 ["Armaria et arcæ habent libros." (S. Hieron. *in S. Matth.* Cap. xxiii. Opp. T. ix. p. 68.)]

armarium and *sacrarium;* beside also that he calleth *titulum Crucis* "the Rood," where findeth he in this sentence the Latin word for his English word "consecrated"? But to the purpose of the Cross, this Canon sheweth, that in old time they used to lay it otherwise than under the title of the Cross; whether they meant thereby the sign of the Cross, or these words, *Jesus Naz. Rex Judæorum*, which was the title of the Cross; as they had in those days many ceremonies grown out of use, and therefore not understood of us.

The third Council is a Canon of the sixth General Council at Constantinople in Trullo, which in the margent he calleth the Council of Chalcedon in Trullo, Can. lxxiii.[6]; which M. Calfhill could not find in that Council, because it is certain, and confessed by Garanza [Carranza[7],] Martiall's author, that the sixth Council of Constantinople in Trullo made no ceremonies [Canons,] but [statements] of the faith, and that those which he setteth forth were made privately by them long after in the days of Justinian: therefore they have neither the authority of Canons, nor be free from suspicion of forgery. And yet the Canon alleged proveth not this Article; for it only commandeth Crosses that were made in the pavement to be put out. Nay, saith Martiall, the prohibition of the Cross to be made on the ground permitteth it to be made in all other places; "for a prohibition restrictive of a thing to be done in one place is a lawful permission for all other places which are not namely included in that prohibition:" and for this he referreth himself to the judgment of the lawyers. But I think his law deceiveth him in this point as much as his divinity almost in every point. For if the King's edict forbid swearing, fighting, brawling in his court, I suppose he doth not permit these things as lawful in all other places. The last Canon, which forbad the laying of the Lord's body in the vestry, doth not lawfully permit it to be laid in the belfry. The captain's prohibition, that no man shall discharge his belly within the precinct of the camp, is not a lawful permission that a soldier may defile a church without the camp. The law that forbiddeth the Prince's image to be made on the pavement is not a lawful permission that the same may be set upon the high altar. What Martiall's law is in these

6 [Calfhill, *Supplem. Observat.* pp. x—xi.]

7 [*Summa*, p. 396. Salm. 1551.]

cases, I know not: but my reason serveth me not to allow of those prohibitions for lawful permission.

And where these Canon-makers say they did "reverence the lively Cross with mind, tongue, and sense," Martiall inferreth that "this word 'sense' declareth that they had a sensible Cross, to which they might shew their reverence with their external senses." Which senses, Martiall? their sight, their hearing, their smelling, their tasting, or their feeling? Did you teach your scholars at Winchester thus to interpret? Was it the Image of the Cross, or the lively Cross, that shewed them that saving health, which they profess to reverence in word and mind? And were you wont to construe *cum* "seeing," *vivifica Crux* "the living Cross," *ostenderit* "doth shew?"—for thus you give me example to play with you. And if one of your boys that learned Terence had so construed, would you not have straightway asked him, *Cujus modi et temporis ostenderit?* If he had answered, "The preterperfect tense," you would have demanded whether "doth" be the sign of that temps, or "have." If "have," then have you not rightly translated *Cum Crux vivifica illud salutare nobis ostenderit,* "Seeing the living Cross doth shew unto us that healthful thing." Wherefore, to leave this trifling, the Canon is this: "Seeing the living Cross" (that is to say, the passion of Christ,) "hath shewed unto us that saving health, it behoveth us to employ all our study, that we may give unto it, by which we are saved from our old fall, that honour which is convenient. Wherefore, giving reverence unto it with mind, speech, and understanding, we command that the figures of the Cross, which are made of some in the ground and pavement, be utterly taken away; lest the trophy of our victory be injured by treading of those that pass over it." It is not without fraud that, beside your false translation, you have omitted *per quam ab antiquo lapsu servati sumus;* lest every popish woman might see that the Canon speaketh not of honour given to the Image of the Cross, whereby we are not saved, but to the passion of Christ.

But Martiall rejecteth the Council of Constantinople, condemning Images, as M. Calfhill doth the second of Nice, allowing them. The best way then, as Augustin counselleth the heretic Maximinus, were to give over the hold of Councils on both sides, and try the matter by the word of God.

It is a fond quarrel that he picketh to M. Calfhill, of the time when the Eliberine Council was kept[1]. If it be ancienter than he supposeth, it is of greater credit; for the latter times were more corrupt. And whereas he girdeth[2] at the marriage of Ministers, because in the twenty-seventh Canon of that Council the Bishop or Priest was forbidden to have any woman to dwell with him, but either his sister or his daughter, being a virgin and professed to God, he sheweth both his falsehood and his folly: his falsehood, for that he translateth *extraneam*, which is a strange woman, "no other woman;" his folly, in seeing the Priest's daughter, he cannot see his wife. But the thirty-third Canon commandeth them abstinence as from their wives, and begetting of children. I answer, if that Canon were not to be understood of a temporal abstinence, the General Council of Nice decreed against it; as appeareth in Socrat. Lib. i. Cap. xi.

But touching the Canon against Images, *Placuit:* "We decree, that Pictures ought not to be in the church, lest that which is worshipped and adored should be painted on the walls;" first he repeateth his principle of law, before set down, for prohibition; that Pictures are only forbidden, and not other Images: as though he that forbiddeth wounding permitteth murdering: beside that they should be simple Images, in which were no picture or painting. Secondly he saith, that Pictures on walls only are forbidden: but therein he lieth; for they are generally forbidden in the church: *ergo* not in walls only. Thirdly he saith, "Here is an evident proof that Pictures were then worshipped. For this argument followeth necessarily upon these words: That was worshipped that was forbidden to be painted in the walls: But Pictures were forbidden to be painted upon walls: *Ergo* Pictures were worshipped. Answer, M. Calfhill." Who would have thought that an usher of Winchester and student in Louvain, that teacheth us an old lawyer's point, would also teach us a new logic point, to conclude affirmatively in the second figure, and that all upon particulars? "Answer, M. Calf.," quod Martiall. Nay, answer goose to such an argument: and reason who will any longer with such an ass about

1 [Calfhill, p. 154. The mistake was assuredly one of considerable moment; and Calfhill was led into it by the Homily *against peril of Idolatry*, which he too closely followed upon more than this occasion.]

2 [Girdeth: sneereth.]

this matter. For I will hearken to his law, seeing his logic is no better: "For the better understanding of a statute or a Canon, divers circumstances are to be considered." This was law enough to make him a Bachelor.

Well, the circumstances are these. The authors of this Canon were Catholic and wise Bishops. The place, Granata, a city in Spain; which had then many infidels, that thought Christians to commit idolatry by having of Images. The time, when they feared persecution; as appeareth by the fifty-ninth and sixtieth Canon. But if we believe Garanza[1] your author, it was about the time of the Nicene Council, when no persecution could be feared: and therefore your cause, which you make the fourth circumstance, is forged; that they feared lest those Images should have been despitefully abused by the Pagans, when they were fled. Neither are you able to prove it; and therefore in the end you conclude, it was but a Synod of nineteen Bishops, whose Decree was undone by the second Nicene General Council, the Council at Frankfort, &c. That the Council of Frankfort condemned the Council of Nice, he only denieth that it did so, but answereth not the authority cited by M. Calfhill. The book of Carolus Magnus against Images he condemneth for a forged tale; although ancient writers make mention of it, and the style of the book doth argue that it was written in that time, if not by the Emperor, yet by his appointment[2]. But seeing he referreth us to the Confutation of the Apology, fol. 328, I will refer the readers to the Defence of the Apology[3] for the same matter.

After this he spendeth certain leaves in defending the credit of Irene, the idolatrous Empress, and in defacing those Emperors that were enemies to Images: wherein he hath the idolatrous historians favourable, not sparing to report whatsoever their malicious enemies could invent to slander them. But hereof I have written somewhat in mine Answer to D. Sander's book of Images, Cap. iv. or iii., and Cap. xv. or xiv.

Now cometh in S. Ambrose extolling the Cross, *Ser.* lvi.: "As a church cannot stand without a Cross, so a ship is weak without a mast. For by and by the Devil doth disquiet it, and the wind doth squat it. But when the sign of the

[1] [Calfhill, p. 154, note 1.]

[2] [Supra, p. 23, n. 5.]

[3] [Bp. Jewel's *Works*, vi. 474. Cf. iii. 257. ed. Jelf.]

Cross is set up, by and by both the iniquity of the Devil is beaten back, and the tempest of wind is appeased." Here Martiall triumpheth against M. Calfhill, that the author speaketh not of a cross-beam in the church, but of the sign of the Cross. But he lieth shamefully: for this writer speaketh not of a material church, chapel, or oratory, but of the congregation of Christ, in which the Cross and passion of Christ hath the same force that the mast in a ship, which is made after the figure of the Cross, and the plough-beam in tillage, &c. His other sentence, *Serm.* lv., is yet more plain against him: *Arbor enim quædam in navi est Crux in Ecclesia, quæ inter totius sæculi blanda et perniciosa naufragia incolumis sola servatur. In hac ergo navi quisquis aut arbori Crucis se religaverit, aut aures suas Scripturis divinis clauserit, dulcem procellam luxuriæ non timebit:* "For the Cross in the Church is as it were a certain tree in a ship, which among the flattering and pernicious shipwrecks of the whole world alone is preserved in safety. In this ship therefore whosoever shall either bind himself to that tree of the Cross, or stop his ears with the holy Scriptures, he shall not fear the sweet storm of luxuriousness," &c. He alludeth to the fable of Ulysses, which tied himself to the mast, and stopped his ears with wax, that he might not hear the song of the mermaids. This sentence (whereof Martiall durst cite but three or four words) declareth, that this author maketh nothing for the title of this Article of erecting the Cross in churches, chapels, &c. And yet, when all is done, I must confess with the learned, that these Sermons were not written by S. Ambrose; but by one Maximus of latter time, Bishop either of Taurinum or of Milan[4].

Concerning the tale that you father upon Sir Ambrose Cave, of an island by Rhodes, and a road there where no anchor nor cable will hold the ship, unless the mariner make the sign of the Cross over the place where he casteth anchor; it may be he reported it as a fond persuasion of superstitious people, but I think not that he gave any credit to it. Popery is full of such tales. But why do you charge M. Calfhill with a lie, for saying that in the popish Catholic time the church of Paul's was twice burned within fifty years' space? Marry, "because it was not on Corpus Christi eve; nor the Communion-table was burned with all the four aisles, within the compass of

[4] [See Calfhill, p. 177.]

three or four hours : therefore it was not the like plague." But how often hath the Sacrament of the altar (your God) been burned, when churches were fired? Mo things, in which there is any diversity, shall be like, by Martiall's logic or law: I cannot tell whether it is, by which he condemneth M. Calfhill for a liar.

Touching Lactantius, he reasoneth to and fro of his authority himself, and yet chargeth M. Calfhill for so doing. Our judgment of Lactantius, as of all old writers, is this: that whatsoever they speak contrary to the truth of the holy Scriptures, we may boldly reject it; whatsoever they say agreeable unto them, we do willingly admit it. The chief matter touching this Article is this; that certain verses are ascribed to Lactantius, exhorting men to worship the Cross; which verses M. Calfhill[1] denieth to have been written by Lactantius: first, because S. Hierom, in the catalogue of his works, maketh no mention of them. But they might be unknown to Hierom, saith Martiall. It is not like they could be unknown to Hierom, and known to Martiall. Secondly, because he speaketh of churches, that were scarcely builded in Lactantius' time. But Martiall proveth that Christians had churches even in the Apostles' time, and ever since; as though any man doth doubt of that, but of such churches as this versifier speaketh of. Thirdly, because the doctrine of these verses, concerning Images, is contrary to that Lactantius taught, and was generally received in his days. Martiall replieth, that all which Lactantius did write against Images was against the false Images of the heathen; and not against the holy Images of the Christians. But Christians in his time had no Images as holy in any use of religion; and his arguments are general against all Images in religion. Finally, it is also manifest that this versifier, making a poetical *prosopopœia*, induceth Christ hanging upon the Cross, and speaking to him that cometh into the church: and therefore no argument of Cross or Image may be rightly gathered out of the poem, whosoever was the author. For immediately after this verse, *Flecte genu, lignumque Crucis venerabile adora*, followeth, *Flebilis innocuo terramque cruore madentem Ore petens humili, lachrymis suffunde subortis:* "Bow thy knee, worship the venerable wood of the Cross," and "Lamentably kissing with humble mouth the earth, which is moist with

[1] [pages 180—4.]

mine innocent blood, wash it over with tears flowing out." By these verses then Martiall may as well prove, that the church-floor was moist with the blood of Christ, as that there was a Cross in the church.

To Lactantius he joineth Augustin, *De Sanctis Hom.* xix.[2], saying that churches are dedicated with the sign of the Cross: where he not only changed the word *charactere* into *mysterio*, but also translated the word *mysterio* "by the sign." Where he confesseth his fault, he may be pardoned; but where he justifieth *mysterio* and *signo* to be all one, he sheweth himself as he is. But how will he persuade us, that those Homilies *De Tempore*, and *De Sanctis*, of which some one is ascribed to so many authors, were either written by Augustin, or by any of those times? The style is so dissonant that any man learned, and of indifferent judgment, will confess: although it is not to be denied but the sign of the Cross was superstitiously abused even in the days of Augustin, and long before. Whereas Augustin reporteth of a woman called Innocentia, which had a canker healed in her breast by the sign of the Cross; if it were a miracle, it proveth not that every church, chapel, and oratory should have a Cross. Great miracles were done by imposition of hands: yet it followeth not therefore that every church must have imposition of hands. Again, not only cankers, but also fistulas, tooth-ache, and many other diseases have been healed by charms. And yet these charms are not justifiable thereby: much less to be brought into the church, as wholesome ceremonies and prayers.

But albeit the Cross be no ordinary mean whereby God useth to conserve health, (saith Martiall,) yet may you not conclude that He hath not ordained it to remain in the Church, for any remembrance of His death and passion. "For think you," (saith he,) "He hath left no more means but the preaching of His word, which every one can hear? Yes, it hath pleased His Majesty to ordain by General Councils the sign of the Cross and Images to be a mean to put us in remembrance of Christ's death," &c. But seeing the Church flourished three hundred years without a General Council; and neither that General Council which was first holden, nor three other which followed, make mention of any such matter; where was the ordinance of God by General Councils for the Cross?

2 [Calfhill, p. 184.]

He will say, it had the appointment of the Prelates of the Church. Which? and when? Every idle ceremony and ungodly heresy that prevailed had the Prelates of the Church either for the authors, or for the approvers. But Christ committed to the Prelates (saith Martiall) the charge and government of His Church. Yea, Sir, to feed them with His word; and not with dumb signs and dead Images, which things He hath forbidden.

Now come we to Paulinus, Bishop of Nola; by whom it appeareth that the sign of the Cross was set up eleven hundred years ago in some churches: but the title of the Article is, that it should be set up in all churches. But Martiall will prove that it was well done by Paulinus, to set up the sign of the Cross in his church, "because he was an holy and learned Bishop; and no Catholic Bishop or General Council did find fault with him: for whatsoever any holy and learned Father did at any time, and was not controlled of any Catholic Father for his doing, was well done, and must be so taken." I deny this *major:* for Augustin was an holy and learned Bishop, which did give the Communion to infants, and thought it necessary for their everlasting salvation; neither was he controlled therefore: yet did he not well, neither was his opinion true. And where Martiall taketh upon him the defence of Paulinus, in commending a woman that separated herself from her husband under pretence of religion, he playeth the prattling proctor; picking of quarrels against M. Calfhill, without all honesty or shame. For he feigneth that the fault is alleged for want of consent of her husband: whereas such separation as he commendeth, without consent, is directly contrary to the doctrine of the Holy Ghost. 1 Cor. vii. v. 5. Likewise, where M. Calfhill nameth a book that the Apostles wrote, Martiall saith it was but of Paul's Epistles. Where he saith it was laid unto diseases, M. Martiall saith it saved a man from drowning. But of these quarrels too much. Martiall confesseth, that where a Doctor swerveth from Scripture, no man ought to follow him. But if Paulinus swerved not from Scripture, when he brought Images into the church, we need not doubt that any man swerved from Scripture; seeing nothing is more plain in all the Scriptures than forbidding of Images and similitudes of any thing to be made or had in any use of religion.

Where M. Calfhill answereth to the Decree of Justinian,

(that no church should be builded before the place were consecrated, and a Cross set up by the Bishop,) that this was a constitution of the external policy, Martiall laboureth to prove that it was religious; and yet at length granteth that it was a matter of external policy. Whereupon I infer, that it was not of necessity; and so the Article is not proved thereby, "That every church should," &c. But it cometh of great wisdom, that he will defend the time of Justinian from ignorance and barbarity, because the civil law was then gathered, and a few learned men were found in the whole world. All this notwithstanding, the barbarians had overcome a great part of the empire, and filled the world with ignorance and barbarousness.

Against the Decree of Valentinian and Theodosius, cited out of Crinitus[1], he hath many quarrels. First, against Petrus Crinitus, who was as good a Clerk as Martiall. Then at the Homily against Images[2], where the printer calleth him Petrus Erinilus. Yet again that Valentinian, not being written at large, is mistaken for Valens, where it should be Valentinianus. "And if Valens and Theodosius had made such a law, what an oversight was it of Eusebius to suppress it!" When Eusebius was dead before any of them were born, it was a great oversight, in Martiall's judgment, to suppress in his story a law made by them which lived near an hundred year after him; so that belike he would have Eusebius to write stories of things to come. But concerning that law of Valentinianus and Theodosius, you shall see more in mine Answer to D. Sander's book of Images, Cap. xiii. or xii.

The rest of this chapter is spent in commending the Church of Rome; whose custom it hath been (saith Martiall) these twelve hundred years to set the sign of the Cross in the church; and Pope Pius the fourth did it himself of late, &c. Concerning the Church of Rome, so long as she continued in true religion, and so far forth as she maintained the truth, as she was greatly commended of ancient writers whom Martiall nameth, so now it is to her greater reproach and shame, *earum laudum et gloriæ degenerem esse,* "that she is grown out of kind and desert of all such praises;" as the Clergy of Rome, writing to Cyprian. Lib. ii. *Epist.* vii.[3]

[1] [See Calfhill, p. 190.]

[2] [Second part of the Homily *against peril of Idolatry.* The typographical mistake was afterwards corrected.]

[3] [Ad Pamel. num. xxxi. Ad Erasm. L. ii. *Ep.* vii. In edit. Oxon.

To conclude, therefore, there is nothing shewed to prove that every church, chapel, or oratory should have a Cross: although in the latter and more corrupt times of the Church, it is declared, that some churches had a Cross; and at length grew to a custom in those parts of the world, that every church had one, and was thought necessary that it should have one.

THE FOURTH ARTICLE.

MARTIALL. *Martiall.* That the sign of the Cross was used in all Sacraments, &c.

FULKE. *Fulke.* That it hath been used in the latter declining times, we will not stand with Martiall: but that in the best and purest age of the Church, by the Apostles and their immediate successors, it was used or allowed, before the Valentinian heretics, I affirm that Martiall cannot prove by any ancient authentical writer, between the Apostles and Irenæus. Wherefore Master Calfhill answereth well, that the ceremony once taken up of good intent, being grown into so horrible abuse, is justly refused of us. Martiall will know what our vocation is; as though we were not able to prove our calling both before God and men. Our Synods he refuseth, because no Council can be kept without the consent of the Bishop of Rome: in which point as many of the Papists are against him, which hold that even a General Council may be kept to depose an evil Pope against his will; so he mistaketh the Tripartite History[1], and Julian [Julius] Bishop of Rome[2], where they speak of General Councils and Synods, to determine of matters of faith; from which the Bishop of Rome, while he was a Bishop, was not to be excluded, because those cases touch all Bishops; dreaming that they speak of all Councils. But long after their times it was practised as lawful for Kings and Bishops of several provinces to gather and hold Provincial Synods, for the state of their several Churches, without the consent or knowledge of the Bishop of Rome: in which some

Epist. xxx. pag. 57.—"Quarum laudum et gloriæ degenerem fuisse, maximum crimen est."]

1 [Lib. iv. Cap. ix. Cf. Socrat. *Ecc. Hist.* L. ii. C. viii.]

2 [See the same sentence in two spurious Epistles attributed to Pope Julius I.—Blondelli *Pseudo-Isidor.* pp. 447, 459.]

things have been determined against the will of the Bishop of Rome, as in the Councils of Carthage and Africa; and in General Councils also, as in that of Chalcedon, Constantinople the fifth and sixth, the Councils of Constance and Basil.

But signing with the Cross is a tradition of the Apostles, and so accounted by S. Basil: therefore we ought not to forsake it for any abuse, (saith Martiall.) But how will S. Basil persuade us of that, when we find it not in their writings? It is more safe therefore to follow his counsel in his short Definitions, *Q.* i.[3], where he affirmeth, that it is not lawful for any man to permit himself to do or say any thing without the testimony of the holy Scriptures. And this we will hold, even with Basil's good leave, against all pretended traditions of the Apostles whatsoever. We know the Apostle willeth us to hold the traditions, either learned by his Epistles, or by his sermons: but what he delivered in his sermons we cannot tell but by his Epistles. Yes, saith Martiall, the Church telleth you of the sign of the Cross. But seeing the Church telleth us of other things, which are left and forsaken; avouching them likewise to be traditions of the Apostles, which ought not to have been so given over, if they had been Apostolic traditions indeed; we see no cause why we may not refuse these as well as those; having no ground of certainty for Apostolic traditions but only the Apostolic writings. Tertullian counteth the tasting of milk and honey after Baptism for an Apostolic tradition, because it was a ceremony in his time as well as crossing. The one was left long ago: why may not the other be forsaken, that hath no better ground, and hath been worse abused?

Concerning the tale of Probianus[4], which followeth next after this discourse, I will refer the reader to mine Answer to D. Sander's book against Images, Ca. xiii., or xii. after the error of his print.

[3] [D. Basilii *Opera Græca*, p. 483. Basil. 1551.—Bellarmin, after having declared that it is uncertain whether these *Regulæ contractiores* were written by S. Basil or by Eustathius Sebastenus, significantly adds, "quod auctor harum Quæstionum, Quæstione 1. & Quæst. 95, non videtur admittere Traditiones non scriptas ... Quare cum valde probabile sit, eas Quæstiones editas esse ab homine parum probatæ fidei, non est cur earum testimonium magni faciamus." (*De amissione Gratiæ*, Lib. i. Cap. xiii. Opp. Tom. iv. 111. Ingolst. 1601.)]

[4] [Calfhill, page 198.]

Where Calfhill thinketh it not meet that we should be restrained to that whereof there is no precept in Scripture, nor they themselves yield lawful cause, Martiall telleth him that he must be restrained, if he will be a good Christian. For there is no precept in express Scripture to believe three Persons and one God in the blessed Trinity, the equality of substance of Christ with His Father in His Godhead, &c., the perpetual virginity of Mary, the keeping of the Sunday, the Sacrament receiving fasting, the Baptism of infants, &c. You see what an Atheist he is, that can find no more certainty in the Scriptures for the blessed Trinity than for S. Mary's virginity; for the Godhead of Christ than for receiving the Communion before other meats. If Papists have no ground of their faith out of the Scriptures, yet we can prove whatsoever is necessary for us to believe. If he dally upon the word "express Scripture," either he answereth not to the same thing whereof he is demanded, or else he knoweth not that an argument rightly concluded out of holy Scripture is as good as the very words of the Scripture: as when I say, If Peter believed and was baptized, *ergo* he was saved, is as true as these words, "Whoso believeth and is baptized shall be saved."

To the second demand, whether the ancient Fathers did attribute such virtue to the wagging of a finger, that the Holy Ghost could be called down, and the Devil driven away by it, Martiall answereth, "It is most evident, that as soon as prayer is duly made, and the sign of the Cross made, the Holy Ghost, according to the promise of Christ, cometh down and sanctifieth, &c., and the Devil is driven away." This is Martiall's evidence: other reason he bringeth none. If he refer the promise and coming of the Holy Ghost to prayer, he playeth the palterer, that, being demanded of the Cross, answereth of prayer. Otherwise, let him shew what promise Christ hath made to the sign of the Cross, or to prayer with the sign of the Cross more than without it. If he cannot, you may easily see his poverty.

To the third, whether they would have refused the Church and Sacraments for want of a Cross, he "believeth verily they would not; for the Sacraments lacketh not the virtue, if the sign of the Cross be omitted: yet the fault is great when the tradition of the Apostles is wilfully rejected." Whether it be like they delivered any needless or unprofitable ceremony, let wise men judge.

After this followeth a long and foolish dialogism about the interpretation of Cyprian's[1] words: "Whatsoever the Ministers of the Sacraments be, whatsoever the hands are that dip those that come to Baptism, whatsoever the breast is out of which the holy words proceed, the authority of operation giveth effect to all Sacraments in the figure of the Cross; and the Name which is above all names, being called upon by the dispensers of the Sacraments, doth all." Martiall so scanneth these words, as though M. Calfhill knew not the difference between the power of God and the ministry of man in the Sacraments, which Cyprian doth plainly distinguish in these words. But to the purpose, Cyprian seemeth to make the figure of the Cross a mean by which God worketh in the Sacraments. But indeed he meaneth, that all Sacraments take their effect of the passion of Christ; as a bare sign and token whereof they used the figure of the Cross, and not as a mean whereby God worketh; seeing it is confessed by Martiall, that "the Sacraments, if the sign of the Cross be omitted, lack not their virtue."

Another foolish brabble and usher-like construing he maketh of Cyprian's[2] words, *De Baptismo: Verborum solemnitas, et sacri invocatio Nominis, et signa attributa institutionibus Apostolicis Sacerdotum ministeriis, visibile Sacramentum celebrant.* For, reproving Master Calfhill for translating *signa attributa institutionibus Apostolicis,* "signs attributed to the institution of the Apostles," he teacheth him to construe "signs attributed by the Apostolical institutions, through the ministry of the Priests." Wherein I marvel that such an ancient student will now suffer the word *attributa* to go without a dative case: which I think he would not have done in his petite school at Winchester. But if I might be bold, under the correction of such a grounded grammarian, to construe the lesson over again, I would give the Latin this English: "The solemnity of words, and invocation of the holy Name, and the signs appointed by the institutions of the Apostles for the ministry of the Priests, doth make the visible Sacrament." And what be those signs? By M. Martiall's leave, the elements; as water, bread, and wine.

[1] [Arnold's. See Calfhill, p. 200.] [2] [Arnold's. Calfhill, 201.]

But then M. Grindall, (whom I laugh to see this wise dialogue-maker to bring in swearing once or twice in this devised talk, as though our Bishops used that vein as commonly as popish Prelates;) M. Grindall, I say, must send me to Saint Anthony's school; because the elements of the Sacraments be of Christ's own institution, and not of His Apostles: wherefore those signs must be other goodly ceremonies; and the sign of the Cross must not be least. But if Martiall ever were a scholar in that school, or any other of any value, he might have learned long ago that *institutio* signifieth not only the first beginning of an ordinance, but also a teaching or doctrine. And so doth Cyprian mean, that by the doctrine of the Apostles the Priests are appointed to use those signs: which if Martiall's ushership will not admit, Cyprian, in telling what maketh the visible Sacrament, hath left out the principal part thereof; namely the element, and that which indeed in it is only visible; for the solemnity of words and invocation are audible rather than visible.

But in this foolish dialogue is cited Justinus, *Apol.* ii.[1], to prove that the old Fathers used the sign of the Cross in all Sacraments. "Justinus Martyr," (saith he, in the place of M. Grindall,) "talking of the Cross, biddeth us view in our minds, and consider with reason all things that are in the world; and see whether *sine hac figura administrentur*, they may be done without this sign." How like it is that M. Grindall should say Justinus biddeth us, when he biddeth the Gentiles, I leave to speak of. But that he speaketh of our Sacraments, how will Martiall prove; when both he speaketh to the heathen, and of heathenish customs and ceremonies, or else civil and natural matters; as of sailing, ploughing, digging, and all handicrafts, whose tools had some figure of the Cross; in which the Gentiles did so fondly abhor and despise Christ for it, whereas it was to be found even in the shape ot man in the trophies and standards of their Emperor, in the consecration of their dead Emperors' Images, whom they worshipped as Gods? For which causes Justinus thought it unreasonable that they should contemn Christ for His Cross' sake. But of using the sign of the Cross in all Sacraments there is no mention in Justinus.

[1] [*Apolog.* i. Opp. p. 90. Lut. Paris. 1615. The first Apology is ranked second in this edition.]

That in Chrysostom's time, and other more ancient Fathers, the sign of the Cross was used at the celebration of the Sacraments, M. Calfhill granteth, as a ceremony; and you confess "it is but a ceremony; and that our Sacraments, lacking the sign of the Cross and that usual ceremony, be perfect notwithstanding." And yet you exclaim against us for omitting a needless ceremony, where we see it hath been turned from that indifferent usage of the forefathers into an idolatrous custom and opinion of necessity.

The credit of Dionysius, for so ancient a scholar of S. Paul as you would make him, is too much cracked by Erasmus[2] to be cured by Martiall.

Where M. Calfhill truly saith, and you cannot deny but he hath as good authority for honey, milk, wine, to be restored in Baptism, and the Communion to be given to children, as you have for the Cross; you answer, Those were altered by the Church of Rome, which hath authority so to do: the Cross still remaineth. But mark what you say: were these traditions of the Apostles? If you say no, the like will I say of the Cross; for the same authority commendeth them all alike for traditions of the Apostles. Well, if they were traditions of the Apostles by the Holy Ghost, which you hold to be of equal authority with the Scriptures, and the Church of Rome hath abolished the one, why may she not abolish the other? so that your answer containeth manifest blasphemy.

To fortify your traditions, you allege that Jesus did many things "which are not written," &c.; but you leave off that which followeth, "But these are written that you might believe, and in believing have eternal life." Jo. xx. And yet S. John speaketh of miracles; not of ceremonies to be used in Baptism, whereunto you apply it. But Jesus Himself saith He hath "many things to say," that the Apostles could not then bear, &c. Joan. xvi.: and you would know in what work of the Apostles those things are written; yea, you would have the chapter noted. Pleaseth it you to look yourself in the Acts of the Apostles, and in their Epistles, &c.; and you shall find, that the Scriptures will instruct the man of God "unto all good works," and make him "wise unto salvation." If

[2] [Vid. *Epist.* præfix. *Paraph.* in 1 Cor.; itemque *Schol.* in S. Hieron. *Catal. Scriptt. Eccl.* Opp. Tom. i. 308. Cf. Coci *Censur.* pp. 50—1.]

these will not serve your turn, seek where you will, and find the Devil and eternal damnation. But, I pray you, could not the Apostles bear the hearing of the sign of the Cross, of salt, oil, spittle in Baptism? Were these such hard lessons to learn, or heavy to bear? If you think they were, I envy not unto you so wise a thought.

But you will teach us, how we shall know that these are traditions of the Apostles. To this inquiry you answer, Even as we know the Gospels and Epistles to be the canonical Scriptures, by authority of the Church; which you think sufficient for that purpose. But so do not we: for although we receive the testimony of the Church, yet we have greater authority out of the Scriptures of the Old Testament, and that Spirit by which they were written, being always the same by which we are persuaded that the Gospels and Epistles are the holy Scriptures. Again, the universal Church of all times and places giveth witness to those writings: so doth it not to these traditions. Therefore we are never the near to know Apostolical traditions by authority of the popish Church; which ascribeth things manifestly contrary to the word of God and writings of the Apostles to Apostolic traditions, as Images, half Communion, private Mass, &c.

After this brabbling of traditions followeth a long brawl about numbers, which the Papists do superstitiously observe; and of the authority of the seventy Interpreters, whose translation, if it were extant[1], no doubt but it were worthy of great reverence: but seeing these questions are fruitless, and impertinent unto the Article, I will clearly omit them.

Martiall, returning to prove that the sign of the Cross was used in consecrating the body and blood of Christ, findeth himself greatly grieved that M. Calfhill calleth the Mass "the sacrifice of the Devil;" wherein be so many good

[1] [Fulke possibly means extant in absolute purity. He could scarcely have been unacquainted with the existence of at least two of the four principal editions of the Septuagint, viz. the Complutensian and the Venetian; the former completed in 1517, the latter published in 1518. The Roman edition was printed seven years after the appearance of the present work, namely in 1587; and the Alexandrian followed in 1707. Vid. Waltoni *Prolegom.* ix. §§. 28—30. *Appar. Biblic.* pp. 332—4. Tiguri, 1673. Grabii *Proleg.* Cap. iii. Oxon. 1707. Le Long *Biblioth. Sac.* Tom. i. p. 185. Paris. 1723.]

things, as the Collects, Gospel, Epistle, *Gloria in excelsis*, &c.: by which reason I might prove a devilish cónjuration, in which be so many names of God, and good words, to be an holy piece of work. Therefore it is not many good parts, abused to make a wicked thing good, that can justify the Mass; which is an horrible blasphemy against the death and only sacrifice of Christ. But M. Calfhill doth not satisfy him, where he, citing out of Albertus Magnus, "that Christ did bless the Sacrament with a certain sign of His hand; as Jacob laid his hands on Joseph's sons, and Christ laid His hands upon the children, and lifted up His hands, and blessed His Apostles," &c., asketh, why we might not say Christ made a sign of the Cross; considering that Chrysostom, Augustin, and Euthymus [Euthymius] testify, that in their time the sign of the Cross was used in consecration? This question (he saith) is not soluted. This is soon answered; because laying on of hands, and lifting up of hands, which be sometime used in blessing, doth not prove a crossing with the fingers of one's hand, as the Papists use; and because the Evangelists, which describe all that He then said or did for us to follow, make no mention of any such sign of hand made by Him in blessing.

The long discourse that followeth of blessing and giving of thanks is needless: for we know and confess, that as they sometimes signify all one thing, so they differ sometimes; and we confess that the bread and wine in the Lord's Supper were blessed, that is to say, sanctified and consecrated; but not with any sign of hand, which is the matter in question, but with the word of God, and with prayer; not only as bodily meats, but as heavenly and spiritual mysteries, to feed the soul. But it is a sport to see how Martiall, when he hath proved that which was not in question; that the bread and wine were blessed and sanctified by Christ, and that they must now be so consecrated by the Church; he runneth away with the sign of the Cross, whereof he hath brought no proof of the use by Christ, saying, "There must be consecration by honouring the words of Christ, and calling upon His name, and making the sign of the Cross: which manner of consecration the Church learned of Christ, and hath continued ever since; so that we may boldly say with Albertus, 'He blessed it with a certain sign of His hand'." But I pray you, Sir, where learned you this sign used by Christ? How prove you that it hath been used ever since? It is enough for Martiall to say, that "all the learning in English Doctors will never be able to prove this assertion of his to be frivolous."

But seeing he is so Greekish to teach M. Calfhill to construe Saint Paul's words[1], *τὸ ποτήριον τῆς εὐλογίας*, &c., and findeth fault with him for giving the aorists the signification of the present temps, let him look in his lexicon, where I ween all his Greek is, how he will abide by this saying, "*εὐχαριστήσας* in Saint Matthew, *εὐλόγησας* [*εὐλόγησεν*] in Saint Luke, *εὐλογοῦμεν* in Saint Paul, have relation to the bread and wine[2], and answer to the question 'whom?' or 'what?,'" seeing *εὐχαριστέω* is no verb transitive; although the Christian writers, as Justinus Martyr, hath feigned a passive unto it.

Again, in the saying of Chrysostom, *Ho.* xxiv. *in* 1 *Cor.* Cap. x.[3], where Martiall will have us mark that the body of Christ is seen upon the altar, let him and his fellows mark, that if it be none otherwise there than as it is seen, it is present only to the faith by whose eye it is seen.

After this tedious treatise of blessing and thanksgiving, he cometh to his old petition or [of?] principle[4], that the signing with the Cross is a tradition of the Apostles; and angry he is, that he should be called on to prove that it is a tradition of the Apostles, whereof he can find no mention in ecclesiastical writers before the Valentinian heretics. And whereas Cyprian, *Ad Panpeium*[5], calleth all traditions to the writings and commandment of the Apostles, he crieth out that Cyprian is slandered, because he himself allegeth the tradition of Christ for mingling of water with the wine. If Cyprian break his own rule, who can excuse him? But if he had been urged as much for the necessity of water as he was for the necessity of wine in the Sacrament, he would have better considered of the matter.

From this matter he descendeth to prove the number of Sacraments to be seven, because Matrimony is of some old writers called a Sacrament[6]; when they mean not a Sacra-

1 [1 Cor. x. 16.]

2 [Compare Fulke's *Defence of the English translations of the Bible*, p. 497. ed. Parker Soc.]

3 [Calfhill, page 232.]

4 [Petitio principii.]

5 [*Pompeium.* Ep. lxxiv. p. 211. ed. Oxon. 1682.]

6 [It is so called in the first part of the Homily *against Swearing*.]

ment in that sense that Baptism is a Sacrament, but generally a mystery. And because M. Calfhill saith that Sacraments were signs ordained of God to confirm our faith, he will prove that we have no Sacraments at all; because Baptism, if it be ministered to men of years, confirmeth not their faith; for they must have their faith confirmed before they be baptized, and so must they that receive the Communion: but when infants be baptized, they have no faith but the faith of the Church; and therefore their faith cannot be confirmed. Did you ever hear such a filthy hog grunt so beastly of the holy Sacraments, that they should be no helps of our father? [faith?] We believe that infants, although they have no faith when they are baptized, yet have their faith confirmed by their Baptism even to their lives' end; and that they which come to the Lord's table with a true faith in God's promises have the same confirmed by the seal of His word, which is that holy Sacrament. Martiall calleth for Scripture. Among a thousand texts, this one shall serve: Abraham "received the sign of circumcision, a seal of the righteousness of faith which he had being uncircumcised." Rom. iv. v. 11. Tell us, Martiall, by thy law, wherefore a seal serveth, if not for confirmation? But what should I talk with them of faith; which, as they have none in the promises of God, so they know not what it meaneth?

To that reason of Master Calfhill, that Matrimony hath no promise of forgiveness of sins, he answereth, denying that every Sacrament hath a promise of forgiveness of sins annexed; and afterward he asketh, Where hath the Supper of our Lord a promise of remission of sins? for sins are forgiven before the Sacrament be received. Is this the divinity of Louvain? Is the holy Supper available neither for confirmation of faith, nor to forgiveness of sins? Wherefore saith Christ of the cup, "This is My blood of the new testament, which is shed for many unto forgiveness of sins?" "Nay," (saith Martiall,) "if there be a remission of sins, then is it a Sacrament propitiatory, contrary to your own doctrine." Nothing the sooner; so long as remission of sins be not tied to the work wrought, according to your heresy, but sealed unto the faith of the worthy receiver. Likewise he quarrelleth against that reason, that Matrimony conferreth no grace; which is easily proved by this, that Matrimony is good, being contracted among

Gentiles and heathen persons. And whereas he bringeth in the blessing[s] of God to married persons, either they be such as pertain to all men in general, and so prove no grace of Marriage in the Church; or else to the faithful only, and so pertain to faith, and not to Marriage; as that the faithful woman shall be saved by[1] bringing forth of children. The question of Marriage after divorcement, because it pertaineth not to the Cross, I will not meddle with it. M. Calfhill hath said more than Martiall can answer.

Touching the popish Sacrament of Penance, which Martiall, and not S. Hierom, calleth "the second table after shipwreck," M. Calfhill hath likewise proved effectually, that it is no Sacrament of Christ's Church. Against which Martiall bringeth nothing but certain sentences of Scripture, to prove how necessary repentance is, after men have sinned, to obtain remission of sins. Whereof S. Hierom speaketh, and not of popish Penance, consisting of Contrition, Confession, and Satisfaction, with their blasphemous Absolution.

Concerning Extreme Unction, that it is no perpetual Sacrament of the Church, it is plain by Scripture; because the gift of healing, which was annexed unto the anointing of oil spoken of in S. James, hath long ago ceased. Wherefore it followeth, that the same ceremony of anointing was temporal; even as the promise of bodily health that was joined to it was temporal. Finally, touching the Council of Trent, that hath allowed all these for Sacraments, how lawful it was, when he that was accused for heresy should be the only judge, I think Martiall by his law could discuss if he list. And as for the safe-conduct granted to the Protestants, they have learned by the case of J. Huss and Hierom of Prague to trust the faith of Papists as much as they like their religion.

To conclude, there is nothing proved in this Article, which pretended that the Cross was always used in the Sacraments: and it is confessed, that when it is used, it is but a ceremony; and such as the want thereof taketh not away the effect of the Sacraments. Wherefore, seeing the Sacraments are perfect without it, they are not to be condemned, which upon good ground and sufficient authority have refused it.

[1] [through. "διὰ τῆς τεκνογονίας." 1 Tim. ii. 15.]

THE FIFTH ARTICLE.

Martiall. That the Apostles and Fathers of the primitive Church blessed themselves with the sign of the Cross, and counselled all Christian men to do the same; and that in those days a Cross was set up in every place convenient for it. MARTIALL.

Fulke. The first controversy is of the signification of this word *benedicere*, which with Martiall is all one with *signare*. For although he find not in the old writers *benedicebant se signo Crucis*, "they did bless themselves with the sign of the Cross," yet he findeth *signabant se signo Crucis*, "they marked themselves with the sign of the Cross," which is all one with him. But not so with us: for there was another use of marking at the first than for blessing. The Christians among the pagans marked themselves with the sign of the Cross, in token that they professed Him that was crucified: afterward, to put themselves in mind of the death of Christ. These were tolerable uses of an indifferent ceremony. The opinion of blessing with the Cross, as M. Calfhill sayeth, was taken (as the term) from superstitious old women. And Martiall cannot deny but the term of "blessing" in that sense is a new signification of the word, and therefore not used of the ancient Fathers: which that he might obscure with brabbling, as his custom is, he repeateth his former jangling of the significations of this word *benedicere*, and how it sometime signifieth to bless with the hands, as when Christ blessed His Apostles and the children; as though to use a ceremony of lifting up or laying on of hands, when He blesseth, is to bless with a bare ceremony of the hands, as they do with their Cross. Nay, he sayeth, to bless with the Cross is as old as Jacob, who with his hands across blessed Joseph's children. The Papists are wise in their generation, when they would not have unlearned men to read the Scriptures: for every child of seven years' age, reading the story of Jacob's blessing, will easily perceive, that his laying of his hands overthwart was not for any blessing with the Cross, but because he was to lay his right hand upon the younger, and his left upon the elder; contrary to their father's placing of them, which would have had his elder son preferred. FULKE.

But seeing Martiall maketh himself so cunning in the significations of *benedicere*, "to bless," which he will not have "to say well," or "pray for" only, &c., but "to sanctify;" let him remember, that in his own sense the Apostle sayeth to the Hebrews, cap. vii. ver. 7, "That which is less or inferior is blessed of the superior:" by which argument he proveth Melchisedech to be greater than Abraham. If then the Apostles and Fathers did bless themselves with the sign of the Cross to sanctify themselves, I demand, whether the sign of the Cross was greater than the Apostles? for no man will say that the Apostles were greater than themselves. If it were not greater, then surely they were not blessed by it. Wherein also the fable of Abdias is convinced, which sayeth of S. Paul *muniens se signo Crucis*, "arming himself with the sign of the Cross." Was the sign of the Cross stronger than S. Paul? for men arm themselves with harness of defence which is stronger than themselves. Was not that πανοπλία, that universal armour or complete harness, which he exhorteth other men to put on, as sufficient to withstand all the assaults of the Devil, sufficient for himself, without the sign of the Cross? But seeing the Apostle there describeth "the whole armour of God," whereof the sign of the Cross is no piece, it is certain that it is no armour meet for the defence of a Christian man. Wherefore your fabling Abdias and counterfeit Clement can carry no credit with wise and learned Christians. Nor yet the examples of Anthony, Martin, Donatus, and Paula, reported of credible writers, yet no Evangelists, which armed themselves with the sign of the Cross, doth either force or move us to imitation, further than they had warrant for their doings out of the holy Scriptures.

Eph. vi.

Where M. Calfhill sayeth, that the Devil[1] delighted in the sign of the Cross, and feigned himself to be afraid of it, that the hermit might run to that sorry succour, and men put more affiance in it, he meaneth, that the Devil delighted in the superstitious opinion of it; for otherwise he doth neither fear nor love the sign of the Cross of itself: for if it had been so terrible to the Devil as Martiall and others do think, Saint Paul would not have left it out of the complete harness of God, whereby all the deceits and fiery darts of the Devil are withstood.

And although the elder and better age used and received

[1] [Not the Devil, but S. Anthony. See Calfhill, p. 252.]

that sign tolerably, yet, considering the shameful abuse thereof, it ought now of right and conscience to be condemned, as M. Calfhill sayeth. But Martiall will none of that: for things good of their own nature must not be taken away nor condemned for the abuse. Very true: but who will grant him that the sign of the Cross is good of itself? It is as much as may be borne to grant it to be a thing indifferent. And whereas Martiall will acknowledge none abuse of that sign, what else should we say but, Who is so blind as he that will not see?

Concerning the authority of the Epistle of Epiphanius, translated by S. Hierom[2], and his fact in rending a veil wherein was painted an Image, as it were of Christ or some Saint, &c., I will refer the reader to mine Answer to D. Sander's book of Images, Cap. iv., or, according to the error of his print, Cap. iii.; where he shall see all Martiall's cavils shaken off, except one, which I think no man ever espied before this wily lawyer: and that is of the word *quasi;* "having an Image 'as it were' of Christ or some Saint;" but not an Image of Christ or of some Saint indeed, for then he would not have rent it: but perhaps it was an Image of Jupiter, or Hercules, &c. But, under correction of Master Usher, this is but a quasy[3] argument that is grounded upon *quasi;* as though it should signify always a thing that is not true, but as it were so, and yet not so. For Cicero, that knew the nature of the word *quasi* as well as Martiall, useth it otherwise: *Illos qui omnia incerta dicunt, quasi desperatos aliquos, relinquamus:* "As for them that say all things are uncertain, let us leave, as men past hope." Will Martiall say they were not past hope indeed? S. Mark sayeth that Christ did teach, *quasi potestatem habens,* "as one that had authority." Will he say He had not authority indeed? S. John saith of Christ, "Who have seen His glory," *quasi Unigeniti,* "as the glory of the only-begotten Son of God." Let Martiall say with the Arrians He was but *quasi Unigenitus,* "as it were the only-begotten Son of God," and not He indeed. Again he sayeth, *Cum fecisset quasi flagellum,* "When He had made as it were a scourge." Master Usher will construe it so, that [it] was not a scourge indeed, because he sayeth "as it were a scourge."

Mark i.

John i.

[John ii. 15.]

2 [Calfhill, pp. 42, 253.]

3 [queasy, sick.]

But Martiall will still urge the fact of Paula in worshipping the Cross of Christ, until it be shewed out of Epiphanius, by better evidence than yet is shewed, that he would have no Cross, no Crucifix, nor Image in the church. A man would think this were sufficient evidence, when he sayeth, *Cum ergo hoc vidissem, in ecclesia Christi, contra authoritatem Scripturarum, hominis pendere Imaginem,* &c.: "Wherefore when I saw this, that in the church of Christ did hang an Image of a man, contrary to the authority of the Scriptures, I rent it," &c. Further evidence out of Epiphanius you may see in the place before cited.

Martiall would have us make a calendar of Christian men, that refused to bless themselves with the Cross: which were an infinite matter, seeing from the Apostles unto the Valentinian heretics it is not read, that any such estimation was of the Cross, that it should be any blessing or confirmation. Master Calfhill's rule, that "we must live not after examples, but after laws," meaning, not follow whatsoever hath been done by good men, but whatsoever was well done, according to the law of God, Martiall rejecteth upon vain, foolish, and frivolous reasons; as, that some examples are to be followed; that the law serveth not for a just man; that custom must be followed where law faileth, &c. Beside that, he slandereth Luther, as one that would have all laws and orders of Princes put away. Again, whereas M. Calfhill sheweth, that the Fathers taught other things more oft and more earnestly than the use of the Cross; as that it was a wickedness to fast on Sunday, or to pray on our knees[1]; beside the oblations on birth-days, milk and honey, with the Communion given to infants, &c.; Martiall answereth, These are abrogated by the Church: this is not. But seeing none of them hath been in worse abuse than this custom of crossing, this ought to be abrogated of every Church as well as those. But whereas Martiall compareth the doctrine of S. Paul, 1 Cor. xi., for covering or uncovering of men and women's heads, and the decree of the Apostles for blood and strangled, Act. xv., with those abrogated customs, he doth very lewdly: for beside that the authority of the one is certain, the other uncertain, and of some forged, the doctrine of S. Paul, as he there delivereth it, is perpetual; and the decree of

[1] [Calfhill, pp. 257, 413.]

the Apostles was never meant of them but to be temporal, for avoiding offence of the Jews.

As touching the credit of the old writers, who had all their errors, we like well the counsel of Vincentius Lirinensis[2], that we should still have recourse for trial to the most ancient; in which we must needs account the writings of the Apostles both of most antiquity and of greatest authority. Wherefore, seeing the manner of blessing with the Cross is not found either in the writings of the Apostles, or in the most ancient Fathers, Justinus, Irenæus, Clemens Alexandrinus, by Vincentius' counsel we may justly account it for a corrupt custom, crept into the Church either by emulation of heretics, or in contention against the pagans.

But Martiall slandereth us, and the Apology of the Church of England, that the chief cause of our separation from the Church of Rome was the evil life of the governors thereof; and vainly spendeth time to prove out of Cyprian, Augustin, and Calvin, that for that cause we ought not to separate ourselves: whereas we are departed out of Babylon, not so much for the abominable life thereof as for the corrupt and false doctrine taught therein; by which it is shewed to be the Synagogue of Satan, and not the Church of Christ. And here Martiall huddleth up a number of quotations for the authority of the Pope and of the Church of Rome; which seeing they have been all oftentimes answered, and by me also in answer to D. Sander's Rock, it were folly here to stand upon them.

But he will not be counted a falsifier of Tertullian, when of divers copies and impressions he wilfully chooseth the worst, that he might wring it to his purpose: although the matter be not worth the strife about it; for Tertullian's judgment of tradition without Scripture in that place is corrupt. For Martiall himself confesseth that a tradition unwritten should be reasonable, and agreeable to the Scriptures; and so he saith the tradition of blessing with the Cross is, because the Apostles by the Holy Ghost delivered it. But who shall assure us thereof? Tertullian and Basil are not sufficient warrant for so worthy a matter, seeing S. Paul leaveth it out of the universal armour of God.

But where M. Calfhill distinguisheth traditions into some

2 [*Advers. Hær.* fol. 4. Paris. 1561.]

necessary, as necessarily inferred of the Scripture; some contrary to the word, and some indifferent; Martiall, like an impudent ass, calleth on him to shew in what Scripture, Doctor, or Council he findeth this distinction of traditions: as though a man might not make a true distinction in disputation, but the same must be found in so many words in Scripture, Doctor, or Council; when he himself cannot deny but the distinction is true, and every part to be found in the Scriptures, Doctors, and Councils. But the examples please him not; for the covering of women, and their silence in the church, are taught in express words of Scripture, and therefore are not necessarily inferred of Scripture: "Therefore there is one lie," quod Martiall. Who would think such a block worthy of answer; which thinketh a truth may not be inferred of the express words of Scripture, when of nothing it can be better inferred? Again, he calleth it another lie, that S. Paul proveth his tradition by the Scripture; for he bringeth no text nor sentence of Scripture to prove that women should be covered in the church. But Martiall doth not only belie M. Calfhill, but also slander S. Paul; seeing he allegeth out of Genesis, both that the man is the image and glory of God, and that the woman was made for man.

The examples of the second sort, as Latin service, worshipping of Images, &c., Martiall will not allow: but the Scripture is plain to them that have eyes, and be not like the Images whom they worship.

Again, he liketh not that there should be any limitation in observing traditions of the Church in things indifferent; as if cases of necessity and of offence might not make a limitation, without contempt of the Church's authority. But he will learn in which kind of traditions we place the signing with the Cross, and the rest named by Basil. I answer, that marking with the Cross, in some respect, as it was first used of the old Fathers, is of the third kind; but as it is used of you Papists, for a blessing and sanctifying, of the second kind. If it be told him, that the Fathers builded some straw and wood as well as gold and silver, he saith those words were meant of manners, and not of doctrine; wherein he sheweth himself a profound student in S. Paul's Epistles. Yet if the Fathers have any private opinions, or that some bastard books be intituled to them, yet will he follow the rule of S. Basil, *Hom. con. Sabel.*[1]*: Dominus,* &c.: "Our Lord hath so taught; the Apostles have preached; the Fathers have observed; the Martyrs have confirmed. It shall suffice to say, I have been so taught." I would he would or could follow this counsel: but he leaveth out all the rest, and taketh but the tail, "We have been so taught." But if he will have us to allow blessing with the Cross, let him begin with the head, and shew where our Lord hath taught it, the Apostles preached it, and so forth continue his gradation to the end.

But hitherto he hath been hammering of tags to his two tagless points, as M. Calfhill nameth them; and now he cometh to work upon his third point, "that a Cross was set up in every place." And first he goeth to work with the authority of Martialis, one of the seventy-two Disciples of Christ; which was as surely a Disciple of Christ as a kinsman of his: of whose credit I have spoken before, and therefore will not here repeat it.

Whereas he is accused of falsifying of Athanasius, he coloureth the matter by following two or three corrupt prints; wilfully refusing the true edition and best reformed according to the most ancient written copies. His leaving out of words material, which he cannot excuse by the print, he defendeth by his written copy, and layeth the fault on the printer. Better a bad excuse than none at all. Lawyers have many such shifts. But the place is *Quæstion.* xvi. *ad Antioch.*[2]*: Quare credentes omnes ad Crucis imaginem Cruces facimus; lanceæ vero sanctæ, aut arundinis, aut spongiæ figuras nullas conficimus; cum tamen hæc tam sint sancta quam ipsa Crux? Responsio. Figuram quidem Crucis ex duobus lignis compingentes conficimus; ut si quis infidelium id in nobis reprehendat quod veneremur lignum, possimus, duobus inter se disjunctis lignis, et Crucis dirempta forma, ea tanquam inutilia ligna reputare; et infideli persuadere quod non colamus lignum, sed quod Crucis typum veneremur: in lancea vero, aut spongia, vel arundine, nec facere hoc nec ostendere possumus:* "Why do all we believers make Crosses after the image of the Cross; but we make no figures of the holy spear, or of the reed, or of the sponge; whereas yet

1 [*Hom.* xxiv. in ed. Bened. Tom. ii.: vel *Opp. Græc.* p. 237. Basil. 1551.]

2 [See Calfhill, pp. 73, 268, 272, 376.]

these are as holy as the Cross itself? The answer. We make indeed the figure of the Cross by putting two pieces of wood together; that if any of the infidels reprehend that in us that we worship wood, we may, by separating the two pieces of wood, and breaking the form of the Cross, account them as unprofitable pieces of wood; and persuade the infidel that we worship not wood, but that we worship the type of the Cross: but in the spear, or sponge, or reed, we can neither do nor shew this."

Here Martiall observeth, that all Christian men made Crosses; yet can he not prove that they did set these Crosses in the church: but that they used them in other places, it appeareth by that they were made so as, the infidels seeing them, they might be taken asunder. But I will observe, that seeing they made no images of the reed, sponge, spear, &c., they made no images of Christ's passion, which the Papists account so profitable.

Secondly, Martiall urgeth, that they worshipped the type of the Cross; which Master Calfhill sayeth is not the figure, but the thing represented by the Cross. And verily the Gentiles should have as great cause to reprehend them for worshipping the shape of a creature, as for worshipping the creature itself. Wherefore, except Martiall will say the Christians made a fond excuse, let him not play the fool so magnifically, in cavilling upon Master Calfhill's interpretation, when he cannot otherwise reasonably defend the author's meaning.

Finally, let Martiall remember that the spear, sponge, and reed be as holy as the Cross itself: and therefore in respect of no holiness thereof the Cross was made rather than the rest; but because the form thereof being easily broken in two sticks, the Gentiles might acknowledge, that the Christians made the Cross neither for the wood nor for the fashion, but for a remembrance of Christ crucified, whom they worshipped.

From the Cross he digresseth awhile to the marriage of vowed Priests; complaining that Innocentius and Siricius, Popes of Rome, are slandered where they are said to take marriage for a satisfying of lusts of the flesh, where they speak only of the marriage of Priests that had vowed to live unmarried: which is false; for they speak of Priests that were married lying with their own wives. *Plurimos enim Sacer-*

dotes atque Levitas, post longa consecrationis suæ tempora, tam de conjugibus propriis, quam etiam de turpi coitu, sobolem didicimus procreasse[1]*:* "For we have learned that many Priests of Christ and Levites, long time after their consecration, have begotten children, as well of their own wives as of filthy copulation." Thus do they account both faults alike. Again, the reasons they bring are such as concern marriage generally; that "they which be in the flesh cannot please God," &c. Read the Epistle of Siricius *ad Himerium Tarraconen.*[2], and Innocentius *ad Victricium*[3]*;* which are all one, word for word, concerning this matter. But where Martiall taketh upon him to charge us with a statute in force against the marriage of Priests in England, unrepealed, he is misconceived. For we have a clause of a statute in force, that all marriages lawful by the laws of God shall be accounted lawful by the laws of the realm. So long therefore as the marriage of Priests may be approved by the law of God, there is no danger in the law of the realm. Concerning the filthy lives of the popish Clergy it is needless to speak, being so well known in the world: and yet it is not their wicked life that separateth us from their synagogue, but their heretical doctrine.

But, returning again to the Cross, he burdeneth M. Calfhill with a lie, because he said that Martiall, having named houses, markets, wildernesses, highways, seas, ships, garments, parlours, walls, windows, armour, &c., where the Cross should be, nameth not the church; whereas a little before he cited out of Chrysostom, that it was used in the holy table at the holy mysteries. But Chrysostom saith not that the Cross was erected and set up, or painted, in any church, although he say the figure thereof was used. Wherefore here is no lie proved.

Touching the saying cited out of Augustin, *Serm.* cxxx.

1 [Siricius Papa, *ad Himerium Tarracon. Episc.* Vid. Gratiani *Decret.* Dist. lxxxii. Cap. iii. *L'Art de vérifier les Dates,* ii. 362. A Paris, 1750.]

2 [Ubi supra, vel apud Crabb. *Concill.* Tom. i. p. 417. Colon. Agripp. 1551.]

3 [Crabbe, i. 455. *Codex Canonum Eccles. Rom.* p. 337. Lut. Paris. 1609.—The fourth Epistle of Pope Siricius is considered spurious, and seems to have been copied from the Epistle to Victricius ascribed to Pope Innocent I. See the latter document in Blondel's *Pseudo-Isidorus,* pp. 551—556.]

de Tempore, although the authority is not greatly to be regarded of those Sermons, yet admit it were Augustin's indeed[1], M. Calfhill saith truly, that he speaketh neither of Martiall's material nor mystical Cross, but of the death of Christ, and the Cross whereon He suffered; as all the discourse of that Sermon declareth: "Before the Cross was a name of condemnation; now it is made a matter of honour: before it stood in damnation of a curse; now it is set up in occasion of salvation[2]." This now Martiall would either craftily or impudently refer to Augustin's time, which is spoken of the time of Christ's passion, when the Cross was set up in occasion of salvation, and not an Idol thereof in Augustin's time.

He complaineth, that to another place of Augustin, wherein mention is made of the sign of the Cross, nothing is said; where nothing needeth, when it is confessed that the sign of the Cross was used in his time. And concerning Constantine's Cross, we have spoken already sufficiently.

To conclude therefore, here is nothing replied in this Article to prove that the Apostles and Fathers of the first Church did bless themselves with the sign of the Cross; although the Fathers of latter time used to mark themselves with that sign, and counselled others so to do. Neither is there any thing but the forged new-found Martial's Epistle, which is worse than nothing, to prove that the sign of the Cross in the first age of the Church was used by the Apostles, or their immediate successors, before the days of Valentinus the heretic.

THE SIXTH ARTICLE.

MARTIALL. *Martiall.* That divers holy men and women got them little pieces of the Cross, and inclosed them in gold, &c.

FULKE. *Fulke.* It is confessed that divers made great account to have little pieces of the Cross, to inclose them in gold, and hang them about them; but their superstition is re-

[1] [It will be found safer to admit that it is S. Chrysostom's indeed. See the commencement of the first Homily *De Cruce et Latrone,* inter Opp. S. Jo. Chrys. Tom. ii. p. 403. ed. Bened. Cf. Calfhill, pp. 63, 277.]

[2] [The latter clause is a very inaccurate rendering of "*πρότερον σύμβολον κατακρίσεως, νυνὶ δὲ ὑπόθεσις σωτηρίας.*"]

proved both by Hieronym and Chrysostom. To Hierom Martiall answereth, that he reproved not the having of those pieces, but the confidence put in them; as the Pharisees did in their phylacteries hanged upon their bodies, and not printing the law in their hearts. Be it so: but what accounteth he the having of them? Even the straining of a gnat: *culicem liquantes, et camelum deglutientes.* Lib. iv. Cap. xxiii.[3] But in other places (saith Martiall) he wisheth himself to kiss the wood of the Cross. *Apol.* iii. *cont. Ruff.*[4] This was a small matter, and yet it was more than having a little piece of the Cross: for he speaketh of his visiting the places of the death, burial, and birth of Christ; in which he might take more occasion of meditation upon the mysteries of our redemption.

To Chrysostom, which counted it impiety in certain Priests, that hanged Gospels about them, and pieces of the coat and hair of Christ, he maketh like answer; alleging out of his *Demonstr. ad Gentiles,* that all the world desired to have the Cross, and every man coveted to have a little piece of it, and to inclose it in gold, &c. And whereas M. Calfhill answereth, that this was no praise of the parties, but a practice of the time, Martiall replieth, that it was a praise of the parties; repeating what Chrysostom doth write in commendation of the sign of the Cross, &c.; whereas indeed Chrysostom, speaking of the matter in question, only sheweth what was the affection of Christians to the Cross, which was sometime the wood of condemnation: which affection, although in some it were immoderate, yet Chrysostom's reason against the Gentiles should not turn him to perpetual shame, (as Martiall saith;) for he proveth that Christ was God, in that He had wrought so great a conversion unto the faith, that no man was now ashamed of the sign of the Cross, which before was a token of condemna-

3 ["Hoc apud nos superstitiosæ mulierculæ, in parvulis Evangeliis et in Crucis ligno, et istiusmodi rebus, quæ habent quidem zelum Dei, sed non juxta scientiam, usque hodie factitant; culicem liquantes, et camelum glutientes." (*Comment.* S. Hieron. Lib. iv. *in S. Matth.* Cap. xxiii. Opp. Tom. ix. p. 68. Basil. 1565.)]

4 [S. Jerom's words are these: "Protinus concito gradu Bethlehem meam reversus sum; ubi adoravi præsepe et incunabula Salvatoris." (*Opp.* Tom. ii. p. 240.) Conf. *Ad Eustoch. Epitaph. Paulæ matris,* i. 172: "Prostrataque ante Crucem, quasi pendentem Dominum cerneret, adorabat."]

tion. To conclude, where Martiall abuseth the words of Christ, *Hæc oportet facere*, &c., "These things ought to be done, the other not omitted," to prove that the fact of having these pieces of the Cross, and inclosing them in gold was good, he must either bring the law of God, as the Pharisees did for tithing of mint and anise, or else we cannot be persuaded that such estimation of pieces of wood is good and godly.

THE SEVENTH ARTICLE.

MARTIALL. *Martiall.* That a Cross was borne at the singing or saying of the Litany, &c.

FULKE. *Fulke.* That Processions came not from Gentility to Christians Martiall will prove, because Processions came from tradition of the Apostles; and that he proveth by a saying of Leo[1]: "Whatsoever is retained of the Church into custom of devotion, cometh of the tradition of the Apostles and doctrine of the Holy Ghost." So is Procession, &c. But the *minor* is false: for the Church of Christ, for many hundred years after Christ, knew no Processions. But if Processions came from the Gentiles, saith Martiall, shall we therefore condemn them? Have we not the liberal sciences and many politic laws from the Gentiles?—as though there were one reason of religion, and politic laws or liberal arts. Deut. xii. The one we are forbidden to learn of the Gentiles; the other, being the gifts of God, we may take them even from the Gentiles. Neither doth Augustin against the Manichees, whom Martiall citeth, Lib. xx. Cap. xxiii. *Con. Faust.*, speak of any heathenish ceremonies received in Christian religion; but of such things as we must have common with them, like the sun and the air, as meat, drink, apparel, houses, &c.

Whether Processions came from the Montanists or Arrians, certain it is they came not from Christ nor His Apostles. Tertullian, a Montanist, maketh mention of certain Stations;

[1] ["Dubitandum non est, dilectissimi, omnem observantiam eruditionis esse divinæ; et quicquid ab Ecclesia in consuetudinem est devotionis receptum, de Traditione Apostolica et de Sancti Spiritus prodire doctrina." (*Sermo* lxxvii. *de jejunio Pentecostes* ii. Opp. T. i. pp. 161—2. Lugd. 1700.)]

but I suppose they were no Processions, but standings[2]. The miracle of water turned into oil, to serve for light in the church, reported by Eusebius[3], I marvel to what end Martiall bringeth forth, and counteth that it was an hundred years before the heresy of Arrius.

The Litany or supplication prescribed by the Council of Mentz[4] Martiall saith the Papists do observe; for they ride not in the Rogation-week, nor wear their copes: but how observe they that the Canon commandeth them, to go barefooted in sackcloth and ashes? The Council of Orleans, anno 515[5], calleth these Litanies Rogations; but of Procession or going abroad it speaketh nothing. S. Ambrose indeed is ancienter than this Council; but whether that Commentary upon the Epistles that goeth under his name were of his writing, it is not agreed among learned men[6]: at least wise there be divers additions, and the written copies vary. Besides that the word whereupon he buildeth, *dies Processionis*, both in written and printed copies is *dies purgationis*, "the days of a woman's purification:" or if algates[7] he will have it *Processionis*, as some printed books have, yet the very circumstance of the place will prove, that it is the days of a woman's

2 [According to Rabanus Maurus, *Statio* signifies "observatio *statutorum* dierum vel temporum." (*De institut. Clericor.* Lib. ii. Cap. xviii. Phorcæ, 1505.) In Tertullian's Montanistic treatise *De Jejuniis*, Cap. xiii., he speaks of "Stationum semijejunia:" by which we are to understand the abstinence, less rigorous than the Lent-fast, anciently observed till the ninth hour, or three o'clock in the afternoon, on the Wednesdays and Fridays throughout the year; which times prescribed for humiliation and other religious duties were the *Stationes*, or "stationary days," of the primitive Church. Vid. Petavii *Animadvers.* in S. Epiphanii *Opp.* Tom. ii. pp. 356—8. Paris. 1622. Bingham's *Antiquities*, Book xxi. Chap. iii. Fleury, iii. 216. Oxf. 1844.]

3 [*Hist. Eccl.* Lib. vi. Cap. ix.]

4 [an. 813. See Calfhill, p. 297.]

5 [A. D. 511. C. xxix. "Rogationes, id est Litanias." (Binii *Concill.* ii. i. 562. Conf. Gratiani *Decret.* De Cons. Dist. iii. Cap. iii.)]

6 [The Commentary upon S. Paul's Epistles was certainly not written by S. Ambrose. It is generally cited under the name of Ambrosiaster, and many ascribe it to Hilary the Deacon; but the Benedictine editors, in their Dissertation upon this point, do not decide the question. Vid. S. Amb. *Opp.* Tom. ii. Append. Tillemont, *Mémoires*, x. 127. A Brux. 1732.]

7 [Algates: at any rate, notwithstanding: probably *all gaits.*]

going forth after her childbirth; and therefore no Procession after the Cross.

And if Agapetus did not devise Processions first, as M. Calfhill saith, your own Canon Law lieth[1], and not he; *De Con. D.* i. *Agapitus*, as your author Garanza citeth it[2].

But, to come near unto the Article, Sozomenus, Lib. viii. Ca. viii.[3], sheweth, that the Arrians at Constantinople began a kind of Procession, with singing of Psalms by course: which John Chrysostom, fearing lest any godly men should be seduced by them, took up the same fashion; and so passed the Arrians in number, *et processu*, "and going forward;" "for silver standards of the Cross, with burning wax candles, went before them." This place sheweth how godly men took up fond ceremonies in emulation of heretics.

But now concerning these silver standards in form of the Cross, which Socrates, Li. vi. Ca. viii.[4], sheweth did serve to carry wax candles or torches burning upon them, to give the people light in the night-season, (for then their Processions were in the night,) Martiall is as mad as a March hare that they should be counted no better than candlesticks or cresset-staves. And yet when he hath prated what he can, for that principal use they served, although it may be that Chrysostom had some superstitious fantasy in the forms also of the Cross, which he devised to be as the standards for the Catholic army to follow, so the same cross staves served both for candlesticks and standards. Howsoever it was, this Procession differed much from our popish Processions, in which Idols are carried about; and not as candlesticks, but candlesticks before them, with candles' light in the day-time, and not in the night.

His surmise that the silver Crosses were set in the church, because no place is mentioned where they left them when they came home, is foolish. They had common theatres and meeting-places, more meet for setting up of such candle-bearing crosses than the churches. The quarrel of the

[1] [The Canon Law, *De Consec.* Dist. i. Cap. xxiii., does not mention anything about Processions.]

[2] [Fulke is mistaken here: for Carranza (*Summa Concill.* p. 252. Salmant. 1551.) quoted Gratian merely with reference to the character of Agapetus; and the words "Hic Dominicas Processiones instituit" are a distinct marginal note.]

[3] [See Calfhill, pp. 298—301.]

[4] [Calfhill, 299.]

four lies I pass over. Let the reader compare both their books, and judge whether Martiall have handled that story with sincerity.

The Council Elibertine forbad candles to be lighted in the day-time in the churchyards: *Ergo* they forbad them not on the Lord's table, quod Martiall. But why then go you with torches and tapers into the churchyard, both in Procession and at burials? And seeing it was an heathenish custom to light them in churches as well as in churchyards, they which forbad the one would not have allowed the other. But you light them not as heathen men, of whom Lactantius speaketh, thinking God to be in darkness, and to have need of light; but *ad signum latriæ demonstrandum*, "to declare a sign of the high service that you owe to God." If it be so, why light you them to Saints; yea, to Images? The Gentiles had as good excuses as you. Nevertheless you are determined to keep your lights still, as you have record and witness out of Eusebius, Athanasius, &c. Indeed there is great reason, because they had candles' light in the night, you will have them in the day. But of light I wish the reader to look more in my Refutation of Rastal's [Rastell's] Confutation, to the thirty-third leaf of his book.

After this followeth a vain discourse, to prove that we are heretics, because we have departed from the unity of the Church, from the Clergy, from the Bishop of Rome, &c. All which is false: for we have not departed from the Church of Christ, which is ruled by His word, nor from the Christian Clergy, nor from any godly Bishop of Rome, in any point in which he departed not from the truth: but we are gone out of Babylon; we have forsaken Antichrist, and all his merchants, that made sale of men's souls. Our prayer in a known tongue, our Communion in both kinds, our reverent administration of the Lord's Supper, have the Scripture for their warrant, and the primitive Church for their witness.

His railing upon Luther I will not deal withal. God hath advanced Luther as His poor witness above the Pope, the proud Antichrist; which maketh all Papists to spite him.

Concerning Justinian's Constitution[5] for Crosses to be borne at the singing of the Litany, it savoureth of the corruption of his time. Such godly Constitutions as he made,

[5] [Calfhill, pp. 135, 189, 304—5.]

as well in ecclesiastical as politic matters, we esteem as the good laws of a foreign Prince are to be regarded.

And at length we come to Augustin the Monk; which, coming from Rome, did more hurt in corrupting true religion than good in planting any religion. And whereas Martiall saith, if our religion came from Eleutherius, it came from Rome; although it were no shame to confess it came from Rome in those purer times, yet Christian religion came to us even from the Apostles, as witnesseth Gildas the Briton[1], being planted here in the reign of Tiberius the Emperor. And as for Augustin, although the King Ethelbert and the people were well prepared before his coming by the Queen and the Bishop that attended upon her, yet, according to his zeal, he took some pains to make the people receive the doctrine of Christ; although in behaviour he was proud, as Galfride writeth, and Beda not altogether denieth but that he seemed so, and in ceremonies superstitious. So that the doctrine of Christ which he taught came from Jerusalem, from whence the Gospel was first preached; his errors and superstition came from Rome. That the Bishops of the Britons refused both his authority and ceremonies, it argueth that Christianity was in this land not subject to the see of Rome. If they refused to join with Augustin in teaching the Saxons, it might be not for that they envied their salvation which were their enemies, but because they would not consent to join in that work with him which sought to bring them into subjection.

Concerning the cruel murder of the Monks of Bangor in Augustin's quarrel, Galfride, a Briton, imputeth no small part of the fault to Augustin[2]: Bede, a Saxon, would have him clear of it. But seeing the threatening of Augustin is agreed upon, and the slaughter followed, it is shrewd evidence against

[1] [Bp. Stillingfleet (*Origines Britann.* pp. 4—6. Lond. 1685.) justly remarks, that "most of our writers" have misunderstood the passage in the *Epistle* of Gildas here referred to; and even the unequalled Ussher has misapplied it. (*Brit. Eccl. Antiqq.* p. 2. Lond. 1687.) Gildas evidently speaks of a twofold shining of the light of the Gospel: the first general, and having reference to the whole world; the second particular, and relating only to Britain. It is with regard to the former, and not the latter, that he, following Eusebius and Tertullian, has mentioned the end of the reign of Tiberius.]

[2] [See before, page 6.]

him. That Augustin's Cross and painted table differeth from that the Papists now use in Procession, Martiall counteth it not material, seeing afterward they received other kind of Images from Rome, and other kind of Images were then used in churches: which yet were hard for him to prove; for the Grecians to this day receive none but painted Images.

The pretence that Master Calfhill saith Augustin might have to excuse him, to feed the eyes of them that never heard of Christ with the image of His death, that, lending their ears, he might instruct their hearts, Martiall will not admit: or if he did admit it, that it followeth not, that they which have not like pretence may not use like example: whereas Master Calfhill doth neither absolutely affirm the pretence, nor allow it to be good.

From this pretence he passeth into a defence of praying to Saints, to justify the popish Litany, "Virgin Mary, pray for us;" which he denieth to be idolatrous, because some steps or shew of Invocation of Saints are found in some old writers; and calleth for Scripture to prove it to be idolatrous, yet refuseth whatsoever Luther, Calvin, or the Magdeburgs have said against it. But, by his favour, I will use one or two reasons out of Scripture to prove it to be idolatrous to call upon the Virgin Mary, or any creature. Saint Paul saith, Rom. x. ver. 14, "How shall they call upon Him in whom they have not believed?" By which it is evident, that none ought, nor can in true faith be called upon, but He in whom we believe; and it is idolatry to believe in any but in God only: wherefore it is idolatry to call upon Mary, or any creature, but upon God only. Again, the Apostle, 1 Tim. ii. ver. 5, saith, "There is but one God, and one Mediator of God and men, the man Jesus Christ;" where the Apostle speaketh not only of redemption, but of prayers, supplications, intercessions, &c.; which overthroweth your blind distinction of Mediator of intercession and redemption.

For keeping the memory of the dead, which Lactantius counteth superstition, you think yourselves clear of it, because Matthew, Peter, and Paul, &c. are alive in heaven. But you must remember that Christ sayeth Abraham, Isaac, and Jacob were alive to God[3]: but in respect of men they are dead; and therefore those memories are not excused of super-

[3] [S. Matth. xxii. 32.]

stition, according to Lactantius' judgment. Further you say, The note that the material Cross is no ensign of Christ hath simple proof. But indeed your assertion, that it should be an ensign of Christ, hath no proof at all.

The book of Carolus Magnus against Images you imagine to have been written by Calvin, or Illyricus, or some other late Protestant: but of the credit and antiquity thereof I have written, against Doctor Sander's book of Images, *Cap. ultimo.* Also concerning the second Council of Nice, which Martiall citeth for Procession with the Cross, Cap. xv. or xiv.

That God would not suffer the bones of Moses to be translated, lest they should have been matter of idolatry, he saith it is no cause why translating of other Saints' bodies should not be permitted; because God "will have mercy upon whom He will have mercy[1]," and be gentle to whom it pleaseth Him. "Hath not the pot-maker power to make one vessel to honour, and another for reproach?" "May He not transfer Peter's bones, and let Moses' alone? May He not make Paul's body to be honoured, and Joseph's obscured; Saint Stephen's shrined, and Samuel's interred? I think you will not deny." These reasons to rehearse, it is a sufficient confutation of them.

But for the high estimation of Reliques, Hierom is of his side against Vigilantius, whom he calleth a famous heretic: and yet no man condemned him for an heretic but Hierom, who rather raileth on him than reasoneth against him. As for Eusebius, although he speak honourably of the bones of Polycarpus, which the Christians gathered and buried, as the parts of an holy Martyr's body, yet he nameth not any worshipping of them, such as the Papists use. But Martiall maketh much ado that Master Calfhill alloweth the excuse which the heathen men made, that they would not deliver the body of Polycarpus, lest the Christians should leave Christ, and begin to worship him; saying it was the instinct of the Devil to deny his body, &c., and so to say. What then? Although they meant cruelly and slanderously against the true Christians, which could neither forsake Christ, nor worship any other[2]; yet the same answer might be well made to

1 [Rom. ix. 18, 21.]

2 ["Ignorantes, quia nunquam Christum relinquere possumus Christiani . . . neque alteri cuiquam precem orationis impendere." See the Epistle of the Church of Smyrna, concerning the martyrdom of

superstitious Papists, who have forsaken Christ, and worship men, yea, dead bones, and them often not of godly men, nor always of men.

That Chrysostom was a great admirer of Reliques I shewed before, insomuch that he would change the kingdom of heaven for the chain that Saint Paul was bound withal[3]: wherein if he spake not excessively, let Martiall follow him. We esteem the kingdom of heaven more than all the Reliques that ever were. And yet we allow a reverent laying up of the bodies and bones of the Saints, so it be without superstition and idolatry, as was meant by the ancient Fathers; although the contrary followed of their too much zeal and carefulness of such small matters.

To conclude, you have heard what can be said for the antiquity of Processions, and bearing of the Cross before them. Whether it be an Apostolic tradition, that was first devised by Chrysostom in emulation of heretics, let the readers judge.

THE EIGHTH ARTICLE.

Martiall. That many strange and wonderful miracles were wrought by the sign of the Cross. MARTIALL.

If this Article were granted in manner and form as it is set down and meant by the author; namely, that God by the sign of the Cross hath wrought miracles; yet doth it not follow that the sign of the Cross is now to be used of us, nor that we should repose any confidence therein. By the rod of Moses great miracles were wrought: yet was neither the sign of that rod to be esteemed, nor hope of health to be placed in it, nor the rod itself to be worshipped. The Apostles by anointing with oil did work great miracles: yet neither the sign of that anointing is of us to be used, nor the oil to be worshipped. Wherefore, if God, to shew the virtue of Him that was crucified, hath wrought miracles by the Cross, or sign thereof, it followeth not that the sign is still to be used, or the Cross honoured, but He that was crucified. FULKE. Mark vi.

S. Polycarp. *Patres Apostol.* ed. Jacobson. Tom. ii. p. 607. Oxon. 1840. Euseb. *Hist. Eccl.* iv. xv. 134. ed. Vales. Ruinart *Acta Martyrum*, p. 37. Veronæ, 1731.]

[3] [See page 110.]

Whereas M. Calfhill said that miracles are done by the Devil and his ministers, although Martiall cannot deny it, yet he saith it followeth not that all miracles, or those of the Cross, were done by the Devil: whereas M. Calfhill's meaning is plain, that we ought not to believe all things that are commended to us by miracles, but to examine all doctrine by the word of God; against which we must believe no miracles, no Prophets, no Angels. Gal. i. But whereas Martiall laboureth to prove that miracles done by sign of the Cross were done by God, he should first have proved substantially that miracles were done indeed by the Cross, and after proved by what power they were done: for we may not believe every report of miracles; especially when they are alleged to confirm false doctrine.

Let us therefore consider the first miracle which he rehearseth of the Cross of Christ that Helena found, if she found any; for Eusebius, that knew Helena, and speaketh much of her commendation, and of her doing at Hierusalem, as I take it, would not have concealed such a notable invention, if any such had been, in his story; and therefore the note in his Chronology seemeth to be a late addition[1]. But to the miracle, that the Cross was discerned from the other two by a sick gentlewoman upon whom it was laid; whereupon, as soon as it touched her, she recovered. This report of Rustinus [Rufinus] seemeth to be uncertain: first, because Ambrose sayeth the Cross was known by the title, without speaking of any miracle: secondly, because the report of other writers is, that the miracle was of a dead woman, and some of two dead persons; whereof to see more, I refer the reader to mine Answer to D. Sander's book of Images, Cap. xiii. or xii.

Concerning the rest of the miracles reported by Paulinus, Epiphanius, Augustin, and others, let them have such credit as their authors deserve; which is not to build faith or doctrine upon them or their writings. Let it be that some were true and wrought by God, yet followeth it not, that all that have been since reported in the popish legends were either true, or not wrought by the Devil: whereabout Martiall maketh much wrangling; but neither affirmeth nor concludeth any thing universally. None use more crossing than witches and conjurers. The Devil seemeth to be afraid to come near them:

[1] [See Calfhill, pp. 321—2.]

certain strange works are brought to pass by them. Let Martiall affirm any virtue included in the Cross or sign thereof absolutely, and then we may deal with him accordingly. For while he telleth us what may be done by faith and the sign of the Cross, and what God hath done by good men with that sign; it is nothing to the authorising of that sign, seeing the Devil by credulity in wicked men hath done the like by the same sign.

And this is a true position of M. Calfhill, though Martiall will not understand it, "That it is not a sufficient proof to make a thing good," or to shew it to be good, (because he cavilleth like a calf at the word of 'making,') "to say that miracles were wrought by it." Martiall asketh first, whether the miracles of Christ were not a sufficient proof of His divine power? where he flieth from the position, which speaketh not of the principal efficient cause, but of a ceremony, a mean, or instrument. More pertinently he asketh of the hem of Christ's coat, Saint Paul's napkins, whether they had not a virtue by his body? I answer, no: no more than Judas' lips that kissed Christ, and Peter's shadow, which could neither be holy nor efficient of any thing, because it was nothing but the privation of the light by coming between of his body. So I say of coats, napkins, ashes of Martyrs, and sign of the Cross: if any miracles were done by means of them, they are not thereby holy, neither have they any virtue in them.

The Lord hath given us a general rule to examine all miracles and miracle-workers by the doctrine they teach; Deut. xiii.: "If there arise among you a Prophet, or dreamer of dreams, (and give thee a sign or wonder, and the sign and the wonder which he hath told thee come to pass;) if he say, Let us go after other Gods, which thou hast not known, and let us serve them; thou shalt not hearken unto the words of that Prophet, or unto that dreamer of dreams: for the Lord your God proveth you, to know whether you love the Lord your God with all your heart, and with all your soul. Ye shall walk after the Lord your God, and fear Him, and keep His commandments, and hearken unto His voice, and ye shall serve Him, and cleave unto Him." By this Scripture we are taught to examine all miracles, whether they tend to the honour of the only true God, and the maintenance of His true worship according to His word: which Martiall himself in a manner confesseth, saying "that miracles done by heretics are not able to commend a thing." But he findeth great fault with Master Calfhill for coupling the generation of a child in adultery, or feeding by stolen bread, to be miracles, because they be not extraordinarily miracles: and yet he cannot deny but they be great wonders; and the reason of the means is all one in both.

Now let us see how he answereth those three reasons of Master Calfhill's why miracles make not for the Cross. And first, he answereth to a question, "Why the dirt in the street, by which Christ wrought a miracle, should not be honoured as well as the Cross on the altar?" He answereth, "Because the Cross was an instrument by which all the world was saved." So was Judas; so was Pilate. The second, he saith "The Cross is a lively representation of Christ's death." Nay, a dumb and dead Idol, which is good for nothing. Abacuc ii. The third, "The Cross is effectuous ever since." A deed [dead] efficient. Fourth, "The Cross is commanded of God to be made and used by divers revelations from heaven." Nay, by the Devil from hell. And yet, if Angels from heaven had taught the Cross to be made and used as another Gospel, as it is accounted of the Papists as great as Circumcision was of the Jews, not preached by the Apostles, nor contained in the Scriptures, we might safely accurse them.

But now to the reasons. The first is, "Why should not such external means as Christ and His Apostles used, and Scripture mentioneth, be had in administration rather than the idle device of man, of which there is no lawful precedent?" Martiall answereth, "The Cross is no idle device, but a tradition of the Apostles, whereof they have lawful precedents." But seeing no precedent is lawful to build our faith upon but the holy Scriptures, which the Papists have not for their Cross, the reason standeth untouched.

The second reason: "If miracles were done by the sign of the Cross, yet not only by it; therefore the Cross should not only be magnified without the rest." Martiall affirmeth that he would not have the Cross magnified without the rest, as prayer and faith. How doth he then magnify the Cross in Julian's story, which was without prayer and faith?

The third reason: "If miracles were done by the Cross, yet it should not be had in estimation, except all other things by which miracles were wrought, as the hem of Christ's garment, the spittle and clay, the shadow of Peter, and napkins of Paul, were likewise honoured and esteemed." Martiall answereth, "This is but his assertion; for which he hath neither Scripture, Council, nor Doctor:" as though an argument *a paribus* were not good, except the conclusion were expressed in Scripture, Doctor, or Council. Yet he replieth, that the Cross is the principal mean by which miracles have been wrought. But the Scripture is against that: for Christ wrought no miracle by the sign of the Cross. Nay, I slander him; for he reasoneth not *ad idem*, but the Cross is the chief and principal instrument of our redemption: yet not holier than the spear, the reed, and the sponge, as Athanasius affirmeth. *Ad Antioch. Quæ.* xvi.[1] But even the hem, the spittle and clay, if he had them, Martiall would honour, worship, and esteem for His sake whose precious body they touched. Then let him worship the sun, that touched Him with his beams of light; or, if that be too far off, let him worship Judas' lips that kissed Him, if he can come by them.

Concerning the person of Helena, I would wish nothing to be spoken of her but to her honour, except in case where her honour should be an hindrance of the honour of Christ. Martiall, to justify her in all things, raileth upon M. Calfhill for charging her with superstition; as though he had been the first that had so written of her, when it is reported of her that she was *usque ad superstitionem pia*, "devout even to superstition." And yet her superstition appeareth not so great in any thing as in this supposed invention of the Cross.

The variety in time that is in the witnesses of the invention of the Cross the blasphemous beast is not ashamed to compare with the appearance of variety which is in the Evangelists: where indeed there is none; whereas this discord cannot be reconciled. Yet will he not have the tale discredited for the discord in time; as though there were none other discord.

The manifest contradiction that is between Ruffinus, saying, *Titulus non satis evidenter Dominici prodebat signa patibuli*, "The title did not shew evidently the sign of our Lord's gibbet," and Ambrose, saying, *Titulo Crux salutaris patuit*, "By the title the healthful Cross was manifestly

1 [Calfhill, 73—4, 272—3.]

known;" this contradiction, I say, he denieth to be any, affirming that a simple logician would prove it to be none; thinking that *satis evidenter*, "evidently enough," would excuse the matter; as though we knew not what *patet* doth signify as well as Master Usher of Winchester.

That a ship would not carry the pieces of the Cross that are shewed in so many places, he counteth it an impudent lie of Calvin; whom he raileth upon like a ruffian, and slandereth like a Devil. Yet Erasmus affirmeth the same in his *Peregrinat. Relig. erg.*[1]*:* and he that will believe neither of them both, let him consider, beside so many whole Crosses as are shewed instead of that one, and of great boards that are kept in many places as part of it, so many thousand churches and abbeys as either now shew or have shewed chips and pieces of it, and he shall not think their report to be incredible.

The talk of the nails, which were but three at the first, and all bestowed at the time of the invention, yet are now multiplied to thirteen or fourteen, which bewrayeth an horrible impudency in the popish idolaters, Martiall refuseth as impertinent: yet will he not confess the forgery; which is a token of a wicked and devilish conscience. Where M. Calfhill sayeth that miracles were not done by the Cross to establish a worshipping or having of it, Martiall requireth proof by Scriptures, Councils, or Doctors. I reason thus *a paribus* out of the Scripture: Miracles were done by oil, shadow, and other things, not to establish a worshipping or having of them: the like reason is of miracles done by the Cross. Beside that the Scripture is plentiful in challenging all honour and worship to the author, and not to the means or instruments. Peter and John, means of the healing of the lame man, refused all honour and worship in respect of his healing, Act. iii. vers. 12: yet were they other manner of means than the Cross ever was in doing of miracles.

That M. Calfhill sayeth, miracles teach us not to do the like, but to believe the like, Martiall sayeth, they teach us to do the like if we may: and he proveth it by him that teacheth that alms covereth sin[2]; who thereby teacheth to do

[1] [The Colloquies of Erasmus are thus condemned in the *Index Expurgatorius* of Cardinal Zapata: "Expungatur totum opus familiarium Colloquiorum." (p. 244. Hispali, 1632.)]

[2] [Ecclus. iii. 30.]

alms, &c. Thus the wise man compareth miracles and men together, facts and doctrine, act and possibility, even as right as a ram's horn. But how shall we come by this power to work miracles by the sign of the Cross? for to assay without assurance of God's power is to tempt God. Therefore we may no more cross us against Devils, because God hath sometime chased them away by that sign, than we may anoint blind men's eyes with clay, to prove if they will see after it, because Christ wrought a miracle by that mean, which, as Martiall saith, teacheth us to do the like if we may. What estimation Paulinus, a superstitious man, had in his piece of the Cross, which was perhaps a piece of another tree than ever came in Jewry, we have not to follow him in his folly.

That miracles wrought of holy men by the sign of the Cross, &c., is not a sufficient reason to prove that the sign of the Cross should be had, kept, set up, and honoured, I have already proved out of the Scripture by the like or equal: and yet it is against reason, when we deny your arguments, whose consequence you ought to prove, that we should be driven to prove that they follow not. Where M. Calfhill sayeth, that miracles only ought not or may not commend a thing, you pick quarrels to him without cause; objecting the miracles of Christ, who took witness not only of His miracles, but also of the holy Scriptures. When you have urged the miracle done by the sign of the Cross, out of Epiphanius, as much as you can, yet proveth it not the honouring and setting up of the sign of the Cross in these days, as M. Calfhill telleth you; seeing that we live not among Turks or Saracens, that we need to have any such sign whereby we might be known to be worshippers of Christ.

But you would fain learn, what if a Portingal, or one of the new-converted islands of India, coming by chance into England, of which he never heard before, and seeing neither Images nor Crosses in church nor street, how he should know in whom we believe. And I would learn of you, what skilleth it, if such a man as never came here, nor ever by any likelihood shall come hither, yet supposed to be driven on a board out of India into England; what skilleth it, I say, if he knew not in whom we believe, and so depart as wise as he came? What remedy, but we must have all places filled with Images and Crosses, for such a man to know what we hold of, who shall be never the better thereby, nor the worse if he know not?

But you think that happily [haply] strangers of Greece, Constantinople, Jewry, and India may come to our coasts; and therefore we ought to have the sign of the Cross in churches, chapels, and highways, to signify of Whom we hold. We have not many such strangers: but when they arrive, we have books of the holy Scripture in Greek, Hebrew, Chaldee, Syrian, Arabic, Sclavonian tongues; in which they may be instructed that are desirous to understand what religion we profess. The Lord God thought it sufficient to have His law written upon great stones, at the entrance into the Holy Land, to let all strangers know both Whom, and after what manner, the people of Israel did honour and serve their God. Deut. xxvii. 3. But as for Images and pillars, He utterly forbad them to set up any for any use of religion. Deut. xii. 1. [3.] & xvi. ver. 2. [22.]

THE NINTH ARTICLE.

MARTIALL. *Martiall.* What commodity every Christian man hath or may have by the sign of the Cross.

FULKE. *Fulke.* Whereas M. Calfhill detesteth the idolatrous Council of Nice the second, by the example of Ambrose, who abhorred the heretical Council of Ariminum, Martiall, willing to justify that rabble of idolaters assembled at Nice, would shew great difference, not only between the Councils, but also between him and Ambrose; saying, that he was a Catholic Bishop, acknowledging obedience and subjection to the Pope's Holiness: as though the Bishop of Rome in his time either required such obedience and subjection, or that Ambrose acknowledged any. But concerning that assembly of Nice, and the authority thereof, how they determined contrary to the word of God, not only in the matter of having and worshipping of Images, but also in other things, I refer the reader to mine Answer unto M. Sander's book of Images, Cap. xv. or xiv.

Of all that M. Calfhill saith against that Council of Nice, Martiall chooseth but one saying of Germanus to defend; wherein he picketh two quarrels against M. Calfhill: one, that he should misunderstand the saying of Germanus, as though he meant that grace were dispensed by Images, where he saith, "An Image is a figuring of holy virtue, and dispensation of grace." But if grace be not dispensed by Images, whether Germanus said so or no, I pray you, to what purpose are they set up in the churches? or what profit may a Christian man have by the sign of the Cross, when Martiall denieth that any grace is dispensed by Images? The second quarrel he picketh is, that M. Calfhill denieth that the virtues of Saints can be seen in their Images, which could not be seen in their persons. Martiall saith, "This reason condemneth the Scripture as well as Images: for the ink and paper hath no mind or sense to hold the power of Christ, and virtue of the Apostles, more than Images have:" as though the Scripture were nothing but ink and paper; or as though that all things that may be learned and understood by hearing may be discerned by the eye, which conceiveth only bodily shapes of things, and cannot attain to see faith, holiness, virtue, &c., whereof no Images can be made.

When M. Calfhill sayeth, that the Image of Mars or S. George, Venus or the mother of Christ, cannot be discerned asunder, Martiall hath nothing to reply, but that we must not suppose to find any Images among the Christians but of Christ and His Saints: so that Images be wise books, which cannot teach their scholars what or whereof they are; but they must learn of the common opinion how to esteem of them. That Images be teachers of pride, avarice, wantonness, &c., as the Prophet sayeth they are the doctrine of vanity and lies, Abac. ii., Martiall saith blasphemously, that Images give no more occasion of vices than the holy Scriptures, of which some wicked men take occasion of drunkenness, whoredom, usury, &c. But seeing the Scripture directly and plainly condemneth all these and other vices as occasion is given by them, howsoever any is taken by ungodly persons; whereas Images, which teach no goodness, but, being gorgeously and whorishly decked with gold and precious stones, otherwise than the Saints delighted, even as in holy Scripture they are counted as stumbling-blocks, so they teach men vainly affected to delight in such things as they see to please the Saints. But Martiall sayeth that gilded Images make men think of the joys of heaven. O ridiculous fantasy! They may sooner make men think of the vanity of the world, to delight in it. But when the Holy Ghost, by the mouth of His Prophets, hath determined that Images are the doctrine of lying and vanity, it were lost labour to dispute any longer what good things they can teach. Jer. x. ver. 8. Abac. ii. ver. 18.

The examples of Ezechias, Josias, and Salomon, he saith are brought to no purpose against Images amongst Christians; as though it were more lawful for Christians than for Israelites to commit idolatry. But the Christians (saith he) direct their hearts, and offer their prayers to God; and therefore there is no mistrust of idolatry amongst them. Why, Martiall? Have not the Papists in England made, and do they not yet still in other places make, vows to the Images that are in such a place and such a place? Do they not travel thither, and offer up both prayers and sacrifice of candles, money, jewels, and other things unto the Images? Have not your Idols given answer? Have they not wagged their heads and lips, &c.? O shameless dogs, and blasphemous idolaters! The Lord so deal with you as you know in your own consciences that the ignorant people have made their prayers even to the stocks and stones, thinking them to have a life and divinity in them: and yet you say there is no mistrust of idolatry, lest you should be driven by example of Ezechias to destroy and break your Images; although otherwise they were not against God's commandment, but even made by His appointment, as the brasen Serpent was. That fond quarrel of yours, that Salomon was not abused by Images, but by women, I leave to women to laugh at your vanity, when they read that by women he was brought to be an idolater and worshipper of Images.

And every child that readeth Chrysostom, *Hom.* liv. *in* viii. *Tom.*, [*Joan.*[1],] can understand, that although occasioned by obstinate Jews, yet he speaketh generally of all obstinate minds, whether they be professors of Christianity or no. *Animo desperato*, &c.: "There is nothing worse than a desperate mind. Although he see signs, although miracles be wrought, yet he standeth still in the self-same frowardness." For an obstinate sinner, that hath professed Christianity, is no more moved with miracles and the sign of the Cross than a Jew or Pharaoh was.

It hath more colour, but not more truth, that Athanasius[2]

[1] [*Opp.* viii. 324. Calfhill, p. 353.]

[2] [*De incarnatione Verbi Dei*, §. 50.]

ascribeth not all effects of conversion of wicked men, &c. wholly and solely to the faith of Christ, when he saith, "Who hath done this," &c., "but the faith of Christ, and sign of the Cross?" Martiall confesseth that faith is able to do it without the Cross, but that God would have the sign of the Cross common with faith. If ye ask in what Scripture God hath revealed this will, he hath nothing to say. Only he denieth M. Calfhill's exposition of Athanasius, that the sign of the Cross was joined to faith, not as a fellow-worker, but as a witness and sign of the faith against the Gentiles, because he hath neither Scripture, Doctor, nor Council for it. Wherein
he lieth shamefully: for the Scripture, shewing that faith only Rom. iii. 28.
is the instrument by which we apprehend God's mercy and our
justification, by which God purifieth our hearts, sufficiently Acts xv. 9.
proveth that the sign of the Cross is no worker in these cases.

Chrysostom, speaking of our conversion, &c. saith, *Hom.* xiv. *in Ep. ad Rom.*[3]*: Unum hoc,* &c.: "We have offered this one only gift of [to] God, that we give credit to Him promising us things to come, and by this only way we are saved." This Doctor ascribeth all to faith; therefore nothing to the sign of the Cross. Whether the Parisians approve Erasmus his censure[4], it is not material. The censure is true, and approved by as wise and well-learned as they.

Touching the next quarrel, that Cyrillus[5] acknowledgeth it no fault of the Christians to make the sign of the Cross at their doors, it is very foolish, as all the rest be: for although he defend it as a good deed, and in his time tolerable, yet if any did worship the wood of the Cross, as Julian charged them, it was a fault, which Cyrillus doth excuse and seek to cover: but of that matter you may read more in mine Answer to D. Sander's book of Images, Cap. iv., or iii. after the error of his print.

That S. Basil alloweth Images in churches, he citeth his Sermon upon Barlaam[6], where he exhorteth painters to set forth the valiant conflicts of the Martyr by their art: but of setting up those tables in churches there is no word. Neither

3 [*Opp.* Tom. ix. p. 584. ed. Ben.]

4 [See Calfhill, p. 361.]

5 [Vid. S. Cyrilli Alexand. Lib. vi. *Contra Julianum,* pp. 194, 195. ed. Ezech. Spanhem.]

6 [*Opp.* Græc. p. 203. Basil. 1551.]

do I perceive he speaketh of other painters than eloquent rhetoricians: for immediately before he saith: *Quin magnificentioribus laudum ipsius linguis cedamus. Sonantiores doctorum tubas ad illius præconia advocemus. Exsurgite nunc, O præclari athleticorum gestorum pictores*, &c.: "But let us give place to more magnificent tongues, utterers of his praises. Let us call hither the louder sounding trumpets of learned men. Arise now, O ye noble painters of the valiant acts of champions," &c. And it is usual among learned men to compare good orators to cunning painters.

The counterfeit Oration of Athanasius[1], brought in the idolatrous Council of Nice[2], we reject as a matter forged by heretics and idolaters. The other Doctors' places, whom he quoteth, are all considered and answered in several places of mine Answer to Doctor Sander's book of Images, before mentioned.

Whether an Image may be made of Christ, which is both God and man, you shall find it more at large entreated in my said Answer, Cap. vii. or vi.

That the Cross in the time of Cyrillus had none Image upon it, it is to be proved by this reason, that Julian would not have omitted to object the worshipping of Images unto Christians, which they condemned in the heathens, if any Images had been upon their Crosses, which he charged them to have worshipped. Concerning the calling of churches by the name of Saints we have spoken already.

That S. Paul joineth not Pictures with Scriptures to be our instruction and comfort, it is an argument of better force than Martiall hath wit to answer. For if any such instruction, comfort, or commodity had any ways come to Christians by Pictures, he would not have written that the Scriptures are

[1] [This must be the fictitious *Liber de passione Imaginis Christi*, called by Crabbe (in Indice Tom. ii. *Concill.*) "luculentus ac pius Sermo", and alleged by Bellarmin (*De Imagg.* L. ii. C. x. et xii.) and many other Romanists in defence of Image-worship. Baronius candidly rejects this history of the fabled Picture of Berytus; (*Annall.* ad an. 787. §§. xxxiv—xlix. Tom. ix. Ant. 1612. *Martyrol.* die Novemb. 9.) and the learned Montfaucon pronounces it to have been the work "imperiti alicujus et infacundi hominis." (S. Athan. *Opp.* ii. 343.) Conf. Raynaudi *Erotemata*, p. 173. Coci *Censur.* pp. 93—95.]

[2] [Sept. Synod. Act. iv. *Concill. Gen.* Tom. iii. p. 472. Romæ, 1612.]

able to make "the man of God perfect, prepared to all good works." 2 Tim. iii. vers. 17. Article iii. [ix.[3]]

THE TENTH ARTICLE.

Martiall. The adoration and worship of the Cross allowed by the ancient Fathers. MARTIALL.

Fulke. Martiall thinketh it not reason that he should prove the adoration of the Cross by some testimony of Scripture, because God hath not so tied Himself to the written letter of the Scripture, that nothing can be taken for truth which is not written in Scripture. But God hath so tied us to the written letter of the Scripture, that we are bound to believe nothing but that which may be proved thereby. The Baptism by heretics, the Baptism of infants, the authority of the Epistle to the Hebrews, of Saint James and Jude, and of all the canonical Scriptures, have proof and approbation out of the holy Scriptures; and are not received of us by the only tradition and authority of the Church; which yet we do not refuse when it is warranted by the holy Scriptures inspired of God. FULKE.

The ancient Fathers, Athanasius, Chrysostom, &c. were not exempted from the infirmity of men, that they could so order their terms as no heretics should take occasion of error by them; when even the terms of holy Scripture are oftentimes abused by them, clean contrary to the meaning of the Spirit, by which they were written.

But Martiall, like a proud fool, disdaineth to be called to define "adoration," because every term is not necessary to be defined. And yet I suppose he would claw his poll twice or ever he could make a true definition of it, or a description either. At the least wise, seeing the word of "adoration" is taken so many ways, but that he would walk under a cloud of ambiguity, he should have expressed what manner of adoration he doth speak of. But he is content to take adoration for bowing down, prostrating, putting off the cap, &c., which he thinketh may be done to a senseless Image, as well as to the Queen's cloth of estate, her privy seal, &c.; as though there were no difference between civil reverence and religious

3 [Calfhill, p. 349.]

worship: and yet I ween no man doeth this honour to those senseless things, although he shew reverence to the Prince at the sight of them.

The second Commandment, Exod. xx., he saith, toucheth not popish Images more than politic images of dragons, eagles, owls, &c. in arms or other pictures. So good a lawyer he is, that he cannot interpret the law according to the matter whereupon it is made, namely religion; but fantasieth, that because Images out of the use of religion be not forbidden to be made by a law of religion, therefore they be not forbidden to be made, no not in the use of religion.

The Prophets, he saith, cry out against the Images of Gentiles: and, by his leave, against the Images of the Israelites also. The Image of the brasen Serpent was a figure of Christ: and yet the Prophets condemned, and Ezechias destroyed the worship of the brazen Serpent.

For the examination of the sentence of Ambrose, *De obitu Theodosii*[1], I refer the reader to mine Answer to D. Sander, of Images, Cap. xiii. or xii.

Augustin, *in Joan. T.* xxxvi.[2], sheweth how reverently the Cross was esteemed of the Romans, that now malefactors were no more punished upon it, lest it should be thought they were honoured if they suffered that kind of death which our Saviour Christ died: as among us, if rascal thieves should be beheaded at the Tower-hill, where only honourable personages use to suffer, it might be said they were honoured with that kind of execution. Hereupon Martiall both foolishly and lewdly dreameth, that if thieves had been put to death upon the Cross, the people were likely to have honoured them for the Cross's sake.

Hierom saith[3], that Paula "worshipped, lying before the Cross, as though she had seen Christ hanging upon the Cross;" yet saith he not that she worshipped the Cross.

Ambrose[4] saith of Helena, that "when she found the Cross, she worshipped the King, and not the tree; for that is an heathenish error, and a vanity of ungodly persons." Where-

1 [Calfhill, pp. 192, 377.]

2 [*Opp.* Tom. iii. ii. 396. ed. Ben. Amst.]

3 [See before, p. 181, note 4.]

4 De obit. Theod. ["Invenit titulum, Regem adoravit; non lignum utique, quia hic Gentilis est error et vanitas impiorum."]

fore if Hierom or any other Father should teach us to worship the Cross as an Idol, we might well say to him, Avoid, Satan. But Martiall, lest he should seem weary of wrangling, scoffeth at M. Calfhill for talking of a wooden tree; as though the matter of a thing might not be named, but where there is difference of matter. Why say we then an earthly or fleshly man, if we may not say a wooden tree, by Martiall's philosophy, lest men should think we talk of watery and fishy men? I had not thought to have named Martiall's term of gentlemen's recognizances, of dragons, eagles, &c. used in this Article, but that he is so captious to take exceptions to M. Calfhill's terms, himself being a lawyer, to trip in a term of law.

That service and worship do so concur together, that the one cannot be without the other, Martiall granteth; although he think M. Calfhill can bring no Scripture, Doctor, nor Council for it; when he bringeth the saying of Christ, Matth. iv. But when he inferreth that we must serve God only, therefore we must worship God only, Martiall bringeth instance of civil service, and worship of parents; when our Saviour Christ speaketh only of religious worship, which the Devil required to be given him, not as God, but as the distributor of all the kingdoms of the world under God.

That Angels are inferior to Christ, which worship Him, Heb. i.
and are not worshipped again, Martiall saith it is an addition unto S. Paul, because in all that Epistle we are not forbidden to worship Angels. But where he proved before that God only is to be worshipped, and the Angel refuseth to be worshipped of John, Apoc. xix. vers. 10, xxii. vers. 8, who was not so mad to worship him as God, but as an excellent creature, what addition can this be to the sense and meaning of the Apostle; especially when he addeth immediately, that they are all "ministering Spirits, appointed to minister for them that shall inherit salvation?" They are appointed of God to serve: they are not set up to be served and worshipped. Their honour and delight is, that God only may be served and honoured.

Out of Damascen[5] he excuseth their worshipping of the

[5] [*De orthodoxa Fide*, Lib. iv. Cap. xii. fol. 152. Paris. 1519.—"Non materiam venerantes, (absit enim,) sed figuram, tanquam Christi signum."]

Cross, for that they worship "not the matter," as wood, copper, &c., "but the figure;" as if it were less idolatry to worship an accident than a substance.

The honour which Peter refused to receive of Cornelius was not such as became the Minister of God; and therefore was reproved by Peter, without counterfeiting of humility. The other examples that Martiall bringeth of civil worship done unto David by Abigail and Nathan be clean out of the purpose.

Concerning the worship of Angels I have spoken immediately before. Martiall slandereth S. John, that he would have worshipped the Angels as God. The conclusion of this argument he thinketh worthy to be hissed at: Angels may not be worshipped: *ergo* much less the Cross. What shall we say to such a Chrysippus, as alloweth not the argument *a majoribus?* The objection of the Cherubims, the brasen Serpent, the oxen, and other Images in the Temple, you shall find answered, Cap. v. or iv. of my Confutation of D. Sander's book of Images.

The seventeen authorities, brought by M. Calfhill against the worshipping of Images, Martiall will answer, if he can: and first, he denieth that Clemens speaketh of Crosses, Crucifix, &c., but of the Images of the Gentiles. Indeed in his days the true Christians had no such Images, that he should speak of them. But consider his reasons that he maketh against the worshipping of heathenish Images, and they serve also to condemn the worship of popish Images.

The fables of the Image of Christ's face, that he gave to Veronica, and sent to Algarus, [Abgarus,] is good draff for such swine as delight in idolatry. But Martiall thinketh, that as our ears call upon us to bow our knees at the name of Jesus, so do the eyes at the sight of the Crucifix. But he must understand, that we worship not the sound of the name of Jesus, rebounding in the air; but the power, the majesty, and authority of Jesus we acknowledge and honour: not called upon by the sound of the name of Jesus, but by the voice of the Gospel, to which the Idol of the Crucifix hath no resemblance; neither is it a lawful mean to stir up our remembrance, because it is forbidden of God.

Where Saint Paul saith, that Christ was described or painted unto the Galatians, we must either say, that the passion of Christ was painted in a table, or else they carried the

Image of the Cross of Christ rent and torn in their minds. "If they might carry an Image in their minds, why might they not have it fair painted in a table? Speak, Master Calf: answer, if you can." O mighty Martiall, withdraw your grim countenance awhile, and give him leave to gather his wits together. First he saith, that Saint Paul speaketh of neither of both your Images, but of the effect and fruit of the death of Christ; which was so lively described before them, that they ought not to have sought any thing more to the sufficiency of His redemption, and their salvation. Secondly, although the sense of hearing be appointed of God, Rom. x., to instruct faith, yet he findeth not the sense of seeing, and especially of Images, which God hath forbidden, admitted to be a mover to Christian devotion, or worship of God. And therefore there is no like reason, that as the story may be carried in remembrance, so the Image may be painted, and set up in the church to be worshipped.

The injunction of kneeling at the Communion intendeth no worship of the bread and wine, more than of the table, the cup, the book, the desk, the wall, &c., before which the people kneel: and therefore it hath nothing like to your kneeling before the Cross; which is not only before it, but also to it, to worship it.

But you think you have an argument to choke us, of the ceremony of swearing upon a book, seeing swearing is a kind of adoration. But, Sir, we swear not by the book, as you Papists do: we call God only to witness. The book is but an external indifferent ceremony, and that rather civil than ecclesiastical; whereas adoration of God by Images is prohibited by God's law. Again, we give no honour at all to the book, as you do to your Images.

That Clemens alloweth the honour given to man, as to the Image of God, we allow very well, because man is a true Image of God. Your blocks and stocks be all false and counterfeit Images.

To Clemens Alexandrinus, Irenæus, and Tertullian, he maketh the same answer, that they speak only of heathenish Images. The like he might say, where they speak against adulteries, that they speak of the adulteries of the heathen, and not of Christians. And the same to Cyprian, Origen, Arnobius, Lactantius, and Athanasius; bringing instance of the civil reverence done to the Prince's seat, and to the Prince himself. And whereas Arnobius[1] saith expressly and absolutely, "We worship no Crosses," he expoundeth it, We worship them not as Gods. Such expositions may avoid all authorities. The Gentiles, which knew the Christians worshipped but one God, did not object worshipping of Crosses unto them as Gods.

Against the authority of Lactantius he bringeth in a verse falsely ascribed unto him, *Flecte genu, lignumque Crucis venerabile adora*, "Bow the knee, and adore the venerable wood of the Cross." If Martiall allow this verse for authentical authority, how will he justify that he said before, they worshipped not the wood, stone, metal of the Cross, but the figure or sign of it?

Against Athanasius he obtrudeth that counterfeit Sermon of the Image of Christ in Berisus [Berytus;] and once again urgeth his forged Question xxxix. *ad Antiochum*, which is Quest. xvi., as we have set it down at large Article v., having in it no such words as he citeth, *Crucis figuram ex duobus lignis componentes, adoramus*, "We, making a figure of the Cross of two pieces of wood, do adore it."

To Epiphanius he answereth, that he speaketh only against women, which offered sacrifice to the Virgin Mary; whereas neither it was lawful that women should offer sacrifice, nor that Mary should be made a God. But indeed Epiphanius speaketh against the adoration of dead men by Images. *Et mortui quidem sunt qui adorantur*, &c.: "And they truly which are worshipped are dead: but they bring in their Images to be worshipped which never lived; for they cannot be dead which never lived." He would have Mary to be honoured, but not with worshipping her Image, for that were idolatry. Martiall hath two strong collections: "If a woman may not sacrifice, *ergo* she may not be head of the Church;" as though it were necessary that the chief governor of the Church should do sacrifice. The other, "That women may not offer external sacrifice: *ergo* there is an external sacrifice that men may offer." As good as this: A woman may not circumcise: therefore Circumcision is in use to be done by men. To

[1] [Minucius Felix, *De Idolor. vanit.* p. 89. Oxon. 1678.—"Cruces nec colimus nec optamus."]

be short, Epiphanius calleth the heresy of the Collyridians, that sacrificed to the Virgin Mary, *hæresis simulacrifica*, "an Image-making heresy."

But lest Martiall should seem to be beaten clean away from Epiphanius, he citeth him, *De vitis Prophet.*[2], alleging a prophecy of Hieremy of the second coming of Christ, which should be *quando gentes universæ ligno supplicabunt*, "when all nations shall make their supplications to wood." Here is either Martiall's sign of the Cross, or an heathenish error commanded by the Prophets, he saith. But if he will boast of the authority of the ancient Epiphanius, he must bring better stuff than this fragment, *De vita et inter. Proph.;* which, following so many Jewish fables, argueth the later Epiphanius, the patron of Images, to be the author, rather than the elder of Cyprus. For this prophecy of Hieremy, even as the fable of the ark swallowed of a stone, &c., savoureth of Jewish vanity. And yet if we should admit it as authentical and true, the sense should rather be, that Christ shall come when all nations shall be idolaters or wood-worshippers, than when all nations should worship the sign of the Cross, as Martiall supposeth: for Christ at His second coming shall scarce find faith. Therefore, infidelity possessing the greatest part of the world, it is more like all nations should worship wooden Idols than Christ, by honouring the sign of His Cross.

To Ambrose, denying that Helena worshipped the wood of the Cross, he opposeth a forged saying of Ambrose[3], cited in the second Council of Nice[4], where lying, forging, and false worshipping did bear all the sway. Concerning the true testimony of Ambrose, read more in mine Answer to D. Sander's book of Images, Cap. xiii. or xii.

To Hierom, not admitting the civil honour used to be given to the pillars and Images of the Emperors, much less adoration of Images in religion, he opposeth his saying *in Psalm.* xcviii.[5], affirming that adoration of the Cross is allowed by him; whereas that Commentary, by learned and indifferent

[2] [S. Epiph. *Opp.* Tom. ii. p. 240. Paris. 1622.—Petavius declares, in his Preface to the reader, that "sexcentæ mendaciorum nugæ" prove the spuriousness of this treatise.]

[3] [Calfhill, p. 173.]

[4] [Vid. Act. ii. p. 413. *Concill. Gen.* Tom. iii. ed. Sirmond.]

[5] [*Opp.* Tom. viii. p. 146. Basil. 1565.]

judges, Erasmus[1] and Amerbachius[2], is proved by many arguments to be none of Hieronym's writing, but of one of much later time. Thus hath Martiall against the true testimonies of the Fathers nothing to oppose, but their counterfeited authorities and false-inscribed writings.

Concerning Hieronym's adoration of the manger and *incunabula*[3], "the cradle" of Christ, which Martiall so often called "the swathling clothes," I have answered before, that he meaneth no such adoration as the Papists give unto their Images, but a reverent estimation, as of an ancient holy monument: wherein yet I will not altogether excuse Hierom of superstitious affection, as I will not charge him with idolatry.

For Chrysostom's judgment of worshipping the Cross, I refer the reader, as before, to Cap. xiii. or xii. of mine Answer to D. Sander's book of Images.

To Claudius, Bishop of Taurino[4], that in all his diocese forbad the worship of the Cross, he answereth, Alphonsus de Castro counteth him for an heretic, and Jonas, Bishop of Orleans, writeth against him. Indeed Jonas writeth against his overthrowing of Images, but he writeth also against the adoration of Images. His words are these, Lib. i. *De cultu Imagin.: Claudius, Præsul Ecclesiæ Taurinensis,* &c.: "Claudius, Bishop of the Church of Taurine, saw his flock (among other things which it did worthy of reformation) to be given to the superstitious, yea, the pernicious worshipping of Images; of which disease some of those parts are sick, of an old-rooted custom," &c. So that not only Claudius, but also Jonas, was directly contrary to this tenth Article.

Touching the brabbling distinction of *Latria* and *Doulia*, I refer the reader to mine Answer to Doctor Sander's book of Images, Cap. vi. or v.; as also for that noble argument that followeth, whereby he would prove that Papists cannot commit idolatry.

That M. Calfhill affirmeth outward profession to be necessary for every Christian man, Martiall saith he condemneth

1 [Videatur *Alienorum Index*, præf. Tom. i. sig. a 6.—"... nihil illic esse arbitror Hieronymi."]

2 [Commentarii, qui "Divo Hieronymo hactenus sunt falso inscripti." (Bruno Amorbachius Lectori. Tom. viii. Tit. vers.)]

3 [See before, p. 181, note 4.]

4 [Turin.]

his doctrine of only faith justifying. Verily, a club is more meet than an argument, to beat it into such an ass's head, that when we teach that only faith doth justify, we say not that God requireth nothing of a Christian man but faith only. Again, who would vouchsafe to answer his quarrelling of true faith without confession? "The rulers believed, but did not confess. John xii. Here was faith," (quod Martiall,) "but no confession." But who will grant that here was a true justifying faith? Likewise this argument: "There is a corporal service of outward gesture due to God: therefore it is no idolatry to kneel before an Image." And again: "Protestants kneel before Images in glass windows, and hold up their hands at Paul's Cross: therefore they defile their bodies with sacrilege. And if they excuse themselves by their good intent, the same will serve the Papists, which adore the Image for that it representeth Christ or His Saints." But Protestants adore no Images with any intent, thou foolish advocate of idolaters, no more than Martiall doth reverence to a dog, when he putteth off his cap, or maketh courtesy in any house where a dog is before him.

"And verily," he sayeth, "a man may as well be suspected for idolatry if he bow before any visible creature, as if he kneel before an Image." But not so probably as Martiall may be suspected to be out of his wits when he maketh such comparisons. The Jews were not only suspected, but also affirmed by the Gentiles to worship the clouds and the power of heaven, because in prayer they looked up to heaven: *Qui puras nubes et cœli Numen adorant*, sayeth the poet of them[5]. Wherefore, by Martiall's comparison, they might as well have prayed before Images.

And where he sayeth that Protestants condemn outward things, except hats, beards, barrel breeches[6], &c., he sheweth his vanity. Our judgment concerning outward things, that serve for order and comeliness, (being not defiled with idolatry and superstition,) is sufficiently known. What we teach of fasting and praying, vowing, &c., it were superfluous here to repeat, when public testimonies of our doctrine are daily given, both in preaching and writing: and surely I am to blame,

[5] [Juvenalis *Sat.* xiv. 97.—"Nil præter nubes et cœli Numen adorant."]

[6] [Fox, ii. 431. ed. 1684.]

that vouchsafe such vain calumniating of any mention. That "not to bow their knee to Baal" is not a peculiar note of God's servants, because other things are required in God's servants than to be free from idolatry, it is a foolish and more than childish quarrel: for in the days of Elias that was a peculiar note to discern them from idolaters, whom God had preserved both from yielding to idolatry in heart, and also from dissembling with outward gesture.

But Martiall would learn whether M. Calfhill, kneeling down before his father to ask him blessing, did not commit idolatry. How often shall I tell him he is an ass, that cannot make a difference between civil honour and religious worship? And once again he must be answered, why the people are suffered to swear upon a book, with their caps in their hands, rather than to kneel before the Cross in doing of their adoration to God. If he will be answered, I will tell him again, partly because it is against civil honesty that the people should stand covered before the Judge; partly because they swear by the name of God, whom they ought to reverence. But kneeling before a Cross, to worship it, is manifest idolatry, and expressly forbidden by the law of God, "Thou shalt not bow down to them, nor worship them." The people are not allowed to put off their caps to the book; neither yet to swear by the book. When Martiall can prove that it is lawful for Christians to worship Images, then we will grant it is uncharitable to judge them idolaters that kneel before them.

But he will not grant the Cross to be "nothing" in that sense that Saint Paul sayeth "an Idol is nothing[1]," because it is a representation of a thing that was. By this reason the Image of Jupiter, Hercules, Romulus, which were men sometime, were no Idols: the Image of the sun, of an ox, an ape, a cat, &c., worshipped of the Egyptians, were no Idols, neither was the worshipping of them idolatry. The questions to be propounded in the Chancery I leave to Martiall to propound himself. But where he sayeth that "no evidence of any idolatrous fact in worshipping the Cross can be shewed in true Christians," I agree with him: but in Papists, if he mean them, great evidence. Who went a pilgrimage to the Roods of Boston, Dovercourt, and Chester? Were they not Papists? Who made the Roods to sweat, to bleed, and to smell sweet,

[1] [1 Cor. viii. 4.]

as D. Read did with his Rood of Becclys? Were they not Papists? Finally, who sayeth and singeth to the Crucifix, *Ave, Rex noster*, &c., "All hail, our King;" "All hail, O Cross, our only hope[2]," &c.? I doubt not but the country of Christian men will judge this as good evidence for pulling down the Cross as Ezechias had for destroying the brasen Serpent.

It is Martiall's "poor judgment," when you see men praying, they be Christian men; therefore they serve God in spirit and truth. But afterward he restraineth it to men that were baptized in Christ: yet may they be heretics, and therefore no true worshippers of God. But that which he spake in way of humility, he will now say stoutly: "Sir, when you see men, that is to say, men that are baptized, men that believe in God, praying, yea, before an Image, and holding up their hands, and knocking their breasts, it is a good consequent to say they be Christian men: *ergo* they serve God in spirit and truth; and we may not judge the contrary." This argument holdeth of the place of stoutness; for other consequence there is none in it, nor yet witty conveyance. For first, when I see men, I must say they be men that are baptized, and believe in God; whereas by sight I cannot perceive that they are baptized: and yet if I know that they be baptized, I cannot tell whether they believe in God as Christians or as heretics, or whether they be hypocrites without faith. How shall I then judge them to be Christian men? Finally, when I see them do an open act contrary to Christian profession, yet, by Martiall's divinity, I may not judge but that they be good Christians, and worship God in spirit and truth: even as by his Canon Law[3] I am taught, that if I see a Priest embracing of a woman, I must judge he doeth it for no harm, but to bless her.

To be short, Martiall's good consequent will make him confess, that all the Protestants "that hold up their hands at Paul's Cross, and say 'Amen' when the preacher sayeth 'God confound the Papists,'" (whereat he scoffeth,) be Christian men, and worship God in spirit and truth. As for their adoration of the Cross, he saith [it] standeth as well with the glory of God as our kneeling at the Communion, putting off

[2] [Calfhill, p. 381.]

[3] [Gloss. in *Decret.* ii. Par. Caus. xi. Quæst. iii. Cap. *Absit.* fol. ccx. Parrhis. 1518.]

our caps to the cloth of estate, to the Prince's letters, bowing to the Prince's person, kissing of the book, &c.: so that with him things by God expressly forbidden stand as well with His glory as things by Him commanded and permitted.

In the end, complaining that Master Calfhill hath not answered him to thirty places out of the ancient writers, whereof let the readers when they have compared judge, he glorieth that his railing and slanderous conclusion is not dealt withal but by silence; which silence he taketh for a confession: but indeed it is a sufficient confutation of such lies and slanders as have no colour of truth in them. Our Saviour Christ, being called a Samaritan, made none answer to it. Socrates, an heathen man, kept silence when a varlet railed on him. Wherefore silence in such a case as this is neither a confession, nor a conviction.

To conclude, I will not altogether refuse, as Master Calfhill doth, to deal with "so lewd an adversary as Martiall is:" but I would wish that the Papists, for their credit's sake, would henceforward set forth a better champion for their causes, or else help him with better weapons to fight in their quarrel. For in this Reply he doth nothing in a manner but either construe like an usher, or quarrel like a dogbolt lawyer.

FINIS.

A DISCOVERY

OF

THE DANGEROUS ROCK

OF

THE POPISH CHURCH.

A DISCOVERIE
OF THE DAVNGEROVS ROCKE OF THE POPISH
Church, commended by Nicholas Sander D. of Diuinitie.

Done by VVilliam Fulke Doctor of diuinitie, and Maister of Pembroke hall in Cambridge.

A DISCOVERY

OF THE

DANGEROUS ROCK OF THE POPISH CHURCH,

LATELY COMMENDED BY NICHOLAS SANDERS, DOCTOR IN DIVINITY[1]; AT WHICH THE CATHOLIC CHURCH OF CHRIST HATH BEEN IN PERIL OF SHIP-WRECK THESE MANY HUNDRED YEARS.

BY W. FULKE,

DOCTOR IN DIVINITY.

Sander. THE Eternal Rock of the Universal Church. "Christ was the Rock." "Another foundation no man is able to put." 1 Cor. iii. and x. SANDER.

The Temporal Rock of the Militant Church. "Thou art Peter; and upon this Rock I will build My Church." Matt. xvi.

Fulke. S. PAUL speaketh manifestly, 1 Cor. iii., of building of the Church Militant; and Christ, Matt. xvi., speaketh of an Eternal Rock, against the which the gates of hell shall not prevail. Therefore your distinction of Eternal and Temporal, Universal and Militant, which is the foundation of all your rotten Rock, is an impudent and blasphemous falsehood. FULKE.

Of the continuance of your Temporal Rock it is in vain to contend, when your Rock is nothing else but an heap of sand and dung, whereon your popish Church is builded.

Sander. To the right worshipful M. Doctor Parker, bearing the name of the Archbishop of Canterbury, and to all other Protestants in the realm of England, Nicolas Sander wisheth perfect faith and charity in our Lord; declaring in this preface, that the Catholics (whom they call Papists) do pass the Protestants in all manner of signs or marks of Christ's true Church. SANDER.

Concerning the omission of titles accustomed to be given to the Archbishop of Canterbury, for which you excuse your- FULKE.

1 ["*The Rocke of the Chvrche. Wherein the Primacy of S. Peter and of his Successours the Bishops of Rome is proued out of God's Worde.* By Nicolas Sander, D. of diuinity.—Lovanii, Apud Ioannem Foulerum. Anno D. 1567." 8vo.]

self, I think M. D. Parker, while he lived, did not much esteem them, given to him by any man, and least of all looked to receive them at such men's hands as you are. But touching the religion and Church whereof he was a Minister, I will answer you in his behalf, and of all other Ministers and members thereof; that no excuse will serve you, upon so slender reasons as you bring, to condemn the same of schism and heresy; nor to defend that Synagogue of Satan, whereof you profess yourself to be a champion, to be the undefiled Church and Spouse of Christ. For think you, M. Sanders, that we will more mislike the Church of Christ, persecuted by the hypocritical cruelty of Antichrist for the space of five or six hundred years before our age, than we do the same, persecuted by the furious rage of heathenish tyrants for three hundred years after the first planting of the same among the Gentiles? And think you if we are now to learn that all that glory and bright shining of Christ's Church promised by the Prophets is spiritual and not carnal, heavenly and not earthly, eternal and not transitory? or that we know not your Synagogue to be the very contrary kingdom, and see of Antichrist, even by that outward glory and glistering pomp of open shew that you boast of, according to the prophecy of Christ in the Revelation? Apoc. xiii. & xvii.

And as for the "city built upon an hill," whereof you have never done babbling, by the plain context of the Gospel [it] is not the whole Church, but every true Pastor and Minister thereof; who are also "the light of the world," "the salt of the earth," and a candle set on a candlestick to give light, not hidden under a bushel to be unprofitable. Matt. v. And Christ hath always been with His Church, although the Church of Rome be departed from Him; and He both liveth and reigneth for ever over the house of Jacob, though He be persecuted in His members by the whore of Babylon; and His name is great among the Gentiles, from the sun-rising to the going down thereof, notwithstanding that all nations have drunk of the cup of her fornications. The prophecies of God's Spirit do not one of them overthrow the other; but the one sheweth how the other is to be understanded.

And whereas you say our Church hath been under a bushel before these fifty years, because no history maketh mention of any congregation professing our faith in any towns or places of divers countries at once, I answer, this is as true as all your doctrine beside: for all ancient histories, that write of the state of the primitive Church, make mention of the same faith which we profess. And although toward the revelation of Antichrist the purity of the faith began to be polluted, yet the substance thereof continued until by Antichrist that great defection and apostasy was made, whereof the Apostle prophesieth, 2 Thess. ii. 3. And yet, even in the time of that apostasy, many histories make mention of the continuance of our faith and Church in divers countries in Europe, namely, England, France, Italy, or although under cruel persecution and tyranny; beside great nations of the East, which never submitted themselves to the Church of Rome, and yet retained the substance of Christian faith and profession, though not without particular errors and superstition. Wherefore, although they that were blind, or far off from the Church of Christ, could not see her glory, although she had been set upon never so high an hill, no more than a city built upon the Alps can be seen in England; yet they that had spiritual eyes, and by God's grace drew near unto His Church, did in the most obscure times (as the world esteemeth them) see the clear beauty of her light, and the glory of the Lord's hill, lifted up above all the hills in the world. Esa. ii.

The heathen tyrants thought by their cruel persecution that they had utterly rooted out the name and nation of Christians from the face of the earth. Nero gloried that he had purged the world of the superstition of Christ, as appeareth in an old inscription in a picture of stone: *Neroni Cl. Cæs. Aug. Pontif. Max. ob provin. latronib. et hiis qui novam generi hum. superstitionem inculcar. purgatam:* "To Nero Claudius, Cæsar Augustus, the greatest Prelate; for that he hath purged the province of thieves, and them that brought in a new superstition to mankind." Likewise another like pillar there is of Diocletian and Maximian, in these words: *Diocletian. Jovius, Maximi. Herculeus,* [Herculius,] *Cæs. Augu. amplificato per Orientem et Occident. nup. Rom. et nomine Christianorum deleto, qui Remp. evertebant:* "Diocletianus Jovius, and Maximianus Herculeus, [Herculius,] Cæsaris [Cæsares] Augusti; having amplified the empire of Rome both in the East and West, and utterly destroyed the name of Christians, which did overthrow the Commonwealth." Another like there is of Diocletian alone: *Diocletian. Cæs. Aug. Galerio in Oriente adoptat. superstitione Christi [Christ.] ubique deleta, et cultu Deorum propagato:* "Diocletianus, Cæsar Augustus, having adopted Galerius in the East, and in all places utterly destroyed the superstition of Christ, and set forth the worship of the Gods." By these inscriptions and glorious titles you see that the heathenish tyrants persuaded themselves that they had utterly defaced the religion of Christ, and destroyed His Church out of the world. What marvel then if Antichrist and his adherents, which to the cruelty of the former tyrants have added most detestable hypocrisy, have thought that they had so wholly subverted the true religion of Christ and His true Church, that the name either of Church or religion might not seem to have remained in the world, but that of the Romish Antichrist? But as Nero, the Pontif. Maximus of Rome, which with Diocletian and the rest were deceived in their time, so their successors in place, office, and wickedness, the Popes of Rome, are likewise disappointed of their cruel purpose.

But M. Sander glorieth, that in all marks and signs of the true Church the popish Church doth excel ours. But first of all, that which is the only true mark and trial of the Church, namely the word of God, he denieth to be a sufficient mark of the true Church: yet had he before confessed the Church to be "the pillar and stay of truth." 1 Tim. iii. But the rule of truth (if we believe our Saviour Christ) is the word of God: John xvii. 17.: therefore the word of God is the only true trial and mark of the Church.

But let us consider his reasons, by which he would persuade us that the word of God is not the chief mark whereby the true Church of God may be known. First he saith, the mark whereby another thing is known ought itself to be most exactly known; whereas we are not agreed what God's word is. Note this reason of his, by which he taketh away all authority and use from the word of God, not only thereby to discern the true Church, but also to teach us any other thing that is needful for us to know. But why, I pray you, are we not agreed what is God's word? Forsooth, because some call only the written letter and the meaning thereof God's word: other think many things are God's word which are not expressly written, but delivered by tradition from the

Apostles, and by the Holy Ghost, which hath written His laws in our hearts. Of this latter sort be the Papists; but they are easily confuted: for this principle must needs stand unmoveable, that God's Spirit is never contrary to Himself. Therefore, seeing the Spirit of God hath pronounced of the Scriptures that they are "able to make" "the man of God perfect, prepared to all good works," 2 Tim. iii. 16, it is certain that God hath revealed nothing by tradition, for our instruction, which is not contained in His word written; much less any thing that is contrary to His doctrine delivered in the holy Scriptures.

His second reason is, that we are not agreed upon the written word of God, because the Protestants do not admit so many books of the Old Testament as the Catholics do. I answer, the Protestants do admit as many as the Catholic Church ever did or doth at this day.

His third reason is, that the meaning of those books which we are agreed upon is altogether in question between us: therefore that can be no mark of the Church which itself is not known. I answer, although heretics, which are overthrown in their own conscience, will acknowledge no meaning to be true but their own, yet are there many principles in the Scriptures so plain as they are granted by both parties, or else cannot without shame be denied of our adversaries; out of which plain, certain, and immutable principles all matters in controversy may be proved, and the same Church also discerned: which is the very cause why the Papists dare not abide the trial by the Scriptures, but fly to traditions, even as their forefathers, the ancient Valentinian heretics, of whom Irenæus writeth, Lib. iii. Cap. ii.: *Cum ex Scripturis arguuntur, in accusationem convertuntur ipsarum Scripturam* [*Scripturarum ;*] *quasi non recte habeant, neque fuit* [*sint*] *ex auctoritate,* [*et*] *quia varie sunt dictæ, et quia non possit ab* [*ex*] *his inveniri veritas* [*ab his*] *qui nesciant traditionem: non enim per literas traditam* [*illam,*] *sed per vivam vocem:* "When they are convinced out of the Scriptures, then fall they to accusing of the Scriptures themselves; as though they were not right, nor of sufficient authority, because they are spoken doubtfully, and that the truth cannot be found of them which know not the tradition: for that was not delivered by letters, but by word of mouth."

Thus much Irenæus of the old heretics: and what his judgment was of the meaning of the Scripture, which M. Sander maketh so ambiguous, he declareth, Lib. ii. Cap. xxxv. [xlvi.]: *Universæ Scripturæ, et Propheticæ et Evangelicæ, in aperto, et sine ambiguitate, et similiter ab omnibus audiri possunt*, &c.: "The whole Scriptures, both of the Prophets and of the Gospels, are open and without ambiguity, and may be heard of all men alike." This speaketh Irenæus, not of every text of Scripture, but of the whole doctrine of the Prophets and Apostles; which is so plain, and easy to be found in the Scriptures, that no man can miss thereof, that seeketh not of purpose to be deceived; as he saith, Cap. lxvii. [lxvi.] of the same book.

1. But M. Sander is content, for disputation sake, to admit God's word for a mark of the true Church, and will prove that it is first with the Papists. For if by God's word we mean the written letter of the Bible, they are before us, because we have none assured copies thereof which we received not of them: for since that day in which S. Peter and S. Paul delivered God's word to the Romans, the Church of Rome hath always kept it without leasing or corrupting.

I answer, we mean not by God's word the written letter only, but receiving and obeying the true and plain sense thereof, to be the mark of the Church. Again, I deny that we had any assured copies of the Old and New Testament of the popish Church; but the one of the Jews in Hebrew, the other of the Greek Church in Greek. And whereas he talketh of a certain day in which S. Peter and S. Paul delivered the Scripture to the Romans, it savoureth altogether of a popish fable. Finally, how the Romish Church in these last days hath kept the Scripture from corruption, although I could shew by an hundred examples, yet this one shall suffice for all: the very first promise of the Gospel that is in the Scripture, Gen. iii., that The Seed of the woman should break the Serpent's head, the popish Church hath either wilfully corrupted, or negligently suffered to be depraved, thus: *Ipsa conteret caput tuum*, "She shall break thine head;" referring that to the woman which God speaketh expressly to The Seed of the woman.

2. The second mark is, that the Papists acknowledge more of the Bible than we do, by the books of Toby, Judith,

Wisdom, Ecclesiasticus, and of the Maccabees. I answer, in that you add unto the word of God, it is a certain argument that you are not the true Church of Christ; for the true Church of Christ hath ever accounted those books for Apocryphal: witness hereof Hieronym, *Præf. in Proverb*[1]: *Sicut ergo Judith, et Tobiæ, et Maccabæorum libros legit quidem Ecclesia, sed eos inter Canonicas Scripturas non recipit; sic et hæc duo volumina legat, ad ædificationem plebis, non ad auctoritatem ecclesiasticorum dogmatum confirmandam:* "Therefore as the Church doth indeed read the books of Judith, Tobias, and of the Maccabees, but she receiveth them not among the Canonical Scriptures; so she may read these two books," (meaning the book of Wisdom and Ecclesiasticus,) "for the edifying of the people, but not to confirm the authority of ecclesiastical opinions."

Neither is Augustin, *De Doct. Christ.* Lib. ii. Cap. viii., (whom M. Sander[2] quoteth,) of any other judgment; but prescribeth rules how the Canonical Scriptures are to be known. And, *Cont. Gaudent. Epist.* Lib. ii. Cap. xxiii.[3], he confesseth plainly, that the book of Maccabees is not accounted of the Jews as the Law, the Prophets, and the Psalms, which our Saviour Christ admitteth as His witnesses: yet it is received of the Church, if it be read or heard soberly. Whereby it is manifest, that the Church in his time received it not absolutely as part of the Canonical Scripture, but under condition of a sober reader or hearer.

As for the Decree ascribed to Gelasius[4], it hath no sufficient credit of antiquity[5]; and much less the late Councils of

[1] [*Opp.* Tom. iii. p. 25. Compare a passage in our sixth Article. It is worthy of observation, that in the old Latin Bibles (for example Paris. 1523,) this Preface is to be found, as well as the other Prologues by S. Jerom: so that we have in the very volume of the Scriptures, as received by the Church of Rome, a remarkable testimony against her modern addition to the Canon.]

[2] [Preface to Archbishop Parker.]

[3] [Cosin's *Scholast. Hist.* p. 98. Lond. 1672.

[4] [A.D. 496. Vid. Gratiani *Decretum*, Dist. xv. Cap. *Sancta Rom. Eccles.*]

[5] [A good deal of uncertainty exists with regard to this Decree, which has manifestly been corrupted; but it would not be difficult to justify the assertion of Mabillon, "nullatenus dubito quin hæc Epistola decretalis Gelasium auctorem habeat." (*De Cursu Gallicano*, ad calc. lib. *De Lit. Gall.* p. 386. Lut. Paris. 1685.)]

Florence[1] and Trent[2] which he quoteth: beside that the same Decree of Gelasius, admitting but one book of Esdras, excludeth the Canonical book of Nehemias[3]; and receiveth but one book of the Maccabees[4], which will do the Papists but small pleasure.

3. The third mark: The popish Church receiveth not only the Hebrew text of the Old Testament, and the Greek of the New, but also the Greek translation of the Septuaginta, and the common Latin translation, to be of full authority; whereas we give small credit to those translations, except they agree with the first Hebrew and Greek copies: therefore the Papists have God's word in more authentic tongues and copies than we have. I answer, the Tridentine Council alloweth none for authentical but the common Latin translation, that is the worst of all. But in that the popish Church admitteth differing translations from the original truth of the Hebrew and Greek text to be of full authority with the truth, it appeareth plainly that she is not the Church of Christ; which either wilfully confoundeth error with truth, or else lacketh the spirit of discretion to know the one from the other. And for more authentic copies, it is impudently said that the Papists do receive: for we receive not only all these which he nameth, but also the most ancient Chaldee

[1] [If the Catalogue of Canonical books here alluded to were genuine, its authorship could be referred only to Pope Eugenius IV.; (see Calfhill, pp. 247—8.) but the large collections of the Councils do not contain this document. (Bp. Cosin, *Schol. Hist.* p. 186.) Carranza, Queen Mary's Confessor, (*Sum. Conc.* p. 626. Salm. 1551.) first set forth this spurious inventory; and Longus a Coriolano, (*Summa*, p. 891. Antv. 1623.) Sixtus Senensis, (*Biblioth.* viii. Hæres. xii. p. 713. Francof. 1575.) Becanus, (*Analogia Vet. ac Nov. Test.* Cap. i. Paris. 1633. *Compend. Manual. Controv.* p. 26. Duaci, 1628.) Bellarmin, (*De verbo Dei*, Lib. i. Cap. iv.) and very many others, have adduced as authentic the interpolated Decree. The Parisian Doctor, Louis Bail, frankly declares: "Revera in hoc nulla fides habenda Carranzæ, qui nonnisi ex falsis Actis Concilii Florentini Decretum istud haurire potuit." (*Summa Conciliorum*, Tom. i. p. 489. Paris. 1659.)]

[2] [Sess. iv.]

[3] [It must be remembered that the name "Esdras" included the books of Ezra and Nehemiah; as in Melito's letter to Onesimus, in the last Apostolic Canon, and in the sixth Article of the Church of England.]

[4] [Ivo (*Decret.* iv. 63.) reads "libros" instead of "librum:" but, at all events, the section relates not merely to the Canonical Scriptures, but to writings read in the church "pro fidelium ædificatione."]

Paraphrasts, and the Syrian text of the New Testament; yea, the Arabical text of the whole Bible, beside all vulgar translations of English, French, Dutch, Italian, Spanish, which the Papists cannot abide. All those, I say, we receive as authentical copies for Christian men to use; but so that the trial of all translations be made by the original truth of the Hebrew and Greek texts, in which tongues the Old and New Testament were first written.

Fourthly, the Papists do translate and expound God's word in all manner of tongues better than we; because they have not only internal vocation, but also external vocation, and commission from the Apostles, by lineal succession of Bishops and Priests; whereas we have no commission but from the Commonwealth, which hath none authority to make Priests, &c.; and yet "how shall they preach if they be not sent?" Rom. x. I answer, concerning translations of the word of God into all tongues, I never saw any; neither is there any translation to be shewed of any Papist into any vulgar tongue. 4.

And as for the external calling of the Papists, I say it is not from any lawful succession of the Apostles and ancient Church, whose faith and doctrine they do not follow in their interpretations. For if lineal succession of Priests and Bishops could make interpretations good, the doctrine of Arius, Nestorius, Macedonius, and many other heretics, whose external calling was according to the lineal and ordinary succession of Bishops and Priests, might be auctorised for Catholic: yea, the Papists might not refuse whatsoever Luther, Bucer, Cranmer, and other have taught, which had the same lineal succession that M. Sander doth now brag of. And as for our external calling, he saith falsely it is of the Commonweal, &c.; whereas it is of the Church, and therefore ordinary and lawful. And the saying of S. Paul, whom he citeth, Rom. the tenth, is of the inward calling and sending by God: whereof our doctrine agreeable with the Scripture, and our whole intent to set forth the glory of God, is a sufficient proof; the one to satisfy men, the other to answer our own conscience.

Fifthly he saith, it is no perfection at all on our side, that we read God's word to the people in our church-service in the vulgar tongue; for thereby we lack the use of the better tongues, as of the Greek and Latin. O master of impudency, what use is there of the Greek and Latin tongues to be read to the people that understand them not? And 5.

why are those the better tongues? He saith they were sanctified on Christ's Cross for all holy uses, and especially to serve God in the time of sacrifice. But how were they sanctified, I pray you? Forsooth, because Pilate wrote the title in Hebrew, Greek, and Latin, that it might be understood of all nations for what crime He was condemned. And is Pilate now become a sanctifier of tongues for God's service? Is the malicious scorn of an heathen tyrant a sanctification of these tongues? O brasen foreheads of shameless Papists! But hear more yet of this impudent stuff.

This sanctification was the cause that the Apostles in the East and West delivered these tongues alone as holy, learned, and honourable; not regarding the infinite multitude of profane and barbarous tongues: whereof it came, that the East Church was called the Greek Church, and the West the Latin Church. But the Scriptures, Acts the second, doth teach us, that the Holy Ghost hath sanctified all tongues of all nations to the praising of God, and that the Apostles delivered the magnifical praises of God in all languages. Acts ii. 11. And although the Greek and Latin tongues were most used and most commonly understood in the Roman empire, yet the Church of Christ was enlarged farther than ever the Roman empire extended, in Persia, Armenia, Æthiopia, India, &c., where there was no knowledge either of the Greek or Latin tongues. And even in the Roman empire, those nations to whom the Latin and Greek tongues were not vulgar used their church-service in other tongues. Hieronym, *in Epitaphio Paulæ ad Eustochium*, telleth, that at the solemn funerals of Paul every nation that was present did sing their Psalms in order in their own language: *Hebræo, Græco, Latino, Syroque sermone Psalmi in ordine personabant:* "In the Hebrew, Greek, Latin, and Syrian speech the Psalms were sung in order." But seeing Master Sander alloweth none other sanctification of the tongues but Pilate's title on the Cross, how is the Hebrew tongue, which was one of the three, and the most principal, as the first tongue of the world, and for the excellency thereof called "the holy tongue;" how is that, I say, shut out from church-service? Why was there not an Hebrew service established by the Apostles as well as the Greek and Latin?

But yet he bringeth another argument, to prove that it is lawful to read service to the people in a tongue which they understand not, by the example of Christ, who in time of His sacrifice did recite the beginning of the twenty-first[1] Psalm, "My God, My God, why hast Thou forsaken Me?" in the Hebrew tongue, which He knew the people did not understand, and did not interpret the same in the vulgar tongue. Good Lord, into what foolishness doth Satan carry their minds that wilfully strive against the truth! For what reason is this? Christ in His private prayer, that concerned His own person, spake with a tongue that was not commonly understood: therefore the ordinary public service ought to be in a strange tongue. Christ compassed about with His enemies, and none within the hearing of Him but the Virgin Mary and John the Evangelist, which loved Him or regarded Him, spake Hebrew: therefore the Priest in the church must speak Latin or Greek.

But when M. Sander hath played with this argument as long as he can, his antecedent is utterly false: for Christ recited not that text of the Psalm in the Hebrew, but in the Syrian tongue, which was the vulgar tongue, understood and spoken of all the people; as is manifestly proved by the word *Sabachtani*, reported by both the Evangelists, Matt. xxvii. Mark xv., which is of the Syrian tongue, whereas the Hebrew text is *Hazabtani*, as I report me to all that can but read two tongues, Hebrew and Syrian. And whereas the malicious hell-hounds said He called for Elias, it was not because they understood Him not, but because they most despitefully mocked His most vehement prayer; taking occasion of the like sound of the name of God and of Elias, as scornful deriders use to do.

Sixthly, lest the Protestants should pass the Papists in any one iota, they have the use of the vulgar tongues in Dalmatia, Assyria, and Æthiopia, which acknowledge the Supremacy of the Bishop of Rome. This is a loud lie: for neither the Church of Dalmatians, Moscovites, Armenians, Assyrians, Æthiopians, nor any other of those East nations that retain the name of Christ, did ever acknowledge the Pope's Supremacy. I know they have feigned fables of letters sent from Preto Joannes[2] and such like; which are mere

1 [Eng. xxii.]

2 [Prester John. See Geddes's *Church Hist. of Ethiopia*, pp. 21—3. Lond. 1696. Mosheim, ii. 423—4. ed. Soames. Paulsen et Moshem.

forgeries, upon the submission of some one poor wanderer that hath come out of those countries.

But M. Sander will shew the cause why all nations are not suffered likewise to use their vulgar tongues in their service. First he sayeth, "Vulgar tongues cause barbarousness;" for the preachers of those countries understand not the Latin and Greek tongues by this means. What an absurd reason this is, experience doth shew. For when or where was greater ignorance in the Clergy than there and at such time as the Latin service was used? How many in all England understood or could read the Greek tongue within these sixty or eighty years? I speak nothing of the Hebrew tongue. Contrariwise, what age was ever more full of liberal knowledge in all sciences and learned tongues than this is; even in England, France, and Germany, where service is used in the vulgar tongue? Therefore the use of the vulgar tongue in church-service is not the cause of barbarousness.

The second reason is, that "necessity" enforceth the Apostolic see to tolerate these nations in their vulgar tongues, because they know none other: but Protestants by schism "are fallen from Latin to English, that is, from better to worse," and therefore not to be tolerated. But indeed the necessity is, because they will not receive your Latin tongue; and our schism is from Antichrist to be joined with Christ, from whose doctrine the Church of Rome by horrible schism is departed: for what the doctrine of Christ is concerning public prayers in a tongue that is not understood, His Apostle Saint Paul hath abundantly taught us, the 1 Corinthes, the xiv. chapter. Finally, we defend that our natural English tongue is better to edify English men than your bald Latin tongue that you use in your popish service is for any use of any man learned or unlearned.

Seventhly, the Papists do not only consider "the written letter, but also the plain meaning of every proposition;" and as the words do sound, so do they understand them: and hereof he bringeth many examples. To this I answer, that if they understand all propositions, as well figurative as plain and proper speeches, as the words do sound, they make monstrous interpretations: as, if they understand this proposition, "The

Hist. Tartar. Eccles. pp. 16—28. Helmst. 1741. Ottonis Frising. *Chronicon*, Lib. vii. Cap. xxxiii. p. 146 Basil. 1569.]

rock was Christ," as the words sound, they make a new transubstantiation of the stone into Christ: or this, "This cup is the new testament," if their interpretation be none other than the sound of the word doth give, they make the new testament to be nothing but a drinking-vessel.

But, to discuss his examples, the first is this text, Matth. 1.
xxvi.: "This is My body:" "Why," saith he, "is this which Christ pointeth to denied to be His body?" I answer, it is affirmed to be His body in that sense that He spake; and otherwise than He meant, it is denied to be His body.

Again, James saith, Cap. ii., "A man is justified of works, 2.
and not of faith only." "Why then are works denied to justify, or only faith taught to justify?" I answer, works are not denied to justify before men; and only faith is taught to justify before God. Rom. iii.

"The doers of the law shall be justified." Rom. ii. "Why 3.
then teach you the law not to be able to be done?" Because the Apostle saith that "of the works of the law none shall be justified before God:" Rom. iii. 20: for if the works of the law could be done by any man perfectly as the law requireth, he should be justified by them, as the text affirmeth.

"'By the obedience of one,' that is Christ, 'many shall 4.
be made righteous.'" Rom. v. "Why then are we denied to be really righteous, and said to be righteous by imputation only?" Because the obedience of Christ is not really our obedience, but by imputation of God through faith.

"The love of God is spread in our hearts by the Holy 5.
Ghost which is given us." Rom. v. "This is more than a bare imputing of righteousness to us." Yea, Sir, but this is not our justification, but an effect thereof: for he said immediately before, that "being justified by faith, we have peace with God."

"Whose sins ye forgive, they shall be forgiven them." 6.
Joh. xx. "Why then are Bishops and Priests denied to forgive sins?" We grant that true Bishops and Elders have authority to forgive sins, in God's name, but not absolutely.

"He that is great among you, let him be made as the 7.
younger." Luke xxii. "Why then deny you that one was greater among the Apostles, and is still among the Bishops their successors?" One was not greater among the Apostles in authority: for their greatness was to be the greatest ser-

vant, and to take the most pains, and to be most humble. Mat. xviii.

8. "'Thou art Peter,' or a Rock; 'and upon this Rock I will build My Church'." Mat. xvi. "Why is the militant Church denied to be built upon S. Peter, and his successors in that chair and office?" The Church is affirmed to be "built upon the foundation of the Prophets and Apostles," and so upon Peter as one of them; in which office he hath no successors.

9. "Keep the traditions which ye have learned, either by word, or by an Epistle." 1 [2] Thessa. ii. "Why then are traditions so despised that the name cannot be suffered in the English Bible?" It may and is suffered in that sense which the Holy Ghost useth it; but not to bring in Prayer for the dead, or any thing contrary to the Scripture, under the name of traditions Apostolic. For the Apostle speaketh only of the doctrine which he delivered to them, either by preaching or by Epistle; which is none other than is contained in the holy Scriptures: for of other traditions, pretended to be of the Apostles, he biddeth them take heed in the same chapter, vers. 2.

10. "He that joineth his virgin in marriage doth well, and he that doth not join her doth better." "Why make you marriage as good as virginity?" For such as have the gift of continence, we grant virginity is better, in such respects as the Apostle teacheth.

11. "Vow ye, and render your vows unto God." Psal. lxxv.[1] "If thou wilt be perfect, go and sell all things which thou hast, and give them to the poor, and follow Me." Mat. xix. "There are eunuchs, which have gelded themselves for the kingdom of heaven." "Obey your rulers, and be subject unto them." "Why then are the vows of poverty, of chastity and obedience, counted unlawful, or men constrained not to perform them?" The first text pertaineth to the old testament: the second is a singular trial to that one place: the third we grant in them to whom it is given: the fourth we never made question about it: but all these are evil-favouredly patched together, to prove the vow of Monkery lawful; which is superstitious for want of God's commandment, blasphemous for the opinion of merit, impossible for the frailty of many men's

[1] [lxxvi. 11.]

nature. As for compulsion, there is none used: for no man is compelled to be rich, unchaste, or disobedient.

"Do ye the worthy fruits of Penance." Luc. iii. "Why 12.
then is Satisfaction and Penance despised with you?" This text is, "Do ye the fruits worthy of repentance." We honour the fruits worthy of true repentance, and exhort all men to bring them forth; but popish Satisfaction hath nothing like to them. For we believe that God doth freely forgive the penitent for Christ's sake.

"The husband and wife being two in one flesh is 'a great 13.
Sacrament' or mystery in Christ, and in the Church." Ephe. v. "Why is then the marriage of faithful persons denied to be a Sacrament?" If you understand a Sacrament generally for every mystery, we may grant you it is a Sacrament: but if you understand a Sacrament specially for an outward sign of God's favour and grace, or a seal of our justification, it is none: for if it were, it should be necessary for all men to receive it. Again, it hath the institution of God before the fall of man; therefore can be no Sacrament of the new testament to testify our restitution. Your common translation turneth the Greek word μυστήριον, which is "a holy secret," oftentime *Sacramentum:* yet I know you would be ashamed to confess so many Sacraments of the popish Church as there be mysteries which he calleth Sacraments: as Ephe. iii. the preaching of the Gospel to the Gentiles he calleth *Sacramentum:* 1 Tim. iii. so he calleth the incarnation of Christ *Sacramentum pietatis.* And are you not ashamed to delude ignorant men with the ambiguous name of a Sacrament?

"Work your salvation with fear and trembling." Phi. ii. 14.
"Why then are you so presumptuous as even by faith to assure yourselves of your salvation?" Because it followeth immediately, that "it is God which worketh in us both to will and to perform according to His good will." For it is no presumption to assure ourselves that the promises of God are true: and he may well fear which is assured to be saved; for faith doth not exclude, but plant in us the fear of God, though not a servile fear. As for the deep secrets of God's predestination, we take not upon us to know them, otherwise than they be revealed by His word. Finally, where you ask whether faith be not "an ordinary gift in the Church," I answer you with the Apostle, that "all men" which are in the

outward face of the Church, and participate the Sacraments, "have not faith." 2 Thess. iii. 2.

8. The eighth mark of the Church, "if not only the plain understanding of any one sentence, but also the circumstance of the place and the conference of God's word be necessary," the Papists have used it in every question. For proof hereof M. Sander referreth us to his Treatise of the Supper of the Lord, Lib. iv., and to his book of Images, Cap. ii. [v.] and xi., and in this book to the Ca. ii. and iv. I answer, you make a light shew for a fashion; but you neither consider the circumstances rightly, nor make any true collation of one place with another, as is proved by the answers of these books. Therefore your academical conclusion is false, heretical, and blasphemous; that "the only word of God, being never so well handled, is no sufficient mark to shew the truth;" when Christ saith, "Sanctify them in Thy truth; Thy word is the truth." Joan. xvii. 17.

9. The ninth: M. Sander saith "the heads of the Church, the Councils, the Bishops, and the ancient Fathers must be judges whether we do well apply the Scriptures or no:" as whether S. Peter be the Rock; which M. Jewel denieth, and he proveth by sixteen Doctors afterward, Cap. iv.; of which proof we shall consider, God willing, in due place. But whereas M. Sander quoteth Aug., *Cont. Julian.* Lib. ii.[1], for his rule of judges, I say he hath no such rule in that book: only Augustin doth convince the arguments of the Pelagians of novelty by the judgment of Iren. Cyprianus, Rhetianus, [Reticius,] Ambrosius, &c., and other which lived before their time, and therefore were no partial judges. So do we convince the popish heresies and their arguments of novelty, not only by the manifest word of God, but also by the testimony of the most ancient Fathers, although we may not admit all that they did write to be true: even as the same Augustin, being pressed with the auctority of Ambrose, Chrysostom, and Cyprian by the Donatists and Pelagians, provoketh from them only to the Scriptures. *De Nat. et Gra.* Cap. lxi.[2] *De Unit. Eccl.* Cap. xvi.[3] *Cont. Crescon.* Lib. ii. Cap. xxxi.[4] *De Gratia Christ.* Cap. xliii.[5] That the allegation of the Fathers

[1] [*Opp.* Tom. x. col. 361. ed. Bened. Amst.]
[2] [Tom. x. col. 106.]
[3] [Tom. ix. 249.]
[4] [Tom. ix. 292.]
[5] [Tom. x. 167.]

sufficeth not of itself, we agree with Master Sander: but that there is any other trial of the truth than Scripture we will never grant; seeing God hath therein delivered His whole doctrine, whatsoever is necessary for us to believe that we may be saved. Joh. xx. 31.

But the Papists, for the tenth mark, "join tradition and 10.
practice of God's Church, which can never deceive a man. 'We think,' saith Chrysostom[6], 'the tradition of the Church to be worthy of belief. Is it a tradition? Ask no further.'" But how shall we prove it to be a tradition of the Church? The Valentinians (as I shewed before out of Irenæus) denied the Scriptures to be sufficient without knowledge of the tradition. Therefore, to discern the tradition of the Church from the tradition of the heretics, we have none other trial but by the Scriptures. Therefore Chrysostom saith, *in* 2 *Cor. Ho.* iii.[7], that S. Paul did write the same things which he told them before in preaching. As for the universal practice either of the Pope's Supremacy, or of the Sacrifice of the Mass, which he braggeth of, shall never be proved, but the contrary.

The eleventh mark is the auctority of "General Councils," 11.
confirming the truth, and condemning heretics: and such he maketh the late Council of Trent to be. But we deny that *Conciliabulum* of a few popish hypocrites to be a General Council; in which no man should have a definitive voice but they that were accused of heresy; and whereof he that is most of all charged with heresy, that is the Pope, is made the supreme judge. Wherefore the Papists have no lawful General Council on their side. Although General Councils, as he confesseth, are no sufficient trial of the true Church; both because they may be hindered many ways, and also because they may err, as did the Councils of Arimine and Ephesus.

In respect of these considerations, he maketh the twelfth 12.
mark to be "the Supremacy of the Pope," which is wholly theirs; for trial whereof this book following was written. But for proof that Christ hath appointed such a judge over all he citeth Joan. xxi., that Christ commanded Peter to feed His sheep; as though that pertained not to every one of the Apostles as much as to Peter. Also Lu. xxii., that Christ, having prayed that Peter's faith might not fail, commanded him, when he was converted from his fall, to confirm his

6 [*In* 2 *Thess. Hom.* iv.] 7 [*Opp.* T. x. p. 443. ed. Ben.]

brethren: which pertaineth only to the person of Peter, and cannot with any cable-ropes be drawn to the Bishop of Rome, or any successor of Peter; for it concerneth his singular, full comfort and duty, in respect of his fall and God's mercy; except that, according to analogy, it may be applied to any man that is so raised after his fall: and so that precept, "Confirm thy brethren," giveth no special commandment to the Pope, but to every man whom God hath mercifully converted as He did Peter.

13. With the twelfth mark M. Sander would have ended, but that the Protestants affirm the lawful preaching of "God's word, and the lawful administration of the Sacraments," to be a mark whereby they will be tried. But seeing lawful preaching and ministering must be tried by God's word, M. Sander first asketh what we call God's word: and secondly he asketh if he have not proved it to be more with them than with us, whatsoever it be. It is like this popish academical Atheist hath proved God's word to be on his side, that will not have it certainly known what God's word is. After this he will prove the Papists to be most lawful preachers, because they are likest to the Apostles, in converting many nations within these nine hundred years, when he saith "no man alive could once hear us peep:" as though controversy [conversion] of nations would argue a true Church. By which reasons not only the Protestants may now prove themselves to be most like the Apostles, in converting so many nations of Europe; but also the Arians, and most of all the Mahumetists, might prove themselves the true Church. It is not, therefore, conversion of nations, but conversion of them to the true doctrine of the Apostles, which maketh us like the Apostles; and the Papists, Arians, and Mahometists most unlike unto them.

And where he saith that no sound of ours was heard in nine hundred years' space by any man alive; to see how impudently he lieth, read Flaccius Illyricus, *in Catalogo Testium veritatis*, and you shall see in all ages what monuments are extant of some few whom God reserved from that general apostasy of Antichrist. Read also the *Acts and Monuments* set forth by M. Foxe, and you shall see the same most plentifully.

He will prove their administration of the Sacraments to be more lawful than ours, because they have five more than we. But I answer, because they have five more than the word of God alloweth, or the primitive Church acknowledgeth; and in the administration of the other they have either altogether perverted the institution, as in the Lord's Supper; or shamefully corrupted it with superstition, as in Baptism; they are not the Church of Christ, but the Church of Antichrist.

When we allege the persecution of the Romish Antichrist 14.
to be the cause that our Church hath not flourished in outward peace, and to be a mark also of the truth of our congregation, "What? Masters," (saith D. Sander,) "Antichrist's persecution shall dure but three years and an half; and is the Pope Antichrist, who hath dured these nine hundred years?" But, good M. Doctor determiner, how prove you that Antichrist's persecution shall dure but three and an half of such years as the Pope hath dured nine hundred? You quote Dan. vii., Apoc. xiii. You might by as good reason say it shall dure but three days and an half. Apoc. xi. 9. Will you take upon you so precisely to determine of the mystical number, which is sometime called three years and an half, sometime forty-two months, sometime twelve hundred and sixty days, sometime three days and an half, sometime a time, and times, and half a time; all which make half a prophetical week, and signify a time determined of God, but not plainly revealed to many? [man?]

Secondly, you ask how it could be "the true Church, against which Antichrist so long prevailed, that no man could tell whether any such were in the earth;" when hell-gates shall not prevail against the true Church. I answer, if you cannot put a difference between impugning and prevailing, you will have much to do to defend your Romish Church to be the true Church against the Turks themselves, who have possessed a great part of that ground which you say pertained once to your Church. But herein appeareth the mark of the true Church, against which the gates of hell have not prevailed; that although Satan was let loose, the whore of Babylon drunken with the blood of her members, her two witnesses slain, she herself driven into the wilderness, her seed persecuted wheresoever they were dispersed, yet she is restored in the sight of the world, her witnesses raised from death to life, the Devil is vanquished, the purple whore of Babylon is fallen, and Antichrist shall at length be thrown into the lake with the Devil and his Angels. "This is the Lord's work, and it is marvellous in our eyes."

15. If either persecution, or not failing in persecution, be a mark of the Church, it is more in the Papists than in the Protestants. For persecution he will prove that they be persecuted by us, as the mother by that child which departeth from her obedience, as Agar and Ismael from Sara. But I answer, we are departed from Agar, under whom we were in bondage, to Sara, by whom we are made children of the heavenly Jerusalem: and even as Agar departed from Sara, so did the Synagogue of Rome from the Catholic Church of Christ. For not failing in persecution, experience teacheth in all countries which have received the Gospel how small punishment the greatest number of Papists will abide for their popish profession: whereas so many thousands of God's Saints being most cruelly murdered by the popish Church, the Church of Christ is not diminished but increased thereby; even as Cyprian[1] saith, "The blood of the Martyrs is the seed of [the] Church."

[16.] If antiquity be a mark, it is proved to be on the Papists' side by this reason: "The Church is all one: the latter part of the Church for nine hundred years last past is on the Papists' side: therefore the former part also." But this reason, standing upon a shameful begging of that which is questioned, is soon turned upon your own neck. The Church is in all but one: but the beginning of the Church maketh not for you: therefore that which you say is the latter part of the Church, being contrary to that former, is no part of the Church: so that by this reason you shall neither have antiquity, or any part of the Church.

But "if you appeal to particular examples," (saith M. Sander,) "I say the Christians in the primitive Church did communicate under one kind at Emaus and at Jerusalem." And I say, M. Sander, if he would burst himself with study, shall never prove it. He quoteth Aug., *De consen. Evang.* Lib. iii. Cap. xxv.[2], whose opinion was that Christ gave the Sacrament at Emaus; but of Communion in one kind he never once dreamed.

[1] [Tertullian, S. Cyprian's "master," used the words, "Semen est sanguis Christianorum." (*Apologet.* ad fin.) See a note in the English translation of his *Works*, Vol. i. p. 105. Oxford, 1842.]

[2] [Tom. iii. Par. ii. col. 101.]

He saith "the Christians did set up Images in the honour of Christ;" quoting Eus. Lib. vii. Cap. xiv.[3]: whereas Eusebius speaketh of heathen men, that "of heathenish custom" did set up Images, and not of Christians.

Dionysius[4], although he be ancient, yet he wrote not in the time of Eusebius, Hieronymus, or Gennadius, and so was known for no writer in the Church for five hundred years after Christ. Wherefore I will not stand about his errors and ceremonies; which yet for the most part are as unlike the popish ceremonies as they are to ours.

Although we have no certainty of the writings of Ignatius which are extant[5], yet is there nothing in them that favoureth the Papists' religion. He nameth a sacrifice which could not be offered without the Bishop. That cannot be the Mass, which every hedge-priest may say. *Ad Smyrn.*[6] "He would have the Emperor obey the Bishop," (saith M. Sander.) *Ad Phil.* But this proveth the Epistle to be counterfeit[7]; for there was no Christian Emperor when Ignatius lived: (although in divine matters the Christian Emperor ought to obey the Bishop, or rather God's word which the Bishop preacheth.) "Also he speaketh of virgins that had consecrated themselves to God[8]." And who speaketh against them

3 [Cap. xviii. ed. Vales. Cf. Calfhill, pp. 28, 29. Bingham, Book viii. Chap. viii. Sect. vi.]

4 [Calfhill, p. 211.]

5 [The genuine Epistles were not at this time separated from those which are confessedly fictitious. Isaac Vossius published the authentic Letters at Amsterdam, in the year 1646; and these were reprinted Lond. 1647, in the *Appendix Ignatiana*, by Archbishop Ussher, who had previously set forth the interpolated Epistles, Oxon. 1644.]

6 [In the Epistle *ad Smyrnæos*, §. viii. it is declared: "Οὐκ ἐξόν ἐστι χωρὶς τοῦ Ἐπισκόπου οὔτε βαπτίζειν, οὔτε ἀγάπην ποιεῖν:" but instead of the last phrase the interpolator has put "οὔτε προσφέρειν, οὔτε θυσίαν προσκομίζειν, οὔτε δοχὴν ἐπιτελεῖν." Consequently Fulke has referred to the surreptitious passage, which is thus rendered by the old Latin interpreter: "non licet sine Episcopo neque offerre, neque sacrificium immolare, neque Missas celebrare." Vid. cl. Usserii ed. p. 118; vel Jac. Fabri Stapulens. edit. sig. D 5. Argent. 1527. *PP. Apostol.* cura Jacobson. Tom. ii. p. 433. Oxon. 1840. Suiceri *Thesaur.* in verb. Δοχή. Tom. i. 960—1. Amstel. 1728.]

7 [The sentence in question occurs in the interpolated Epistle *ad Philadelphenos*. Videatur Usserii edit. p. 99.]

8 [Usser. p. 97. In the old Latin version of this passage there is

which having the gift of continency do keep virginity? In the same Epistle he affirmeth both Peter and Paul to have been married[1], and will not condemn the marriage of Church Ministers.

"He commendeth the Lent-fast." *Ad Antioch.*[2] Choose, M. Sander, whether your Decretals lie of Thelesphorus that invented the Lent-fast[3], or that this is a counterfeit Epistle of

an error, which by some has been considered a corruption. (See Sir H. Lynde's *Case for the Spectacles*, p. 67. Lond. 1638.) The word "animabus" has been inserted instead of "precibus:" but probably the mistake was originated by the reading of "ψυχαῖς" for "εὐχαῖς." This note may remain, though it is certain that Sanders had in view a sentence which appears in the spurious Epistle *ad Antiochenos*. (Usser. p. 158.)]

1 [This well-known but inconclusive statement is found in the same interpolated Letter to the Philadelphians. (ut sup. p. 98.) Ussher, in the seventeenth chapter of his *Dissertatio*, has mentioned many particulars connected with this counterfeit testimony; and Daillé perversely makes use of it as the ground of his fortieth argument against the remains of S. Ignatius. (*De lib. suppos. Dionys. et Ignat.* p. 353. Genevæ, 1666.) Romanists have endeavoured to suppress this unfriendly evidence, such as it is, by vitiating the passage whether in MS. or print; and of course the simplest remedy is that suggested by the Vatican Expurgatory Index; viz. "verba illa, 'et Pauli et aliorum Apostolorum,' videntur e textu abradenda." (p. 116. Romæ, 1607: pp. 101—2. Berg. 1608.) We may see this recommendation transcribed and adopted in the *Bibliotheca Patrum*, Tom. iii. p. 22. Paris. 1610; *Magna Bibliotheca*, Tom. i. p. 85. Colon. 1618; and *Maxima Bibliotheca*, T. ii. P. i. p. 83. Lugd. 1677. It is alluded to also in the notes of Martialis Mæstræus, p. 17. ad fin. Tom. xiii. *Mag. Bibl. Patt.* Paris. 1654.]

2 [Fulke's reference here evidently belongs to a preceding place. Lent is spoken of in the utterly false Epistle to the Philippians; (Usser. p. 186. Conf. Dallæum, *De Jejun. et Quadrag.* p. 417. Davent. 1654.) a document of sufficient validity for Mr. Taylor's purposes. (*Ancient Christianity*, i. 119. Lond. 1839.)]

3 [Gratiani *Decret.* Dist. iv. Cap. iv. *Statuimus;* an Ordinance noted for the memorable Gloss upon its commencement: "Statuimus, i. e. Abrogamus." (See Bp. Jewel's *Works*, Part i. p. 33. ed. Parker Soc. Donne's *Pseudo-Martyr*, p. 112. Lond. 1610.) Blondel has with reason called the author of this feigned Decree an "impostor;" (*Pseudo-Isidor. et Turr. vap.* p. 188.) and Bp. Gunning (*Paschal or Lent Fast*, p. 94. Oxf. 1845.) observes, that the foundation of the error, with regard to the alleged institution of Lent by Telesphorus, was a forgery "practised upon" the Chronicle of Eusebius; into which, after the

Ignatius. In the Epistle *ad Phil.*[4], where he commendeth the forty days' fast, the Wednesday and the Friday fast, he saith farther: *Quicunque Dominicum aut Sabbathum non jejunaverit, præter unum Sabbathum Paschæ, ipse est Christi interfector:* "Whosoever shall not fast the Lord's day or Sabbath, beside one Sabbath of Easter, he is a murderer of Christ." If this be true antiquity, why doth the Church of Rome omit fast on Sunday? If it be counterfeit, why is not M. Sander ashamed to allege it?

"Justinus[5] witnesseth that water was mingled with wine." Yea, but it was to allay the strength of the wine, not that it was necessary for the Sacrament; though afterward it grew to a superstitious observation. "He saith further, the Deacons carried the consecrated mysteries to them that were absent; which Calvin reputeth an abuse." If they carried the bread and the wine as the Sacrament, it was an abuse not to be warranted by God's word. But seeing the Deacon's office was to minister to the poor, I think rather they carried it as the alms of the Church to such as were needy.

What Pius[6] decreed we find in no writer of credit. As for the Pope's Law, it is no good evidence; having a bushel of dross and counterfeit dregs to one grain of good and true

story of Chochebas, as Scaliger declares, "intruserunt editores de Quadragesimæ jejunio a Telesphoro instituto." (*Animadvers.* p. 216. Vid. Euseb. *Chron.* Gr. p. 212: Lat. p. 167. Amstel. 1658.)]

4 [Usser. ut sup. 186; vel Fabri Stapul. edit. sig. C 5. Argent. 1527. The true reading is this: "Quicunque Dominicam aut Sabbatum jejunaverit, præter unum Sabbatum Paschæ, ipse est Christi interfector." Conf. Can. Apostol. lxvi. Hooker, Vol. ii. pp. 417—18. Oxf. 1841.]

5 [*Apol.* i. §. lxxxv. *Opp.* p. 97. Lut. Paris. 1615.]

6 [Gratiani *Decr.* De Consec. Dist. iii. Cap. xxi. Blondellus, p. 194. With respect to the supposed injunction of Pope Pius I., for the observance of the feast of Easter upon the Lord's day, it is to be remembered, first, that this Epistle is spurious; and secondly, that the Chronicle of Eusebius has been basely interpolated for the purpose of maintaining the falsehood. Scaliger assures us, that "Quæ Pio attribuuntur in editionibus de Resurrectionis Dominicæ die Dominico celebrandæ institutione, ea in nullo veterum codicum comparent. Sed Marianus a Beda, Beda a libro Hermæ apocrypho in sua Chronica traduxerunt; et ab illis in Eusebianum textum ab editoribus admissa sunt." (*Animad.* p. 219. Cf. Eusebii *Chron.* Lat. p. 168: Græc. p. 212. Gunning, ut sup. pp. 95—6.)]

antiquity. Indeed Eusebius testifieth that Victor, Bishop of Rome, did excommunicate the Bishops of Asia about the celebration of Easter: but he testifieth also that Victor was sharply rebuked by divers other godly Bishops, namely by Irenæus of Lyons, and Polycrates of Ephesus, for so doing. Euseb. Lib. v. Cap. xxv.[1]

"Tertullian[2] saith, All doctrine is false and lying, that agreeth not with some Apostolic Church." And such is the doctrine that the Church of Rome holdeth; which agreeth with no Apostolic Church, no not with the ancient Apostolic Church of Rome. But our doctrine agreeth with all the Apostolic Churches that ever were planted in the earth, and continued in the doctrine of the Apostles.

Tertullian, a Montanist[3], speaketh indeed of oblations for the dead; but they were none other than such as they offered for the birth-days, and that was thanksgiving. He speaketh of Prayer for the dead, which he received of Montanus the heretic. The Stations he speaketh of were no gaddings, but standings[4]. The visitation of Jerusalem is denied to no man that will take the pains to go thither: neither was it ever like to popish pilgrimage, which is to run a whoring after Idols.

We confess with S. Cyprian[5], that the bread in the Sacrament is "changed, not in shape but in nature," to be the flesh of Christ; understanding nature for property, and the flesh of Christ to be received spiritually.

In public offences we would have confession to be made publicly before the Elders of the Church, as Cyprian would them that fell in persecution: but of popish Auricular Confession he never spake one word. We acknowledge the forgiveness of sins by the Ministers to be ratified by God; not binding God's judgment to it, but it to God's judgment.

[1] [ed. Musc. xxiii—xxvi. Calfhill, p. 269. Tassin, *Hist. Litt. de la Cong. de S. Maur*, p. 637.]

[2] [*De præscript. Hæreticor.* Cap. xxi.]

[3] [Calfhill, 257.]

[4] [Bingham's *Antiq.* B. xxi. Chap. iii. Hooker, v. lxxii. 8. p. 416. ed. Keble, 1841. See note 2, page 183.]

[5] [The passage quoted by Sanders is contained in the supposititious treatise *De Cœna Domini;* (ad calc. *Opp.* S. Cypriani, p. 40. ed. Fell.) the author of which, Arnoldus Carnotensis, lived about the year 1160.]

We grant that temporal punishment for satisfaction of the Church ought to be appointed unto public offenders; which may be released upon their hearty repentance, and is no more like to popish pardons than the stews and market of Rome is like the Church of God.

The rest which he huddleth up together, I will answer as briefly. S. James his chair was esteemed but as a monument of antiquity, and no holiness put in it. Euseb. Lib. vii. Cap. xv.[6] The solemn dedicating of churches was no more like popish hallowing of churches than Christian preaching and praying is like to conjuration. Euseb. Lib. ix. Ca. x.[7] The strait life of Heremites was as like the popish Heremites that dwelt at every good town's end, where the other dwelled in the wilderness, as the city and the desolate wilderness are alike. Ruff. Li. xi. C. iv.[8]

Driving of Devils by Holy Water was no ordinary ceremony, but a miracle once wrought by the Bishop of Apamea; who, when the temple of Jupiter could not be burned with fire that was set unto it, after he had prayed, caused water signed with the Cross to be sprinkled on the altar; which being done, the Devils being driven away, the temple was set on fire and burned. Theodor. Lib. v. C. xxix.[9] The auctority of unwritten traditions is so defended by Basil, *De Sp. Sanct.* xxvii.[10], that he affirmeth, "Whatsoever is not of the holy Scriptures is sin." *Mor. Diff.* [*Def.*] lxxx.[11]

Prayer to Saints, as the dregs of that time, I leave to be sucked up of the Papists. Repentance, but no popish Sacrament of Penance, is commended by S. Ambrose. The name of the Mass is not in Ambrose, *Ep.* xxxiii.[12]: for *missam facere* signifieth "to let go," or "let pass," not "to say Mass." The name of Sacrifice signifieth a sacrifice of thanksgiving.

The Canon of the popish Mass is not in Ambrose, but the form of celebration of the Communion in his time. *De Sacr.* Li. iv. Ca. v. & vi.[13] Chrysostom reciteth the text of S. James only to prove that God forgiveth sins at the

6 [Cap. xix. ed. Vales.]

7 [Lib. x. Cap. iii.]

8 [Rufini *Hist. Eccl.* ii. iv.]

9 [Cap. xxi. edit. Vales.]

10 [See Calfhill, p. 266.]

11 ["Πᾶν τὸ ἐκτὸς τῆς θεοπνεύστου γραφῆς, οὐκ ἐκ πίστεως ὄν, ἁμαρτία ἐστίν." (Ἀσκητικά. π'. *Opp. Græc.* p. 437. Basil. 1551.)]

12 [See before, p. 81.]

13 [Calfhill, p. 202.]

prayers of the Elders; not speaking of the ceremony of Extreme Unction, used by the Papists. *Et De Sacer.* Li. iii.[1]

Hieronym, *ad Vilant.*[2], alloweth not the superstitious use of burning candles in the day-time. That he will not allow Bishops to beget children, it sheweth his errors, condemned by the Nicene Council by the persuasion of Paphnutius. Socr. Li. i. Cap. xi.[3] Hieronym speaketh not of a certain number of prayers, to confirm the use of your beads; but of a certain number of the verses of the holy Scripture, to be learned as a talk [task] to the Lord. *Ad Furian.* [*Furiam*[4].]

That he which hath had two wives could not be a Priest in Hieronymus' time, that was a little of that chaff which afterward overwhelmed the good corn in the Church of Rome. Hierom affirmeth that he, as helper unto the writing of Damasus, Bishop of the city of Rome, did answer the synodical consultation that came from the East and the West. What is this to any purpose of the Papists? Not only the Bishop of Rome was consulted, nor he always; except the matter concerned the whole Church, when no member should be left unconsulted, and not made privy.

Finally, that Augustin saith, that the fire by which some shall be saved after this life is "more grievous than any pain of this life," *Psal.* lxxvii.[5], he saith the contrary, *De fide, ad*

1 [*Opp.* Tom. i. p. 384. ed. Bened.]

2 [*Adversus Vigilantium.* Opp. Tom. ii. p. 123. Basil. 1565.]

3 [*Hist. Eccles.* i. xi. ed. Vales.]

4 ["De Scripturis sanctis habeto fixum versuum numerum: istud pensum Domino tuo redde." (*Opp.* T. i. p. 82.)]

5 [*In Psal.* xxxvii. fol. 55. Lugd. 1519.—"...gravior tamen erit ille ignis quam quicquid potest homo pati in hac vita." A spurious passage, similar to this, is twice inserted in the Canon Law, (*Decr.* i. Par. Dist. xxv. Cap. v. & ii. Par. Caus. xxxiii. Qu. iii. *De Pœnit.* Dist. vii. Cap. vi.) and ascribed to S. Augustin: "Hic ignis, etsi æternus non sit, miro tamen modo gravis est. Excellit enim omnem pœnam quam unquam aliquis passus est in hac vita, vel pati potest." The work here cited is the fictitious treatise *De vera et falsa Pœnitentia*, which the Master of the Sentences also has adduced, (Pet. Lombardi *Sententt.* Lib. iv. Dist. xx. fol. 338. Paris. 1553.) and which is referred to by the present Bishop of Exeter in his valuable *Letters to Charles Butler, Esq.*, p. 117. Lond. 1826.—S. Austin's sentiments respecting Purgatory may be learned from his *Summes* by Crompton, pp. 164—7.

Laurent. Cap. lxviii.[6]; where he denieth that text of Scripture to be understood of punishment after this life, and sayeth the whole matter of Purgatory may be inquired of as a matter uncertain. The like *De octo Dulcitii Quæst.* xci[7]. et *Cont. Pelag. Hypog.* Lib. v.[8]; he knoweth heaven and hell, and utterly denieth the third place to be found in the Scriptures. By which it appeareth, that this error of Purgatory was but very young in Augustin's time.

And now you see what antiquity he can boast of: for when he hath wrested and wrong[9] all that he can, scarce two or three errors have any shadow of antiquity, and those not in the greatest matters; whereas the whole substance of the doctrine of faith in God, justification by Christ, the true worship of God, the virtue of Christ's death, the infirmity of man, the right use of the Sacraments, the auctority of the holy Scriptures, and a number more of such principal heads of Christian learning, in which we differ from them, he is as silent as a stone.

The seventeenth mark is the name of "Catholics," which 17.
M. Jewel confesseth to have been of late given to the Papists; which, among other things, stayed S. Augustin in the right faith, as he confesseth, *Cont. Epist. Manich.* Lib. iv[10]. But seeing the name of Catholics was falsely given to you, which are now rightly called by the name of your arch-heretic the Pope Papists, the only name of Catholics, which was given to you by yourselves to shadow your heresies, cannot prove you to be Christians, or your Church to be Catholic; especially seeing you lack the truth, which Augustin in the same place confesseth to be more worth than either succession, antiquity, the name of Catholic, or any other thing else.

The eighteenth mark is "the succession of Priests and [18.]
Bishops," even from the seat of Peter unto Pius the fifth, in whose time this book of M. Sander was written: which mark is approved by Augustin, by Irenæus, by Tertullian, by Op-

Lond. 1625, or from Ussher, *Answer to a Challenge*, pp. 183—4. Ib. 1631.]

6 [*Enchirid. ad Laur.* Opp. Tom. vi. coll. 162—3.]

7 [Quæst. i. *Opp.* vi. 93—4.]

8 [*Opp.* T. x. Append. p. 26. This work is doubtless counterfeit.]

9 [wrung.]

10 [Or rather *Cap.* iv.; for it is a single book. *Opp.* viii. 110.]

tatus, and by Hieronym, as he saith, being one of the most evident of all other: but therein he belieth all these Fathers whom he citeth; who never alleged the bare succession of place and persons, but joined with the continuance of doctrine, received from the Apostles, against new and late-sprung-up heresies. Augustin shall speak for the rest; who, after he hath alleged unto the Donatists the successions of Bishops from Peter in the unity of the Catholic Church, among which was never a Donatist, the judgment of the Bishop of Rome in absolving of Cecilianus, and many such-like reasons whereunto he thinketh the Donatists should yield, yet in the end he addeth these words[1]: *Quamquam nos non tam de istis documentis præsumamus, quam de Scripturis sanctis:* "Although we do not so much presume of this [those] documents as of the holy Scriptures."

These eighteen marks M. Sander will have to be more richly seen in them than in the Protestants: but what marks they are, and how they are to be found in their Church, I have briefly shewed. But now he cometh to a general challenge, to prove that we have nothing which they lack, and we lack many things which they have. "First, they have a justifying faith as well as we; but not justifying alone, but with charity, which is the life of faith." But charity is a fruit of a living and unfeigned faith, not the life thereof; 1 Tim. i. 5.; the effect, not the cause: and we hold with Saint Paul, "that a man is justified by faith without the works of the law;" Rom. iii.; for charity is no instrument to apprehend the mercy of God, but faith only: therefore faith only doth justify. We are "justified" *gratis*, "freely, by His grace:" Rom. iii. 24: therefore nothing can come in account of justification before God but only faith; which seeing the Papists have not, they have not a justifying faith.

We have two Sacraments, and they have seven: but seeing they have five more than Christ instituted, and have perverted the one, and polluted the other, they have but one Sacrament at the most, and that horribly profaned; I mean Baptism. "We have an inward priesthood," he saith, "to offer up Christ in our hearts; and they offer Him both in hearts and hands." But our spiritual priesthood is not to

[1] [*Epist.* Fortunati, Alypii, et Augustini ad Generosum. *Opp.* S. Aug. Tom. ii. col. 92. ed. Ben. Amst.]

offer up Christ, but "spiritual sacrifices, acceptable by Christ;" 1 Pet. ii. 5; Heb. xiii. 15; and they are horrible blasphemers that take upon them to offer up Christ, whom none could offer but Himself, by His eternal Spirit. Heb. ix. 14.

He saith that the Papists "believe as well as we, that Christ by one sacrifice paid our ransom for ever, when they shew it to the eye in the oblation of their Mass;" than the which nothing can be more contrary to the holy sacrifice of Christ once offered, and never to be repeated, because He found "eternal redemption" thereby. Heb. x. 14; ix. 12, and 25, &c.

He addeth, that they believe Christ to be the Head of the Church, "and shew it by a real figure of one head in earth," meaning the Pope, whom now he maketh a figurative head; as though Christ were not present with His Church, or that His Church were a monster with two heads.

As laymen receive the Communion in both kinds with us, so they do with them in Austria by the Pope's dispensation; as though Christ's commandment and institution were not sufficient without the Pope's dispensation. Wherein also he affirmeth a monstrous absurdity, that the Sacrament was not instituted in two kinds, to be so received; but by an unbloody sacrifice, to shew the nature of His bloody sacrifice, in which His soul and blood was separated from His body and flesh: and yet he saith the body and flesh of Christ is not [as] well contained in the cup as His blood in the paten, with the body and form of bread, and no separation of the one from the other, and no more contained or distributed by both than by one alone: which saying is to be received with whoops and hisses of all men that have their five wits.

They have Marriage, he saith, in greater price than we, because they teach it to be a Sacrament: but we find it not instituted by Christ to be a Sacrament of the new testament; therefore we receive it as an holy ordinance, containing also a great mystery, but yet no Sacrament. But if it be an holy Sacrament, why do you think it unmeet for Ministers of the Church? and why doth your Pope Siricius[2], or

[2] [Crabbe *Concill.* Tom. i. p. 417. Colon. Agripp. 1551. Extracts from this Epistle, ascribed to Pope Siricius, are contained in the Canon Law. *Dist.* lxxxii. Capp. iii, iv. The words alluded to occur also in an

rather some counterfeiting Canonist in his name, call holy Matrimony a living in the flesh, such as cannot please God? But although Marriage be "honourable in all men," you say it is not so in them that have gelded themselves for the kingdom of heaven; who have no more possibility to marry than a gelded man to beget children. You were best then to tell the Apostle that his saying was too general; for he should have excepted them that so gelded themselves. But S. Paul saith, notwithstanding your impossibility, "If a virgin do marry, she doth not sin." 1 Cor. viii. [vii.] 28. You will reply, he speaketh of them that have not vowed: and how prove you that Christ speaketh of them that have vowed longer than God would give them grace to live chaste; which he affirmeth to be a peculiar gift, and not in the power of every man? Matt. xix. 12. But what if your popish geldings, by neighing at every man's wife, and by tumbling in all beds, where they are not kept out by force, prove themselves to be stone horses; are they still in the number of those that, having gelded themselves for the kingdom of heaven, may not possibly marry, and yet neither will nor can possibly live chaste?

But omitting these things which they have as well as we, now he cometh to those things which we lack, and yet many of them are very necessary; as Insufflations, that is, blowing upon; Exorcisms, that is, conjuring; holy Oil in Baptism, Chrism in Bishopping, external Priesthood, Sacrifice, Altars, Censing, Lights, and so forth; a large rabblement of popish errors, and superstitious ceremonies. And that we say falsely, in saying these are naught, he proveth by S. Paul's saying to the Galathians, *præterquam quod accepistis,* "beside that you have received;" for once, saith he, we have received those things of our ancestors: as if S. Paul had not spoken of the Gospel, but of beggarly ceremonies; which, because they are another Gospel and way of salvation, brought in by the Pope, than S. Paul delivered to the Galathians, we hold the Pope and them justly accursed. "But we justify them," saith he, "by the word of God:" not written, I am sure; but by your counterfeit word of traditions, and, as you say, by books of ancient

Epistle to Exuperius, attributed to Pope Innocent I., and cited in Cap. ii. of the same Distinction.]

Fathers; and yet not by books of the most ancient Fathers, in whom is little or nothing at all of such dross and chaff, among a great deal of good corn.

"But seeing we made no new religion in those and such-like things," saith he, "but keep the old, humility, obedience, and unity is our fault, if we have any." O faultless hypocrites! if the older truth had never been revealed unto you, against your old heresies, your faults had been the less; but now your darkness being convinced of the light, your pride, rebellion, and schism from Christ and His Church is and appeareth most heinous and manifest.

Now seeing M. Sander dare not encounter with us in this very point of our contention, he feigneth an idol of an adversary, to shew his manhood upon before his friends, that they may praise him for a worthy champion. He imagineth that we reply, that Luther and Calvin did so change popish religion as Christ and His Apostles did change the Jewish religion; and then he layeth on load, that Luther and Calvin's authority is not like to Christ's: whereas we make no such comparison; but affirm that these godly preachers were sent of God, so to reveal and discover the idolatry and corruptions maintained in the Church, as Elias, Elizeus, Oseas, and the other Prophets were sent to restore and reform the true worship of God, corrupted and decayed among the Israelites; reproving and reforming all things according to the infallible rule of God's word.

And whereas he trifleth of the continuance of the sacrifice of Christ, according to the order of Melchisedech, I say it is horrible blasphemy to make any successors unto Christ in that Priesthood which the Holy Ghost saith[1] He hath ἀπαράβατον, "such as passeth not from Him by succession to others, because He liveth for ever." And whereas he quoteth Irenæus, Lib. iv. Cap. xxxii., and Augustin, *in Psal.* xxxiii. *De Civi. Dei*, Lib. xvii. Cap. xx. *Cont. adv. Leg.* Lib. i. Cap. xviii., read the places who will, and he shall find, that these Fathers speak not at all of any propitiatory sacrifice of Christ's very body and blood in the Sacrament, but of the sacrifice of thanksgiving, which the Church throughout all the world doth offer to God, in the celebration of the holy mysteries, for their redemption by the death of Christ. But

1 [Heb. vii. 24.]

it is sufficient for blind and obstinate Papists to see the book's margent painted with quotations of Doctors by them which peradventure never turned the books themselves, but borrowed their quotations of other men.

But M. Sander saith, whereas we pretend that Luther and Calvin do all things according to God's word, they are "the more to be abhorred," not only because the one is contrary to the other, but also because they "pretend to have their doings figured and prophesied in the Gospel; whereas there is but one Christ, which hath been born and died but once: therefore these men have no power to abrogate the Mass, or to take away the key of ancient religion." To their dissension I answer, it is not in many points, but in one, and that not of the greatest weight. As for their pretence of their doings to be figured or prophesied in the Gospel, it is a dream of M. Sander's drowsy head; for they make none such, but they shew the abuses of the Romish Church by the doctrine of God's word: and by the same they shew the way to reform them and this to the glory of Christ, who died but once: they abrogate the Mass, by which it should follow, if it were of any force, that He should die often; for without death, and "shedding of blood," there is no sacrifice for remission of sins. Heb. ix. 22, and 26.

If we deny the Mass to be that they say it is, he answereth, that as he doth not read that the Jewish Priests did err "concerning the substance of their public sacrifice," so is it less possible "that the universal Church of Christ should err in that public act wherein Christ is sacrificed." Here is a wise argument, having neither head nor foot, nor any joint to hang together. For whatsoever M. Sander readeth, we read that Urias the High Priest made an heathenish altar in the Temple, at the commandment of the King Achas, and offered sacrifice thereon. 2 Reg.[1] xvi. We read also in Josephus, that Caiaphas[2] and divers other of the High Priests were Sadducees, which could not but err in

[1] [Kings.]

[2] [It does not appear from Josephus (*Antiqq. Judaic.* Lib. xviii. Capp. iii, vi.) that Caiaphas was a Sadducee. He states (L. xx. C. viii.) that Ananus the son of Ananus, who is called Ananias in the Acts of the Apostles, belonged to this sect. Compare Acts xxiii. 2—9: v. 17. Lightfoot's *Temple Service*, Chap. iv.]

the substance of their public sacrifice,[3] when they believed not the resurrection, seeing the end of their sacrifices was to signify the eternal redemption by Christ.

Now to the second part of the argument I say, the universal Church did not err; though the schismatical Synagogue of Rome departed from Christ's institution. But M. Sander chaseth us away with this double negative, "No, no, Masters, Antichrists [Antichrist's] you may be; Christ [Christ's] you cannot be." God's curse light on him that would have any other Christ than Jesus, the Son of God and Mary, which sitteth at the right hand of His Father in heaven. But it is your Antichrist of Rome, that usurpeth not only the office, but also receiveth the name of Christ and God of his antichristian Canonists: which I know you will not deny, though your face be of brass, because the books may be shewed to any man that list to see them[4].

After his large excursion, he returneth to D. Parker, whom he would advise to revolt to the popish Church: but he, (God be thanked,) having ended his days in the Catholic Church of Christ on earth, is now received into the fellowship of the triumphant Church in heaven. I pass over how maliciously he raileth against the blessed Martyr Tho. Cranmer; for defence of whose learning and godliness I refer the reader to his story, faithfully set forth by M. Fox[5]. All other Archbishops of Canterbury, he saith, from Augustin sent thither by Gregory, were of their popish profession. Of a great number it is as he saith, but not of all. For the opinion of the carnal presence of Christ in the Sacrament was not received in the Church of England for two or three hundred years after Augustin's arrival; as that Homily, which that reverend Father, Matthew, late Archbishop of Canterbury, caused to be translated and imprinted, doth manifestly declare[6].

And whereas he scorneth at the persecuted congregation of Wickleve, Husse, and the Poor Men of Lyons, boasting of the external pomp and visor of glory that was in the Romish Church; I have sufficiently answered before, that both the

3 [Jackson's *Works*, Tome i. iii. xv. p. 471. Lond. 1673.]

4 [Calfhill, note 3, pp. 5, 6. ed. Parker Soc.]

5 [*Acts and Mon.* iii. 531—563. Lond. 1684.]

6 [See before, p. 7.]

apostasy of the Church of Antichrist, and the persecution of the Church of Christ, was so described and prophesied before, that neither the one nor the other should trouble any man's conscience with the strangeness thereof, so long as the truth of the little flock, and the falsehood of the revolted multitude, are manifestly tried by the authority of the Scriptures.

The conclusion of all his Preface is, that which was the cause of this treatise, that there "never lacked a chief Bishop in Saint Peter's chair;" whose Supremacy being "granted, all other controversies be superfluous." Yea, verily, all Scriptures, Doctors, and Councils be needless, where there is such a person always at hand, who cannot err in any thing that he commandeth men to believe or do. And contrariwise, if there be any necessary use of Scriptures, Doctors, Councils, learning, tongues, &c., there is no such chief Bishop on earth. But what say you, M. Sander, did there never lack a Pope to sit in Peter's chair? Was that see never void many days, many months, and many years together? And when there was two Popes or three Popes at once, and that oftentimes, who sat in Peter's chair? You will say, One of them: but which, you cannot tell. Whose voice should the people obey as Christ's Vicar? The one cursed, the other absolved; the one commanded, the other forbad. Is not all your bragging of Peter's chair, and unity, thereby proved to be nothing else but a mere mockery?

The Lord Jesus confound Antichrist with the breath of His mouth, and with His glorious appearance; and defend His Church in truth and holiness for ever and ever. Amen.

THE FIRST CHAPTER.

SANDER. *Sander.* The state of the question concerning the Supremacy of Saint Peter, and of the Bishops of Rome after him.

FULKE. *Fulke.* Upon our denial of the Supremacy of the Pope, and of S. Peter, he saith we deny "all primacy and chief government in the Church." Whereupon he raiseth three questions to entreat of.

1. "Whether it be against the word of God that there should be in His Church any primacy or chief authority."

"Whether S. Peter had the same primacy, or no." 2.

"Whether the Bishop of Rome had it after S. Peter." 3.

To which we answer, with distinction of the words Primacy and Church, that we affirm there is a spiritual and eternal primacy of the universal Church; which is proper only to our Saviour Christ; which never was given to Peter, nor to any mortal man. Likewise we affirm, that in particular Churches there is and must be a primacy of order; which is temporal, according to the disposition of the Church. And such primacy in the College of the Apostles might Peter have for some time: but that he had it not always, it appeareth in the Council of the Apostles, in the fifteenth of the Acts, of which James in a manner, by all writers' consent, was President and Primate; and, upon the controversy being throughly debated, pronounced the definitive sentence, Ἐγὼ κρίνω, &c.; according to which the Synodal Epistle to tho Churches of Antiochia, Syria, and Cilicia was written, in the name of "the Apostles, Elders, and brethren."

But concerning S. Peter, M. Sander moveth new questions. First, whereas Christ promised that Simon should be called Cephas or Peter, which is "a stone" or Rock, Joh. i.; and afterward performed His promise when He chose him to be an Apostle, Mar. iii. Luk. vi.; and thirdly, when Simon confessed His Godhead, the reason of the promise was declared, that He would build His Church upon that Rock; the question is, whether Peter himself be that Rock upon which Christ would build His Church, or Christ Himself, or the faith and confession of Peter.

M. Sander, the spokesman for the Papists, passing over the second question, that is, whether Christ Himself, whom Peter confessed, by [be] this Rock, denieth the faith or confession of Peter to be the perfect sense of that promise; affirming the Rock on which the Church is builded to be S. Peter, not barely confirmed, but in respect of the promise past, the present confession, and the authority of feeding Christ's sheep given him after His resurrection; of which four conditions the Protestants (he saith) do lack no less than three. But what do the Papists lack, when in their sense they exclude "the Rock Christ," the only "foundation," than the which "none other can be laid," 1 Cor. x. 4; 1 Cor. iii. 11, by any wise builder of the Church? Yet seeing M. Sander is so desirous to have Peter to be the stone whereof Christ speaketh, laying first Jesus Christ to be the head corner-stone, I will frankly yield unto him that which he could never win by force, that Christ, saying to Peter, "Thou art Peter; and upon this Rock" or stone "will I build My Church," meaneth even Peter himself, upon whom He would build His Church; but so that He maketh not Peter a singular Rock or stone to bear the whole building, (for then He should put Himself out of place,) but one of the principal stones of the foundation, even as all the Apostles and Prophets were; for so the Holy Ghost speaketh, Ephe. ii. vers. 20: "Being builded upon the foundation of the Apostles and Prophets, Jesus Christ being the head corner-stone; in whom all the building being compacted groweth unto an holy temple unto the Lord."

Now let us consider whether any singular authority was committed to Peter, when he was willed to feed the sheep of Christ. M. Sander saith yea, because it was said to him alone, "Feed My sheep," and no particular flock named, it must needs be meant the whole flock. Mark these main pillars of the popish Rock. Christ said only to Peter, "Come after Me, Satan, for thou art an offence to Me," &c.: therefore Peter only was an enemy of Christ. If the Pope must needs have the one text as peculiar to him, let him take the other also. Again, Peter himself saith to the Elders, "Feed as much as in you lieth the flock of Christ." 1 Peter v. Here is no particular flock named: therefore he meaneth the whole universal flock. But he urgeth farther, that as Peter loved Christ more than the rest, so he did feed the flock of Christ above all other Pastors. But if labouring in preaching the Gospel be the feeding of Christ's flock, not Peter, but Paul laboured more than he, and all the rest of the Apostles. 1 Cor. xv.

The answer of the Protestants to his demand, "why Peter alone, in presence of other Apostles, was commanded thrice to feed the sheep," (that by thrice confession and injunction to feed he might abolish the shame of his thrice denying, and know that he was restored to his Apostleship, from which he deserved to be deprived,) M. Sander liketh not for three causes. First he saith, he had not lost his Apostleship, because his fault was not externally proved, nor confessed in judgment, nor stubbornly defended, &c.; as though Christ, which knew and foretold his infirmity before he fell, had need of external proofs, or a Commissary's court, to deprive Peter of his office. O blockish reason! Although neither Calvin nor Beza do affirm that he was altogether excluded from his office by his fault, but that he deserved so to be; and therefore had need especially to be confirmed by our Saviour Christ more than the rest, as his offence was more shameful than of any of the other. Therefore the second reason that he bringeth of his restitution, if he had lost it, is superfluous: Joh. xx.: for he was none otherwise restored than the rest were; but at this time especially confirmed, as his special case required.

His last reason is, that "admit Peter had not been restored before this time, yet now he was restored to a greater authority than any other Apostle had received at any time:" and whereas we reply that all the Apostles were equal, by testimony of Cyprian and Hierom, he answereth by distinction, forsooth that they were equal in Apostleship; and yet Peter was chief of the Apostles, and an ordinary chief Shepherd or high Bishop, wherein they were all inferiors to him, and he was their Primate and their head; and this distinction he promiseth to prove exactly hereafter. In the meantime it is a monstrous paradox, that all the Apostles should be equal with Peter in Apostleship, and yet Peter be the chief of the Apostles. He that can prove inequality to be where he granteth equality to be, and in the same respect, is a strange logician. Finally, whereas some men, granting Peter to be the Rock, deny the honour to his successors, he will prove that the Bishop of Rome, and none other, hath all that authority which Peter sometime had; and consequently that the Protestants come nearer to the nature and condition of Antichrist than any Pope of Rome ever did or can do.

THE SECOND CHAPTER.

Sander. That there is a certain primacy of spiritual government in the Church of Christ; (though not properly a lordliness, or heathenish dominion.) And in what sort this ecclesiastical primacy differeth from the lordly government of secular Princes, and how it is practised by the Bishop of Rome. Also the Apostles' strife concerning superiority is declared. That there was one greater among the Apostles to be a ruler and as a minister do not repugn. The pre-eminence of Priests SANDER.

above Kings. A King cannot be supreme governor in all ecclesiastical causes, because by right and law he cannot practise all ecclesiastical causes. The High Priest is preferred before the King by God's law. The evil life of a Bishop taketh not away his authority. The differences between the Bishop of Rome and temporal Princes. That Moses was a Priest.

FULKE.

Fulke. The ecclesiastical government of the Church is a ministry or service, by the authority of Christ and His Apostle Peter; and therefore neither properly nor unproperly a godliness, [lordliness,] or heathenish dominion; but altogether as unlike to it as our Saviour Christ, the pattern of all true Ministers, was unlike to an earthly lord or an heathen Prince. But whereas M. Sander in the first sentence of this chapter saith, "That no man properly can be lord among the Christians, where all are servants indifferently, under the obedience of one true Lord and Master Jesus Christ," he sheweth himself not only to be a Papist, but also an Anabaptist. For the common service that we owe unto Christ hindereth not but that a Christian man may be lord and King over his fellow-servants and brethren in Christ as properly as ever he might be before the incarnation of Christ, who saith Himself that His kingdom "is not of this world;" who Himself was obedient and taught obedience both to God and Cæsar, to each in things that belonged to them: and that dominion which He forbiddeth unto His Apostles, like to the Princes of the nations; Luc. xxii. Matth. xx.; and which S. Peter forbiddeth the Elders of the Church, 1 Pet. v., is not prohibited to all Christians, but to the Ministers of the Church only, in respect of their ministry.

And yet that there ought to be a government of the Church, and some kind of primacy also, it is clearer by the Scriptures than that it need any proof; especially such slender proofs as M. Sander bringeth: and namely, where he citeth this text, "Feed My sheep," to signify that Peter should give every man his due portion and just measure of victuals in convenient time; which thing neither Peter did, neither was he able to do; and much less any man in succession to him, which is not equal in gifts with him. And therefore the example of a steward, who may provide for a competent number of one family, is fondly applied to make one steward over the whole world, beside Him that is almighty. For although the Apostles were not limited to any certain congregation, but were generally ambassadors into all parts of the world, yet were they not appointed to give to every man his due portion, but to appoint Pastors in every Church and town for that purpose; Tit. i. Acts xiv. verse 23; and they themselves to proceed in matters pertaining to their general commission.

And therefore although M. Sander, in applying these words of Hieronym, *Cont. Luciferianos*[1], which he calleth *exsortem quandam et eminentem potestatem,* "a certain peerless and high power," and of Cyprian, Lib. i. *Ep.* iii.[2], of "one Priest in the Church for that time," &c., true [to] every several Pastor, or, as he termeth them, parish Priest, dealeth more honestly than other Papists, that draw the same testimonies as proper to the Pope's sovereign auctority; yet in that he argueth that the like should be in the whole Church militant which is in every parish, it is out of all compass of reason: for that which is possible in the one is altogether impossible in the other. And the argument is no better than if we should say, there is one steward in every College or great house: therefore there is one steward over all the world.

And whereas he would prove his matter good by that S. Matt., cap. x., rehearsing the names of the Apostles, calleth Peter "the first," it is too childish and frivolous. For in every number one or other must be the first; and it seemeth that Peter was first called to the office of Apostleship: therefore his primacy was of order, and not of auctority. Neither is he always first named: for Gal. ii. 9, where the question is of the dignity of the Apostles, James is named before Cephas or Peter; as he was indeed elected to be the principal Minister at Hierusalem, by consent of most ancient writers. Neither doth it follow, that because the High Priest of the old law was called *Princeps populi,* "a Prince of the people," therefore Peter was made Prince of all Christian men. For neither was the High Priest alone called the "Prince of the people," as M. Sander seemeth to say; neither had Peter by those words, "Feed My sheep," any auctority committed unto him more than to the rest of the Apostles. As for the name of Lord, or term of dominion, sometime given by ecclesiastical writers

1 [*Opp.* Tom. ii. p. 139.]

2 [Ad Cornel. Ep. lix. *Opp.* p. 129. ed. Oxon.]

to the Bishop or his government, we strive not about it; so there be no such dominion by him exercised as Christ and His Apostles forbiddeth, and as we see to be usurped and practised by the Pope of Rome and his Clergy, howsoever M. Sander in terms of distinction would seem to shadow it. But he will shew out [of] one of these places which we allege, as if it did utterly forbid all superiority among the Disciples, Luke xxii., that the ecclesiastical primacy is clearly established and confirmed.

First, he saith most untruly, that we deny all superiority among the disciples of Christ, as though we denied all government among Christians; except he do childishly understand the disciples of Christ for Ministers ecclesiastical only: and yet we deny not all superiority among them, but that kind of primacy which the Pope claimeth, and tyrannically usurpeth. Secondly, he maketh a long preamble before he come to the matter; that although the Apostles did divers times strive for the primacy, as in the way to Capharnaum, Mark ix.; upon the request of Zebedee's wife, Mark x.; and after His last supper, Luke xxii.; yet Christ never denied that there should be one greater among them, and often signified that the same should be S. Peter; especially when He said, "Thou art Peter; and upon this Rock I will build My Church." If you demand why they strove for Supremacy when He had determined it, he yieldeth a substantial reason; because, while Christ lived upon earth, it was in His free choice to have appointed it otherwise, until at the last, in the twenty-first of John, He said unto him, "Simon, thou son of Jona," &c. By these it appeareth that M. Sander confesseth, that no text of Scripture proveth the Supremacy of Peter more directly and plainly than this of John xxi.: which when every child seeth how little force it hath to prove it, you may easily judge that the Papists themselves, against their own consciences, do enforce all other texts uttered before to establish it: and namely this of Luke xxii.; in which he saith that Christ, taking up the strife that was among His Apostles about the primacy, ended His talk at last with Simon Peter, shewing him to be that one that was greater than the rest.

What ass, if he could speak with man's voice, would reason thus; that because Christ, converting His speech from exhorting all His Apostles to admonish Peter of his special danger he stood in by his infirmity, signified that Peter was greater than all the Apostles? But we must hear him compare these words of Christ, Luke xxii., with the words of S. Matthew and Mark in other places; which he saith the Magdeburgen. Cent.[1] doth "huddle up," as [if] they were all one, whereas they differ much.

The words of Christ, Matt. xx. and Mar. x., are these: "Whosoever among you will be greater, let him be your servitor; and whosoever among you will be first shall be your servant." In Saint Luke xxii.: "He that is greater among you, let him be made as the younger; and he that is chief as he that ministereth." M. Sander will have great difference to be in these sayings. First, generally, that the former sentence speaketh not of the greatness among ecclesiastical officers, but all Christians: which is utterly false; because this kind of greatness is prescribed unto them to whom external dominion is forbidden. But that is not to all men, but unto the Apostles only and their successors: therefore this kind of greatness is proper only unto them. For he speaketh not of greatness by humility only, but of greatness without foreign dominion and worldly dignity, and joined with service; which is peculiar to the ministry ecclesiastical. Secondly, he maketh six frivolous differences; which either are false, or else make no diversity in the sense of the places.

The first: Matthew and Mark speak of any man, "Whosoever;" S. Luke of one man, which by the article ὁ is pointed out. If the article ὁ do always point one certain man, it is somewhat that M. Sander saith: but if ten thousand times and more (as every man meanly learned in the Greek tongue doth know) it signifieth not one certain man, then is this a fond difference.

The second: The other speak of a desire to be great, "Whoso would be great;" S. Luke of the effect already present, "He that is greater." But the words of S. Matt., xviii. ver. 4, overthrow this difference with the former: for there ὁ μείζων, "the greatest," is taken for any one that shall humble himself as a child, and not for one made Primate of the Church.

The third difference is, that the letter [latter] speak of him that would be μέγας, "great;" S. Luke of him that is μείζων, "greater;" by which is meant "the greatest of all,"

[1] [*Cent.* i. Lib. ii. Cap. vii. 525—6. ed. Basil.]

after the Greek phrase. But that μέγας in the others signifieth "the greatest," according to the Hebrew phrase, it is manifest by the word used by both, which call him also πρῶτον, "the first" or chiefest of all. Therefore these three differences are not worth three chips.

The fourth: S. Matthew calleth him that would be great δοῦλος, "a servant;" S. Luke giveth no name of service to him that is greater, but he is willed to be younger or underling. Yet S. Luke in another place, cap. ix. vers. 48, calleth him μικρότερος, "the least," which shall be the greatest. But what fond quarrelling is this! Doth not the Pope call himself "Servant of the servants of God?" By which he acknowledgeth that the greatest service belongeth to him that claimeth the greatest dignity; though indeed he yield no service, but usurpeth all tyranny. Is M. Sander now ashamed of that service, that the Pope by solemn title hath so long professed?

As for a pre-eminence of order, we deny not but it was among the Apostles, and must be in every several company; although it be not necessary that it should be perpetual in one man, but as every Church shall ordain: but a primacy of authority over all the Church, we utterly deny that ever it was granted to Peter, or any man, by our Saviour Christ. M. Sander citeth Ambrose, *in Luke* xxii., to prove it: *Qui lapsus es*, &c.: "Thou which didst slide before thou didst weep, after thou hast wept art set upright; that thou shouldest rule others, who before hadst not ruled thyself." "Lo," (saith he,) "Peter did rule others." A great miracle: but doth it follow, that either he ruled all men, or that he ruled his equals the Apostles? of whom the same Ambrose saith: *De Spiritu Sancto*, Lib. ii. Cap. xii.[1]: *Nec Paulus inferior Petro; quamvis is Ecclesiæ fundamentum, et hic sapiens architectus, sciens vestigia credentium fundare populorum:* "Neither was Paul inferior to Peter; although he was the foundation of the Church, and Paul a wise builder, knowing how to found the steps of the people believing." And again, in his book *De incarnatione Domini*, Ca. iv.[2]: *Hic, inquam, ubi audivit, Vos autem quid Me dicitis? statim, loci non immemor sui, primatum egit: primatum confessionis utique, non honoris; primatum fidei, non ordinis*: "This Peter, I

[1] [*Opp.* Tom. iv. col. 254. Lut. Paris. 1661.]
[2] [*Opp.* iv. 290.]

say, when he heard, 'But what do you say that I am?' immediately, not forgetting his place, executed his primacy: verily the primacy of confession, not of honour; the primacy of faith, not of degree." By these places of Ambrose it appeareth what government and primacy was granted to Peter, and how he exercised the same.

The fifth difference is, "that the other Evangelists say absolutely, Let him be a minister and a servant; in S. Luke it is said, with a great moderation, Let him be made as the younger, and as he that ministereth." If this be a good argument to prove that the ministry is more truly a greatness than a ministry, the Arrians may deny by the like that Christ is more truly a man than the Son of God; because Saint John sayeth, "We saw His glory, as the glory of the only-begotten Son of God." O beastly absurdity! And yet he sayeth, "If any man say that there was not one certain man greater among the Apostles, who might be as the younger, it is plain contradiction to Christ, and he is Antichrist." But where, on God's name, sayeth Christ, that there is one certain man greater among the Apostles?

The last, and the least difference is, "that the greater man is evidently named a little after, when Christ saith to S. Peter, 'Simon, Simon, behold Satan hath desired to sift you as it were wheat: but I have prayed for thee, that thy faith shall not fail: and thou, being once converted, confirm thy brethren.'" Master Sander asketh what other thing it is for Peter to confirm his brethren, but to practise and exercise his greatness over them; for every one that confirmeth is greater than they which are confirmed. Who ever did read such impudent assertions? Peter's faith was confirmed by Mary Magdalen: therefore she was greater than Peter. Paul was confirmed by Ananias: therefore he was greater than Paul. Aquila and Priscilla confirmed Apollo: therefore they were greater than he.

To conclude, if ὁ μείζων in S. Luke xxii. do necessarily prove that there was one certain man among them "greatest," then ὁ μικρότερος in the ix. of Luke, 48, doth prove that there was one "least" among them: "He that is least among you all," (saith our Saviour Christ,) "even he shall be the greatest." And lest M. Sander should renew his difference of μέγας and μείζων, it may please him to understand, that the contention was among the Apostles, τίς ἂν εἴη μείζων αὐτῶν, "which should be the greater" or greatest "of them:" which question our Saviour Christ doth not decide, if M. Sander's difference of μέγας and μείζων in this place may stand. Wherefore hitherto Peter hath found no Supremacy; and much less the Pope, by prerogative of his chair; who cannot be said to sit in Peter's chair, except he taught Peter's doctrine: which if he did teach, as he doth the contrary, yet Peter's auctority could no more be derived to him than the auctority of Moses to every one of the Scribes and Pharisees which did sit in Moses' chair.

He citeth Ambrose to prove that there is a prelacy or preferment in the Church, because he forbiddeth contention thereabout; as though there could not be a prelacy or preferment of every Bishop over his Church, but there must be one Bishop over all the Church. The like he allegeth out of Bede, which speaketh expressly of all the teachers of the Church, and not of one Pope over all. The conclusion of his disputation is, that the ecclesiastical primacy doth in all points resemble (as much as it possibly may) the primacy of Christ: and therefore he that denieth the primacy among the Apostles to be a true primacy in his kind is blasphemous against Christ Himself. Nay rather, he that communicateth with any man that which is peculiar to our Saviour Christ, that He only should be, as S. Paul speaketh of Him, ἐν πᾶσι Αὐτὸς πρωτεύων, "Himself the Primate in all things," Col. i. 18, which is the "Head of His body," which is "the Church," is found a manifest blasphemer of our Saviour Christ. But that they which excel among the Apostles, and their successors the Bishops, may be humble and yet great, after the example of our Saviour Christ, is no question at all: but that any hath such greatness in auctority as our Saviour Christ hath over His whole Church is the thing we deny.

If Gregory affirm that Peter "by God's commission had the primacy of the holy Church," and was "grown in power above the rest," it is no marvel, seeing he was so near to the open manifestation of Antichrist; which succeeded him the next save one; whose tyranny began to increase long before Gregory's time: yet was he in his pretended primacy more modest than any that followed him to this day; utterly refusing and condemning as profane, proud, and blasphemous against Christ, the title of Universal Bishop[1], which John of Constantinople did usurp, and other Bishops would have given to him.

And whereas M. Sander frameth an objection of our part, that no man can be both a minister and a governor; therefore no ecclesiastical Minister can be a governor; he playeth with his own shadow. For we deny not but a Minister of the Church, which is a servant, is also a governor. But we affirm that his government is spiritual, not worldly; unlike to the earthly government of this world, even as the kingdom of Christ is not of this world. But it followeth not, because that every Bishop and shepherd is a governor, therefore there must be one Bishop and shepherd governor of them all; other than our Saviour Christ, the arch or "head Shepherd," and "Bishop of our souls." 1 Pet. v. 4, and 1 Pet. ii. 25.

M. Sander commendeth the saying of Leo Bishop of Rome to Anastasius Bishop of Thessalonica[2]: *Qui se,* &c.: "He that knoweth himself to be set over some men, let him not disdain to have some man preferred before him." But he proceedeth: *sed obedientiam quam exigit etiam ipse dependat:* "but such obedience as he requireth of other, let him yield himself." By this saying it appeareth, that although Leo take [so] much upon him as to hear the controversies that cannot be determined by the Metropolitans, yet he acknowledgeth, that in equity he was bound to yield that obedience to others which he required of others, if he himself were in fault.

But M. Sander maketh another objection for us, on this manner: The Princes of the Gentiles do also serve their subjects in conserving peace, keeping out their enemies, &c.: but the Clergy must be altogether unlike to temporal governors: therefore there must be no primacy or government among them, although it be joined with service. Once again I say, we make no such objection: but we answer the Anabaptists that so object, that the government of the Clergy, as it differeth in matter which is spiritual, so also it differeth in form and manner from the regiment temporal; which is with outward pomp of glory, and with the material sword; and this with all humility, and with the sword of the Spirit. Con-

[1] [*Opp.* Tom. ii: *Ep.* Lib. iv. Capp. lxxvi, lxxviii, lxxx, lxxxii, lxxxiii. Lib. vi. C. cxciv. Antv. 1572.]

[2] [*Epist.* xii. alias lxxxiv. *Opp.* i. 224. Lugd. 1700.]

trariwise, M. Sander answereth this objection so as he both strengtheneth the hands of the Anabaptists, and sheweth himself little to differ from their opinion. First therefore he saith, that "Christ forbiddeth His Apostles and Bishops such a dominion as is used among the Princes of the earth; not altogether such as ought to be among them." But that He speaketh not of tyrannical dominion, it appeareth by the title of Εὐεργέται, "Benefactors," which their subjects did give them for their bountifulness towards them, in preserving them from enemies, in peace and wealth. Secondly he saith, "that although the King be never so good, yet it is not the kingly, but the priestly power, which God chose from the beginning to rule His people withal. And although Kings serve God's eternal purpose, and they are commanded to be obeyed, yet the making of Kings over God's own people at the first came not of God by way of His merciful election, but by way of His angry permission." What Anabaptist could speak more heretically or seditiously against the lawful auctority of Kings and Princes?

But let us see his reason. "Nemrod," he saith, "was the first King we read of, which either by force usurped, or was advanced by evil men." I answer, if Nemrod was the first that usurped auctority as a tyrant, yet was he not the first that exercised kingly auctority lawfully, neither was he ruler over God's people. But what will he say of Melchisedech, King of Salem? Was not he elected of God at the first, both to be a King, and a figure of the King of Kings; who should not have had that dignity, if it had not been of itself both lawful and godly? Secondly he saith, "God was angry with His people for asking a King, when they had a Priest to rule them." I answer, He was not angry for their asking of a King, but for refusing of a Prince ordained by Him; which was Samuel, a Levite indeed of the family of Cohath, but no Priest of the family of Aaron: for in his days were High Priests, Eli, Achitob, Achimelech. But after the days of Eli, which was both High Priest and Judge, Samuel was ordained Prince or Judge of the people; having auctority above Achitob or Achimelech the High Priests in his time: which were sufficient to decide the controversy of the Supremacy, if M. Sander would give place to the Scriptures.

But who can discharge him of Anabaptistry, where he

denieth the making of a King to be God's institution; affirming it to be "the fact and consent of men, allowed indeed by God;" when the Apostle expressly sayeth it is "God's ordinance," Rom. xiii.? And where he saith that Abel, Noe, Abraham were directly from God chosen to be Priests as Aaron, he sayeth most untruly; for they had in their family the principality of civil government as directly as they had the Priesthood: but neither of both in such sort as Aaron had the Priesthood; in whom the one was distincted from the other. And of Abraham it is testified that he was "a Prince ordained of God." Gen. xxiii. 6. He setteth forth the excellency of Priests by their auctority in making Christ's body "with their holy mouth," as Hierom speaketh. But that proveth not the Supremacy of one Priest above all men, nor of one Priest above another.

As for the ordaining of Peter to be general shepherd, and high Bishop of the whole flock, by commanding him to feed His sheep, when he can conclude it out of that Scripture in any lawful form of argument, we will yield unto it. But this is intolerable impudency, that, pretending to shew how much the Pope is more excellent than any King, he asketh, "To what Christian King did Christ ever say, 'As My Father sent Me, I send thee?'" as though Christ had ever said so to Peter in singular, and not to all His Apostles in general, "As My Father sent Me, so I send you." Joan. xx. Concerning the Rock that He would build His Church upon, and the feeding of Christ's sheep and lambs, we shall have more proper place to examine afterward what Supremacy they give to the Pope, or to Peter either. His farther raving against the dignity of Kings, who list to see, let him turn to the 57th page of his book, Cap. ii.: and yet I cannot omit that he saith, that "the pomp of a King is most contrary of all other degrees to the profession of Christian faith;" and maketh worldly pomp as unmeet for a King as for a Bishop.

"But the Scripture" (he saith) "never calleth any King Head of the Church." Neither do we call any King Head of the Church, but only Christ: but in every particular Church the Scripture alloweth the King to be the chief Magistrate, not only in governing the Commonwealth, but also in making godly laws for the furtherance of religion; having all sorts of men, as well ecclesiastical as civil, subject unto him, to be governed by him, and punished also, not only for civil offences, but also for heresy, and neglect of their duties in matters pertaining to the religion of God. For although many civil Magistrates at the first were enemies of the Gospel, yet was it prophesied, that "Kings should be nursing fathers, and Queens nursing mothers" unto the Church. Es. xlix. Again, it is an impudent and gross lie, when he saith that God was angry "because the government of the High Priest was rejected, and a kingly government called for." For they rejected not that government of the High Priest, but of Samuel the Judge, who was no High Priest, although he was a Prophet; neither was there ever any High Priest Judge but only Eli.

"But if all Supremacy be forbidden over the whole Church militant," (saith M. Sander,) "it is forbidden likewise that there should be any superior in any one part of the Church." And this he proveth by a jolly rule of logic: "For the parts, (according to their degree,) are of the same nature whereof the whole is." O subtile reason! by which I will likewise conclude, There may not be one schoolmaster for all the children of the world; therefore there may not be one schoolmaster for one town in all the world: There cannot be one physician for all the world; therefore there may not be a physician for every city: yea, there cannot be one Priest for all the Churches in the world; therefore there may not be a Priest in every parish. Again, he reasoneth thus: "If a King be supreme head over his own Christian realm, it must be by that power which he either had before his Christianity, or beside it: for by his Christianity it is not possible that he should have greater power than the Apostles had." I answer, the King's Supremacy is perfectly distinct from any power the Apostles had. For although he have authority over ecclesiastical persons, and in causes ecclesiastical, according to God's word, yet is he no ecclesiastical officer, but a civil Magistrate; having chief authority in all causes, not absolute to do what he will, but only what God commandeth him; namely, to provide by laws that God may be truly worshipped, and all offences against His religion may be punished.

And whereas M. Sander inferreth, that an ethnic Prince or Turk may be supreme head of our Church, we utterly deny to any such the name of an head, which cannot be a member: but even an ethnic Prince or Turk may be chief Magistrate over the faithful; and make laws for the maintenance of Christian religion, as an hypocrite Christian may. They are also to be obeyed in all things that are not contrary to God. Nabuchadnezer, Darius, Cyrus, Artaxerxes, which were heathen Princes, made godly laws for the true worship of God, and furtherance of His people; as in the prophecy of Daniel, the books of Ezra and Nehemiah, it is manifest. S. Paul appealed to Nero the Emperor. Eusebius testifieth, Lib. vii. Cap. xxiv.[1], that the Christians, in a matter of a Bishop's election, and for a Bishop's house, were directed by the decree of Aurelianus an heathen Emperor. And this notwithstanding, the Church is always under the sovereign authority of Christ, and the spiritual government of her several "Pastors and teachers," when [whom] Christ, ascending into heaven, ordained for her edification and unity, and not one Pope over all. Eph. iv. 13.

But now he will enter one degree farther, and suppose "that a King may be as good as it is possible for any mortal man to be, or as any Bishop and Priest is; yet he can neither baptize, consecrate, forgive sins, praise, excommunicate, bless, nor be judge of doctrine, by his kingly authority. If he can do none of those, he cannot be supreme governor in all ecclesiastical causes." I deny this argument: for his Supremacy is not to do those things, or any of them, but to provide and command that they may be done as they ought to be.

But he riseth up again and saith, that "whosoever hath sovereign authority, either in civil matters or ecclesiastical, he may in his own person execute any of those things which any of his inferiors may do." So he saith, "The King, if he will, may be Judge in Westminster-Hall, Shrieve, and Constable: yea, he may play the tailor, master-carpenter, or tanner." It is marvel he saith not that he may be both a King and subject. "Likewise the Primate" (he might as well say the Pope) "may help a Priest to Mass, carry the Cross in procession, dig a grave," &c. I deny this rule to hold in all things. For there are some things that the Prince may not do for lack of knowledge; and some things for lack of calling; and yet he may command both to be done. For controversies of law he may not decide, except he have knowledge of the law; nor minister physic, except he have knowledge in physic: yet he may command both lawyers

[1] [Cap. xxx. p. 282. ed. Vales.]

and physicians to do according to their knowledge. Likewise to preach, baptize, &c., he may not, because he lacketh calling; for none may do those things lawfully but he that hath a special calling: but he may command those things to be done, and to be well done, according to God's law, whereof he ought not to be ignorant; and for that purpose is especially commanded to study in the book of God's law, that not only in matters concerning his own person, but in matters concerning God's honour, he may cause all men to do their duty. Deut. xvii. 18. So did David, Salomon, Jehosaphat, Ezechias, Josias, command the Priests to offer up the sacrifices, and to do their duty; which it is not lawful for their Kings to execute.

And is it so strange a matter, that a popish King may not command his Chaplain to say Mass, or to say his Mass reverently and orderly, as the laws of Popery do require? If he may command over those matters, which yet he may not do himself, let M. Sander see how his rule holdeth, that whosoever hath authority in any matters may do all things himself which any of his inferiors may do, or which he may command to be done. Whereupon he concludeth, that "the King hath no right or supreme power at all in ecclesiastical causes, (unless it be committed to him from the Bishop:)" so that a King, if he be a Bishop's Commissary, may do that by M. Sander's exception, which neither by commandment of God, nor his kingly power, he hath auctority to do.

Another argument he bringeth as good as this, that "the lesser authority doth not comprehend the greater:" and therefore M. Horne must answer him, whether to preach, baptize, forgive sins, &c., be greater or lesser ministry than the King's authority. If it be greater, then it cannot be comprehended in the King's authority, which is lesser. What that reverend Father, the Bishop of Winchester, hath answered, it may be seen in his book against M. Feckenham. But to talk with you, M. Sander, what if I grant that the ecclesiastical ministry is not comprehended in the King's authority? Will you thereupon infer, that the King's authority is not to command the Ministers of the Church in these matters to do their duties according to the word of God? Indeed you conclude so; but your argument is naught: for the King is God's Lieutenant, to see both the Church and the Commonwealth to be well ordered. And the same thing may be greater and lesser than another in divers respects. As in authority of commanding the King is greater than the physician: in knowledge and practice of physic the King is less than the physician. So in authority of commanding the Prince is greater than the Minister: but in authority of ministration he is less; and no inconvenience in the world to the dignity of either estate or calling.

The Bishop of Winchester's examples, M. Sander saith, are evil applied: for they only shew what was done, and not what ought to have been done; and so for many circumstances are subject to much wrangling. 1. For either he was no good Prince which meddled with disposing of holy matters; 2. or in that deed he was not good; 3. or he did it by commission from a Prophet or an High Priest; 4. or he was deceived by flatterers; 5. or he was enforced by necessity. But all these quarrels notwithstanding, the examples of Scripture are so many and so plain, that M. Sander's wrangling cannot obscure them. David, a good Prince, did well in appointing the Levites and Priests to their several offices, and forbidding the Levites to carry the Ark and the vessels thereof, without any commission from Priest or Prophet, but only by the word of God; not deceived by flatterers, nor enforced by necessity. 1 Chron. xxiii. 25. Salomon did the like about the Temple: he deposed Abiathar the High Priest, and set Zadoc in his room[1]. 1 Reg. ii. 27 and 35. And such are the examples of all the godly Kings of Judah; which, being commended in the Scripture, are not uncertain, deceitful, or unknown in their circumstances; but much more certain arguments for the authority of Princes in ecclesiastical matters

[1] [As the conduct of Solomon in deposing Abiathar affords the only example that can be adduced from Scripture to justify the deprivation of Bishops by mere secular power, it is important to shew that the learned Mason was much mistaken when he allowed, that on this occasion "a King deprived one that was a lawful High Priest." (*Of the English Ministry*, Book iii. Chap. ii. p. 219. ed. Lindsay, Lond. 1734.) It is certain that Zadok was the heir of the line of Eleazar, the elder son of Aaron; (1 Chron. vi. 3—8: 50—53.) and consequently Abiathar, whom Solomon deposed in fulfilment of the Lord's denunciation against the house of Eli, was not the rightful High Priest, but he was of the family of Ithamar. (1 Chron. xxiv. 3.) The course of succession in the latter case was this: Eli, Phinehas, Ahitub, Ahimelech, Abiathar.]

than this text which he citeth, "Feed My sheep," to forbid them.

But here he will ask "whether a Christian King be Peter's sheep or no?" I answer, by propriety no; but a sheep of Christ's, as Peter is. Nevertheless, admit Peter to be a shepherd, and the King to be his sheep, what then? Forsooth it is against the law of nature for a sheep to rule his shepherd. I grant, in those things in which the one is shepherd, and the other a sheep. But I ask of him, is not a King also in some respect called in Scripture a shepherd? If he doubt, Esa. xliv. 28, and Jere. xxiii. 4. may resolve him. And is not Peter and Paul in this respect also sheep? If he deny it, let the Apostles speak for themselves: "Let every soul be subject," &c. Rom. xiii. If now I should reason that it is against the law of nature that the sheep should rule his shepherd, I am sure he would answer with making a diversity of respects. You may then see what a wise argument he hath made, that may be turned back on his own head. Wherefore here is no such impossibility as he inferreth; but that a King in some respect of ecclesiastical government may be above his own Pastor, as in other respect he is under him.

M. Sander will go forward for all this, and putteth [the] case that a Bishop should come to a Christian King, as Ambrose did (*Ep.* xxxiii.[1]) to Emperor Valentinian, offering his body and goods to his pleasure; but the thing which the Emperor unlawfully required he would not yield unto: what could the Emperor do to him? He could not excommunicate him: and if he imprisoned him, or put him to death, he did but as Nero or the Turk might do. "Therefore, if the King be never so much christened, he hath no power over the Bishop's soul." If it were possible for the Pope to require an unlawful thing, I might put the like case of his Holiness. What if a Christian man should come to him, &c., he might excommunicate him, as Caiphas did all that confessed Christ: he might imprison him, as Annas did the Apostles: he might command him to be smitten, as Pashur did Jeremy, and Ananias Paul, &c. Therefore, if he were never so much a Pope, he hath no power over a Christian man's soul. Mark the pith of M. Sander's arguments. But if Auxentius the heretic should have come to that Emperor, had the Emperor none authority

[1] [*Epistt.* Lib. ii. xiv. *Opp.* Tom. v. col. 209.]

to call a Synod to inquire of his heresy; and, he being found an heretic, to have condemned him therefore? In these doings he had done as Constantine about Arius and Donatus; and not as Nero with Peter and Paul.

But Ambrose his authority is cited, *Ep.* xxxii.[2]: *Si vel Scripturarum seriem*, &c.: "If we call to mind either the process of holy Scriptures, or the ancient times, who can deny but that in a cause of faith, in a cause I say of faith, Bishops are wont to judge of Emperors, not Emperors of Bishops?" And who saith the contrary, but that in causes of faith the Emperor is ordinarily to be instructed of the Bishops, and not the Bishops of the Emperor? or that the Prince hath absolute authority in matters of religion to do what he will? when we say that in all things he must follow the direction of God's word; the knowledge whereof, especially in difficult matters, he is to receive of the Ministers of the Church; as of the lawyers the knowledge of law, although he be bound to see justice executed.

But M. Sander will know how a King shall correct or depose a Bishop. I answer, if his crime be apparent, even as Salomon deposed Abiathar: if it be doubtful, by order of judgment and trial according; of civil Judges, if it be a civil crime; and ecclesiastical, if it be heresy that he is accused of. If he cannot be condemned upon just trial, he is to be absolved. If this will not satisfy the King, he hath no farther lawful authority by any Supremacy; and if he proceed further, he exerciseth tyranny. And Augustin doth justly complain of the importunity of the Donatists; which, when the cause had been decided by certain Bishops, deputed by the Emperor, they would never be satisfied; but still appealed to the Emperor, and "accused the Bishops that were appointed their judges before the earthly King." M. Sander urgeth that word vehemently, that he calleth Constantine "an earthly King:" and yet he is so blind that he will not see, that the same earthly King, which assigned those Bishops to be judges, was still acknowledged of all parts to be the supreme governor. *Ep.* xlviii.[3]

But omitting the words of men, he will prove the dignity of High Priests above faithful Princes by the authority of God in the Old Testament; Levit. iv: because there God assigneth

[2] [*Opp.* v. 204.] [3] [al. xciii. *Opp.* Tom. ii. col. 178.]

a sacrifice for the sin of every degree of men, according to their dignity: and first beginneth with the High Priest; next whom is the whole people; third the Prince; and last of all every private man. There is no doubt but the High Priest, as he was an image and figure of Christ, was chief in dignity: although in other respects he was inferior to the Prince; as Aaron was to Moses, Achitob or Achimelech to Samuel, Abiathar and Zadoc to David and Salomon. The like is confessed of every Minister of the Gospel: and therefore the authority of Philo and Theodoretus, which he useth in this point, might have been spared. And yet may a wicked Minister be deposed by a godly Prince. Abiathar, in the Temple, at the altar, in the holiest place, and sacrificing, was greater than Salomon: yet was he justly deposed by Salomon for his treason.

Master Sander chargeth us to affirm, that the evil life of a Bishop taketh away his authority: which he denieth to be so, as long as the Church doth tolerate and permit them in their places. Whereupon he concludeth, that though the Bishop of Rome have never so much abused his office, yet he cannot leese [lose] his primacy. Indeed the abuse of the man taketh not away the authority of the office: but if the office be perverted from the right use, and degenerated into an heathenish tyranny, as the Bishop of Rome's place hath been many hundred years; the name of a Bishop only, and that scarcely remaining; we justly affirm that such dignity as that see had by consent of men, it hath clean lost by abuse of their authority.

Moreover he saith it hath no colour of truth, that we affirm the Pope to govern, not as a Pastor, but to bear a sovereignty, as Princes of the world; and that he will shew by six differences, which he will consider in order.

1. First, no man succeedeth in that chair by right of inheritance. The like I may say of the German Emperor: therefore this is no difference.

2. Secondly, it is not obtained by right of battle, invasion, or otherwise, but by election. So is the Emperor at this day, only by election. And if Master Sander be not too impudent, he will not deny but there hath been bickering and intruding by force into that chair; and, that is worse, entering by simony, murder, treason, and devilish sorcery.

The third: neither child, nor woman, nor infidel, nor 3.
Catechumeni, can be chosen Bishop of Rome. No more can any such be chosen Emperor, by the golden Bull, and law of the election. And yet, seeing boys are made Cardinals, which be electors of the Pope, and eligible, there is none impossibility but a boy may be chosen Pope, as well as a woman hath been Pope; Joan I mean. John the XXIII.[1] was condemned in the Council of Constance[2] for an infidel, which denied the immortality of the soul.

The fourth: the election of the Bishop of Rome, as of all 4.
other Bishops, pertaineth only to ecclesiastical persons: a King may be chosen by the people without the Clergy. To this I say, that the Bishop of Rome was wont to be chosen as well by the people as by the Clergy: and so is the Emperor chosen by as many Bishops as civil Princes, except in case of equality of voices. Neither is the Clergy ever excluded in any lawful election of any King, where he is made by election.

The fifth: to omit the Bishop of Rome's temporal dominion, 5.
which he confesseth to be but accessory to his bishoprick, in his ecclesiastical government he useth not that force and power which worldly Princes do: he compelleth none, no not the Jews in Rome, to baptism. No more doth the Emperor. But what means useth he to depose Kings, and absolve their subjects from their oath of obedience, where he judgeth them for heretics? How maketh he wars, and setteth all the world in an uproar, to defend his usurped dignity and false doctrine? Doth he not by force compel Christians to his filthy idolatry, or else cruelly murdereth and tormenteth them?

The sixth: the Bishop of Rome (as Bishop) never punisheth 6.
them with the material sword which forsake his Church. No; but as Antichrist and a tyrant he imprisoneth them, hangeth them, drowneth them, burneth them: "not as a Bishop," saith M. Sander, "but as a temporal Prince and

[1] [In a note placed before the Acts of the Council of Constance, Joverius thus candidly accounts for the fact, that this Pope is sometimes styled John XXIII., and at other times XXIV.: "Varietas oritur ex Joanna illa Maguntina, quæ Joannes Anglicus dicta est; quæ a quibusdam in catalogo Pontificum recensetur post Joannem VII., imperante Lothario, ab aliis vero omittitur." (*Sanctiones Eccles.* Class. i. fol. 128, b. Paris. 1555.)]

[2] [Sess. xii. hab. an. 1415.]

lord; as Moses, being one of the Priests of our Lord, was also master of civil government." Behold, this deviser of differences at length maketh him a civil Prince and temporal lord, from whom he had laboured by so many differences to distinguish before.

But now lest you should espy his impudent conclusion, he draweth into a new controversy, whether Moses were a Priest. And first he will prove that Moses was a Priest by the Scripture, Psal. xcviii. [xcix.], where it is said, *Moses et Aaron in Sacerdotibus Ejus.* If he will not allow the Hebrew word *Cohanim* to signify Princes, as it doth in divers other places, yet saith not the Psalm that Moses and Aaron were both Priests, but that "among His Priests" they were such as "called upon His name," and were heard; and Samuel, who followeth in the same verse, confessed now by Master Sander to be a Levite, forgetting that before he made him High Priest.

But farther to prove that Moses was a Priest, he citeth Augustin, Hieronym, Gregor. Naz., Dionys., and Philo; but all to small purpose for his cause. It must needs be confessed that Moses, as all the Patriarchs before him in their families, was a Priest before the distinction of the two offices was made, when Aaron and his posterity only were chosen to be Priests, after which time he was no longer a Priest; neither did he any thing as a Priest, but as a Prophet, and as a Prince. But admit he were both a Prince and a Priest, yet he commanded Aaron as a Prince, and not as a Priest: for Aaron was High Priest, and therefore could have no Priest above him. By which it is inferred, that the office of a Prince is to command the High Priest; and so was it always practised by all godly Princes.

But Master Sander, returning to his last and least difference, affirmeth that the Bishop of Rome never condemneth any man for heresy or schism to corporal death in his own person, nor teacheth that they may be condemned of other ecclesiastical persons. But who understandeth not this mockery? For as well it may be said, The King never hangeth any man in his own person; therefore none are executed by his authority; as, The Pope never condemneth any to death in his own person; therefore he persuadeth not his religion with fire and sword. But will the Pope and the Bishop, that are so mild and gentle, suffer them whom they condemn for heresy to escape their hands before they have delivered them to death? O cruel and shameless hypocrites!

"Nevertheless," Master Sander saith, "they have power over men's souls by that which our Saviour said to Peter, 'To thee I will give the keys of the kingdom of heaven,' &c.; which words are derived to the Bishop of Rome by means of the chair of S. Peter." A strange kind of derivation never touched in the Scripture. "To which words the said Bishop referreth all his power: whereas worldly Princes appeal to the law of the Gospel neither in getting, nor governing, nor establishing their dominion and power." Mark well this English Anabaptist. Is not this the law of the Gospel, "There is no power but of God; and the powers that be are ordained of God," Rom. xiii. 1, for getting of dominion and power? And is not this the law of the Gospel for their governing; that governors are sent of God "for the punishment of evil doers, and for the praise of them that do well?" 1 Pet. ii. vers. 14. And for the establishing of their dominion, is not this the law of the Gospel, "Give unto Cæsar the things that belong to Cæsar?" Matthew xxii. verse 21. And again, we "must be subject of necessity; not only for fear, but even for conscience." Rom. xiii. verse 5.

As for the Pope's piety and lenity wherewith he ruleth, when all the world seeth how proudly and tyrannically he behaveth himself, it were folly to spend many words about it. As for his gentle terms of "Sons" and "Brethren," wherewith he saluteth Princes and Bishops, and the "Servant of the servants of God," which he calleth himself, [they] be simple and short clokes to hide his horrible presumption and tyranny; wherewith he not only most shamefully revileth most Christian Princes, as it appeareth in that traitorous Bull which came from him against our most gracious sovereign Lady, but also taketh upon him to depose them from their estate royal; usurping to himself the name of "Holiness," of "Head of the Church," &c., of Christ, of God Himself, and calleth Princes his "vassals," &c.; of which blasphemies his Canon Laws are stuffed full: and therefore it is too far in the day for M. Sander to make us think there is no difference between white and black, pride and humility, gentleness and cruelty, holiness and hypocrisy, faith and falsehood, vice and virtue.

THE THIRD CHAPTER.

SANDER. *Sander.* Of the divers senses which are in the holy Scripture; and namely about these words, "Upon this Rock I will build My Church;" and which is the most literal and proper sense of them.

FULKE. *Fulke.* To contend about the diversity of senses, it were to take up a new controversy. I admit that which Master Sander confesseth, the literal sense only to be of force to convince the adversary; and the literal sense not to be always according to the grammatical sound of the words, but according to the most plain meaning of the speaker. As when Christ sayeth to Peter, "To thee I will give the keys of the kingdom of heaven," He meaneth not material keys of iron, but authority in the kingdom of heaven; as keys are delivered by the master to his steward, but not as keys of a city are delivered; which betoken the giving of possession of that city, to be governed by him which receiveth the keys, (as Master Sander saith.) For that was no part of Christ's meaning, to resign the government of His Church to Peter; for such giving of keys is of the subjects to their superior: but to make him one of the stewards of His great house, to open and shut, according to His appointment. Otherwise, only Christ "hath the key of David, which openeth, and no man shutteth; and shutteth, and no man openeth." Apocalypse iii. verse 7.

Likewise when He saith, "Thou art Peter," I confess and agree with Master Sander, that the literal sense is not, Thou art a natural stone; but, Thou art that toward My Church which a stone is toward the house that is builded upon that stone: but so that Peter is not the only foundation, nor the corner-stone, which is only Christ, but one of the twelve stones of the foundation; as it may more plainly appear in the Apocalypse, the twenty-first chapter, and the fourteenth verse.

Furthermore I confess, that whatsoever by necessary conclusion may be gathered of any true literal sense is of equal authority with the word of God with that which is expressed in plain words: as the consubstantiality of Christ with God the Father, the blessed Trinity, and such-like. But whereas M. Sander joineth to these not only the perpetual virginity of the Virgin Mary, which is not certainly though probably to be gathered, but also Transubstantiation, the Sacrifice of the Mass, and Purgatory, against which the sense of the Scripture is manifest, I will not admit them for examples.

But to come to his purpose, he findeth in the ancient Fathers four divers senses of these words, "Upon this Rock I will build My Church[1]:" whereof three he rejecteth as unperfect, which have ancient writers, as he confesseth, for their authors; the last he hath no ancient writer to defend.

The first, that Christ is that Rock on whom the Church is builded; which Augustin holdeth.

The second, that every disciple of Christ is the Rock; which is Origen's opinion.

The third, that Peter's faith or confession is the Rock; which is Chrysostom's judgment.

The fourth, which is his own, and therefore he calleth it "the perfect sense," is, that Peter, concerning his office in God's Church, through the promise of Christ which is past, and the faithful confession of His Godhead which is presently made, and the power of feeding His sheep which then was to come, is this Rock upon which the Church is built. Here I wish the reader to note, that the Papist rejecteth three senses of three several ancient writers, and maketh the fourth himself; that you may see with what equity they exclaim against us, if upon never so good ground we depart from the interpretation of the ancient Fathers. But now let us see what reasons he hath to confute these three Doctors' opinions as insufficient interpretations.

First he sayeth, "If Augustin's sense were true, all the three other should be void." Indeed, his own sense, understanding Peter to be a singular Rock more than the other Apostles, is made void thereby, as it is false. But the other two may stand very well with Augustin's meaning: for he meaneth not Christ barely, but Christ whom Peter and every true disciple of faith confesseth to be the Rock of the Church. Neither doth the word "Thou" hinder this sense; seeing Augustin understandeth Peter to be a denominative *a Petra,* "of the stone:" nor the word "I will build;" for notwithstanding He

[1] [The various bearings of this declaration in S. Matth. xvi. 18 are accurately pointed out in note Q in the English translation of Tertullian's *Works,* Vol. i. Oxf. 1842. pp. 492—497.]

had begun to build His Church before, yet He would build still, and that more magnifical than before.

The sense of Origen he rejecteth as not literal; upon which I will not stand.

The sense of Chrysostom he refuseth, saying, "The faith of Peter is not the only Rock whereupon the Church shall be builded; for then it had been built upon the faith of John Baptist before this time." A pithy argument; as though there is any more than "one faith," Ephesians iv. verse 5, which is the same in Peter and in John, and in all the other Apostles; the same, I say, in kind, not in number. Neither did Chrysostom mean that the singular faith of Peter were the Rock of the Church; but the same one faith and confession embraced of every member thereof.

That He sayeth "I will build," whereas He had already begun to build, and did then presently build, what inconvenience is it, but in a quarreller's mind? He speaketh of the future tenses, to signify the great amplification of His Church which He would make by the preaching of the Apostles.

But of all senses Master Sander liketh his own best, as perfect, and containing all the other therein. For first, saith he, "If Peter be the Rock, then Christ that made him is much more, as the Giver and Author of his power." But I deny that Christ did give the same that He is Himself; that is, to be the only singular foundation, Rock, and corner-stone of His Church.

Secondly, he saith, "If Peter in respect of his confession be a Rock, then his confession is a Rock." But then say I, they that make the same confession are as much a Rock as he.

Thirdly, he saith, "If Peter, being captain-disciple of all that ever were, be a Rock, then all other disciples that are contained in him as in the chief may also be this Rock." Who had thought Peter had been such an universal thing to contain all disciples in him? Doth not this contain manifest blasphemy, to make all disciples contained in Peter; which are contained only in Christ, as the members in their mystical body, whereof He only is chief Head, Sovereign, Captain, or what other name of superiority can be devised?

But now that he hath made such a monstrous jumbling of three opinions in one, he is not ashamed to charge Master Jewell for leaving the most literal sense, and mingling three opinions of these four in one; as though his sense, which is farthest off from the meaning of Christ, were the only or most literal sense. But seeing he wisheth Master Jewell or any of us to discuss the meaning of Christ particularly with all circumstances, for my part, considering all circumstances, I think the most simple and plain meaning of Christ is, that Peter is a Rock or stone upon which the Church is builded; but none otherwise than every one of the Apostles is, Ephe. ii. and 20 verse, and in the Apocalypse, the xxi. chapter, and 14 verse: of which M. Sander also confesseth every one to be a Rock in his kind.

But now let us see the five circumstances by which Master Sander will prove Peter for to be such a Rock as none of all the rest of the Apostles is but he.

The first: Christ promised Simon, before he confessed, that he should "be called Peter;" which was the first cause of being the Rock. John i. Admit this to be a promise, and not an imposition of a name, in respect of the gifts of fortitude and constancy wherewith He would endue him, this proveth him not to be a singular Rock.

The second: he was named Peter before he confessed; which was the performance of the promise, Mark iii. I doubt not but that he had confessed Christ before he was made an Apostle, although he had not made that solemn confession expressed in Matthew xvi. Wherefore this circumstance is a frivolous argument. And his brother Andrew, which first brought him to Christ, confessed Jesus to be the Messias before Peter was come to Christ.

The third: when he had confessed the Godhead of Christ, which was the fruit of the gift and of the promise, Christ pronounced him to be such a Rock whereupon He would build His Church; which was the reward of his confession. But all the Apostles made the same confession: therefore the same reward was given to all, that they should every one be a Rock or stone on which the Church should be builded.

The fourth: Christ prayed that Peter's faith might not fail; which was the warrant of the perpetuity of his strong confession. Luke xxii. Christ prayed for all His Apostles, Joan. xvii. The special prayer for Peter was in respect of his greater weakness when he was left to himself.

The last: to shew what strength Peter should give to his

brethren after his conversion, Christ bade him feed His lambs: whereby he was made such a Rock, whereby He should stay up His Church, by teaching and ruling the faithful, as whose voice the sheep should be bound to hear in pain of damnation. First I answer, that the strength or confirmation which he should give to his brethren was not all one with his feeding of the lambs; but was used to the strengthening of his weak brethren, the rest of the Apostles, whom after his marvellous conversion he did mightily confirm, though in his fall he was shewed to be the weakest of all. Then I say, the feeding of the sheep of Christ was committed to him with the rest of the Apostles; in which he had no prerogative of auctority given, but an earnest charge to shew his greater love by greater diligence in his office. So that hitherto Peter is none otherwise a Rock than every one of the Apostles is.

THE FOURTH CHAPTER.

SANDER. *Sander.* Divers reasons are alleged to prove (chiefly by the circumstance and conference of holy Scripture) that these words, "Thou art Peter; and upon this Rock I will build My Church," have this literal meaning: Upon thee, O Peter, being first made a Rock, to the end thou shouldest stoutly confess the faith, and so confessing it, I will build My Church. The promise to be called Peter was the first cause. Why the Church was built upon him, the Protestants cannot tell. Which is the first literal sense of these words, "Upon this Rock will I build My Church."

FULKE. *Fulke.* First it is to be remembered, that M. Sander, in the chapter before, rejecting the interpretation of three of the greatest Doctors of the Church, Origen, Augustin, and Chrysostom, not only is bound in equity to give us the same liberty which he taketh himself, but also to confess that these three principal Doctors, following other senses than his, were ignorant of that which he and all other Papists make to be the chief article of Christian faith; namely, of the Supremacy of Peter, when they acknowledged not Peter to be the Rock whereupon Christ would build His Church; and therefore would never have subscribed to his book, which he instituteth [intituleth] *The Rock of the Church.*

But now to the argument of this chapter. Chrysostom is cited to prove, that where Christ saith to Peter, "Thou art Simon the son of Jona: thou shalt be called Cepha, which is by interpretation Peter," a new name is promised to Simon. *In Joan. Hom.* xviii.[1] *Honorifice,* &c.: "Christ doth fore-speak honourably of him: for the certain foretelling of things to come is the work only of the immortal God. It is to be noted, that Christ did not foretell at this first meeting all things which should come to pass afterward to him. For He did not call him Peter; neither did He say, 'Upon this Rock will I build My Church;' but He said, 'Thou shalt be called Cephas.' For that was both of more power, and also of more auctority." There is nothing in this sentence but that we may willingly admit. Peter was not yet instructed, that he might be one of the twelve foundations of the Church, as he was afterward. And that Chrysostom judged no singular thing to be granted by that saying of Christ, Matt. xvi., to Peter, appeareth by his words, *in Evang. Joann. Præf.*[2], where he applieth the same to John: *Tonitrui enim filius est Christo dilectissimus, columna omnium quæ in orbe sunt Ecclesiarum, qui cœli claves habet:* "For the son of thunder is most beloved of Christ, being a pillar of all the Churches which are in the world, which hath the keys of heaven."

Neither doth Cyrillus, whom he citeth, make any thing for his purpose. *In Joan.* Lib. ii. Cap. xii.[3] *Nec Simon,* &c.: "And He telleth aforehand that his name shall be Peter, and not now Simon: by the very word signifying that He would build His Church on him, as on a Rock and most sure stone." These are the words of Cyrillus; but that he meaneth not his person, but his faith, he sheweth manifestly in his book *de Trinit.* Lib. iv.[4], speaking upon the text

[1] [*Opp.* Tom. viii. p. 112. ed. Ben.]

[2] [*In S. Joan. Hom.* i. Opp. viii. 2.]

[3] [fol. 36, b. Paris. 1508. Sanders certainly used the translation of S. Cyril's Commentary by Georgius Trapezuntius. This volume is remarkable for the extraordinary insertion of four intermediate books, from five to eight inclusive, which were written by Judocus Clichtoveus, who is consequently styled by Cave "maleferiatus iste nebulo." (*Hist. Lit.* i. 392. Oxon. 1740.) Clichtoveus, however, has been most unjustly accused of forgery, for he used much precaution to prevent mistake: but the result of his attempt to supply the deficiency, in order, as he said, to render the work "uniforme et continuum," has shewn that Dr. James's apprehension of "great danger" was not without foundation." (*Bastardie of the false Fathers*, p. 67.)]

[4] [ad init.]

of Matth. xvi., the ground of M. Sander's book: *Petram opinor per agnominationem nihil aliud quam inconcussam et firmissimam Discipuli fidem vocavit; in qua Ecclesia Christi ita firmata et fundata esset ut non laberetur:* "I think he called a Rock by denomination nothing else but the most unmoveable and steadfast faith of that Disciple; on which the Church of Christ should be so established and founded that it should not fall." Here is another principal Doctor joining with Chrysostom against M. Sander, who affirmeth that the Rock is nothing else but Peter's faith.

After these he nameth Theophylact[1] and Euthymius, two late writers, but he citeth nothing out of them presently. But after shewing the force of God's promise to be effectual to work all means necessary for the performance of it, he citeth out of Euthymius, *in Luke* vi.[2], that it was like that in John i. Christ promised that Simon should be called Peter, and in Luke vi. [Mark iii.] called him Peter. All this needed not: we doubt not but Simon was called Peter. Yea, but Cyrillus saith, *in Joan.* Lib. xii. Cap. lxiv.[3], that "he, being Prince and head, first cried out, saying, 'Thou art Christ, the Son,'" &c.: therefore he was head, before his confession, by promise and name. I will not here say how contrary M. Sander is to himself, which in the Cap. iii. said that his Supremacy was granted to him as a reward of his confession; but I will answer Cyrillus by himself, *in Joan.* Lib. iv. Cap. xxviii.[4], that Peter was *ordine major*, "superior in order," to avoid confusion; not in degree, dignity, or auctority.

And whereas M. Sander urgeth so vehemently, that the name of Peter was not given for his confession, but was singular to him by promise; so that it belonged literally to no Prophet, Apostle, nor Disciple, but only to him and his successors; it is a most fond and frivolous matter: for the name of Bonarges was specially given to the sons of Zebedee in respect of their excellent gifts, and at the same time that the name of Peter was given to Simon: which seeing it pertaineth not to their successors which have not the same gifts, no more doth the name and dignity of Peter pertain to any that sit in his chair; if ever he had any fixed chair among the Gentiles, which by God's ordinance was

1 [*Comment. in S. Joan.* Cap. i. p. 580. Lut. Paris. 1635.]
2 [*In S. Marc.* iii. 16. *Comm.* ii. 50. Lips. 1792.]
3 [fol. 219, b. ed. Lat. sup. cit.]
4 [fol. 101.]

appointed to be the principal Apostle of the Jews. Moreover, where he laboureth tooth and nail to prove that these words, "Upon this Rock I will build My Church," are to be referred to Peter, as I said before, I will grant even as much. But that Peter by these words was made a singular Rock, more than all the Apostles, upon which the whole Church is builded, I utterly deny; neither shall he be ever able to prove it. For it is an impudent lie, "that only Peter at this time had this high revelation, to acknowledge Christ to be the Son of God:" for he answered in the name of all the rest, who believed the same which he in their name confessed. Did not Andrew before Peter acknowledge Him to be the Messias? Did not Nathanael, which was none of the Apostles, acknowledge Him to be "the Son of God," and "the King of Israel?" Joan. i. 49.

But he reasoneth substantially when he saith, "Thou only art the Rock, because thou alone hadst this name, &c., promised; thou alone hadst it given; thou alone didst confess Me; and to thee alone I say, 'Thou art Peter;'" as though a man may not have a name whose signification is common to many. Salomon alone was promised to be called, and was called, Jedidiah; that is, the beloved of God. Shall we therefore reason that Salomon only was beloved of God? As for that he only confessed, I have shewed before that it is false: for Christ, saying "Thou art Peter," meaneth not to say Thou only art a Rock; but Thou well answerest thy name, which signifieth a Rock or stone; and I will indeed use thee as a Rock or stone to build My Church upon: yet not meaning the person, but the office and doctrine of his Apostleship.

But now hath M. Sander no less than twenty-one reasons to prove that Peter is the Rock here spoken of; which although they may for the most part be easily avoided, yet I will grant that Peter is one of the twelve stones whereupon the Church is builded, but not the only stone.

Therefore his first four arguments I deny. First, Simon is alone promised to be called Peter. Second, he alone is called Peter. Third, Christ speaketh to him alone, saying, "And I say to thee," &c. Fourth, Christ saith of him alone, "Thou art Peter." Therefore Simon alone is the Rock of the Church. Let him prove the consequence if he can. The next five, which prove that these words are to be referred to Peter, although that they be not very strong, yet I grant the words may be aptly referred to Peter. The reasons are: first, upon the pronoun: the second, the word "Rock" of which Peter is named: third, the conference of them together: fourth, the word "I will build:" fifth, the word "My Church."

The tenth argument I deny; that Christ, by saying to Peter, "Feed My lambs," "Feed My sheep," made him the head-stone of God's militant Church, next unto Christ.

The eleventh, that Peter is shewed to be the Rock spoken of by giving of the keys, I confess: but seeing the keys are given to all the Apostles, this proveth Peter to be none otherwise a Rock than every one of them. That John received the keys I shewed even now out of Chrysostom.

The twelfth, that the property of a Rock in constant withstanding of tempests agreeth with Peter, I grant: and so it doth to the rest of the Apostles, for whom Christ prayed as He did for Peter; who also strengthened and confirmed their brethren as Peter did.

The thirteenth: I confess that hell-gates shall not prevail against the Church, nor against any member thereof; which is a small reason to make Peter supreme head thereof.

The fourteenth, which is the authorities of those Doctors that teach Peter to be the Rock, whom he nameth, when he citeth their sayings, or quoteth their places, I will severally consider.

The fifteenth: their reasons also, when I see them, to derive Peter's authority to his successors, I will weigh likewise.

The sixteenth, the practice of fifteen hundred years, I deny.

The seventeenth: I deny that all General Councils, or any General Council for six hundred years after Christ, acknowledged Peter to be the Rock in that sense the Papists do now.

The eighteenth: if the confession of Peter be the Rock, yet it is none inconvenience that the Church should be builded thereon, which began to be builded on the same confession offered by John Baptist.

The nineteenth: though you confound the divers senses given by the Fathers in your fourth sense, yet that proveth not your sense to be true.

The twentieth: seeing the Apostles are certain foundations and Rocks upon which the Church is builded, I confess that Peter must needs be one: but that he was the most principal

Rock in respect of his name Peter, which is "a stone," I say it followeth no more than that Salomon was best of all men beloved of God because of that name Jedidiah, which signifieth "beloved of God."

The twenty-first: that all the Protestants do not agree in the interpretation of these words, "Upon this Rock I will build My Church," it proveth not your exposition to be true: for neither do all the old Doctors, nor yet the new Papists, agree in one and the same interpretation of this text. And oftentimes it may invincibly be proved, that an heresy hath no ground out of such a text of Scripture, although the true and natural sense thereof cannot be found at all.

THE FIFTH CHAPTER.

Sander. It is proved out of the ancient Fathers, that S. Peter is this Rock whereupon the Church was promised to be builded, otherwise than M. Jewell affirmeth. SANDER.

Fulke. That Peter was a Rock or stone upon which the Church was builded is granted of us; but that he alone was a Rock for the whole Church to be builded upon we deny: and M. Jewell[1] rightly affirmeth, that the old Catholic Fathers have written and pronounced not any mortal man, as Peter was, but Christ Himself the Son of God, to be this Rock whereon the whole Church is builded. But M. Sander will prove (if he can) out of the old writers, that not only Christ is the chief Rock, but Peter also is another Rock; so that the Church, by his doctrine, is builded upon two Rocks. And this he will shew, first, by their words; secondly, their reasons; thirdly, and by the same places which M. Jewell allegeth for the contrary opinion. FULKE.

The decretal Epistles of Anacletus, Pius, Fabianus, &c., which in his own conscience he knoweth to be forged[2], he omitteth, and beginneth with Tertullian, *De Præscrip. advers. Hæres.*[3]:

[1] [*Reply to Harding's Answer*, Art. iv. Works, Part i. p. 340. ed. Parker Soc.]

[2] [Sanders nevertheless asserts, that testimonies from them are "most unjustly rejected of the Protestants." (*Rocke of the Churche*, p. 139.)]

[3] [Cap. xxii. *Opp.* p. 209.]

Latuit aliquid Petrum, ædificandæ Ecclesiæ Petram dictum? "Was any thing hid from Peter, which was called a Rock of the Church which was to be builded?" This is granted, that he was a Rock or stone whereon the Church is builded: and the same Tertullian, in his book *de Pudicitia*[1], saith of this whole text, that this was conferred to Peter personally; and pertaineth to none other but such as he was, namely, an Apostle or Prophet: *Secundum enim Petri personam spiritualibus potestas ista conveniet, aut Apostolo aut Prophetæ:* "For according to the person of Peter this power shall belong to spiritual men, either to an Apostle or to a Prophet." Where is then the succession of the Bishop of Rome?

But Hippolytus saith: *Princeps Petrus, fidei Petra*[2]*:* "Peter is chief, a Rock of faith." He meaneth a strong preacher of faith; not a Rock whereon faith is builded.

Origenes, *in Exod. Ho.* v.[3], calleth S. Peter *Magnum illud*, &c.: "that great foundation and most sound Rock, whereupon Christ hath builded His Church." But let Origenes expound himself: *In Matth.* Cap. xvi.[4]: *Si autem super unum illum Petrum arbitraris universam Ecclesiam ædificari a Deo, quid dicis de Jacobo et Joanne, filiis tonitrui, vel de singulis Apostolis? Vere ergo ad Petrum quidem dictum est, Tu es Petrus; et super hanc Petram ædificabo Ecclesiam Meam; et portæ inferorum non prævalebunt ei: tamen omnibus Apostolis, et omnibus quibusque perfectis fidelibus, dictum videtur, quoniam omnes sunt Petrus et Petræ; et in omnibus ædificata est Ecclesia Christi; et adversus nullum*

[1] [Cap. xxi. *Opp.* 574. In this place Tertullian, then a Montanist, denies the transmission of the power of binding and loosing.]

[2] [These words (alleged by Baronius also, ad an. xxxi. num. xxvii.) are found in the tenth section of the spurious tract *De consummatione Mundi*, according to the version by Joannes Picus. Aubertus Miræus has wrongly distinguished this treatise from the *Homilia de Christo et Antichristo;* (Schol. in S. Hieron. *Lib. de Viris illust.* Cap. lxi.) and it is strange that its genuineness should have been maintained by Bishop Bull. (*Defens. Fid. Nic.* Sect. iii. Cap. viii. §. 4. *Opp.* p. 220. Lond. 1703.) See Todd's *Discourses on the Prophecies relating to Antichrist*, i. 218. Dubl. 1840.]

[3] [*Opp.* Tom. ii. edit. Ben. Paris. 1733. Berington and Kirk's *Faith of Catholics*, p. 157. Lond. 1813: pp. 139—40. Ib. 1830.]

[4] [Vid. Origenis *Commentaria*, ed. Huet. Par. i. p. 275. Rothom. 1668.]

eorum qui tales sunt portæ prævalent inferorum: "But if thou think the whole Church is builded by God upon that one man Peter, what sayest thou of James and John, the sons of thunder, or of every one of the Apostles? Therefore it was indeed truly said unto Peter, 'Thou art Peter; and upon this Rock I will build My Church; and the gates of hell shall not prevail against it:' yet it seemeth that it was spoken also to all the Apostles, and to all the perfect faithful, because they are all Peter and stones; and on them all the Church of Christ is builded; and against none of them which are such the gates of hell shall prevail." By this you see how Origen is none of his, howsoever he abuse his name.

Next he citeth Cyprian, Lib. i. *Ep.* iii.[5] & Lib. iv. *Ep.* ix.[6], which sayeth that the Church was builded upon Peter: which we confess, as upon one of the foundation-stones. But the same Cyprian, *De simplicitate Prælatorum*[7], saith: *Hoc erant utique et cæteri Apostoli quod fuit Petrus; pari consortio præditi et honoris et potestatis: sed exordium ab unitate proficiscitur, ut Ecclesia una monstretur:* "The rest of the Apostles were even the same thing that Peter was; endued with equal fellowship both of honour and auctority: but the beginning proceedeth from one, that the Church might be shewed to be one." This speaketh Cyprian upon the very text now in discussing.

Consequently he citeth Hilary, Lib. vi. *de Trinit.*[8], *Petrus,* &c.: "Peter lieth under the building of the Church:" and *in* Cap. *Matth.* xvi.[9]: *O in nuncupatione,* &c.: "O happy foundation of the Church in having the new name pronounced!

5 [al. *Ep.* lix. *Opp.* p. 131. ed. Fell.]

6 [*Epist.* lxvi. p. 168.]

7 [vel *De unitate Ecclesiæ,* Opp. pp. 107—8. edit. Oxon. 1682. One of the most glaring depravations ever attempted by Romanists has been exhibited in this treatise. (See the *Conference betwene Rainoldes and Hart,* pp. 210—17. Lond. 1584. Bilson's *True Difference,* pp. 65, 66. Oxf. 1585. *Cyprianus redivivus,* by Dr. James, at the end of his *Ecloga Oxonio-Cantab.* Lib. ii. p. 117. Lond. 1600; and *Corruption of the true Fathers,* pp. 1—32. Ib. 1611.) In the sentence cited by Fulke, after the word "proficiscitur," the clause "Primatus Petro datur" was inserted; and after "Ecclesia una," the text was further interpolated by the addition of "et Cathedra una."]

8 [§. 20. *Opp.* col. 891. ed. Bened.]

9 [num. 7. col. 690.]

and O Rock, worthy of the building of that Church which should dissolve the laws of hell!" But the same Hilary sayeth of Christ, *De Trinit.* Lib. ii.[1]: *Una hæc est felix fidei Petra, Petri ore confessa, Tu es Filius Dei vivi:* "This is that only happy Rock of faith, confessed by the mouth of Peter, 'Thou art the Son of the living God.'" And again, Lib. vi.[2]: *Super hanc igitur confessionis Petram Ecclesiæ ædificatio est:* "Upon this Rock of confession is the building of the Church." And again[3]: *Hæc fides Ecclesiæ fundamentum est. Per hanc fidem infirmæ* [al. *infirmes*] *adversus eam sunt portæ inferorum. Hæc fides regni cœlestis habet claves,* &c.: "This faith is the foundation of the Church. By this faith the gates of hell are of no force against it. This faith hath the keys of the kingdom of heaven," &c. Therefore not the person of Peter is the Rock for all the Church to be built upon.

S. Ambrose hath the next place, whom he citeth, *Ser.* lxvi.[4]: *Si ergo,* &c.: "If Peter then be a Rock upon which the Church is builded, he doth well to heal first the feet; that even as he doth contain the foundation of faith in the Church, so in the man he may confirm the foundation of his members." Of the auctority of this Sermon I will not dispute[5]. It shall suffice that Ambrose, *in Ps.* xxxviii.[6], saith: *Quod Petro dicitur, Apostolis dicitur. Non potestatem usurpamus, sed servimus imperio:* "That which is said to Peter is said to the Apostles. We usurp not power, but we serve under commandment." By this saying of Ambrose, Peter is so a Rock and foundation as the other Apostles are; and not a Rock to bear all the building himself.

S. Basil is alleged, *in Conc. de Pœnit.*[7]: *Petrus Petra est,* &c.: "Peter is a Rock through Christ the Rock. For Jesus giveth His own dignities: He is a Rock, and maketh a Rock."

[1] [n. 23. c. 800.]
[2] [§. 36. col. 903.] [3] [num. 37. c. 904.]
[4] [The passage adduced by Sanders occurs in *Sermo* xi. *in Festo SS. Apostolorum Petri et Pauli:* S. Ambros. Opp. Tom. v. col. 141. Lut. Paris. 1661.]
[5] [Its authenticity, however, cannot be so easily admitted. It is contained in the Appendix to the fifth tome of S. Augustin's works, (col. 237. ed. Bened.) where it is numbered *Sermo* cci., olim xxvi., *de Sanctis.*]
[6] [*Opp.* ii. 744.] [7] [*Opera Græca,* p. 244. Basil. 1551.]

This proveth not Peter to be the only Rock of the militant Church, as M. Sander would make him.

After him he citeth Hierom, *in* xvi. *Matth.*[8]*: Ædificabo Ecclesiam Meam super te:* "I will build My Church upon thee." "Behold," saith M. Sander, "the Church promised to be built upon a mortal man." If he say true, Christ saith in vain that "flesh and blood" made him not Peter. But the same Hieronym interpreteth that power, there given to Peter, to pertain to every Bishop and Priest as much as to Peter: and, *Contra Jovinian.* Lib. i.[9], he writeth: *At dicis, Super Petrum fundatur Ecclesia; licet id ipsum in alio loco super omnes Apostolos fiat, et cuncti claves regni cœlorum accipiant, et ex æquo super eos Ecclesiæ fortitudo solidetur: tamen propterea inter duodecim unus eligitur, ut, capite constituto, schismatis tollatur occasio:* "But thou sayest, The Church is founded upon Peter; although in another place the same is done upon all the Apostles, and they all received the keys of the kingdom of heaven, and the strength of the Church is grounded equally upon them: yet for this cause one is chosen among the twelve, that, the head being appointed, occasion of division might be taken away." You see now that Peter is no more a Rock or foundation than the rest; neither hath any more auctority of the keys than the rest; although, by his judgment, he was chosen to be the chief or first in order, to avoid strife; not in dignity, or auctority.

Chrysostom is cited, *ex var. in Matth.* [*locis,*] *Hom.* xxvii.[10]: *Princeps,* &c.: "Peter, Prince of the Apostles, upon whom

[8] [*Opp.* Tom. ix. p. 49.] [9] [*Opp.* T. ii. p. 35.]

[10] [The words cited by Sanders (p. 143.) are these: "Princeps Apostolorum Petrus, super quem Christus fundavit Ecclesiam, vere immobilis Petra, et firma confessio;" and they are to be met with in a work which is not genuine. (See Jewel, Vol. iii. pp. 98, 463: v. 156. ed. Jelf, Oxf. 1848.) Nothing can be more evident than S. Chrysostom's denial that the Church was founded upon S. Peter's *person;* for the language of this "Prince of interpreters" is: "*τῇ πέτρᾳ . . . τουτέστι, τῇ πίστει τῆς ὁμολογίας.*" (*In S. Matth. Hom.* liv. Opp. Tom. vii. p. 548. ed. Ben. Compare Barrow, *Of the Pope's Supremacy,* p. 87. Lond. 1680.) In the Homily *upon S. Peter and Elias,* the authenticity of which is most uncertain, the following passage may be seen: "Petrum illum, Apostolorum Coryphæum, fundamentum immobile, Petram quæ frangi nequit, Ecclesiæ Principem," &c.; (*Opp.* ii. 731.) and the spurious Sermon *De negatione Petri* contains the expressions "Princeps Apostolorum," "Petram Ecclesiæ," &c. (*Opp.* viii. ii. 138.

Christ founded the Church, a very immoveable Rock, and a strong confession." M. Sander would have us note that Peter is called "confession;" that when he saith the Church is builded upon faith and confession, we might understand no man's faith and confession but Peter's; as though all the Apostles had not the same faith, and made not the same confession. But notwithstanding that Chrysostom doth often acknowledge Peter to be the Prince of the Apostles, yet he willeth us to consider that his principality was not of auctority, but of order: *Jam et illud considera, quam et Petrus agit omnia ex communi Discipulorum sententia; nihil auctoritate sua, nihil cum imperio:* "Now also consider this, how even Peter doth all things by the common decree of the Disciples; nothing by his own auctority, nothing by commandment." *Ex.* [*In*] *Act. Ho.* iii.[1] Also, *in* ii. *ad Gal.*[2], he doth not only affirm that Paul was equal in honour with Peter, but also that all the rest were of equal dignity: *Jamque se cæteris honore parem ostendit; nec se reliquis illis, sed ipsi summo*[3] *comparat; declarans quod horum unusquisque parem sortitus sit dignitatem:* "And now Paul sheweth himself equal in honour with the rest; neither doth he compare himself with the rest, but even with the highest himself; declaring that every one of them hath obtained equal dignity."

Now followeth Epiphanius, *in Anchor.*[4]*: Ipse Dominus,* &c.: "The Lord Himself did constitute him chief of the Apostles; a sure Rock upon which the Church of God is built; and the gates of hell shall not prevail against it. Now the gates of hell are heresies and auctors of heresies. For by

Conf. pag. 9.) Barrow (ubi sup.) has inadvertently adduced an extract from the first fictitious *Sermo in Pentecosten:* (Opp. iii. 790.) and with respect to the Power of the keys, when S. Chrysostom had stated that it was granted not to S. Peter only, but to the rest of the Apostles, the Jesuit Petrus Possinus has taken care to add the surreptitious words "successoribusque suis." (*Catena Græcorum Patrum* in S. Matth. Tom. i. p. 232. Cf. Barlow's *Brutum Fulmen,* pp. 79—80. Lond. 1681.)]

[1] [*Opp.* Tom. ix. p. 23.] [2] [Tom. x. pp. 684—5.]

[3] ["Coryphæo;" which is the term employed by some of the Fathers, when they attribute to S. Peter a primacy of order.]

[4] [§. ix. *Opp.* Tom. ii. p. 14. Paris. 1622. There is nothing in the original equivalent to the words "*Ipse Dominus constituit eum,*" which Sanders has quoted, following the version by Janus Cornarius. p. 364. Basil. 1578.]

all means faith in him was established, which received the key of heaven." That Peter was chief of the Apostles in order we strive not: that he was a sure Rock we grant: but that he alone was the Rock of the Church we deny. The same Epiphanius acknowledgeth the Bishop of Rome to be fellow-minister with every Bishop, and no better; and therefore, setting forth the Epistle of Marcellus to Julius Bishop of Rome[5], he giveth this superscription: *Beatissimo comministro Julio, Marcellus in Domino gaudium:* "To his most blessed fellow-minister Julius, Marcellus wisheth joy in the Lord."

The place of Cyrillus which followeth I have set down and answered in the chapter before.

After him Theodoretus[6] allegeth Psellus: *In Petro,* &c.: "In Peter, the Prince of the Apostles, our Lord in the Gospels hath promised that He will build His Church." Damascen[7] and Euthymius[8], later writers, are alleged to the like effect. All which prove nothing but that Peter is a Rock, which we confess; as every one of the Apostles is.

Then followeth Augustin in his Retractations[9]; which leaveth it to the choice of the reader, whether he will understand Peter, figuring the person of the Church, to be the Rock spoken of by Christ, or Christ whom he confessed. But that Peter, as Bishop of Rome, should be the Rock, he saith nothing. Again, leaving it to the reader's choice, he sheweth he had no such persuasion of the Rock of the Church as M. Sander teacheth.

5 [*Hæres.* lxxii. Opp. p. 271. ed. Cornar.]

6 [*In Cantic. Canticorum:* Opp. Tom. i. p. 349. Colon. Agripp. 1573. The genuineness of this Commentary is doubted by many critics. Vid. Cavei *Hist. Lit.* i. 407. Oxon. 1740. Fabricii *Biblioth. Græc.* Vol. viii. p. 283. Hamb. 1802. *Acta Eruditorum,* Supplem. Tom. ii. Lipsiæ, 1696. p. 418.]

7 [Sanders has alleged the *Historia SS. Barlaami et Josaphati,* of which Raynaud remarks that "supposita videtur." (*Erotemata,* p. 137. Lugd. 1653.) It is true that the Roman Martyrology (die Novemb. 27.) ascribes the work to Damascen; but Raderus maintains that Joannes Sabaita was the author. See his Isagoge to the *Scala Paradisi* of Climacus, sig. e ij. Lut. Paris. 1633. Cf. Fabricii *Bibl. Eccles.* ad Sigeb. Gemblac. Cap. 75. p. 102. Hamb. 1718.]

8 [Vid. Euthymii Zigabeni *Comment. in Evangel.* Tom. i. P. ii. p. 650. Lipsiæ, 1792.]

9 [Lib. i. Cap. xxi. *Opp.* Tom. i. col. 23.]

After him Prosper Aquitanicus, and Leo with Gregory, two Bishops of Rome, say nothing but that Peter was a Rock; which we grant without controversy.

Last of all the Council of Chalcedon is cited, *Act.* iii.[1]: *Petrus Apostolus est Petra et crepido Ecclesiæ:* "Peter the Apostle is a Rock and a shore[2] of the Church;" which M. Sander translateth "the top of the Church." Indeed the Legates of the Bishop of Rome uttered such words; which may be well understood, as all the rest of the Fathers, that Peter was one of the twelve foundations of the Church. But that the Council acknowledged not the Bishop of Rome to have such authority as is pretended, appeareth by the sixteenth Action of the Chalcedon Council[3]; where, notwithstanding the Bishop of Rome's Legates[4] reclaimed, and Leo himself refused to consent, yet by the whole Council it was determined that

[1] [*Concill. Gen.* Tom. ii. p. 244. Romæ, 1609.]

[2] [Or support. The word is "κρηπὶς," *fundamentum.*]

[3] [*Concilia Generalia*, ii. 420. Dionysius Exiguus has not inserted the twenty-eighth Canon of this Council in his *Codex*, (p. 133. ed. Lut. Paris. 1609.) lest he should injure the papal assumption of pre-eminence. Gratian has attempted to accomplish his purpose in another way, viz. by shameless corruption of the text: for whereas in the original we find "ὁρίζομεν," "*definimus*," he has adopted the term "*petimus*." Instead of "*senior* Roma," the rendering of "πρεσβυτέρα Ῥώμη," he has "*superior* Roma." Thirdly, in order to depress Constantinople, which, according to the Decree, was to have "ἶσα πρεσβεῖα," "*æqualia* privilegia," with Rome, Gratian introduces the word "*similia*:" and lastly, in direct opposition to the Canon which ordains, "καὶ ἐν τοῖς ἐκκλησιαστικοῖς," that "*even in* ecclesiastical matters" Constantinople should be honoured like imperial Rome, he boldly puts forward the reading "*non tamen* in ecclesiasticis rebus." (*Dist.* xxii. Canon *Renovantes*, Cap. vi.)]

[4] [Petrus de Marca, Abp. of Paris, (*De concord. Sacerd. & Imper.* Tom. ii. p. 29. Par. 1669.) has pointed out a memorable instance of falsification in the "Sententia" of the papal Legate Paschasinus. The words "Caput universalis Ecclesiæ," applied to Pope Leo, and also the expressions "Petri Apostoli præditus dignitate," are not to be found in the Greek. Compare the passage as given by Crabbe, (*Concill.* i. 945. Colon. Agr. 1551.) in what he calls the "Epistola Paschasini et aliorum," with his own Latin text of the third Act of the Chalcedonian Council; (p. 847.) and also the "Exemplar Sententiæ," transmitted by S. Leo to the Bishops of France, (*Opp.* i. 301. Lugd. 1700.) with the original Greek in Sirmondus (*Concill.* ii. 244.) and Binius. (Tom. ii. P. i. p. 192.)]

the Archbishop of Constantinople should have equal authority with the Archbishop of Rome in the East; only the title of priority or seniority reserved to the Bishop of Rome[5].

To conclude, M. Jewell said truly, for all M. Sander's vain and childish insulting and impudent railing, that no mortal man, but Christ only, is the Rock and foundation of the Church: albeit that Peter and all the Apostles, in respect of their office and doctrine, were foundation-stones whereon the Church was builded; Jesus Christ being the corner-stone, and only one general foundation.

THE SIXTH CHAPTER.

Sander. The divers reasons which the Fathers bring to declare why S. Peter was this Rock do evidently shew, that he was most literally this Rock, whereupon Christ would build His Church. How Peter beareth the person of the Church. SANDER.

Fulke. That he was a Stone or Rock whereon the Church is builded hath been often granted; but that he only was such a Stone is still denied. First, Basil, *adversus Euno.* Lib. ii.[6], is cited, with his reason: *Petrus,* &c.: "Peter received the building of the Church upon himself, for the excellency of his faith." I answer, so did the other Apostles, for the excellency of their faith; for continuance whereof Christ prayed, as well as for Peter's faith. John xvii. FULKE.

The second, Hilary, *de Trinit.* Lib. vi.[7], saith: *Superemi-*

[5] [Though the Pope might possess a primacy of order and precedency, he had not that of jurisdiction or monarchical power. In the last Act of the Council of Chalcedon, two corruptions may be noted in the Latin text. First, where the judges declared that, according to the Canons, the Archbishop of ancient Rome was to have the first place among other Prelates, (πρὸ πάντων μὲν τὰ πρωτεῖα, "the primacy before all others,") the Latin falsely attributes to him "*omnem primatum.*" Again, when the Legate Lucentius affirmed, that the Apostolic throne commanded that all things should be done in the presence of the deputies, (ἡμῶν παρόντων πάντα πράττεσθαι,) the translator thus perverts his statement: "Sedes Apostolica nobis præsentibus *humiliari non debet.*" (*Concilia Generalia,* ii. 430, 431. Romæ, 1609. See Comber's *Church History cleared from Roman Forgeries,* pp. 111—12. Lond. 1695.)]

[6] [Conf. Coccii *Thesaur. Cathol.* Tom. i. p. 800.]

[7] [*Opp.* col. 904. ed. Bened.—If Romanists had any ground for believing S. Hilary to be on their side, they would not have en-

nentem, &c.: "Peter, by confession of his blessed faith, deserved an exceeding glory." And so did the rest of the Apostles, by their confession of their blessed faith, obtain an exceeding or passing glory, *ultra humanæ infirmitatis modum,* "beyond the measure of man's infirmity:" which words also Hilary hath, lest you should think he preferreth Peter in auctority before the other Apostles. For Peter's faith and confession he did before interpret to be the Rock of the Church; which, because it was common to all the Apostles, he maketh their authority equal[1]: *Vos, O sancti et beati viri,* [*et*] *ob fidei vestræ meritum claves regni cœlorum sortiti, et ligandi atque* [al. *ac*] *solvendi in cœlo et in terra jus adepti!* "O you holy and blessed men, which for the worthiness of your faith have obtained the keys of the kingdom of heaven, and have attained to auctority to bind and loose in heaven and in earth!" And if you urge that Peter spake, when all the rest held their peace, yet is that primacy but of order, not of authority: for they all believed as Peter confessed; and Peter confessed in the name of all the rest.

The third, Cyprian, *ad Jubaianum*[2]: *Ecclesia, quæ est una,* &c.: "The Church, which is one, is founded by our Lord's voice upon one which hath received the keys of it." This reason, saith he, can bear but one such Rock; for if there were more Rocks at once, there should be more Churches. But it is reason that Cyprian should expound himself, which by founding meaneth the beginning of the foundation, as he saith, *De simplicitate Prælat.*[3]: *Loquitur Dominus ad Pe-*

deavoured to suppress his evidence. When he had declared, (*De Trin.* Lib. ii. §. 23.) "Unum igitur hoc est immobile fundamentum; una hæc felix fidei Petra, Petri ore confessa, 'Tu es Filius Dei vivi,'" Erasmus felt authorised to insert this marginal note: "Petram interpretatur ipsam fidei professionem;" and (*in S. Matth.* xvi. 18.) cited S. Augustin also to justify the assertion contained in the margin, viz. "Ecclesia non est fundata super Petrum." However, the Spanish Inquisitors, in defiance of the judgment of S. Hilary and S. Augustin, have sentenced to extermination both the text and margin of Erasmus. See Bp. Barlow's *Brutum Fulmen*, p. 38. *Index libror. prohib. et expurg.* edit. 1667. p. 289.]

[1] [col. 901.] [2] [*Epist.* lxxiii. edit. Fell. p. 203.]

[3] [Fulke quotes this important passage as it is found in the old editions, Venet. 1547; Lugd. 1550. After the words "Pasce oves Meas" Bishop Fell (*Opp.* 107.) inserts the sentence, "Super unum

trum, &c.: "The Lord speaketh to Peter, 'I say to thee,' saith He, 'that thou art Peter; and upon this Rock I will build My Church; and the gates of hell shall not prevail against it. To thee will I give the keys of the kingdom of heaven; and whatsoever thou shalt bind upon earth shall be bound in heaven; and whatsoever thou shalt loose on earth shall be loosed in heaven.' And to the same after His resurrection He saith, 'Feed My sheep.' And although He giveth to all His Apostles after His resurrection equal power, and saith, 'As My Father hath sent Me, so also do I send you:' 'Receive the Holy Ghost:' 'Whose sins you forgive, they shall be forgiven; and whose sins you retain, they shall be retained;' yet, that He might shew the unity by His authority, He disposed the beginning of the same unity, beginning at one. For verily the rest of the Apostles were even the same thing that Peter was; endued with equal fellowship both of honour and of power: but the beginning proceedeth from unity, that the Church might be shewed to be one." Thus far Cyprian: by which we see that there is but one beginning; yet all the Apostles are equal. This unity of beginning of building Tertullian also, *Lib. de Pudic.*[4], sheweth to have been in Peter, when he was the first that preached after the ascension of Christ.

The fourth, Augustin, *Hom. de Pastoribus*[5]: *Dominus*, &c.: "Our Lord hath commended unity in Peter himself. There were many Apostles; and it is said to one, 'Feed My sheep'." Here he will have Peter to represent Christ, the only good Shepherd: although the words import no such thing; but only a mystery of unity, which is but frivolously gathered by the author of that book or homily, untruly ascribed to S. Augustin[6]: where yet he will not have Peter to be the head; but to bear a figure of the body of Christ, which is the Church. Whereupon his words follow soon after: *Nam et ipsum Petrum,*

ædificat Ecclesiam Suam," which appears in Gratian's *Decretum* also, an unexceptionable witness against the interpolations in this treatise. (*Caus.* xxiv. Qu. i. Cap. xviii.) See before, p. 283; and cf. Polani *Syllog. Thes. Theol.* Par. ii. p. 380. Basil. 1601.]

4 [Vide supra, p. 282.]

5 [*De Scripturis Sermo* xlvi. Tom. v. col. 169. ed. Ben. Amst.]

6 [This Homily on part of Ezek. xxxiv. is not spurious. See Calfhill, page 67. ed. Parker Soc.]

cui commendavit[1] *oves Suas, quasi alter alteri, unum Secum facere volebat; ut sic ei oves commendaret, ut esset Ille Caput, ille figuram corporis portaret, id est Ecclesiæ; et tanquam sponsus et sponsa, essent duo in carne una:* "For He would make even Peter, to whom He commended His sheep, as one to another, one with Himself; that He might so commend His sheep to him, that He Himself might be the Head, and Peter might bear the figure of His body, that is, of His Church; and so they might be as the bridegroom and his spouse, two in one flesh." These words shew how vain M. Sander's collection is for Peter's headship; beside that he citeth the words otherwise than they are in the author, even as his note-book served him.

The fifth reason is uttered by Hierom, *adversus Jovinianum*, Lib. i.[2], answering the objection of Jovinian, and intending to prove that John the virgin was as excellent as Peter the married man: *At dicis*, &c.: "But thou sayest, The Church is built upon Peter; albeit the self-same thing in another place be done upon all the Apostles, and all do receive the keys of the kingdom of heaven, and the strength of the Church be grounded equally upon them: yet therefore one is chosen among twelve, that, a head being made, the occasion of schism may be taken away[3]."

Here he would have three things to be noted. First, "that the Church is so built upon Peter the Rock, that in the same place where it is built upon Peter, the like is not done

[1] [MSS. *commendabat.*] [2] [See before, p. 285.]

[3] [S. Jerom in continuation asks, "Sed cur non Joannes electus est virgo?" and he replies, "Ætati delatum est; quia Petrus senior erat." Baronius (ad an. xxxii. num. vi.) has cited this passage. He had, however, on a previous occasion (ad an. xxxi. §. xxiv.) unfortunately used the following language: "Ex his apparet quam turpiter errent, qui primatum putant Petro collatum quod senior cæteris esset." S. Jerom therefore, in the opinion of this Cardinal, has fallen into "a shameful error" relative to S. Peter's primacy. But the matter does not end here: for Hen. Spondanus, who epitomised the Annals of Baronius, denies that any deference was shewn to S. Peter's age, "*ut hæretici contendunt.*" (p. 16. Mogunt. 1618.) Consequently this writer, disfiguring the statement of his author, declares that S. Jerom was an heretic!—"En dignum Censorem, qui inter Romanæ vel Hispanicæ Inquisitionis tortores cooptetur." (Casauboni *Exercitt.* p. 257. Lond. 1614.)]

upon the other Apostles." But seeing he himself before urged the future tense, "I will build," this collection is false. Christ promiseth that He will build His Church upon Peter; but when He buildeth, He useth all the Apostles as well as Peter.

Secondly, "that the Church is equally built upon all the Apostles." Therefore not more on Peter than on the rest.

Thirdly, "that one is chosen head, to avoid schism."

But "if all be equal," he asketh "how one may be head?" I answer, even as the foreman of the jury in some respects is chief, and yet they are all equal. But he answereth, "They are equal in authority as Apostles, but not as Bishops." But seeing the office of every Apostle is above the office of every Bishop, it will follow that every Apostle, as Apostle, is above Peter as Bishop of Rome; which were a perilous matter for Master Sander to admit. Howbeit, concerning this distinction of his, more is to be said in a more proper place. In the mean time he urgeth, that Peter was chosen of Christ to be head, to avoid strife and schism: which reason, seeing it holdeth always, there ought always one head to be chosen to be a head and perpetual Rock, by succession. I answer, the reason of avoiding schisms may gain so much, that in every Church, such as the first of the Apostles was, such an head for such purpose may be chosen: but it will not enforce one head, being a mortal man, over all the Church, which no one man can keep in unity. And how convenient the headship of the Romish Church is to avoid schisms, let so many schisms as have been made even for the attaining of the same headship bear witness: whereof one continued thirty-nine years.

As for Leo, Bishop of Rome, it is well known he was too much addict to maintain the dignity of his see; and yet he was far from the tyranny which the later Bishops usurped and practised, under pretence of Peter's Supremacy. His words are cited, *in Ann. Ass. Ser.* iii.[4]: *Super hoc Saxum,*

[4] [*Opp.* Tom. i. p. 53. Lugd. 1700. The words "hoc Saxum" and "soliditatem," adduced by Sanders, are not to be found in the original. Besides, in the end of his extract he omits "FIDEI," and inserts "ROCK." By these means S. Leo's teaching is basely misrepresented: for, according to him, the height of the Church was to rise upon the firmness of *the Faith,* ("in hujus *Fidei* firmitate,") and not upon the strength of S. Peter's person. He proceeds to say, "*This confession* the gates of hell shall not master, the bands of death shall not bind;

&c.: "Upon this Stone, this soundness and strength, I will build an everlasting temple; and the height of My Church, which is to reach to heaven, shall rise in the strength of this Rock." A great extolling of Peter, usual to the Bishops of Rome: but yet no more is said of him than may be truly said upon every one of the Apostles.

The sixth reason is uttered by Augustin, *Ep.* clxv.[1]: *Petro, totius Ecclesiæ figuram*, &c.: "Our Lord said to Peter, bearing the figure of the whole Church, 'Upon this Rock I will build My Church'." And again, *in Joan. Tr.* cxxiv.[2]: *Ecclesiæ*, &c.: "Peter the Apostle, by a generality that was figured, did bear the person of the Church, by reason of the primacy of his Apostleship." Here he maketh much ado about his primacy, by reason whereof he beareth the figure of all the Church; willing to infer, that because he was Primate of the Apostles, and in respect of his primacy represented the whole Church, therefore he was sovereign ruler and general officer of the whole militant Church[3]. But it followeth not, that every one which is made an attorney or proxy, to receive a thing for a whole commonalty, is thereby made general ruler of all that commonalty.

The Papists themselves[4], in the Council of Basil, discharge

for that word is the word of life:" "*Hanc confessionem* portæ inferi non tenebunt, mortis vincula non ligabunt; vox enim ista vox vitæ est."]

[1] [al. liii. *Opp.* Tom. ii. 91. Fortunati, Alypii, et S. Aug. *Ep. ad Generosum.*]

[2] [*Opp.* Tom. iii. P. ii. col. 599.—S. Augustin's interpretation of the Rock is made known in the sentences subjoined: "Ideo quippe ait Dominus, 'Super hanc Petram ædificabo Ecclesiam Meam,' quia dixerat Petrus, 'Tu es Christus, Filius Dei vivi.' Super hanc ergo, inquit, Petram, quam confessus es, ædificabo Ecclesiam Meam. Petra enim erat Christus: super quod fundamentum etiam ipse ædificatus est Petrus. 'Fundamentum quippe aliud nemo potest ponere, præter id quod positum est, quod est Christus Jesus.'"]

[3] [With reference to this point, see the first four chapters of the Jesuit Fitzherbert's *Obmutesce to the Ephphatha of D. Collins*: ed. an. 1621.]

[4] [The treatise in question, proving the superiority of a General Council to a Pope, cannot with accuracy be attributed to a "Papist." It is extant in the Appendix or "Farrago" of documents annexed by Crabbe to the Acts of the Synod of Basil. (Vid. Tom. iii. 303. Colon. Agr. 1551.)]

us of this conclusion; where they agree to the sentence of John, Patriarch of Antiochia, which citeth Augustin[5] to witness that Peter received the keys as minister of the Church.

And Augustin writeth, *De Agone Christ.* Cap. xxx.[6]: *Non enim sine causa inter omnes Apostolos hujus Ecclesiæ Catholicæ personam sustinet Petrus: huic enim Ecclesiæ clavis* [*claves*] *regni cœlorum datæ sunt,* [*cum Petro datæ sunt.*] *Et cum ei dicitur, ad omnes dicitur, Amas Me? Pasce oves Meas*: "For not without cause among all the Apostles Peter sustaineth the person of this Catholic Church: for to this Church the keys of the kingdom of heaven are given. And when it is said unto him, it is said to all, 'Dost thou love Me?' 'Feed My sheep.'"

By this sentence it is plain that Christ, after Augustin's mind, preferred not Peter in power before all the rest; but to receive equal power with the rest, he made him as it were the attorney of the rest. So that, all these reasons duly considered, the sayings of the Doctors, which affirm Peter to be a Rock or Stone on which the Church is builded, do not prove that he was an only foundation of the whole Church: but with the rest of the Apostles he was one, and the first, of the twelve stones whereon the Church was founded; and that in respect of his office and doctrine, not of his person, as he was a mortal man.

THE SEVENTH CHAPTER.

Sander. The authorities alleged by M. Jewell[7], to prove that Peter was not this Rock, prove against himself that Peter was this Rock; although they prove that there was another kind of Rock also beside him; which thing we deny not. SANDER.

Fulke. The first authority is Gregorius Nyssenus, *in loc. Vet. Test.*[8]: "'Thou art Peter; and upon this Rock I will FULKE.

[5] [Whose testimony is inserted in the Canon Law. (*Decr.* ii. Par. Caus. xxiv. Qu. i. C. vi.)]

[6] [*Opp.* Tom. vi. col. 190. Cf. Fitzherbert, ut sup. p. 98.]

[7] [*Works,* Part i. p. 340. ed. Parker Soc.]

[8] [*Opp.* Tom. i. p. 994. Paris. 1615. It is almost universally believed, that the *Testimonia adversus Judæos* here referred to are not an authentic composition. Of this opinion were Cave, (*Hist. Lit.* i. 245. Oxon. 1740.) Scultetus, (*Medull. Theol. Patt. Syntag.* p. 888.

build My Church.' He meaneth the confession of Christ: for he had said before, 'Thou art Christ, the Son of the living God'." M. Sander replieth, that it is neither said, "that Peter was not this Rock," nor "that Christ was this Rock," but that the confession of Peter was the Rock, which he granteth; and therefore Peter much rather must be the Rock: for his confession, "which cometh from his soul and heart, as from a fountain or spring," is greater than the act of confession. First, I deny his argument: because Peter's confession came neither from his soul nor heart, but from God, which revealed the truth unto him, as Christ saith, "Flesh and blood," &c. Secondly I say, Gregory meaneth by Peter's confession Him which Peter confessed; namely Christ, which is the only Rock of the Church, whereon the whole Church is builded; as his words do sound: "for he had said before, 'Thou art Christ,'" &c.

But M. Sander, reasoning like a learned Clerk, findeth fault with M. Jewell's argument, comparing it to this: "There cometh eloquence from a man, but he is not eloquent:" "Peter's confession is the Rock; therefore Peter is not the Rock." Would a man think that a Doctor in Divinity should either be so ignorant in the art of reasoning, or so impudent in perverting a good reason, that a very child might reprove either the one or the other? I appeal to logicians, whether this reason of M. Jewell's, The Rock cometh from Peter by con-

Francof. 1634.) Oudin, (*Comment.* i. 601. Lips. 1722.) Hottinger, (*Dissertt. miscell. Pent.* p. 81. Tiguri, 1654.) Rivetus, (*Crit. Sacr.* iii. xxiii. p. 350. Genev. 1642.) and Du Pin. (*Eccl. Hist.* i. 261. Dubl. 1723.) Their argument against the genuineness of the treatise is, that S. Chrysostom is herein cited: but this difficulty was entirely removed by the Vatican librarian Zacagnius, who, in the year 1698, first published the original Greek text, with four new chapters which complete the work. (*Coll. Monum. vet.* pp. 288—329.) He has made it manifest that the compilation consists of twenty-two chapters: but of these only eighteen were translated from an imperfect manuscript by the former editor Laurentius Siphanus; who, when he came to the spurious addition, complains in the margin, (*Opp.* i. 992.) that his author in very many places "fœdissime corruptus et mutilatus est." It is in this "pannus Nysseni operi assutus" that the mention of S. Chrysostom is found, as well as the sentence alleged by Bishop Jewell, which is hence deprived of all validity. Vid. Zacag. p. 326. not. 3.; et *Præfat.* pp. xxxviii—ix.]

fession; *ergo*, Peter is not the Rock, be like this argument, Eloquence cometh from Cicero; therefore Cicero is not eloquence; and not, as M. Sander inferreth, *ergo*, Cicero is not eloquent. But he hath another example: "A man's oration is eloquent; therefore the man himself is eloquent: so Peter's confession is the Rock; therefore Peter himself is the Rock." I deny the resemblance; for there is resembled the adjective in the one, and the substantive in the other. But thus he should compare them: Tully's defence of Milo is an eloquent oration; therefore Tully is an eloquent oration. Which reasoning is no more absurd than this of M. Sander: Peter's confession is the Rock; therefore Peter is the Rock. Contrariwise you may reason: Peter's confession was the Rock; therefore Peter was rocky or stony.

The second authority is Hilary: *Hæc una est*, &c.: "This is that only blessed Rock of faith, that Peter confessed with his mouth." M. Sander cavilleth, that this is not spoken upon the words said to Peter, but upon the words spoken by Peter. But beside that the whole context of the place is against him, both in that Lib. ii. *De Trinit.*[1], and also Lib. vi.[2], *Super hanc confessionis Petram Ecclesiæ ædificatio est,* "Upon this Rock of confession is the building of the Church," which M. Sander would avoid by bringing in of two Rocks, Christ and Peter, the particle exclusive shutteth him clean out of the doors; for Hilary saith not, that Christ is a Rock, but that He is the only Rock. Therefore this is but one Rock, and one building; and not, as M. Sander saith, two Rocks, and two buildings; for as well he might say two Churches. Now where Hilary upon Matthew[3] acknowledgeth Peter to be a Rock and foundation of the Church, it is answered before, that he was one of the twelve foundations spoken of Apoc. xxi. in a far other meaning than Christ is the only Rock.

The third authority is Cyrillus, *Dial.* iv. *de Trini.*[4]: "The Rock is nothing else but the strong and assured faith of the Disciple." "This," saith M. Sander, "is that I would have:" for this Disciple was S. Peter; and the Rock here spoken of is nothing else but S. Peter's faith: therefore it is not Christ. Nay, rather, the Rock is nothing but S. Peter's faith: there-

1 [§. 23. col. 800.]
2 [§. 36. c. 903.]
3 [Cap. xvi. n. 7. col. 690.]
4 [*Opp.* v. i. 507. Paris. 1638.]

fore it is not his person, and so no mortal man. For those words, "nothing but Peter's faith," do not exclude Christ; because faith cannot be without necessary relation unto Christ: but they exclude the person of Peter as a mortal man; because flesh and blood revealed not this confession unto him, but the heavenly Father.

The fourth authority is Chrysostom[1]: "Upon this Rock, that is, upon this faith and this confession, I will build My Church." M. Sander saith, "He that believed and confessed was Peter, and not Christ:" *ergo*, the Rock is Peter, and not Christ. Although this argument have no consequence in the world, yet, to admit that it doth follow, I will reply thus: But he that believed and confessed was not Peter only: therefore Peter only was not this Rock.

The fifth is Aug. *De verbis Dom.*[2]: "Christ was the Rock, upon which foundation Peter himself was also built." M. Sander asketh, if one Rock may not be built upon another, as Peter upon Christ? Yes, verily; but Peter none otherwise than the rest of the Apostles, who were all foundation-stones, laid upon the great Corner-stone, or only Foundation-rock, Jesus Christ.

S. Augustin[3] again addeth in Christ's person: "I will not build Myself upon thee, but I will build thee upon Me." M. Sander, following the allegory of building, confesseth that Christ is the first and greatest Stone; upon which by all proportion the second stone that should be laid must be greatest that can be gotten next the first. If this be so, it is marvel the Angel, which shewed unto John the building of the heavenly Jerusalem, shewed him not this second stone by itself, but the twelve stones lying equally one by another upon the main foundation. Apo. xxi. Whereby we see that M. Sander uttereth nothing but the visions of his own head.

The sixth is Origenes, in fourth sentence, [second sense[4],] *in* xvi. *Mat.*[5]: "He is the Rock, whosoever is the disciple of Christ." M. Sander reciteth this sense as not literal: and see-

[1] [*Opp.* Tom. vii. p. 548. See note 10, p. 285.]

[2] [*In Joan. Evang.* Cap. xxi. Tract. cxxiv. *Opp.* T. iii. P. ii. col. 599.]

[3] [*Serm.* lxxvi. *de verb. Evang. Matth.* xiv. Cap. i. *Opp.* T. v. c. 290.]

[4] [See page 273.]

[5] [*Commentar.* i. 275. ed. Huet.]

ing Peter is a Disciple, and the first, he will prove Peter, next to Christ, to be the chief Rock. Indeed, according to this sense, it must needs be that Peter is one principal Rock, among so many thousand Rocks: but because he is named first in the catalogue of the Apostles, it is a sorry reason to make him so to excel, that he is one Rock that beareth all the rest. But M. Jewell is frantic in M. Sander's opinion; that, denying any mortal man to be this Rock, now proveth every mortal man that is Christ's disciple to be this Rock. Nay, rather, M. Sander is brain-sick, that cannot understand this reason: Every Christian is such a Rock as Peter was: therefore Peter in being a Rock was not made Pope, or head of the universal Church. Origenes proceedeth: "Upon such a Rock all ecclesiastical learning is built." "But S. Peter is such a Rock," (saith Master Sander:) "*ergo,* upon him all ecclesiastical learning is built. Who would wish such an adversary as M. Jewell is, who proveth altogether against himself?" Nay, who can bear such an impudent caviller, that findeth a knot in a rush[6]? For your conclusion is granted, M. Sander, that all ecclesiastical learning is built upon S. Peter: but so it is built upon every true disciple of Christ, by Origen's judgment.

Again Origen saith[7]: "If thou think that the whole Church is built only upon Peter, what then wilt thou say of John, the son of thunder, and of every of the Apostles?" First, M. Sander chargeth the Bishop for leaving out in English this word *illum,* so that he should have said "upon that Peter;" whereby he accuseth him to deny that Peter is a Rock; which is an impudent lie. Secondly, when this authority doth utterly overthrow his whole building of the popish Rock, he can say nothing but that John was a mortal man; and so were all the Apostles as well as Peter: therefore M. Jewell said not truly, that the old Fathers have written "not any mortal man, but Christ Himself, to be this Rock," when John and all the Apostles be Rocks: as though there were no difference between the only foundation and Rock of the whole Church, which is Christ, and all the other stones that are built upon it.

Last of all Origen saith[8]: "Shall we dare to say that

6 ["Nodum in scirpo quæris." (Erasmi *Adagia,* fol. xxxviii. Argent. 1510.)]

7 [See before, pp. 282-3.]

8 [loc. sup. cit.]

the gates of hell shall not prevail only against Peter? or are the keys of the kingdom of heaven given only to Peter?" M. Sander answereth, "It is enough that the gates of hell shall least of all prevail against Peter: he hath chiefly the keys of heaven." But what reason hath he for this impudent assertion? "Peter of all the Apostles first confessed in the name of the whole Church." Admit this were true, as it can never be proved, that this was the first time that any of the Apostles confessed Christ; yet no primacy of superiority is hereby gained, if the sentence, as Origen expounded it, pertaineth to every faithful disciple. What advantage M. Sander hath taken of the Bishop's allegations, let the readers judge.

THE EIGHTH CHAPTER.

SANDER. *Sander.* The conclusion of the former discourse, and the order of the other which followeth.

FULKE. *Fulke.* The conclusion consisteth of seven points. In the first he repeateth what he would have men think he hath gained in his former discourse, concerning Peter to be the Rock of the Church whereon it is built.

In the second, for continuance of the building promised, "there must be always some mortal man; which, being made the same Rock by election, and afterward by revelation, should make the same confession, whensoever he is demanded or consulted in matters of religion." If this were true, there were no necessity of the holy Scriptures; neither yet of Synods and Councils; if one Pope were able to resolve all the demands moved by all men of the world.

In the third he sayeth, "If there must be some such one Rock, it is not possible it should be any other but the Bishop of Rome." First, because he alone hath been the first and chief in all assemblies. Secondly, he only sitteth in Peter's chair. Thirdly, and the consent of the world hath taken him so, ever indeed; but by the adversaries' confession above a thousand years. But, God be thanked, the Church hath no need of any such Rock: neither is any such taught Ephe. the fourth; where the order of the building thereof, and of all necessary builders of faith and doctrine, are fully set forth.

And the three reasons are all false, in manner and form as they are universally set down, as in their proper places shall be shewed.

In the fourth he glorieth, that he hath chosen to prove that point which of all other is most hard, "that all the Apostles were not the same thing that Peter was." And first he will ask, "in what Gospel or holy Scripture it is written, that every other Apostle was the same Rock which Saint Matthew testifieth Saint Peter to have been?" I answer, not only by necessary collection out of many places of Scripture, which he himself acknowledgeth to be the literal sense as well as that which followeth the sound of words, it is proved, but also in plain words of Saint Paul, Ephe. the second, verse 20; where the Church is "builded upon the foundation of the Apostles and Prophets, Jesus Christ being the head corner-stone:" and Apo. xxi. verse 14; where the twelve precious stones, the foundations of the wall of the city, had on them "the names of the twelve Apostles of the Lamb."

The fifth is either thus, or nothing at all; for it is not noted in him as the other be: If Cyprian or Hierom were alleged for this equality, "it were sufficient for him to say they were no Evangelists; for he sheweth it written, 'Thou shalt be called Cephas[1],' and 'Thou art Peter'." You see these

[1] [The Jesuit Nicolaus Serarius (*Comm. in lib. Machab.* &c. p. 599. Mogunt. 1600.) conceives, that in this Syriac name there was a "suavis allusio" to the Greek word κεφαλή; and this interpretation is sanctioned by many pontifical authorities. For example, Pope Innocent III. affirms, that "licet Cephas secundum unam linguam interpretatur Petrus, secundum alteram exponitur Caput;" (*De sacro Altaris mysterio*, Lib. i. Cap. viii. fol. 5. Lips. 1534.) and elsewhere in similar language, "Tu vocaberis Cephas; quod etsi Petrus interpretatur, Caput tamen exponitur." (Innoc. P. III. *Epistt. Decret.* Lib. ii. p. 514. Colon. Agripp. 1606.) The third spurious Epistle of Anacletus, who was Bishop of Rome toward the end of the first century, is professedly the most ancient evidence on behalf of this supposed derivation; (Blondelli *Pseudo-Isid.* p. 139. See Bp. Ridley's *Works*, p. 180. ed. Parker Soc.) and of course Gratian avails himself of a testimony so simple and conclusive as "*Cephas*, id est *Caput* et principium." (*Dist.* xxii. Cap. ii.) It is remarkable that Burchard and Ivo (*Decret.* Par. v. Cap. 269.) give the passage thus: "ut reliquis omnibus præesset Apostolis Cephas; id est, ut Petrus principatum teneret Apostolatus:" but Turrian endeavours to defend the Pseudo-Anacletus against the Centuriators. (*Adv. Magdeburg. Cent.* Lib. ii. Cap. iii. Florent. 1572.) S.

men, that brag of the Doctors, will be holden by them as long as they list.

The sixth: whereas all holy Scriptures is on the popish Catholics' side, he lamenteth the unhappiness of these days, in which men altogether unlearned in them, by the bare naming of God's word, "have among peddlers won their spurs, and among the ignorant have gotten the opinion of knowledge." As truly as none but peddlers and ignorant men embrace this doctrine which we teach, so truly all Scriptures be on M. Sander's side. Among so many Princes, noblemen, and excellent learned men as at this day acknowledge this doctrine to be the truth, M. Sander's head was very sleepy, when he could see none but peddlers and ignorant persons.

The seventh: he will take upon him to shew by what means Saint Peter excelled the other Apostles, and sheweth in what order he will proceed: which, seeing it is contained word for word in the titles of the seven chapters next following, I thought it needless here to rehearse.

Isidore of Seville, who occasionally errs in his *Origines,* is mistaken about the name Cephas; (Lib. vii. Cap. ix.) and as to what Du Pin (*Not.* in loc.) justly calls the "allusio parum solida" found in the works of S. Optatus, (*De Schism. Don.* L. ii. p. 31. Antverp. 1702.) it occurs in a place allowed to be otherwise interpolated; and Baldwin confesses that the words "unde et Cephas appellatus est" appear to be those "ineptæ alicujus glossæ ad marginem temere adscriptæ, et deinde abs librariis contextui insertæ." (Vid. Priorii et variorum *Annott.* in ed. Paris. 1679. p. 35.) Baronius therefore need not have been so well contented with the etymology in question, (ad an. 31. §. xxvii.) which was slighted by Æneas Sylvius before he became Pope Pius II. (*Commentt. de gestis Basil. Conc.* Lib. i. p. 13. edit. princ.: p. 12. Basil. 1551. Conf. ejusdem *Germaniam,* Cap. lxxxvii. Argent. 1515.) It may be added, that the *Index Auctorum damnatæ memoriæ,* issued by Mascaregnas, Inquisitor General of Portugal, contains the not surprising admonition, "Caute legenda Opera Æneæ Sylvii;" (p. 88. Ulyssip. 1624.) and he himself, in his Bull of Retractations, (Binius, iv. i. 739.) entreats that those things written against the papal claims, while he bore the heathenish name Æneas, might not be put in competition with his tenets when he had been transformed into a Christianized Pontiff: "Æneam rejicite, Pium recipite," &c. His *Commentaria* were reprinted in 1535 by Orthuinus Gratius, in the *Fasciculus rerum expetendarum ac fugiendarum,* which, as well as the work in a separate form, was proscribed by the Venetian Inquisitors in their *Cathalogus librorum hæreticorum,* an. 1554, republished by the Rev. Joseph Mendham in the year 1840.]

THE NINTH CHAPTER.

Sander. That Saint Peter passeth far the other Apostles in some kind of ecclesiastical dignity. SANDER.

That S. Peter had some excellent gifts, peradventure more than some of the Apostles; that he had great dignity among the Apostles, may easily be granted: but that he had auctority over them, such as the Pope claimeth over all Bishops, is of us utterly denied. Neither doth any one, nor all together, of M. Sander's thirty-four arguments prove that he had one jot of auctority over his brethren. FULKE.

First: He was "first" in order of numbering of the twelve Apostles.

Second: He was "promised to be called Cephas before the twelve were chosen."

Third: He was "named Peter at the time of the choice:" *ergo*, he had the Pope's auctority over them.

Who would grant the consequence of these arguments? Let us see what the other be.

Fourth: It was "said to him alone, 'Thou art Peter; and upon this Rock I will build My Church.'" I deny that it was said to him alone: for all the Apostles were likewise Rocks, upon which He would build His Church.

The like I say of the fifth, that "the keys of the kingdom of heaven were promised to him alone:" for every one of the Apostles received them as well as he; being ordained with equal power of binding and loosing, of remitting and retaining sins. Matt. xviii. 18; Joan. xx. 23. Notwithstanding the words at one time were spoken to Peter alone, yet did they give him no singular auctority.

The sixth: "Christ paid tribute for Peter, as under-head of His family:" *ergo*, he was greater than the rest. A fond argument. This *didrachma* was paid for every man in the city where he dwelt: and because Peter had a house and a family in the city, Christ paid for him with whom He lodged, and Himself.

But if you draw it into an allegory, these absurdities will follow: first, that Christ maketh His Church and spiritual kingdom subject to tribute; yea, to Moses' law, by which that kind of tribute was due. Secondly, you divide Christ's Church into two households. *Didrachma* was to be paid for the head or first-born of every house. And you shew your ignorance in referring this payment to Num. iii., which was only for the first-born, whereas this was for all men. And for the first-born was due five siccles, [shekels,] whereof every one was half an unce [ounce] of silver at the least: whereas *didrachma*, containing but two *drachmas*, whereof every one was equal with the Roman penny, could be but sixteen pence at the most of our money.

It is a strong argument, that the payment of tribute, which argueth subjection, should make Peter so great a lord that he should be out of all subjection: which if Chrysostom had considered, he would not have grounded Peter's primacy upon so frivolous an argument[1].

The seventh: Christ preached "out of Saint Peter's boat, to shew that in his chair His doctrine should always be steadfastly professed." An argument to be answered either with laughing or hissing.

The eighth: Though "all the Apostles were to be sifted, yet Peter's faith alone is prayed for." This is utterly false: for Christ prayed for all His Apostles' faith, Joh. xvii. If specially for Peter, it was in respect of his greater danger, and not in respect of his greater dignity.

The ninth: "Peter first entered into the sepulchre:" *ergo*, he was made Pope. He entered for farther confirmation of his faith concerning Christ's resurrection. This may be imputed to diligence, but not to dignity.

Tenth: "The Angel saith, 'Tell His Disciples and Peter';" naming him severally, because of his shameful fall he had more need of comfort.

The eleventh: "Ambrose[2] thinketh Peter was the first man that saw Him." Nay, rather, the soldiers which kept the grave saw Him before Peter; and the women also; which

[1] ["Because then Christ was a first-born Child, and Peter seemed to be first of the Disciples, to him they come." (S. Chrys. *Hom.* lviii. *on S. Matth.* Library of Fathers, Vol. xv. p. 786. Oxf. 1844.)]

[2] [*Comm. in Evang. Luc.* Cap. xxiv. Opp. Tom. iii. col. 232. Conf. S. Luke xxiv. 34. 1 Cor. xv. 5.]

would give them dignity above Peter, if first seeing were a matter to argue dignity or auctority of the seer.

The twelfth: "Only S. Peter walked on the sea: that signifieth the world to be his jurisdiction." As he walked by faith, so by weakness of faith he began to sink. And the sea that he walked on was but a lake or mere; and therefore cannot well signify the whole world. Beside, the argument is as sure as if it were bound with a straw.

Thirteenth: "S. Peter is shewed to have loved Christ more than the rest, and is alone commanded to feed His sheep." He had good cause to love Him more, because greater sins were forgiven him: but it is false that he only was commanded to feed Christ's sheep, for all the Apostles were likewise commanded.

Fourteenth: "It is said to Peter, 'Thou shalt stretch forth thy hands,' and 'Follow thou Me:' by which a particular kind of death on the Cross is prophesied." A violent death, but no particular kind of death, is shewed by these words. And although it were, yet Peter in being crucified was made no greater than Andrew, who was crucified also, if the stories of both be true.

Fifteenth: "Peter answered always for the Apostles: *ergo* he was chief." No more than the foreman of the jury. Although it is not true that he always answered for the rest; for sometime Thomas, sometime Philip, sometime Judas, answered. John xiv.

Sixteenth: "Peter pronounced Judas Iscariot deposed." That was by special instinct of the Holy Ghost, and by no ordinary authority.

Seventeenth: "After the sending of the Holy Ghost, Peter above all the rest first taught the faith." Chrysostom and Cyril saith he did it by the consent of all the rest, who all stood up together with him; although one spake, to avoid confusion, when the apology was made to answer the slanderous scoffers. But before that they taught every one alike.

Eighteenth: "The multitude converted said to Peter and to the other Apostles, but to Peter by name, 'What shall we do?'" If this prove any thing, it proveth the equality of the Apostles; that, having heard one man preach, they demand not of him alone, but of all the rest with him, what they shall do.

Nineteenth: "Peter made answer for all, that they should repent and be baptized." It was good reason, seeing he made the apology for all.

Twentieth: "Peter did the first miracle after the coming of the Holy Ghost; and by healing the lame's feet shewed mystically that he was the Rock, to establish the feet of other." I answer, John healed him as much as Peter, by Peter's own confession, Act. iii. 12, and the lame man's acknowledging the benefit to be received equally from both, in holding Peter and John.

Twenty-first: "Peter confessed Christ first; not only before private men, but at the seat of judgment. Act. iv." It is false that Peter confessed Christ first before private men; and at the seat of judgment he confesseth equally with John.

Twenty-second: "Peter alone gave sentence with fulness of power upon Ananias and Sapphira." Not by ordinary power, but by special revelation, and direction of the Holy Ghost; whatsoever Gregory, a partial judge in this case, doth gather.

Twenty-third: "Peter was so famous above the rest, that his shadow was sought to heal the diseased." This was a singular and personal gift, which the Pope hath not; therefore it pertaineth nothing to him.

Twenty-fourth: "Peter did excommunicate, and enjoin penance to Simon Magus, the first heretic." Peter denounced God's judgment against him; but not by way of excommunication. And yet the argument is naught, as all the rest are, though the antecedents were granted.

Twenty-fifth: "Peter was the first that raised a dead body to life, namely Tabitha, after Christ's ascension." This is neither proved to be true; neither, if it were, should Peter thereby have greater auctority than his fellow-Apostles, which likewise raised the dead; and peradventure before Peter, although S. Luke make no mention of them.

Twenty-sixth: "Peter had first by vision, that the Gentiles were called to believe in Christ." This is false; for Paul had that in vision before him. Act. ix. & xxvi. 17.

Twenty-seventh: "God chose that the Gentiles should first of all hear the word of the Gospel by Peter's mouth, and should believe. Acts xv." This is false; for Peter saith not "first of all," but "of old time:" and the eunuch of Ethiopia was baptized by Philip before Cornelius of Peter.

Twenty-eighth: "Prayer was made for Peter by the Church; which was not so earnestly made for any other Apostle that we read of." Their earnest prayer for Peter is set forth to shew that God at their prayer delivered Peter; not that Peter was thereby shewed to be greater in auctority.

Twenty-ninth: "Paul and Barnabas came to Jerusalem to the Apostles, to fetch a solution from Peter, Act. xv., as Theodoret noteth[1]." But S. Luke noteth, that they came to all the Apostles and Elders at Jerusalem, and not to Peter only; nor for his solution, but for the solution of the Council.

Thirtieth: "In the Council, Act. xv., Peter did not only speak first, but also gave the determinate sentence." Both the parts of this proposition are false: for Saint Luke testifieth there was great disputation before Saint Peter spake. Also Saint James, as President of the Council, gave the definitive sentence; according to whose words the synodical epistle was written in the name of all the Apostles and Elders at Jerusalem.

Thirty-first: "Saint Paul came to Jerusalem to see Peter, as Chrysostom sayeth, because he was primus, first or chief." But Saint Paul himself affirmeth in the same place, and divers other, that he was equal with Peter and the highest Apostles. Galatians ii. 8; 2 Corinthians xii. 11.

Thirty-second: "Peter was either alone, or first and chiefest, in the greatest affairs of the Church." The greatest affair of the Church was the preaching unto the Gentiles; in which Peter was neither alone, nor first nor chiefest; but Paul chiefest. Gal. ii.

Thirty-third: "Peter was sent to Rome, to occupy with his chair the mother Church of the Roman province, and chief city of the world; and there vanquished Simon Magus, the head of heretics," &c. All this is uncertain, being not found in the Scriptures; but those stories which report it convinced by Scriptures to be false in divers circumstances.

Thirty-fourth: "Peter's chair and succession hath been

[1] [Sanders (*Rocke*, p. 200.) refers to "Ep. ad Leonem:" but Crakanthorp remarks, that of the Epistles which bear the name of Theodoret "two are most eminent; that to Dioscorus, and the other to Pope Leo. That the former is forged the other doth demonstrate... so, vice versa, that the latter is forged is demonstrated by the former." (*Vigilius Dormitans*, p. 444. Cf. p. 417. Lond. 1631.)]

acknowledged of all ancient Fathers," &c. Although the see of Rome, appointed for the seat of Antichrist, hath of old been very ambitious; yet it is a fable that [it] hath been acknowledged by all ancient Fathers to have the auctority which the Bishops thereof have claimed. For Irenæus rebuked Victor for usurping. All the Bishops of Africa in Council withstood Innocentius, Zozimus, Bonifacius, and Cæbastinus, [Cœlestinus,] alleging for their auctority a counterfeit Decree of the Council of Nice[1], as we have shewed before in the first treatise[2]. The like may be said of the Councils of Chalcedon[3], of Constantinople, the fifth[4], &c., which withstood the Bishop of Rome's auctority in such cases as he pretended prerogative.

To conclude, neither any one, nor all together of these thirty-four reasons prove Peter to be greater in auctority than the rest of the Apostles; and much less the Bishop of Rome to be greater than Bishops of other seats.

THE TENTH CHAPTER.

SANDER. *Sander.* That the Apostles, beside the prerogative of their Apostleship, had also the auctority to be particular Bishops: which thing their name also did signify in the old time.

FULKE. *Fulke.* ALTHOUGH the Apostles had all such auctority as every particular Bishop hath, yet had they not two offices, but one Apostleship; no more than a King, although he have all auctority that every Constable hath, is thereby both a King and a Constable, but a King only. Neither doth their staying, or as he calleth it residence, in some particular city, prove that the Apostles either were or might be Bishops; that is, give over their general charge, and take upon them a particular; or still retaining their general charge, to exercise the office of a Bishop any longer than until the Church was perfectly gathered where they remained. For although the Holy Ghost distinguished their universal charge into several parts, to avoid confusion; as in making Peter chief Apostle of the Circumcision, and Paul of the Gentiles; yet were they not thereby made Bishops. And although the consent of writers

[1] [Supra, pp. 70—1.]

[2] [Viz. *A Retentive, to stay good Christians in trve faith and religion, against the motiues of Richard Bristow:* p. 44.]

[3] [See before, pp. 288—9.] [4] [General Council, A.D. 553.]

is, that James was Bishop of Jerusalem; yet, following the course of the Scriptures, we must hold that James, by decree of the Holy Ghost, was appointed to stay there, not as a Bishop, but as an Apostle, for the conversion of the Jews, which not only out of all Jewry, but out of all parts of the world, came thither ordinarily to worship. Of S. Peter's sitting at Antioch as Bishop we find nothing in the Scriptures; and less of his removing to Rome. But we find that when Peter came to Antioch, Paul withstood him to his face, and reproved him openly: which he might not well have done, if Peter had been supreme head of the Church, and in his own see, as M. Sander doth fantasy.

Where he allegeth the text *et episcopatum ejus accipiat alter*, "and let another take his bishoprick," to prove that Judas and so the Apostles were Bishops, it is too childish and fond an argument; seeing the Greek word which S. Luke useth, and the Hebrew word which the Prophet useth, signifieth generally a charge or office, and not such a particular office of a Bishop as now we speak of.

He citeth farther Theodoret, *in* iii. Cap. i. *ad Tim.*[5], to prove that the name of an Apostle in the primitive Church did signify such a Bishop. But how greatly Theodoret was deceived appeareth by this, that he citeth for proof Philip. ii.; Epaphroditus to be the Apostle of the Philippensians, because S. Paul saith of him, "Epaphroditus your Apostle, and my helper:" whereas he meaneth that he was their messenger; using the word ἀπόστολος in the general signification for "a messenger," and not for the name of such an officer as an Apostle or Bishop. He nameth also Titus and Timotheus, which in the Scripture are never called Apostles: likewise the Apostles and Elders at Jerusalem; which were indeed the true Apostles of Christ's immediate sending, and not Bishops ordained by men. And whereas Hierom saith that "all Bishops be successors of the Apostles," he meaneth manifestly in auctority within their several charges, and not that the Apostles were Bishops. Likewise where Augustin saith that "the Bishops were made instead of the Apostles," it rather proveth that the Apostles were no Bishops: for then, if the Apostles were Bishops, he should say, Bishops were made instead of Bishops.

5 [*Opp.* Tom. ii. p. 181. Colon. Agripp. 1573.]

The last reason is, that if the office of Bishops had not been distinct in the Apostles from their Apostleship, that office would have ceased with the Apostleship: for the whole being taken away, no part can remain, except it had another ground to stand in beside the Apostleship, as the bishoply power had. Indeed, if the Apostleship had ceased before Bishops had been ordained, bishoplike power would have ceased with it: but seeing the Apostles ordained Bishops and Elders in every congregation, to continue to the world's end, the Bishop's office hath not ceased, though the office of the Apostles is expired. Wherefore, seeing neither by Scripture, reason, nor Doctors, this distinction of offices in the Apostles can be proved; when Peter is called Head, Prince, Chief, First, Captain of the Apostles, by Cyril, or any ancient writer, we must understand, as Ambrose teacheth, "a primacy of confession or faith, not of honour or degree." *De Incar. Dom.* Cap. iv.[1]

THE ELEVENTH CHAPTER.

SANDER. *Sander.* How far S. Peter did either excel or was equal with the Apostles in their Apostolic office. Wherein divers objections are answered, which seem to make against S. Peter's Supremacy.

FULKE. *Fulke.* But that necessity enforceth him, M. Sander thinketh it [a] sin of curiosity to inquire of that equality or inequality of the Apostles, "whereas it should suffice us to follow the present state of the universal Church practised in our time:" as though the universal Church of any time did ever acknowledge the Pope to be supreme head; although a great part of the world hath of long time so taken him. He thinketh it out of controversy that S. Peter was the first of the Apostles, as S. Matthew saith *primus*, "'the first,' Simon, which is called Peter." And he is not content that he was first in the order of numbering, but he will have him first in dignity, because he is always named first. But that is neither true, nor a good reason if it were true, because he is named first, therefore he is of greatest dignity: but Gal. ii. 9, James, and Cephas, and John are said to have been "pillars" of the Church, and yet Paul equal with them. Although if

[1] [*Opp.* iv. 290. Lut. Paris. 1661.—"Primatum confessionis utique, non honoris; primatum fidei, non ordinis."]

we granted greatest dignity to Peter, yet thereupon did not follow greatest authority. For these three Apostles last named were of greatest dignity among the Apostles, yet not of greater authority than the rest. And although the ancient Fathers of the word *primus* have derived the name of *primatus*, or "primacy," yet have they also expressed wherein this primacy doth consist; namely, not in authority, but in order: neither doth those names, Prince, Chief, Head, Top, Guide, Mouth, Greatest of the Apostles, used by some of them, signify his authority over them, but his dignity amongst them.

But if you ask him wherein Peter was chief, he answereth, "The question is curious: for in the nature and order of the Apostleship every Apostle was equal with all his fellows; and so is every Bishop, Priest, King, Duke, Knight, with every one of his degree." If this be as he saith, then was Peter chief neither as Apostle nor Bishop. "But there may be another thing" (saith he) "coincident to some degree of men, not necessary for the [their] being, but for their well-being." One therefore was set over the Apostles for unity's sake, and to avoid schisms, as Cyprian and Hierom write in places before cited. This must needs be a primacy of order, and not of authority: for among men of equal authority, as he confesseth the Apostles were, one may be chosen as the President or Primate, to avoid confusion, the austerity [authority] remaining equal to every one; but one cannot be preferred in authority to remain still equal with his fellows in authority.

But whereas Optatus, Lib. ii. *De schism. Don.*[2], and Leo, *ad Anastas. Ep.* lxxxii.[3], are cited to prove that the same primacy, which Peter some time [sometimes] (but yet not always) had among the Apostles, should be retained in succession of his chair, to maintain unity among all men, it hath no ground in the holy Scriptures: and yet those good men were far from imagining such an absolute power of Peter's successor as M. Sander defendeth in the Pope; although sometimes he do handle it so nicely, as it might seem to be a thing of nothing wherein the Pope is above his fellow-Bishops. Where I said that Peter had not always the primacy of order among the Apostles, it is proved both by the xv. of the Acts, where James was President of the Council; and Gal. ii., not only where

2 [p. 39. ed. Mer. Casaub. Lond. 1631.]

3 [lxxxiv, alias xii. Vid. Quesnelli edit. p. 224.]

James is named before Peter, but also where Peter abstained and separated himself, after certain came from James, fearing them of the Circumcision, lest he should have been evil thought of, as he was before for keeping company with Cornelius; and in divers other places of the Acts of the Apostles.

But M. Sander will add another truth to the former doctrine of Peter's primacy; namely, that, seeing the Apostles needed no head, because they were not in danger of error, the head was appointed over them for an example of the Church afterward, when that personal privilege of the Apostles ceased to be in their successors. But how will he prove that the privilege of not erring hath continued in Peter's successors more than in the successors of all the Apostles? Forsooth, because Christ prayed that Peter's faith might not fail, that he might confirm his brethren. I have often shewed that He prayed for the perseverance of all His Apostles: and the cause of His special prayer for Peter was proper to Peter's person; therefore cannot be drawn to his successors. And what madness is it to defend that the Pope cannot err, when Pope Honorius was condemned for an heretic both by the sixth [General] Council, [the third] of Constantinople, and by the Decree of Leo II., Bishop of Rome, confirming the same Council! *Act.* xviii.[1] *Ep.* Leon. II. *ad Constant.*[2]

But M. Sander concludeth, to answer the argument of the equality of the Apostles, that Paul was equal with Peter in Apostleship; but by the appointment and will of Christ Peter was head, "to shew that His Church, having one Pastor in it above the rest, is one, as a kingdom one by having one King in it." Howbeit we find the will of God for the Supremacy and headship of Christ over all His Church, to make it one, in the holy Scriptures; when of Peter's headship or Supremacy there is never a word. And Paul saith that he was "nothing inferior to the highest Apostles:" 2 Cor. ii. [xii. 11:] if nothing absolutely, then was not Peter his superior in any respect.

That Paul reprehended Peter, M. Sander saith he might do it by equality of his Apostleship. If that be so, why may not every Bishop reprehend the Pope by equality of bishoprick? If you grant they may, then have you so many Canons against you as you can never save their authority, and

[1] [Joverius, Class. i. fol. 83.] [2] [Ib. fol. 85, b.]

abide by your confession. But this fault, you say, with Tertullian, was "of conversation, not of preaching;" that Peter might not seem to have erred in doctrine. Nevertheless it cannot be excused but Peter also erred in doctrine: not in the general doctrine of the abolishing of the law, or of Christian liberty, but of bearing too much with the Jews in prejudice of the Gentiles, whom he compelled to Judaism, and in derogation of the truth of Paul's doctrine: which dissimulation he entered not into for any worldly respect, but because he was deceived in opinion; thinking that in that case he ought so to have done, before he, being reprehended by Paul, saw the inconvenience, and then mildly yielded to the correction. But in this humble submission, saith Master Sander, "Peter proved himself to be the head of all the Apostles; seeing Christ had said, 'He that is greater among you let him be as the lesser.'" Indeed he shewed herein such greatness as Christ commendeth; but no headship or authority over his brethren.

Cyprian, *ad Quintum*[3], saith he, "did not judge this reproving of Peter to be an argument against his Supremacy, but a witness of his humility:" but he giveth us this much to understand, that if he had challenged primacy, he had taken upon him arrogantly. His words are these: *Nam nec Petrus, quem primum Dominus elegit,* &c.: "For neither did Peter, whom our Lord chose the first, and upon whom He builded His Church, when Paul did strive with him about Circumcision afterward, challenge anything insolently; or take upon him arrogantly to say that he had the primacy, and that he ought rather to have been obeyed of novices and after-comers: neither did he despise Paul, for that he was before a persecutor of the Church, but he did admit the counsel of truth."

The like saith Augustin for his humility, but as a later writer more pregnant for his primacy: *De Bap. cont. Don.* Lib. ii. Cap. i.[4] *In Scripturis,* &c.: "We have learned in the holy Scriptures, that Peter the Apostle, in whom the primacy of the Apostles in so excellent grace hath the preeminence, when he used to do otherwise than the truth required about Circumcision, was corrected of Paul, who was admitted after him to be an Apostle." In this saying the primacy is of time and order; not of dignity and authority.

3 [*Ep.* lxxi. pp. 194-5. ed. Fell.]
4 [*Opp.* Tom. ix. col. 65. ed. Ben. Amst.]

But Gregory, much later than Augustin, granteth to Peter not only a primacy, but also a majority: *in Ezech. Hom.* xviii.[1] *Quatenus*, &c.: "That he who was chief in the top of the Apostleship should be chief also in humility." And again: *Ecce a minore*, &c.: "Behold, Peter is reproved of his lesser; and he disdaineth not to be reproved: neither doth he call to mind that he first was called to the Apostleship." These words make Peter greater none otherwise than that he was first called to the Apostleship; which argueth small authority over his juniors.

Hereupon he taketh occasion to inveigh against the pride of Luther, Zwinglius, Calvin, &c., and their bitter dissensions; shewing how far they are unlike to the Apostles. It is not to be doubted that they were many degrees inferior to the virtue and holiness of the Apostles: but yet as well in humility as all other virtues, if they come not nearer to them than the Pope and his pompous Clergy, let God and all indifferent men be judges.

Moreover, whereas it is objected against the Supremacy of Peter, that the Apostles sent him to lay hands upon those whom Philip the Deacon had baptized; he answereth, that proveth no more their equality than when "the Canons of a Cathedral church do choose their Dean or Bishop to go about business of the Chapter," it proveth the Dean and Bishop to be inferior to the Canons. But, by his favour, where the Dean or Bishop are sent about business, it argueth the Bishop and Dean, in respect of those [that] business, to be inferior to the whole Chapter; as Peter and John were to the whole College of the Apostles: though the Bishop or Dean in other respects be superior to the Canons; and Peter and John were equal to every one of the Apostles.

Wherefore M. Sander's conclusion is upon a false supposition, that Peter had authority to depose the Apostles, if they had fallen as Judas did; therefore the Pope hath the like over Bishops. For neither had Peter any singular auctority to depose any of his fellow-Apostles, no more than he had to choose one in place of Matthias; nor the Bishop of Rome over other Bishops ever had of right, but by concession, election, or usurpation.

[1] [fol. lxxxi, b. Parrhis. 1512.]

THE TWELFTH CHAPTER.

Sander. That S. Peter's prerogative above the other Apostles is most manifestly seen by his chief bishoply power. How Christ loved Peter above others. SANDER.

Fulke. M. Sander, fantasying that he hath proved Peter superior to the Apostles, not in their Apostleship, but in his bishoply degree, doth yet again distinguish the order and office of a Bishop from the authority and jurisdiction of the same. And in order and office he confesseth that all Bishops of the world are equal; as Hierom sayeth, *ad Evagrium*[2], and Cyprian, *De unitate Ecclesiæ*[3]; but not in authority. But seeing he rehearseth the testimony of Hierom imperfectly, I will set it down at large, that you may see whether it will bear his distinction. He writeth against a custom of the Church of Rome, by which the Deacons were preferred above the Priests, whom he proveth by the Scripture to be equal with Bishops, except only in ordaining: *Quid enim facit, exempta [excepta] ordinatione, Episcopus,* &c.: "For what doth a Bishop, excepting ordination, which a Priest or Elder doth not? Neither is it to be thought that there is one Church of the city of Rome, and another of the whole world. Both France, and Britain, and Africa, and Persia, and the East, and India, and all barbarous nations, worship one Christ, observe one rule of truth. If auctority be sought, the world is greater than a city. Wheresoever a Bishop be, either at Rome, or at Eugubium, or at Constantinople, or at Rhegium, or at Alexandria, or at Tunis, he is of the same worthiness, and of the same priesthood. Power of riches and baseness of poverty make not the Bishop higher or inferior: but they are all successors of the Apostles." FULKE.

And lest you should think he speaketh only of equality in order and office, and not in authority, he doth in another place shew that the authority of every Priest is equal with every Bishop by God's disposition; and that the excelling of one Bishop above other Priests came only by custom: *In Titum,* Cap. i.[4]: *Sicut ergo Presbyteri sciunt se, ex Ecclesiæ consuetudine, ei qui sibi præpositus fuerit esse subjectos;*

2 [Supra, p. 33.] 3 [See before, pages 283, 290-1.]
4 [*Opp.* Tom. ix. p. 245. ed. Erasm.]

ita Episcopi noverint se, magis consuetudine quam dispositionis Dominicæ veritate, Presbyteris esse majores: "Therefore as Priests do know, that by custom of the Church they are subject to him that is set over them; so let Bishops know, that they are greater than Priests rather by custom than by truth of the Lord's appointment." If the authority, then, and jurisdiction of Bishops dependeth upon custom, and not upon God's appointment, Peter was not by our Lord's appointment preferred in bishoplike authority before the rest of the Apostles; nor the Bishop of Rome before other Bishops and Priests; but only by custom, as Hierom saith. S. Cyprian's words also infer the same[1]: *Episcopatus unus est; cujus a singulis in solidum pars tenetur:* "The Bishop's office is one; whereof every man doth partake the Bishop's office wholly." Now if authority and jurisdiction do pertain to the Bishop's office, every Bishop hath it wholly; as, (to follow M. Sander's example,) whatsoever is incident to the nature or kind of a man is equally in every man.

But now the greatest matter resteth, to prove how S. Peter had more committed to his charge than the rest of the Apostles; and that he taketh on him to prove by this reason: Peter loved Christ more than all the rest of the Apostles: therefore He gave him greater authority in feeding His sheep than to the rest. But I deny the argument. For Peter loved Christ more than the rest, because Christ had forgiven him greater sins than to the rest: Luc. vii. 47: in consideration whereof He required greater diligence in doing his office; but gave him not a greater charge or authority.

Now where M. Sander reasoneth, that Peter loved Christ most because Christ first loved him most, and Christ loved him most because He would make him governor of His Church, it is a shameful petition or begging of that which is in question. For the nearest cause of Peter's greater love was the greater mercy which he found: which mercy, proceeding from the love of God, as the first and infinite cause, can have no higher, superior, or former cause. But Peter, in respect of greater love shewed to him, in that greater sin was forgiven him, was bound to shew greater love toward Christ; which He required to be shewed in feeding His sheep: yet this proveth not that greater authority was given him, or that

[1] [*De unit. Eccl.* Opp. 108.]

he did feed more than all men; for S. Paul saith truly of himself, "I have laboured more than they all." 1 Cor. xv. 10. Whereby it appeareth, that Peter as a man was not equal with Christ in the effect [affect] of excellent love, which was in Him incomparable.

And whereas M. Sander talketh so much of his commission of feeding, I say, these words, "Feed My sheep," &c., be not words of a new commission, but words of exhortation, that he shew exceeding diligence in the commission equally delivered to all the Apostles: "As My Father hath sent Me, so I send you." Joan. xx. 21. But the ancient Fathers expound it so that it might seem to be a singular commission to Peter. It cannot be denied but divers of the ancient Fathers, otherwise godly and learned, were deceived in opinion of Peter's prerogative; which appeareth not in the Scriptures, but was challenged by the Bishops of Rome; which seemed to have a shew of some benefit of unity to the Church, so long as the empire continued at Rome, and the Bishops of that city retained the substance of Catholic religion. Yet did they never imagine that such blasphemous and tyrannical authority, yea such false and heretical doctrine, as afterward was maintained under the pretence of that prerogative, should or ought to have been defended thereby.

But let us see what M. Sander can say out of the ancient writers. August., *in Hom. de Past.* Cap. xiii.[2], writeth: *Dominus,* &c.: "Our Lord hath commended unity in Peter himself. There were many Apostles, and it is said to one, 'Feed My sheep.' God forbid there should now lack good Pastors [...] but all good Pastors are in one, they are one." This maketh nothing for Peter's authority over the rest: but only the author supposeth the unity of all Pastors to be allegorically signified, in that Christ speaketh that to one which is common to all good shepherds; namely, to feed His sheep. And again, *de Sanct. Hom.* xxiv.[3]: *In uno Petro,* &c.: "The unity of all Pastors was figured in one, Peter." So might it well be, without giving Peter authority over all Pastors.

Chrysostom is the next; Lib. ii. *de Sacerdotio*[4]; who saith that Christ did ask whether Peter loved Him, not to

2 [*Opp.* T. v. col. 168. §. 30.]
3 [al. *De Scripturis Serm.* cxlvii. Opp. v. 489.]
4 [*Opp.* Tom. i. pp. 371, 372. ed. Ben.]

teach us that Peter loved Him, but to inform us *quanti Sibi curæ sit gregis hujus præfectura*[1], "how great care He taketh of the government of this flock." Here he would have us mark, that Chrysostom calleth it a rule and government of the flock which Christ intendeth. Yea, Sir, we see it very well; but you would make us blind, if we could not see, that Chrysostom speaketh not of a general rule granted to Peter only, but of the government of every Church by every Pastor. And therefore you dance naked in a net, when you allege the words following absolutely, as though they pertained to Peter only; *Petrum Christus auctoritate præditum esse voluit*, &c.; whereas Chrysostom, speaking to every Priest, and shewing how careful he ought to be in his office, in respect of his high calling, and the excellent dignity thereof, saith: *Etiamne nunc nobiscum contendes, fraudem istam tibi non bene ac fœliciter cessisse, qui per eam universis Dei optimi maximi bonis administrandis sis præficiendus; quum præsertim ea agas, quæ cum Petrus ageret, illum Christus auctoritate præditum esse voluit, ac reliquos item Apostolos longe præcellere?* "Wilt thou then still contend with us, that this fraud hath not happened well and luckily to thee, which by it art to be made overseer of all the goods of God almighty; especially when thou doest those things, which when Peter did, Christ would have him to be endued with authority, and also far to excel the other Apostles?"

Here M. Sander will have us note three things: 1. Peter's authority: 2. passing the Apostles: 3. far passing. We mark them all, that they are directly overthrowing M. Sander's Rock of the popish Church. For they declare, that Peter in doing those things was endued with authority, and far passed the other Apostles; even as every Priest, (to whom Chrysostom speaketh,) when he doth the same things, is endued with the same authority, and far passeth all other men. So that here is none other authority nor excellence of Peter than such as is common to all Ministers in executing their charge; and was common to all the Apostles, when they did the same things that Peter did. For Chrysostom proveth to Basil, that he did him no hurt, when by policy he caused him to be called to the ministry against his will; seeing that thereby he was made partaker of the reward of the faithful and wise servant, and

1 ["quantum cordi Sibi esset hujusmodi gregis præfectura."]

equal in authority with Peter, if of love towards Christ he would diligently feed His flock. So that Leo[2] had no just cause to say, that, in respect of any greater authority, "Peter had a special care of feeding the sheep committed to him;" but rather in respect that he had greater cause to love Christ, which had so mercifully forgiven him so shameful a fall.

But Arnobius[3] is a less partial witness than Leo, a Bishop of Rome; and he, upon the Psal. cxxxviii., writeth thus: *Nullus Apostolorum nomen,* &c.: "None of the Apostles received the name of a Pastor: for our Lord Jesus Christ alone said, 'I am the good Pastor;' and again, 'My sheep follow Me.' Therefore this holy name, and the power of this name, after His resurrection He granted to Peter repenting; and He that was thrice denied gave to His denier that power which He had alone." Arnobius (saith he) noteth none of the Apostles ever to have had the name of a Pastor given to him by Christ, beside S. Peter alone. But I demand of M. S. where he hath in Arnobius this word "ever?" for he saith that Peter had this name after the resurrection, which none of the Apostles had before. He writeth against the Novatians, which denied help to such as repented after Baptism; proving by example of Peter that they are to be received, seeing Christ gave him greater dignity after his repentance than he had before his fall: but that Peter had greater authority than the rest of the Apostles, he never thought or said. M. Sander cutteth off both the head and the tail in this discourse, lest the meaning of Arnobius might appear; for thus he writeth: *Dicis certe baptizatis non debere pœnitentibus subveniri. Ecce Apostolo pœnitenti succurritur, qui est Episcoporum Episcopus; et major gradus additur [redditur] ploranti,*

[2] [*Epist.* x. *ad Episc. per provinc. Viennens. constit.* Opp. i. 217. Quesnel admits that the words "*præ* cæteris" in this sentence should most probably be "*pro* cæteris." (*Not.* p. 435.)]

[3] [*Comment. in Psal.* sig. x 3. Argentor. 1522. Erasmus, who first published this work, vainly endeavours (in his dedicatory Epistle to Pope Adrian VI.) to vindicate its authorship for Arnobius Afer, when it really belongs to Arnobius Junior, who lived a century and a half later. See the *Conference betwene Rainoldes and Hart,* p. 505. Lond. 1584. Ger. Jo. Vossii *Hist. Pelag.* Lib. i. Cap. xi. p. 50. Amstel. 1655. Ussher's *Letters,* p. 436. Lond. 1686. Jortin's *Life of Erasmus,* i. 302. Ib. 1758. Mosheim's *Eccles. Hist.* Vol. i. p. 454. ed. Soames, Lond. 1841.]

quam sublatus est deneganti. Quod ut doceam, illud ostendo, quod nullus Apostolorum nomen Pastoris accepit, &c.: "Indeed thou sayest that such as repent, being baptized, ought not to be helped. Behold the Apostle repenting is helped, which is a Bishop of Bishops; and a greater degree is restored to him weeping, than was taken from him denying. Which that I may teach, this I shew, that none of the Apostles received the name of a Shepherd," &c. Again, in the end, following the words before cited by M. Sander, he saith: *Ut non solum recuperasse quod amiserat probaretur, verum etiam et multo amplius pœnitendo, quam negando perdiderat, acquisisse:* "He gave His denier that power which before His resurrection He alone had; that he might be proved not only to have recovered that which he lost, but also to have gotten much more by repenting than he lost by denying." This speaketh Arnobius of the general authority which Peter had over all the Church; as every Apostle had likewise, and was a Bishop and overseer of Bishops as well as Peter, and a Pastor of the universal Church; which thing Arnobius never did deny.

These therefore be M. Sander's arguments: None of the Apostles had the name of a Pastor before Christ's resurrection; *ergo* they never had it. Peter was called to greater dignity after his fall than he had before; *ergo* he was greater than his fellow-Apostles. Again, Peter was a Bishop, or an overseer of Bishops; *ergo* he was Bishop over the Apostles.

Next Arnobius is cited Ambrose; *in* xxiv. *Luc.*[1]*;* who first said that Peter was "everywhere either alone or first;" and then, upon these words, "Peter, dost thou love Me," saith: *Dominus interrogat*, &c.: "Our Lord asked not to learn, but to teach whom He, being to be lifted up into heaven, did leave to us as the Vicar of His love. For so thou hast it, 'Simon, thou son of John, dost thou love Me? Yea, Lord, Thou knowest that I love Thee. Jesus saith to him, Feed My lambs.' Peter, being privy of a good conscience, doth testify his own affection, not taken for the time, but already well known to God: for who else were able to profess this thing of himself? And because he alone amongst all professeth, he is preferred before all." M. Sander omitteth the conclusion: *Major enim omnibus charitas:* "For the greatest

[1] [*Opp.* Tom. iii. coll. 232, 233.]

of all is charity." So Peter is hereby declared to have the greatest love, but not to have the greatest authority.

M. Sander urgeth, that he is the "Vicar of Christ's love" and pastoral office. The one indeed Ambrose saith; the other Sander sayeth, but is not able to prove: no, not by that which followeth in the same place of Ambrose, that Peter had committed to him to feed, "not only the lambs with milk, as at the first; nor yet the little sheep, as at the second time, but the sheep; to the end that he, being more perfect, might govern the more perfect." For every one of the Apostles had the same charge to feed the sheep of Christ, and not the lambs or little sheep only. Neither doth the word of government help him. For every Apostle had the like government over the whole flock which Peter hath; and there is an ordinary government in every particular Church, 1 Co. xii., which proveth not the governors to be rulers one over another. Wherefore this collection is not only vain, but also ridiculous, that Peter should have authority to govern Patriarchs, Archbishops, and Bishops, as well as Parish Priests, because he must feed the sheep of Christ.

I will not here stand to discuss how properly the distinction of lambs, little sheep, and sheep, is observed by Ambrose; but taking it according as he distinguisheth it, yet here is nothing given to Peter but primacy of love, or, as elsewhere he saith, of order; but of authority singular here is nothing at all: and that his conclusion declareth sufficiently: *Et ideo, quasi perfecto in omnibus, quem caro jam revocare non posset a gloria passionis, corona decernitur:* "And therefore a crown is decreed to him, as to one perfect in all things, whom the flesh could not call back from the glory of suffering." This conclusion M. S. (as his manner is) hath left out; by which it is apparent, that Ambrose inferreth no singularity of authority in Peter, as more perfect than the rest of the Apostles; but as perfect in such degree as the rest of the Apostles, which were likewise prepared to martyrdom, were equal with him therein.

The testimony of Bernard, a late writer, though he were no flatterer, yet I receive not; as of one which was deceived with the common error of his time.

But in sign that Peter was general Shepherd, saith M. Sander, it is not read that he was "ordained Bishop of any other than of Christ; yet did he with two other Apostles ordain S. James Bishop of Jerusalem," as Eus. Lib. ii. Cap. 0. [i.] writeth. There is no doubt but James was acknowledged by the Apostles to be appointed by the Holy Ghost to remain at Jerusalem; though not as a particular Bishop, but as an Apostle of the whole Church. But as we read not that Peter was made Bishop by any man, so we read not that he was made Bishop by Christ.

Yet Arnobius, *in Psa.* cxxxviii.[1], saith he was made "a Bishop of Bishops:" *Ecce Apostolo pœnitenti succurritur, qui est Episcoporum Episcopus:* "Behold the Apostle being penitent is succoured, which is a Bishop of Bishops." He asketh if "any thing could be spoken more plainly?" Yes, verily, you had need of plainer speeches than this, to prove that he was Bishop of the Apostles. For admit that he was an "overseer" of particular Bishops, as the word Ἐπίσκοπος doth signify, yet it followeth not that he was an overseer or Bishop of the Apostles. In which sense Clemens also (if the Epistle were not counterfeit[2]) might justly call James "a Bishop of Bishops;" and not, as M. Sander answereth, that he was an Archbishop of inferior Bishops, but an Apostle, overseer of particular Bishops.

That Cyprian, *ad Quintum*[3], saith, *Neque quisquam*, &c.: "Neither doth any of us make himself a Bishop of Bishops," he answereth, that although no man may make himself, yet Christ may make a man a Bishop of Bishops: but where findeth he that Christ maketh the Pope a Bishop of Bishops? How Peter might be called a Bishop of Bishops, I have shewed before. But the Council of Carth. iii., Cap. xxvi.[4],

[1] [Supra, pag. 319.]

[2] [Which it is. *Ep.* i. *ad Jacob. frat. Dom.*]

[3] [The words "Neque enim quisquam nostrum Episcopum se Episcoporum constituit" are not found in the Epistle to Quintus, but in S. Cyprian's address at the opening of the Council of Carthage in the year 256. (*Opp.* p. 229. ed. Fell.) In this passage there is an evident allusion to the presumptuous interference of Stephen, Bishop of Rome, in a matter of discipline not under his diocesan control. Abrahamus Bzovius, in his *Pontifex Romanus*, when speaking of the Pope's thirty-seventh title, "Judex Episcoporum," thought it altogether necessary to insert the clause "præter Romanorum Pontificem" as a qualification of S. Cyprian's language. (p. 473. Colon. Agripp. 1619.)]

[4] [Joverius, Class. ii. fol. 18, b.—"Ut primæ sedis Episcopus non

forbiddeth that the Bishop of Rome, or any other Primate, should be called "the Prince of Priests, or Highest Priest, or by any such like name, but only the Bishop of the first seat."

Yet Optatus feared not to write thus, Lib. vii. *De schism.*[5], of S. Peter: *Præferri Apostolis omnibus meruit*, &c.: "He deserved to be preferred before all the Apostles; and he alone received the keys of the kingdom of heaven, to be communicated unto the rest." Master Sander confessing, and truly, that the Apostles "took the keys belonging to their Apostolic office immediately of Christ," saith they received the keys of their bishoplike office of Peter. But what lock was there that they could not open and shut by their Apostolic key, when Christ saith, 'Whatsoever you bind or loose,' and 'Whose sins soever you forgive or retain;' which was the power of their Apostolic keys? If the Apostolic keys were so sufficient, what need they any bishoplike keys? Into these absurdities both he and Optatus do follow; whiles the one will urge a prerogative of Peter, the other will forge a bishoplike office in the Apostles, whereof the Scripture giveth us no instruction.

As for Leo and Gregory, Bishops of Rome, although they were not come to the full pride of Antichrist, yet the mystery of iniquity having wrought in that seat near five or six hundred years before them, and then greatly increased, they were so deceived with the long continuance of error, that

appelletur Princeps Sacerdotum, aut Summus Sacerdos, aut aliquid hujusmodi, sed tantum primæ sedis Episcopus." (See before, page 71.) This Decree is alleged by Ivo (Par. v. Cap. 57.) and Gratian. (*Dist.* xcix. C. iii.)]

5 [*Opp.* pp. 101—2. Antverp. 1702. S. Jerom (*De Viris illust.* Cap. cx.) expressly states that the work of S. Optatus *De schismate Donatistarum* was comprised in *six* books, and the author's own testimony (Lib. i. Cap. vii.) agrees with this assertion. The seventh book was added in small type in the edition published by Franciscus Balduinus in 1563. Mr. Husenbeth (*St. Cyprian vindicated*, p. 19. Norwich, 1839.) has cited the chapter adduced by Sanders, but afterwards (p. 61.) mentions the seventh book against Parmenian as that "which some critics indeed have rejected as of doubtful authenticity." Vid. Du Pin *Præfat.* §. ii. Fabricii *Biblioth. Eccles.* i. 200—1. *Bibl. med. et inf. Latin.* v. 498—9. Joan. Fabric. *Hist. Bibl. Fabr.* i. 73. Wolfenb. 1717.]

they thought the dignity of Peter[1] was much more over the rest of his fellow-Apostles than the holy Scriptures of God (against which no continuance of error can prescribe) doth either allow or bear withal. Wherefore, although he have some shew out of the old writers, yet hath he nothing directly to prove that Peter did excel the other Apostles in bishoplike authority; and out of the word of God no one jot or tittle that Peter as a Bishop excelled the other Apostles, not as Apostles, but as Bishops.

THE THIRTEENTH CHAPTER.

SANDER. *Sander.* That the pastoral and chief Bishop's authority of Saint Peter was an ordinary authority, and therefore it must go for ever unto his successors; whereas the Apostolic authority, being extraordinary, hath no successors in it. The Church never lacked a visible Rock.

FULKE. *Fulke.* THAT the office of Apostles, which had general charge to preach over the whole world, is ceased with the Apostles' lives, it is indeed granted of us: but that their Apostolic authority was extraordinary, or that all their authority is so determined that it hath no successors in it, we do utterly deny. For the same authority of preaching, of ministering the Sacraments, of binding and loosing, which the Apostles had, is perpetual in the Church, in the Bishops and Elders, which are all successors of the Apostles. And if the Apostolic authority hath no successors in it, what meaneth the Pope, almost in every Bull and decretal Epistle, to brag so much of the Apostolic authority, and to ground all things *Apostolica authoritate,* "by the Apostolic authority?" By which it is evident, that M. Sander's new distinction of "Apostolic" and "Bishoplike" authority in the Apostles is not acknowledged by the Popes themselves; but invented lately by such as he is, to have a starting-hole, to seem to avoid such arguments and authorities as prove all the Apostles equal in authority.

But let us see what reasons he hath to prove that S. Peter's pastoral authority was ordinary, and must go to his successors, more than the pastoral authority of every Apostle.

First, S. Peter, being but one man, was not able to preach

[1] [Palmer's *Treatise on the Church,* Vol. ii. pp. 491—2. Lond. 1838.]

to all men at once, nor to govern nations newly converted; therefore he had twelve companions adjoined to him: but, the world being converted, it is easy for the Pope without such fellows to govern all the faithful, by help of many inferior officers: as though the Church had not inferior officers in the Apostles' time. If S. Peter then was not able to rule, which had such great gifts, much less the Pope, which is nothing comparable with him in gifts, and is often a wicked man and an heretic, is able to govern all the Church: for he hath not so great an help of the conversion of the world as he hath a want of Peter's gracious gifts, meet for such a government.

Secondly, he would have us mark "the peculiar names of a Rock, of a Pastor, and of a Confirmer of his brethren, which are given by Christ to S. Peter alone; which argue that Peter's Supremacy must necessarily continue for ever." But who will grant to M. S. that Christ gave these peculiar names to Peter alone? Indeed, that which is meant by the names is ordinary and perpetual in the Church. Peter was a Rock; not his person, but his doctrine, that remaineth still in the Church. He was a Shepherd and confirmer of his brethren; and there be now many Shepherds and confirmers of their brethren.

Thirdly, he saith the Church never wanted a visible Rock on the earth, beside the eternal Rock Christ; who in this life "might be so strongly fastened in the faith of Christ, the great Rock, that he (though not for his own sake, yet for the Church's sake,) might be able to stay up all other small stones which joined [leaned] unto him," until Christ came in the flesh; who likewise appointed Saint Peter and his successors to be this ordinary Rock, as Adam, Enos, Henoch, Noe, Abraham, Isaac, Jacob, Moses, Aaron and his successors, who sat in the chair of Moses until the coming of Christ.

Against this I say, that the Church militant on earth hath her foundation in heaven, and not on earth: therefore the Church hath not a visible Rock on earth. Again, it is not true that some one hath always been this visible Rock on earth. For who was greater, Abraham or Melchisedech? Out of all controversy Melchisedech. Then was not Abraham the only Rock. After the death of Jacob and the twelve Patriarchs, who was the visible Rock until Moses was called? And yet had God a Church among the Jews all that time. Thirdly, who is so impudent to say, that all the successors of Aaron were so strongly fastened in the faith, that they were able to stay all the small stones that leaned upon them? Was not Urias the High Priest an idolater? 2 Reg. xvi. What were Jason, Menelaus, Lysimachus, by the report of the book of Maccabees? Was not Caiphas and Annas Sadducees, by the testimony of S. Luke, Act. v., and of Josephus[1]? Where is then the visible Rock, whose faith never failed, &c.? We see there was none such before Christ: therefore there need to be none such after Him.

His fourth reason is of "the name of a Pastor," which signifieth an ordinary office: "for as the sheep continue after S. Peter's death, so must there be also a Shepherd, as Peter was." But how proveth he that Peter was an only Shepherd? Forsooth Chrysostom saith, Lib. ii. *De Sacerdotio*[2], *Christus sanguinem,* &c.: "Christ hath shed His blood to purchase those sheep, the care of whom He did commit both to Peter and to Peter's successors." But whom doth Chrysostom take for Peter's successors? the Bishops of Rome only? No, verily, but all true Pastors of the Church, as his words going before do manifestly declare: *Neque enim tum volebat testatum esse quantum a Petro amaretur; siquidem id multis nobis argumentis constabat. Verum hoc Ille tum agebat, ut et Petrum et cæteros nos edoceret, quanta benevolentia ac charitate erga Suam Ipse Ecclesiam afficeretur; ut hac ratione et nos quoque ejusdem Ecclesiæ studium curamque toto animo susciperemus:* "For His purpose was not then to testify unto us how much He was beloved of Peter; for that was evident unto us by many arguments. But this thing then He intended, that He might teach both Peter and all us what benevolence and love He beareth toward His Church; that by this reason we also might take upon us with all our heart the love and charge of the same Church." This sentence sheweth, that Chrysostom accounted himself and every true Pastor of the Church a successor of Peter; and not the Bishop of Rome alone.

As for Leo, a Bishop of Rome, I have often protested that

1 [See before, p. 246, n. 2.]

2 [*Opp.* Tom. i. p. 372. ed. Bened.]

he was more addicted to the dignity of his see than the Scripture would bear him; and therefore was overruled and resisted in the General Council of Chalcedon.

His fifth argument is a rule of law: "Where the same reason is, the same right ought to be[3]." The reason of Peter's confession and power is such as agreeth to any ordinary office of the Church: therefore the office of Peter being a Rock, of strengthening his brethren, and feeding Christ's sheep, is an ordinary office. But I say that Peter's confession made him not a Rock, but declared him so to be; being appointed of Christ for one of the twelve foundations of the Church. The office of strengthening and feeding, as it was not singular in Peter, so it is not ordinary that it should be singular in any man.

His sixth reason: "Irenæus, Optatus, and Augustin did reckon up such successors of Peter as had lived till every of their ages or times:" therefore Peter had successors in his pastoral office. It is not denied but he had them, and other Bishops also, successors in his pastoral office; at least the Bishops of Antioch, where by your own confession he was Bishop before he came to Rome. Therefore his succession was not singular to the Bishops of one see.

His seventh reason: "No man may preach to them to whom he is not sent:" therefore there must be "a general Pastor," to send other to preach to them that are not converted, to plant new bishopricks, to control them that are negligent, to supply the things that lack, to excommunicate such as live in no diocese, &c. For sending he quoteth Rom. x., where mention is only of the sending of God, and [not] of the sending by men. But all his questions and doubts may be answered. Either the whole Church in General Councils, or every particular Church in their Synods, as they shall see most expedient, may send preachers; as the Apostles and Elders sent Peter and John into Samaria; and order all such matters as he imagineth must be done only by the Pope. But he asketh, "Who shall summon all other Bishops to General or Provincial Councils?" And I ask him, who summoned the four great and principal General Councils, and so many Provincial Councils, but the Emperors and Princes in whose dominion they were gathered? So that here is no necessary affairs of the Church, that doth

[3] ["Ubi eadem ratio, idem jus."]

require one general Pastor, or Pope of Rome, when all things may and have been done best of all without him.

As for placing of Bishops in sees vacant, uniting of two bishopricks in one, or dividing one into two, may better be done by the auctority of those Churches, with consent of their Princes, who seeth and knoweth what is needful in those cases, than by one, which, sitting in his chair at Rome, requireth half a year's travel from some part of the world to him, before he can be advertised of the case, and yet must understand it by hearsay, and therefore not able to see what is expedient so well as they that are present, and see the state of the matter.

Finally, it is against all likelihood that Christ would make such a general Shepherd over all His flock, as many thousand sheep, which live under the Sophi, [Cophti[1],] the Cham, the Turk, can have none access unto for such things as are supposed necessary to be had, and to be obtained from him only. Wherefore, if the Pope were Head of the Church, such as by cruelty of tyrants are cut from him should be cut from the body of the Church. Yea, if heathenish tyrants could so much prevail as they do in hindering this government of the Pope, (pretended to be so necesssary,) the gates of hell might prevail against the Church, contrary to the promise of Christ.

THE FOURTEENTH CHAPTER.

SANDER. *Sander.* That the ordinary auctority of S. Peter's primacy belongeth to one Bishop alone. The whole government of the Church tendeth to unity.

FULKE. *Fulke.* CONCERNING Peter's primacy, as there is little in the Scriptures whereupon it may be gathered, so I have shewed that it was not in him perpetual: for there are greater arguments to prove the primacy of James. Again, the greatest shew of Peter's primacy that we read of in the Scriptures is the primacy or head Apostleship of the Circum-

[1] [It is said that in some ancient monuments the Egyptians are named "Ægophti," and hence "Cophti" or "Copti." See Brerewood's *Enquiries*, p. 156. Lond. 1635. Pagitt's *Christianography*, pp. 37, 88. Ib. 1674. Baronius, *Annall.* Tom. vi. in Legat. Eccl. Alexand. pp. 712, 713. Antverp. 1658.]

cision. So that, if one Bishop should succeed him in that primacy, he must be chief Bishop over the Jews, and not over the Gentiles: for the chief Apostleship over the Gentiles was by God committed to Paul. Galat. ii. 7, 8. But if M. Sander say, as he doth in another place, that the Pope succeedeth both these Apostles, and therefore hath both their auctority; first, he overthroweth his own Rock of the Church, which he will have to be Peter alone. Secondly, his argument of unity, which he urgeth in this chapter, he subverteth, if the Pope's auctority be derived from two heads. Thirdly, he destroyeth his own distinction of bishoplike and Apostolic auctority, if the Apostolic auctority of Paul should descend to the Pope by succession.

Now let us consider what weighty reasons he hath to prove the title of this chapter. S. Peter's auctority was "specified" before the auctority was given to the rest of binding and loosing. Mat. xviii. Therefore, seeing it was first in him alone, it ought to descend to one Bishop alone. But let M. Sander shew where it was given to him alone, or promised to him alone either. For the promise, "Thou shalt be called Peter," gave him no auctority; nor yet the performance thereof, "Thou art Peter." But still the auctority is promised, "I will build," "I will give," (I reason as M. Sander doth of the future tense:) which promise, being made Matth. xvi., is performed Matth. xviii., not to Peter only, but to all the rest; and so all auctority is given in common. Johan. xx.

But S. Cyprian, *ad Jubaianum*, saith, that Christ gave the auctority first to Peter: *Petro primus* [al. *primum*] *Dominus* (*super quem ædificavit Ecclesiam, et* [*unde*] *unitatis originem instituit et ostendit,*) *potestatem istam dedit, ut id solveretur in terris,* [*cœlis,*] *quod ille solvisset* [*in terris.*] This doth M. Sander translate, "Our Lord did first give unto Peter," &c.; whereas he should say, "Our Lord was the first[2] that gave to Peter (upon whom He builded His Church, and instituted and shewed the beginning of unity,) this power, that whatsoever he loosed, it should be loosed in earth." This proveth that the auctority came first from Christ, but not that it was given first to Peter. And if we should understand it so that it was first given to Peter, yet

[2] [The reading is "primum" not only in Bp. Fell's edition, p. 201, but in the Venice impression of 1547, p. 491, and in that prepared by Erasmus. Tom. ii. p. 107. Lugd. 1550.]

he meaneth not that it was given to reside in his person; but that in him, as the attorney of the rest, it was given to them also, as he saith, Lib. i. *Ep.* iii.[1]*: Petrus tamen, super quem ædificata ab eodem Domino fuerat Ecclesia, unus pro omnibus loquens, et Ecclesiæ voce respondens, ait, Domine, ad quem ibimus,* &c.: "Yet Peter, upon whom the Church had been builded by the same our Lord, as one speaking for all, and answering in the voice of the Church, saith, 'Lord, whither shall we go?'" &c.: as he spake for all, so he received for all[2]. Which thing if it had been so, (as we find not in the Scripture,) yet could it have been no ordinary matter, to descend to one by succession. For the power being once received by one in the name of the rest, and by him delivered to the rest, it should be continued in succession of every one that hath received it, and not every day to be fetched anew from a several head. For that beginning came from unity, which Cyprian speaketh of, when Peter, being one, was the voice and mouth of the rest, and so received power for the rest; which being once received, the Church holdeth of Christ, and not of Peter or his successors; no more than a corporation holdeth of him that was their attorney, to receive either lands or authority from the Prince, but holdeth immediately of the Prince. Wherefore this argument followeth not; although the authority had begun in one, that it should continue in one.

The second reason is, that the most perfect government is meet for the Church: but "most perfection is in unity:" therefore there ought to be one chief governor of all. This one Chief Governor is our Saviour Christ; Ruler both in heaven and in earth: who, ascending into heaven, did not appoint one Pope over all His Church; but Apostles, Evangelists, Prophets, Pastors, and Teachers; that we might "all meet in the unity of faith," and grow into "a perfect man." Eph. iv. 11, 13.

The third reason is, that "the state of the new testament must be more perfect than the law:" but in the law there was one high Pastor, the High Priest on earth: therefore there must be one now also, and much rather. I answer, we have Him indeed, our Chief Bishop and High Priest, of whom the

[1] [*Epist.* lix. ad Cornel. *Opp.* p. 131. ed. Ox.]

[2] [This last clause seems to have been given by Fulke as part of the extract from S. Cyprian, but erroneously.]

Aaronical Priest was but a shadow; namely, Jesus Christ, whose government is nothing less perfect and beneficial to His Church in that He sitteth in heaven; and hath, as before is cited, left an ordinary ministry on earth, in many Pastors and Teachers over every several congregation; and not in one Pope over all, which could not possibly either know or attend to decide the one thousand part of controversies, which are determined by the auctority of Christ's law, and such Ministers as He hath ordained.

The fourth reason is of auctority. Cyprian, *ad Jubaianum*[3]*: Ecclesia, quæ una est,* &c.: "The Church, which is one, was founded by our Lord's voice upon one which received the keys thereof." And again, *De simplicitat. Prælat.*[4]*: Quamvis,* &c.: "Although Christ, after His resurrection, giveth equal power to all His Apostles, and sayeth, 'As My Father sent Me, so do I send you:' 'Receive the Holy Ghost: If you remit to any man his sins, they shall be remitted; and if you retain them, they shall be retained;' yet, that He might shew the unity, He disposed by His auctority the original of that unity, beginning of one." But Cyprian proceedeth: *Hoc erant,* &c.: "Verily the rest of the Apostles were the same thing that Peter was; endued with equal fellowship both of honour and of power: but the beginning proceedeth from unity, that the Church might be shewed to be one." These words are plain to declare, that Cyprian acknowledgeth no inequality of the Apostles, in respect of any auctority they had: also that the building of the Church upon one, and the receiving of the keys of one, was not an ordinary office to descend by succession, but a singular privilege for that one time; to shew the beginning, and not the continuance, of the power to proceed from one, but to be held always of One, which is Jesus Christ; without any shadows of one Bishop on earth to signify the same, when Christ is revealed "with open face" unto us now sitting in heaven. 2 Cor. iii. 18.

The like thing teacheth Optatus, Lib. ii. *De schism.*[5]*: Ut in una,* &c.: "That in one chair in which Peter sat

[3] [*Epist.* lxxiii. p. 203.]

[4] [*De unitate Ecclesiæ,* Opp. pp. 107—8.]

[5] [p. 31. ed. Du Pin. With respect to the evidence derived from Optatus, see Chillingworth's *Religion of Protestants,* Chap. v. Works, pp. 294—5. Lond. 1742. Poole's *Testimony of St. Cyprian against Rome,* p. 129. Ib. 1838.]

unity might be kept of all men; lest the rest of the Apostles should every one challenge a chair to himself: so that he should now be a schismatic and a sinner, that against a singular chair should place another. Therefore in that one chair, which is chief in gifts, Peter sat first." His meaning is to defend the unity of the Church against the Donatists: but of the auctority of Peter's chair over all other Bishops' chairs, if he had spoken any thing, M. Sander would not have concealed it; which doth us great wrong to think that we cannot distinguish a chair of unity from a chair of auctority.

The place of Hierom, *Cont. Jovin.* Lib. i., hath been answered once or twice[1]; shewing that among the Apostles, which were equal, Peter was chosen to be Primate, to avoid contention; which was a primacy of order, and not of auctority. As for the collection of Leo, Bishop of Rome, that Peter's primacy was "a platform for other Bishops," to understand that they must have a Bishop over them, if the very Apostles had an head among them, [it] savoureth of the ambition incident to that see which was appointed to be the seat of Antichrist: although neither Leo himself challenged so much as the Pope doth now; neither the Bishops of his time would yield unto him in so much as he challenged. For beside the whole General Council of Chalcedon, that concluded against him about the privileges of the Bishop of Constantinople; wherein they made him equal with the Bishop of Rome, the title of seniority only reserved; it appeareth by his Epistles that many Bishops acknowledged not such primacy over them as he claimed; whereof he complaineth in divers of his Epistles.

The place of Cyprian, Lib. i. *Epist.* iii.[2], "that heresies have sprung because one judge is not acknowledged instead of Christ, for the time, to whom the whole brotherhood might obey," he cannot deny but it is meant of Cyprian of one judge in every diocese: but he reasoneth *a fortiori*, that there ought to be much rather one judge over all the world. Howbeit I have shewed the inconsequence of this argument by example of one physician, one schoolmaster, one judge in temporal matters over the whole world; to whom it is as impossible to discharge such an office over all as it is profitable for one such to be in every town. He saith that "particular flocks are voluntary, and likewise particular Pastors; but one

[1] [Supra, p. 292.] [2] [*Ep.* lix. p. 129. ed. Fell.]

flock and one Pastor is of absolute necessity on earth." Indeed, the limits of particular flocks, and the persons of particular Pastors, are left to the appointment and choice of the Church. But that there should be particular flocks and Pastors, it is of God's ordination, though God by His Apostles appointed it to be so: yet is it of as absolute necessity, while the Church is dispersed in divers places of the world, as that there is one flock, and one Shepherd over all, Jesus Christ. And yet he is not ashamed to challenge us, pag. 298, "Let the text be named where Christ did institute many parishes:" whereas he himself, pag. 294, quoteth Tit. i. and Act. xiv., which places prove that Christ did institute many parishes; except he will say the Apostles did it without the institution of Christ which he confesseth they did not without the special inspiration of the Holy Ghost; or else will say, that the inspiration of the Holy Ghost, in the ordinance of many parishes, differeth from the institution of Christ.

But he that wrangleth thus impudently and unreasonably against the plain institution of many parishes by Christ, bringeth "a plain text where it is said, 'Feed My sheep,' to one Pastor." Hath this man any forehead, think you, that calleth this a plain text to prove that there should be one Shepherd upon earth over all the flock, because Christ upon special occasion exhorted one man to feed His flock? Are all things that were spoken to him singular unto him? Christ said to him, and to none other of the Apostles, "Come after Me, Satan; thou art an offence to Me; for thou savourest not the things that are of God, but of men." Christ said to Peter, and to none other, "Put up thy sword into thy scabbard." Christ said to Peter, and to none other, "Thou wilt deny Me thrice." O painted Rock of the popish Church! that hath no better ground than this saying, "Feed My sheep;" when he that challengeth auctority hereby of all other feedeth least, and poisoneth most.

But let us return, and see what auctority of old Fathers he hath to prove one pastoral pre-eminence over all the Church. Cyprian, Lib. i. *Ep.* viii.[3]: *Deus unus est, et Christus unus, et una Ecclesia, et Cathedra una, super Petram Domini voce fundata:* "There is one God, and one Christ, and one Church, and one chair, founded upon Peter by our Lord's voice." Hear [Here] I say, first of all, that he doth

[3] [*Epist.* xliii. p. 83. ed. Oxon.]

falsify Saint Cyprian's words, turning *Petram* into *Petrum*[1]; so that his saying is, "There is one chair, by our Lord's voice founded on the Rock. Another altar or a new Priesthood cannot be appointed, beside one altar and one Priesthood. Whosoever gathereth elsewhere scattereth abroad," &c. But if the word were *Petrum*, and not *Petram*, yet the whole discourse of that Epistle sheweth, that Cyprian meaneth by these words to set forth not the pastoral pre-eminence of one man over the whole Church, but one Bishop in every diocese. For he writeth against five Elders or Priests, which had chosen one Felicissimus, a schismatic, to be Bishop in Carthage against him.

But what other malicious ignorance or shameless impudence is this, that he perverteth the saying of Christ of Himself to the Pope, "There shall be one sheepfold, and one Shepherd?" Joan. x. Yet see his reason: "A flock of sheep is one by force of one Pastor: therefore, if the Pastor on earth be not one, the flock is not one on earth." If this argument be good, how is the flock one upon earth when there is no Pope? For the see hath been void divers times many days, many months, and sometime many years. How was the flock one when there were two or three Popes at once, and that so often, and so long together? Therefore the flock on earth is one, by that one only Shepherd Jesus Christ; whose divine voice all the sheep hear, though in His humanity He be ascended into heaven; and not by any one mortal man, to whom they cannot be gathered, neither, being so far abroad dispersed, can hear his voice.

And the whole order of the Church on earth tendeth to an unity in Christ; and not in one man whatsoever, as one general Pastor. For if that one should be an heretic, and all the Church tend to unity in him, the whole Church should be wrapped in heresy with him. That divers Popes have been heretics, as Liberius, Anastasius, Vigilius, Honorius, John the XXIII., in known condemned heresies, it is too manifest by records of antiquity that it should be denied. Wherefore Christ instituted no such ordinary auctority, to be limited in one succession, that it should have pre-eminence and jurisdiction over all the Church: seeing unity is best maintained in doctrine by His word, in government by the discipline by Him appointed. And unity in truth cannot be had at the

1 [It would appear that "Petrum" is the correct reading.]

hands of a man which is a liar: and experience sheweth, that the jurisdiction which the Bishop of Rome hath claimed hath been occasion of most and greatest schisms and dissensions that have been in particular Churches; when no man would obey his ordinary Pastors and Bishops without the appealing to the see of Rome: beside so many schisms as have been in the same see; which have set all the Christian world together by the ears, while they were divided in factions; some holding with one Pope, and some with another, and some with the third, and some with none of them all.

THE FIFTEENTH CHAPTER.

Sander. That the Bishop of Rome is that one ordinary Pastor who succeedeth in S. Peter's chair, and is above all Bishops, according to the meaning of God's word. Why S. Peter died at Rome. S. Augustin's mind touching the Supremacy of the Pope of Rome. SANDER.

Fulke. THE first reason is, that although Peter at the first was rather high Bishop of the Circumcision than of the Gentiles, yet because he did "at length settle himself at Rome by God's appointment, and left a successor there," he sayeth he "may well affirm that the Bishop of Rome's primacy is warranted by God's word." A strange kind of warrantise: for to omit that the primacy over the Gentiles by God's word is given to another, namely to Paul, from whom he can never prove that it was taken afterward; where hath he any word of God to prove that by His appointment Peter settled himself at Rome, and appointed there a successor? FULKE.

He quoteth Irenæus, Lib. iii. Cap. iii., who reporteth that Linus, the first Bishop of Rome, was ordained not by Peter only, but by Peter and Paul the Apostles, who founded the Church there[2]: even as Polycarpus by the Apostles in Asia was made Bishop in Smyrna; which Church, with the Church of Ephesus, founded by Paul, and continued by John, the Apostles, he citeth as witnesses alike with the Church of Rome of the tradition of the Apostles, against Valentinus and Marcion, which, being void of Scriptures, bragged of the tradition of the Apostles: but of Peter's primacy, or his successors over all Bishops, Irenæus saith not a word. No more

2 ["Fundantes igitur et instruentes beati Apostoli Ecclesiam, Lino episcopatum administrandæ Ecclesiæ tradiderunt."]

doth Tertullian, whom likewise he quoteth, *De præscript.*[1]; but, even as Irenæus, would have the tradition of the Apostles, against those heretics that boasted of it, to be tried by the confession of those Churches that were founded by the Apostles.

His second reason is upon a false supposition, that he hath already proved Peter alone to be the Rock, to have chief authority in feeding, &c.; all which things are untrue.

That Peter came to Rome[2], he is not content that it be testified by all ancient ecclesiastical writers, but he saith it is witnessed by the express word of God; 1 Pet. v.: "The Church which is gathered together in Babylon saluteth you[3]." Although the history of Peter's coming to Rome, and sitting there twenty-five years[4], testified by so many

1 [Cap. xxxvi.]

2 [Sanders (*Rocke*, p. 308.) remarks, that "some brainesick men woulde now persuade the contrarie." So early as the year 1520, a curious treatise was published by Ulricus Velenus, to prove "Apostolum Petrum Rhomam non uenisse, neque illic passum." Bishop Fisher wrote a reply: (Olearii *Biblioth.* i. 406. Jenæ, 1711.) and the best work upon the negative side of the question is Care's *Modest Enquiry whether St. Peter were ever at Rome, and Bishop of that Church.* 4to. Lond. 1687.]

3 [" Tametsi enim veteres existimaverint D. Petrum vocabulo Babylonis significasse urbem Romam, probabilis est Scaligeri conjectura, qui ex ipsa Babylone scriptam a Petro putat Epistolam hanc ad Judæos dispersos, qui habitabant in provinciis quarum Synagogæ pendebant a Patriarcha Babylonico." (De Marca, *De concord. Sacerd. et Imp.* Lib. vi. Cap. i. Tom. ii. p. 174. Paris. 1669.)]

4 [It is not easy to ascertain precisely what can have originated the idea of this fabulous duration of S. Peter's episcopate. Vedelius supposes that the vulgar opinion was founded on the assertion of Eusebius, that the Apostle went to Rome in the second year of Claudius, and suffered martyrdom in the last year of the reign of Nero, between which limits intervenes the space of a quarter of a century. (*De Cathedra Petri*, Lib. ii. Cap. xv. p. 296. Franeker. 1640.) Antoine Pagi's conjecture, however, is much to be preferred; namely, that the error was produced by a misapprehension of a passage in the second chapter of the treatise *De mortibus Persecutorum*, written by Lactantius, (or Lucius Cecilius, according to Le Nourri.) Here it is declared that, after the ascension of the Saviour, the Disciples "dispersi sunt per omnem terram ad Evangelium prædicandum, sicut illis Magister Dominus imperaverat; et per annos xxv., usque ad principium Neroniani imperii, per omnes provincias et civitates Ecclesiæ fundamenta miserunt. Cumque jam Nero imperaret, Petrus Romam

writers[5], is proved false in many circumstances by the plain word of God, yet I am content to admit that he came thither toward the latter end of Nero's reign. But that in his Epistle he sent salutations from Rome, I cannot admit, seeing that in such manner of salutations men use not to write allegorically; albeit that in the Revelation of Saint John Rome, the see of Antichrist, is mystically called Babylon. But Babylon, from whence S. Peter did write, is more probably to be taken for a city of that name in Egypt, where Mark was with him; whom the consent of antiquity affirmeth to have been Bishop of Alexandria, a city of Egypt also: who could not have been with him at Rome, seeing it is manifest by the first and second of the Epistle to the Galathians, and by divers of Saint Paul's Epistles, that if ever Peter was at Rome, it was but a short time in the latter end of Nero his empire; whereas Mark died in the eighth year of his reign, before Peter could be at Rome. For in the tenth year Paul was brought prisoner to Rome, Saint Luke accompanying him; who would not have omitted to shew that Peter was there to have met him, as the rest of the brethren did, if he had then been at Rome. Again, Paul, in so many Epistles as he writeth from Rome, sending salutations from mean personages, would not

advenit," &c. The period, then, which has reference to the preaching of all the Apostles equally, seems to have been wrongly considered to relate to S. Peter's possession of the Roman see. (*Critica Histor.—Chronol. in Annales C. Baronii*, Tom. i. p. 37. Colon. Allob. 1705.) François Pagi, who edited this work in its completeness, and was nephew to the author, has adopted the same explanation of this difficulty in his *Breviarium Gestorum Pontiff. Rom.* T. i. p. 3. Lucæ, 1729.]

5 [The *Chronicon* of Eusebius is "in primis" cited by Baronius, (ad an. 44. §. xxv.) and likewise by Bellarmin, (*De Rom. Pont.* Lib. ii. Cap. iv.) as bearing witness that S. Peter was Bishop of Rome for five and twenty years: but, as Joseph Scaliger observes, "Græca non habent." (*Animadvers.* p. 189.) The interpolation appears in the Latin version by S. Jerom, (p. 44.) who has repeated the statement in his Catalogue of Ecclesiastical Writers. (Cap. i.) For such occasional depravations S. Jerom prepares us by saying in his *Præfatio in Chronica*, "Et Græca fidelissime expressi, et nonnulla quæ mihi intermissa videbantur adjeci, in Romana maxime historia." It is strange that the learned Benedictine Clémencet should speak of "les 25 années de Pontificat, que la Chronique d'Eusebe donne à Saint Pierre." (*L'Art de vérifier les Dates*, ii. 356. A Paris, 1750.)]

have omitted mention of Peter, if he had been there. Saint Luke then, affirming that he tarried two years in prison at Rome, which must be until the twelfth year of Nero, it followeth that, if Peter came, he came very late to Rome, within two year before his death; at which time it was not possible that Mark, which was dead four years before, could be at Rome with him. Wherefore Babylon in that text cannot be taken for Rome.

Another reason of the Pope's Supremacy he maketh, that Peter not only came thither, but also died there. A simple reason why the city of Rome should have that prerogative, because she murdered the Apostles. Rather might Jerusalem claim it, in which Christ the Head of all died.

After this he telleth the fable, out of the counterfeit Egesippus[1], of Simon Magus flying in the air, and the Emperor Nero his great delight in his sorcery. The credit of Egesippus he defendeth, by blaming his translator for adding names of cities which had none such when Egesippus lived[2]. But

[1] [*De excidio Hierosolymitano,* Lib. iii. Cap. ii. fol. xxix. Colon. 1544. —For the remains of the true Hegesippus, who wrote about the year 170, and is placed by S. Jerom before Justin Martyr, (*De Vir. illust.* Cap. xxii.) vid. Grabii *Spicileg.* ii. 205—13. Oxon. 1714. Routhii *Reliquiæ Sacræ*, i. 191—203. Ib. 1814. The variations in the name of the Pseudo-Ben-Gorion are Josephus, Joseppus, Josippus, Igisippus, Egesippus, Hegesippus; and Colomesius speaks of the depravation of his title in manuscripts which belonged to Isaac Vossius. (*Paralipom.* Opp. p. 695. Hamb. 1709.) Bishop Pearson believed him to have been an author of the fourth or fifth century; (*Lect.* iii. *in Acta Apostol.* §. iv.) but Gerard Vossius more prudently places him amongst historians "incertæ ætatis." (*De Hist. Lat.* Lib. iii. Par. ii. p. 219. Amst. 1697.) Elsewhere, (*De Hist. Græc.* ii. viii.) he assents to the likelihood of Joseph Scaliger's opinion, that Gorionides lived at all events after the year 600; and Cap. xiv. he represents him as "infimæ antiquitatis scriptorem," one who existed not long after A. D. 968. Oudin is not satisfied with this degree of lateness, but brings Hegesippus down to 1120. (*Comm.* ii. 1026.) Tillemont declares that "On ne sçait quel est cet auteur, ni en quel tems il a vécu;" (*Mémoires*, Tome i. p. 240. A Brux. 1732.) and Struvius determines that he was not an impostor. (*Dissert. de doctis Impostoribus*, §. v. p. 11. Jenæ, 1710.) But whether he be considered an author or a compiler, or whether his work be vitiated or not, it is certain from the antiquity of two MSS. described by Mabillon that he must have flourished before the seventh age. (*Iter Italicum*, p. 14. Lut. Paris. 1724.)]

[2] [Sanders is not by any means the only Romanist who has ap-

that Simon Magus shewed no experiment of sorcery before Nero, as this counterfeit Egesippus reporteth, it is plain by Plinius, Lib. xxx. Cap. ii. *Natur. Histor.;* who, shewing how desirous Nero was, and what means he had, to have trial thereof, yet never could come by any. It was a practice of old time to feign such fables for love of the Apostles: as Tertullian witnesseth, *De Baptis.*[3], of a Priest of Asia, that was convicted and confessed that he feigned for the love of Paul a writing unto Tecla, in which many absurd things were contained. Again, so many apocryphal Gospels, Epistles, Itineraries, and Passions, as are counterfeited under the name of Apostles and ancient Fathers, who knoweth not to be fables and false inventions? Among which this fable of Simon Magus and Peter is one.

pealed with confidence to the Pseudo-Hegesippus. The Jesuit Coster cites his evidence as genuine. (*Enchirid. Controvers.* p. 131. Colon. Agripp. 1599.) Likewise Bellarmin, (*De Rom. Pont.* L. i. C. xxiii. et Lib. ii. Cap. iii.) saying in the latter place that he was "vicinus Apostolorum temporibus." But since this perplexing writer makes mention of Constantinople, a name not heard of till the year 330, we must concur in the judgment of Baronius: "Feruntur Hegesippi nomine Commentarius de excidio Ierosolymitano, et ad ipsum apposita Anacephaleosis: sed alterius plane auctoris est opus, qui (ut alias diximus) post tempora Constantini floruerit." (*Annall.* Tom. ii. ad an. 167. §. xv.) Gretser, in the first volume of his *Defensio Controv. Bellarm.*, (col. 1660. Ingolst. 1607.) asks with reference to Whitaker's proof that this work was not composed by the ancient Hegesippus, "Quis ex eruditiorum numero abnuit?" In his second volume, however, (col. 672. Ib. 1609.) he seems to hesitate, and affirms that "it is not so evident that these Commentaries were not written by the old Hegesippus as that the sun does not shine at midnight;" using the argument of Sanders, that interpolations may have been inserted at a succeeding time.]

3 [Cap. xvii. Rigaltius remarks that the name of Thecla had crept from some margin into the text. The *Acts of Paul and Thecla* were rejected as apocryphal by S. Jerom, (*Catal. Scriptt. Eccl.* Cap. vii.) and were afterwards condemned by Pope Gelasius in the year 496. (Gratiani *Decret.* Dist. xv. C. iii.) Baronius endeavours to maintain their credit, (*Martyrol.* die Septemb. 23.) and quotes in their favour a spurious Epistle of S. Jerom to Oceanus. (See before, p. 97, note 7.) Grabe has published this curious narrative both in Greek and Latin. (*Spicil.* Tom. i. pp. 95—127.) Conf. Fabricii *Cod. Apoc. Nov. Test.* ii. 794—6. Hamb. 1703. Schmidii *Decas Dissertt.* Apostoli uxorati, p. 364. Helmst. 1714.]

That S. Luke maketh no mention of Peter's death, he preventeth the objection, because he continued not his story so far: which [no] doubt (saith he) he would not have omitted, "if he had gone so far forward in his story." But seeing he brought Paul to Rome, both in his journey and in his history, why maketh he no mention of Peter's being there; which, if their story were true, must have sit there twenty years before?

To omit therefore the four causes why Peter should die at Rome; whereof three are taken out of a counterfeit August., *De Sanctis Hom.* xxvii.[1], the fourth out of Leo and Gregory, Bishops of Rome; he cometh to decide the controversy between the Greeks and Latins, who was first successor of Peter, Linus or Clemens; taking part with them that affirm Clemens: although Irenæus, the most ancient writer of any that is extant, name Linus: who was not a Grecian far off, but a Frenchman at Lyons, near hand to Italy: whose authority although he reject in naming Linus to be ordained Bishop by both the Apostles, yet he glorieth much that he calleth the Church of Rome *maximam, et antiquissimam,* &c.[2], "the greatest, and the most ancient, and known to all men; founded and settled by two most glorious Apostles, Peter and Paul." And again: *Ad hanc Ecclesiam,* &c.: "To this Church, by reason of the mightier principality, every Church, that is, the faithful that are every where, must needs agree[3]." But he proceedeth, and sheweth the cause why: *In qua semper ab hiis qui sunt undique conservata est ea quæ est ab Apostolis traditio:* "In which always that tradition which is from the Apostles hath been always kept of them that are round about."

M. Sander calleth it wilful ignorance in M. Jewell, that saith "the mightier principality" spoken of in Irenæus is meant of the civil dominion, and Roman empire; whereas it hath relation to the former titles of commendation, that it was "the greatest," and "the most ancient:" the greatest, he

[1] [alias *Serm.* ccii. in Append. Tom. v. ed. Ben. col. 138. This Sermon is found also among the works of S. Ambrose, (v. 142. Lut. Paris. 1661.) and those of S. Maximus Taurinensis. (Raynaudi *Heptas Præsulum,* p. 231. Par. 1671.)]

[2] [*Adv. Hær.* Lib. iii. Cap. iii. See Beaven's *Account of S. Irenæus,* pp. 63—68. Lond. 1841.]

[3] [" convenire," should *resort.*]

saith, because it was founded by Peter, the greatest Apostle. But so saith not Irenæus: for he saith it was founded "by two most glorious Apostles," and not by Peter alone. It was then greatest, because the greatest number of Christians were in Rome, as the greatest city. But how is it "the most ancient" but in respect of Peter's seniority; for otherwise Jerusalem and Antioch were ancienter in time? I answer, two ways. First, it is sophistical to urge the superlative degree grammatically: as when we say *potentissimo Principi*, "to the most mighty Prince," *doctissimo viro*, "to the best learned man," &c., we do not mean that no Prince is equal or superior in power, nor that no man is equal or superior in learning, to him whom we so commend; but to shew the power and learning of those persons to be excellent great. Secondly I answer, that Irenæus speaketh conjunctly it is sophistical to understand severally. He saith there is no Church of such greatness, so ancient, and so well known, as the Church of Rome.

From this blind collection out of Irenæus he cometh down groping to Cyprian; who, speaking of certain factious heretics that sailed from Carthage to Rome, to complain of Saint Cyprian and other Bishops of Afric to Pope Cornelius, [saith:] Lib. i. *Ep.* iii. *ad Cor.*[4]: *Audent et ad Petri*, &c.: "They dare carry letters from schismatical and profane men unto the chair of Peter, and the principal Church, from whence the priestly unity began: neither consider that they are Romans, whose faith is praised by the report of the Apostle; unto whom falsehood can have none access."

In this saying we must note the privileges of S. Peter's Supremacy to be at Rome. 1. "This [There] is S. Peter's chair; that is, his ordinary power of teaching," &c. Nay, rather, the Bishop's seat; which he and Paul did set up there, as Irenæus sheweth. Li. iii. Ca. iii. 2. "There is the principal Church, because the Bishop of Rome succeedeth the Prince of the Apostles." Nay, rather, because it is the greatest Church, being gathered in the greatest city of the world; as Irenæus also calleth it. 3. "The priestly unity began not in Rome, but in Peter: therefore there is the whole authority of Peter." The argument is naught: the beginning of unity proveth not authority. 4. "This word 'unity' doth import, that as Peter

[4] [*Epist.* lix. pp. 135—6. ed. Fell.]

alone had in him the whole power of the chief Shepherd, so Cornelius his successor hath in him the same power." This argument is of small importance; for neither had Peter alone such power, nor any of his successors. 5. "Where he saith infidelity can have no access to the Romans, what other thing is it than to say, [that] in the Church of Rome he ruleth for whose faith Christ prayed?" Luc. xxii.

Christ prayed for the faith of all His Apostles, and of all His disciples to the end of the world. Joan. xvii. Beside this, Master Sander translateth *perfidia*, which signifieth falsehood or false dealing, "infidelity." Secondly, that which Cyprian saith of all the faithful Romans, he draweth to his Pope. Thirdly, where Cyprian sheweth how long they shall continue without falsehood; namely, so long as they retain the faith praised by the Apostle, he maketh it perpetual to the see of Rome; whereas the Romans themselves write to Cyprian of those praises of the Apostle: *Quarum laudum et gloriæ degenerem fuisse, maximum crimen est:* "Of which praises and glory to be grown out of kind, it is the greatest crime[1]." Finally, if Cyprian had thought the Pope and Church of Rome could not err, he would never have maintained an opinion against them; as he did in rebaptizing them that were baptized by heretics.

The sixth: We must "add hereto, that Cyprian calleth Rome *Ecclesiæ Catholicæ matricem et radicem*, 'the mother and root of the Catholic Church'." Lib. iv. *Epist.* viii.[2] We find not Rome so called there. We find that Cyprian and his fellows exhorted all such troublesome persons as went over sea, and carried false tales, *ut Ecclesiæ Catholicæ matricem et radicem agnoscerent et tenerent*, "that they would acknowledge and hold the mother and root of the Catholic Church:" by which words they dissuaded them from joining with schismatics; who, being condemned in one Church, would gad up and down for absolution in another.

The seventh: "Did not S. Cyprian confess Cornelius to have received the appellation of Basilides lawfully out of Spain?" Li. i. *Ep.* iv.[3] There is no word of any such confession or appellation in that Epistle. But rather, if you

1 [See before, p. 159.]

2 [*Epist.* xlviii. p. 91. ed. Ox.]

3 [*Ep.* lxvii. pp. 172—3.]

suppose an appellation and a restitution by the Bishop of Rome, Cyprian and thirty-six Bishops with him determine the same restitution to be void and of none effect: *Neque* [*Nec*] *rescindere ordinationem jure perfectam potest, quod Basilides, post crimina sua detecta, et conscientiam* [*etiam*] *propria confessione nudatam, Romam pergens, Stephanum collegam nostrum, longe positum, et gestæ rei ac* [*tacitæ*] *veritatis ignarum, fefellit; ut ambiret* [*exambiret*] *reponi se injuste in episcopatum, de quo fuerat juste depositus. Hæc* [*Hoc*] *eo pertinent,* [*pertinet,*] *ut Basilidis non tam abolita sint quam cumulata delicta: ut ad superiora peccata ejus, etiam fallaciæ et circumventionis crimen accesserit. Neque enim tam culpandus est ille, cui negligenter obreptum* [*est,*] *quam hic execrandus, qui fraudulenter obrepsit. Obrepere autem* [*si*] *hominibus Basilides potuit, Deo non potest; cum scriptum sit, Deus non irridetur:* [*deridetur:*] "Neither can it make frustrate the ordination lawfully made, that Basilides, after his crimes were detected, and his conscience opened by his own confession, going to Rome, hath deceived our fellow-Bishop Stephen, being far off, and ignorant of the matter and of the truth; that he might ambitiously seek to be unjustly restored into his bishoprick, from which he was justly deposed. These things tend to this end, that the offences of Basilides are not so much abolished as increased: so that to his former sins the crime of deceitfulness and circumvention is added. For neither is he so much to be blamed, who was negligently deceived, as he is to be abhorred, which did craftily deceive him. But if Basilides could deceive men, he could not deceive God; seeing it is written, 'God is not mocked'."

Here is no lawful appellation spoken of, but the Bishop of Rome's sentence pronounced void; and he blamed for his negligence and rashness, to meddle with matters whereof he could have no knowledge, by means of distance of place. But if M. Sander reply, that he is not reproved for taking such appellations, he must hear what Cyprian saith of such appellations, which began to be used in his days, unto Cornelius, Bishop of Rome, immediately after the words cited by him, Lib. i. *Epi.* iii.[4], of those schismatics that were so bold as to sail to Rome, and carry letters as above: *Quæ autem causa veniendi, et pseudo-Episcopum contra Episcopos fac-*

[4] [Supra, pag. 341.]

tum nunciandi? Aut enim placet illis quod fecerunt, et in suo scelere perseverant; aut si displicet, et recedunt, sciunt quo revertantur. Nam cum statutum sit omnibus nobis, et æquum sit pariter et justum, ut uniuscujusque causa illic audiatur ubi est crimen admissum; et singulis Pastoribus portio gregis sit ascripta, quam regat unusquisque et gubernet, rationem sui actus Domino redditurus; oportet utique eos quibus præsumus non circumcursare, nec Episcoporum concordiam cohærentem sua subdola et fallaci temeritate collidere; sed agere illic causam suam, ubi et accusatores habere et testes sui criminis possint: nisi paucis desperatis et perditis minor videtur esse auctoritas Episcoporum in Africa constitutorum; qui jam de illis judicaverunt, et eorum conscientiam, multis delictorum laqueis vinctam, judicii sui nuper gravitate damnarunt: "But what cause had they to come, and to report that a false Bishop was made against the Bishops? For either that which they have done pleaseth them, and they continue in their wickedness; or if it displease them, and they go back from it, they know whither they should return. For whereas it is decreed of us all, and is also meet and right, that every man's cause should be heard there where the crime was committed; and a portion of the flock is committed to every Pastor, which every one ought to rule and govern, as he that shall yield an account of his doings to the Lord; verily it behoveth them over whom we have rule not to run about, neither by their crafty and deceitful rashness to craze the concord of Bishops agreeing together; but there to plead their matter, where they may have both accusers and witnesses of their crime: except the authority of the Bishops ordained in Africa seemeth to a few desperate and wicked fellows to be less; which have already judged of them, and condemned their consciences, bound with the weight of their judgment in many cords of their offences." This place of Cyprian declareth not only that the Bishops of Africa had decreed against such appellations; but also that they thought their authority nothing inferior to the Bishops of Italy, nor to the Bishop of Rome himself.

The eighth note out of Cyprian is, that he "required Stephanus the Pope to depose Marcianus, the Bishop of Arles in France: which to do in another province is a sign that the Pope of Rome is above other Bishops." If it were true that

M. Sander sheweth, it might prove the Bishop of Rome to be a Primate or Metropolitan: it could not prove him to be a Bishop over all the world. But it is utterly false that he saith, "Cyprian required the Pope Stephen to depose him:" for he was deposed by the judgment of all the Bishops of the West Church; *ab universis Sacerdotibus judicatus,* "condemned of all the Priests." Only he exhorteth Stephen of Rome, which was negligent in this behalf, to join with the rest of the Bishops of France in ordering of another Bishop in his stead; who long since hath been excommunicated, and deposed from his place, for taking part with Novatian the heretic. And lest you should think the whole matter to be referred to the Bishop of Rome, these are his words in the same Epistle: Li. iii. *Ep.* xiii.[1]: *Idcirco enim, frater charissime, copiosum corpus est Sacerdotum; concordiæ mutuæ glutine, atque unitatis vinculo copulatum: ut si quis ex collegio nostro hæresim facere, et gregem Christi lacerare et vastare tentaverit, subveniant cæteri; et, quasi Pastores utiles et misericordes, oves Dominicas in gregem colligant:* "For therefore, most well-beloved brother, the body or fellowship of Priests is plentiful; being coupled together by the glue of mutual concord, and the band of amity: so that if any of our company shall assay to make an heresy, or to rent or waste the flock of Christ, the rest should give aid; and, as profitable and merciful Shepherds, gather again the Lord's sheep into His fold."

The ninth note is, that notwithstanding Cyprian "dissented from Pope Stephanus in opinion concerning the baptizing of such as had been baptized by heretics, yet he denied not his prerogative; but kept still the unity of the militant Church, in acknowledging the visible head thereof." He quoteth his *Ep. contra Stephan.*[2], wherein is no word of acknowledging the Pope's prerogative: but contrariwise every child may see, that seeing he did boldly dissent in opinion from the Bishop of Rome, and wrote against him, he held no such prerogative of that see as the Papists now maintain, that the Bishop of Rome cannot err. Indeed Cyprian professeth, that notwithstanding he differed from him in opinion, yet he would not depart from the unity of the Church. But what is this for acknowledging of a visible

[1] [*Epist.* lxviii. p. 178.] [2] [*Ep.* lxxiv. p. 210.]

head; whereof M. S. speaketh much, but Cyprian never a word; neither in that place, nor in any of all his works?

The next authority is Hippolytus; whose words Prud[entius] rehearseth: *Peristeph. in Passion. Hip.*[1]: *Respondet, Fugite,* &c.:

> "His answer was, O flee the schisms
>   Of cursed Novat's lore:
> And to the Cath'lic folk and flock
>   Yourselves again restore.
> Let only one faith rule and reign,
>   Kept in the Church of old:
> Which faith both Paul doth still retain,
>   And Peter's chair doth hold."

No doubt this was a good exhortation, so long as the temple of Peter and Paul at Rome did hold the old Catholic faith: from which seeing the Pope is now fled, we may not honour the empty chair of Peter, to think there is his faith where his doctrine is not.

After Hippolytus followeth Sozomenus[2]; who reporteth that Athanasius, and certain other Bishops of the Greek Church, came to Rome, to Julius the Bishop there, to complain that they were unjustly deposed by the Arians. Whereupon the Bishop of Rome, finding them upon examination to agree with the Nicene Council, "did receive them into the communion; as one that had care of them all, for the worthiness of his own see; and did restore to every of them their own Churches," &c. Here M. Sander hath his nine observations: he delighteth much in that number. But it shall not need to stand upon them. It is confessed that in Sozomenus's time, the writer of this story, who judgeth of things done according to the present state in which he lived, the see of Rome was grown into great estimation; and counted the first see, or principal in dignity of all Bishops' sees in the world. Yea, it is true that Socrates, a writer of histories as well as he, sayeth, that, long before his time, the Bishop's

1 [*Opp.* fol. 180, b. Antverp. 1540.

> "Respondit, Fugite, O miseri, execranda Novati
> Schismata: Catholicis reddite vos populis.
> Una fides vigeat, prisco quæ condita templo est;
> Quam Paulus retinet, quamque cathedra Petri."]

2 [Lib. iii. Cap. viii. ed. Lat. Conf. Cassiodorii *Hist. Tripart.* L. iv. C. xv.]

see of Rome, as well as of Alexandria, was "grown beyond the bands [bounds] of Priesthood into a foreign lordship and dominion." Soc. Lib. vii. Cap. xi.[3] But if we consider the records of the very time in which Julius lived, we shall not find that the dignity of his see was such, as that he had such authority as Sozomenus ascribeth to him; and much less such as M. Sander imagineth of him.

In Epiphanius there is an Epistle of one Marcellus, which, beside that he called him his fellow-minister, acknowledgeth no such dignity of his see. Lib. iii. To. i.[4] And Sozomenus himself testifieth that the Bishops of the East derided and contemned his commandments: Lib. iii. Cap. viii.: and, Cap. xi.[5], they were as bold to depose him, with the Bishops of the West, as he was to check them, that they called not him to their Council. Wherein, as I confess, they did evil: yet thereby they shewed evidently, that the Christian world in those days did not acknowledge the usurpation of the Bishop of Rome, as M. Sander saith they did. Neither durst they ever to dissent from him, if it had been a Catholic doctrine received in the Church, that the Bishop of Rome is head of the Church, Bishop of all Bishops, judge of all causes, and one which cannot err. As for Athanasius, Paulus, &c., and other Bishops, being tossed to and fro by their enemies, no marvel if they were glad to find any comfort at the Bishop of Rome's hands, having first sought to the Emperors for refuge; of whom sometime they were holpen, sometime they were hindered, as information was given either for them or against them.

But "Arnobius," he sayeth, "giveth a marvellous witness for the Church of Rome," *in Psal.* cvi.[6]: *Petrus, in deserto,* &c.: "Peter, wandering in the desert of this world, until he came to Rome, preached the Baptism of Jesus Christ, in whom all floods are blessed from Peter unto this day. He hath made the going forth of the waters into thirst; so that he which shall go forth of the Church of Peter shall perish for thirst."

3 [Fulke translates the Latin of Musculus: "ultra Sacerdotii limites ad externum dominatum progresso."]

4 [*Opp.* Tom. i. p. 834. ed. Petav.]

5 [pp. 589, 591. edit. Musc. See Du Moulin's *Defence of the Catholicke Faith,* pp. 421—23. Lond. 1610.]

6 [sig. p 7. Vide supra, p. 319, n. 3.]

It is a marvellous wit of M. Sander, that can find such marvellous prerogative of Peter in this place, which Arnobius would have in the example of Peter to be understood of all men: *Quid est Ascendunt? Disce in Petro; ut quod in ipso inveneris, in omnibus cernas. Ascendit Petrus,* &c.: "What meaneth this, 'They go up as high as heaven'? Learn in Peter; to the end that that which thou shalt find in Peter thou mayest see in all men. Peter went up as high as heaven when he said, 'Although I should die with Thee, yet will I not deny Thee,'" &c. And so applying the understanding of the Psalm to Peter, and in him to all Christians, he cometh to that marvellous testimony of the Church of Rome which M. Sander reporteth; shewing how, after his repentance, God exalted him to be a preacher of that Baptism of Jesus Christ, in whom all floods are blessed from Peter to this day. Where M. Sander useth a false translation; saying the floods are blessed of Peter, and expoundeth the floods to be the Churches; whereas Arnobius speaketh of all waters, which in Christ are sanctified to the use of Baptism, from the Apostles' time until this day. But it is a Catholic argument, that whosoever goeth out of the Church of Peter goeth out of the Church of Christ: therefore Rome is the mother Church, and Peter the head thereof. Even like this: Whosoever goeth out of the Church of Paul, or of any of the Apostles, wheresoever they planted it, doth perish: therefore Corinth and Paul, or any other city and the Apostle that preached there, may be taken for the head and Pastor, and mother Church of all other. Yet is this with M. Sander a marvellous testimony.

Optatus succeedeth Arnobius: *Cont. Pamen de nat.* [*Parmen. Donat.*] Lib. ii.[1]: *Negare non potes,* &c.: "Thou canst not deny but that thou knowest that to Peter first the Bishop's chair was given in the city of Rome; in which Peter, the head of all the Apostles, hath sit; whereof he was also called Cephas[2]: in which chair unity might be kept of all men; so that he should be a schismatic which should place any other chair against the singular chair." [...] "Unto Peter succeeded Linus: unto Linus succeeded Clemens:" and so nameth all the Bishops until Siricius, which lived in his time[3]; of

[1] [Lib. ii. Capp. ii, iii.]

[2] [See page 302, note.]

[3] [It is certain that Optatus wrote about A.D. 370, and that the

whom he saith, *qui noster est socius*, "which is our fellow." In this sentence Optatus laboureth to prove against the Donatists, which were schismatics, that there is but one Catholic Church, from which they were departed. He useth the argument of unity, commended in Peter's chair; whom he calleth head of the Apostles in respect of unity, and not of authority: which appeareth by this, that in the end he accounteth Siricius, Bishop of Rome and Peter's successor, not head of all Churches, nor universal Bishop of all Bishops, but *socius noster*, "our fellow" or companion; as one consenting with him in the unity of that Church which was first planted by the Apostles; and not as a general governor of the universal Church of Christ. Wherefore, although Optatus do more than was necessary urge this argument of the unity of Peter's chair, yet his meaning was, not to set forth an unreproveable authority thereof, such as the Pope now challengeth, but only to make it the beginning of unity.

At length he cometh to S. Hierom, in an Epistle to Damasus[4], out of which he gathereth divers sentences: *Mihi cathedram*, &c.: "I thought it best to ask counsel of the chair of Peter, and of the faith praised by the mouth of the Apostle. [..] I speak with the successor of a fisher, and with a disciple of the Cross. I, following none first but Christ, am joined in communion with thy blessedness; that is, with the chair of Peter. Upon that Rock I know the Church to be builded. Whosoever shall eat the lamb out of this house, he is unholy. If any man be out of the ark of Noe during the time of the flood, he shall perish. [...] I know not Viiatis; [Vitalis;] I despise Melitius; [Meletius;] I have no acquaintance with Paulinus. Whosoever doth not gather with thee, he doth scatter abroad: that is, he that is not of Christ, is of Antichrist." The conclusion openeth all the matter. As long as Damasus Bishop of Rome gathereth with Christ, that is, maintaineth true doctrine, Hierom will gather with him; who professed before that he would follow none as first but Christ. For he would not have gathered with Liberius Bishop of Rome, whom he confesseth to have subscribed to the Arians that were heretics. *In Catal. Script. Ecclesi.*[5] What

pontificate of S. Siricius did not commence till the end of the year 384. The text has consequently been corrupted.]

[4] [Supra, p. 120, n. 1.]

[5] [Cap. xcvii.]

mockery is it then to draw the commendations of a good Catholic Bishop, maintaining true doctrine, to every Bishop sitting in that seat, agreeing neither in doctrine nor manners with that Christian predecessor!

Augustin must succeed Hierom; who, in his clxvi. Epistle[1], giveth us this rule: *Cœlestis Magister*, &c.: "The heavenly Master maketh the people secure concerning evil overseers; lest for their sakes the chair of healthful doctrine should be forsaken. In which chair evil men are ever constrained to say good things: for the things which they speak are not their own; but they are the things of God."

Here, sayeth Master Sander, "we have a chair of healthful doctrine," and that is afterward called the chair of unity: therefore it is not the chair of every Bishop, which are many, and of which many have been heretics, but the only chair of the Bishop of Rome; in which chair the Pope, be he never so evil, "is constrained to say good things," and cannot err. But seeing I have often proved that many Bishops sitting in that chair of Rome have spoken evil things, and were filthy heretics, it followeth that this is not a wooden chair that Augustin speaketh of, but the chair of true doctrine; such as the chair of Moses was, in which not only Aaron and his successors, but even the Scribes and Pharisees did sit; having the authority of Moses, while they uttered nothing but that which God delivered by Moses. But when they preached false doctrine they did not sit in the chair of Moses, but in the chair of pestilence, as the Pope and all other heretics do. He talketh much of unity in S. Peter, in his chair, seat, and succession; as though any of these were worth a straw, without unity in S. Peter's doctrine, which was the doctrine of Christ.

But Saint Augustin, *Contr. Epist. Fundament.*[2], confesseth that the succession of Priests from Saint Peter unto this present time stayed him in the Catholic Church. It is true he confesseth that this succession among many things was one that stayed him. And yet he acknowledgeth that the manifest truth *præponenda est omnibus illis rebus quibus in Catholica teneor*, "is to be preferred before all things by which I am stayed in the Catholic Church;" namely, before

[1] [alias *Ep*. cv. §. 16. *Opp*. ii. 229.]

[2] [Supra, p. 56.]

antiquity, consent of nations, miracles, succession of Bishops, and the name of Catholics.

Likewise, rehearsing the same things in a manner against the Donatists, which Master Sander hath not omitted, *Epist.* clxv.[3], he sayeth: *Quamvis non tam de istis documentis præsumamus, quam de Scripturis sanctis:* "Although we presume not so much of these documents as of the holy Scriptures." Wherefore, as the argument of succession was well used against heretics, so long as there was succession of doctrine with succession of persons; so now to allege the only succession of persons, where the doctrine is clean changed, is as foolish and ridiculous as by shewing of empty dishes to prove abundance of victuals; or shewing vessels full of filthy waters, to prove that they are full of good wine; because meat of old time hath been served in such dishes, and wine preserved in such vessels.

But if the authority of one man, as Saint Augustin was, seem little, M. Sander bringeth the two Councils, gathered in Africa and Numidia[4] against the Pelagians; which sent their Decrees to the see of Rome, "that the authority of the Apostolic see might be given to them." *Epi.* xix. [xc.[5]] If they required the Bishop of Rome to agree with them in the truth, what prerogative of Supremacy do they grant unto him[6]? Nay, rather, they do privily reprehend him, that he had so long suffered the Pelagian poison to be spread under his nose in Europe; and the doctrine neither called to examination nor confuted; yea, rather seemed to consent to the den of the Bishops of the East, that Pelagius was justly absolved.

But Pope Innocentius himself praiseth them, *Ep.* xci.[7], that they had kept the customs of the old tradition in referring the matter to his see; and saith, "that the Fathers, not by human but by divine sentence, have decreed, that whatsoever was done in the provinces afar off they should not account it before to be ended, except it came to the knowledge

3 [See page 242.]

4 [At Carthage and Milevis; both held in the year 416.]

5 [alias clxxv. S. Aug. *Opp.* T. ii. col. 470.]

6 [In addressing Innocent I., Bishop of Rome, the Fathers of this Synod of Carthage use the words "Domine frater."]

7 [al. clxxxi. ubi supra, col. 484.]

of this see; where whatsoever had been justly pronounced should be confirmed by the authority of this see; and those other Churches should take it, as it were waters which should flow from their own native fountain." We know the ambitious Epistle of Innocentius; if it be not counterfeited, because many patches thereof are found in other decretal Epistles; but we deny that the authority which he pretended was acknowledged by these two Councils. Yes, saith M. S., the Fathers of the Milevitan Council[1] say, *Arbitramur*, &c.: "We think these men that have so pernicious and froward opinions will give place more easily to the authority of your Holiness, being taken out of the authority of the holy Scriptures; by help of the mercy of our Lord Jesus Christ, [God,] which vouchsafeth to rule you when you consult, and to hear you when you pray." By these words they shew, that they hope the heretics, being reproved by the Bishop of Rome out of the word of God, will the rather give place: without imagining that the Bishop of Rome's authority is so stablished by the Scriptures, that whatsoever he decree contrary to the Scriptures, the same should be embraced.

But a farther confirmation of the Epistle of Innocentius he bringeth out of Aug., *Ep.* cvi.[2], where he saith Pope Innocent "did write an answer" to the Bishops, in ["to"] "all things, as it [was right, and as it] became the Prelate of the Apostolic see." But these words neither prove that Epistle to be written by Innocent; nor, if it were, do allow his pretended authority; because that was no matter whereof they required his answer[3]. But, to put it out of doubt, both these Councils have decreed against the usurpation of the Romish see: as the Council Milevitan, Cap. xxii., decreed that no man should appeal out of Africa, under pain of excommunication[4].

The last authority cited out of Augustin is Epistle clxii.[5]; speaking of the Church of Rome, *in qua semper Apostolicæ cathedræ viguit principatus,* "in which always the principality of the Apostolic chair hath flourished." A matter often

[1] [The second Synod of Milevis, anno 416. Vid. S. August. *Opp.* Tom. ii. c. 473. *Epist.* clxvi.]

[2] [alias clxxxvi. col. 506.]

[3] ["Scripsimus . . literas familiares." (S. Aug. loc. cit.)]

[4] [See note 2, page 71.]

[5] [al. xliii. *Opp.* ii. 69.]

confessed, that the Fathers, especially of the later times, since Constantine advanced the Church in wealth and dignity, esteemed the Church of Rome as the principal see in dignity; but not in absolute authority, such as in process of time the Bishops of Rome claimed and usurped. For even the same Augustin, with two hundred and sixteen Bishops, refused to yield to the Bishop of Rome, claiming by a counterfeit Canon of the Council of Nice to have authority to receive appeals out of Africa; *Epi. Con. Aphr. ad Bonifac.;* which they count an intolerable pride and presumption; and, *in Epist. cont.* [*Conc.*] *Aphri. ad Cœlestinum*[6], *fumosum typ*[*h*]*um seculi*, "a smoky pride of the world," which the Pope claimed; and an absurd authority, that one man should be better able to examine such causes than so many Bishops of the province where the controversy began, and by the old Canons should be ended.

To Augustin he joineth Prosper, Bishop of Rhegium[7] in Italy, which affirmeth in *Lib. de Ingrat.*[8], that "Rome the see of Peter was the first that did cut off the pestilence of Pelagius: which Rome, being made head unto the world of pastoral honour, holdeth by religion whatsoever it doth not possess by war." And again[9]: Rome, "through the primacy of the Apostolic Priesthood, is made greater by the castle of religion than by the throne of power." First, how untruly he boasteth that the see of Peter was the first[10] that did cut off

6 [Supra, note 1, pp. 70—1.]

7 [It is not certain, nor even probable, that S. Prosper was more than a layman.]

8 [Cap. ii. *Opp.* p. 548. Colon. Agripp. 1609: vel in Clerici *Append. Augustin.* p. 5. Amst. 1703.

..."Pestem subeuntem prima recidit
Sedes Roma Petri: quæ pastoralis honoris
Facta caput mundo, quidquid non possidet armis,
Relligione tenet."]

9 [*De vocatione omnium Gentium*, Lib. ii. Cap. xvi. *Opp.* p. 846. The author of these books is not known. (Tillemont, x. 129.) They are found amongst the works of S. Ambrose; but are unquestionably not his, inasmuch as they mention the Pelagians who arose after his death. Erasmus attributes them to Eucherius of Lyons: others assign them to Hilary, of Arles, Syracuse, or the friend of Prosper: Gerard Vossius and Cave plead for Prosper of Orleans; and Quesnel (*Dissert.* ii.) is in favour of Pope Leo the Great.]

10 [The meaning of the word "prima" in the passage above quoted

the heresy of Pelagius, you may easily see by that the Council of Africa did before condemn it, and had somewhat ado to persuade Innocentius Bishop of Rome to it. Whereby you see that Prosper was over partial to the see of Rome: to whom yet he ascribeth a principality or primacy of honour, not of power or auctority.

The testimonies of Leo and Gregory, Bishops of Rome, as always, so now I deem to be unmeet to be heard in their own cause: though otherwise they were not the worst men; yet great furtherers of the auctority of Antichrist, which soon after their days took possession of the chair, which they had helped to prepare for him. The last testimony out of Beda, which lived under the tyranny of Antichrist, I will not stand upon. M. Sander may have great store of such late writers to affirm the Pope's Supremacy.

THE SIXTEENTH CHAPTER.

SANDER. *Sander.* That the good Christian Emperors and Princes did never think themselves to be the supreme heads of the Church in spiritual causes; but gave that honour to Bishops and Priests, and most specially to the see of Rome, for S. Peter's sake, as well before as after the time of Phocas. A Priest is above the Emperor in ecclesiastical causes. The Oath of the royal Supremacy is intolerable. Constantine was baptized at Rome. Phocas did not first make the see of Rome Head of all Churches.

FULKE. *Fulke.* Concerning the Supremacy of our Sovereign, which this traitorous Papist doth so maliciously disdain, although it be expounded sufficiently by her Majesty in her Injunction not to be such as he most slanderously doth deform it, yet I will here, as I have done divers times before in answer to these Papists, profess, that we ascribe no Supremacy to our Prince but such as the word of God alloweth in the godly Kings of the old testament, and the

from the *Carmen de Ingratis* has been disputed. It may have reference to Rome as the *principal* witness against Pelagianism; or, with greater likelihood, this Apostolic see may be named *first* in the order of the narrative, rather than with respect to time. In the fourth chapter S. Prosper speaks of two African Synods, (query, whether those of Carthage and Milevis? if not, certainly both of Carthage,) which had decreed "quod Roma probet, quod regna sequantur."]

Church hath acknowledged in the Christian Emperors and Princes under the new testament.

First, therefore, we ascribe to our Prince no absolute power in any ecclesiastical causes, such as the Pope challengeth, but subject unto the rules of God's word. Secondly, we ascribe no Supremacy of knowledge in ecclesiastical matters to our Prince; but affirm that she is to learn of the Bishops and teachers of the Church, both in matters of faith and of the government of the Church. Thirdly, we allow no confusion of callings; that the Prince should presume to preach, to minister the Sacraments, to excommunicate, &c.; which pertain not to her office. But the Supremacy we admit in ecclesiastical causes is auctority over all persons, to command, and by laws to provide, that all matters ecclesiastical may be ordered and executed according to the word of God. And such is the true meaning of the Oath that he calleth blasphemous and intolerable. And as for examples of honour given to the Bishops by Christian Princes, which he bringeth forth, they deny not this Supremacy, nor make any thing against it.

The first is of the Emperor Philippus, counted of some for the first Christian Emperor[1], although it be not like to be true; yet admitting the story written by Eusebius[2] to be so, this Prince without due repentance offered himself to receive the holy mysteries; and being refused by the Bishop of the place, took it patiently, and submitted himself to the discipline and order of the Church. I answer, this example toucheth not the auctority he had in ecclesiastical causes:

[1] ["Qui primus Romanorum Principum Christianus fuit." (Vincent. Lir. *Advers. Hœres.* fol. 23, b. Paris. 1561.) "Hic primus Imperatorum omnium Christianus fuit." (Pauli Orosii *Histor.* Lib. vii. Cap. xx. fol. cccix. Colon. 1561.) In the worthless Acts of the Martyr Pontius, (de quo plura apud Bolland. ad diem 14. Maii,) published by Surius, (Tom. vii.) and cited by Baronius, (ad an. 246. §. ix.) it is stated that the Emperor Philip and his son were converted by this Saint, and baptized by Pope Fabianus. Eusebius, in the place presently referred to, relates what he has written as a report; "κατέχει λόγος," "fama est;" and elsewhere (*De vit. Const.* iv. lxii.) distinctly affirms, that of all the Roman Emperors Constantine was the first who received Baptism.]

[2] [*Eccl. Hist.* Lib. vi. Cap. xxxiv.]

for in receiving of the Sacraments the Prince differeth not from a private person.

But he pusheth at M. Nowell with a two-horned argument, called a dilemma. "If the Priest in these causes be superior to the Emperor, other causes be greater or lesser than these. If they be greater, the Emperor, which is not supreme governor over the lesser causes, cannot be in the greater: if they be lesser, then the Priest, which governeth the Emperor in greater causes, must needs govern him in lesser causes." These horns are easily avoided, not by distinction of the causes, but of the governments. The government of the Prince is one, and of the Priest another: this spiritual, the other external; and therefore no contrariety between them. For put the case, that Philippus had seen the Bishop profane the Sacrament, in ministering to infidels, or otherwise uncertainly behaving himself in his office, might he not justly have punished him, as supreme governor over the Bishop even in those matters? I say not to do them; but to see that they be well done, and to punish the offenders: neither is the meaning of the Oath any other. And according to this meaning, M. Nowell, M. Horne, and M. Jewell dare warrant the King to be supreme governor in all ecclesiastical causes; although it please M. Sander to say the contrary of them: whose traitorous quarrelling upon the words of the Oath ought not to trouble any man's conscience; when the meaning is publicly testified, both by the Prince, and by the whole consent of the Church.

The next example is of Constantinus the Great; which, in the Synod of Nice, when the Bishops had offered unto him bills of complaint, one against another, without disclosing the contents of them, he said, as Ruffinus reporteth, Lib. x. Cap. ii.[1]: *Deus vos constituit Sacerdotes*, &c.: "God hath made you Priests, and hath given you power to judge of us also; and therefore we are rightly judged of you: but ye cannot be judged of men. For which cause expect ye the judgment of

[1] [*Histor. Eccles.* Lib. i. Cap. ii. p. 233. edit. Basil. 1549. This chapter is remarkable for having supplied words which are cited in the Canon Law to prove that the Pope, being God, cannot be judged by men: "nec posse Deum ab hominibus judicari manifestum est." (*Decret.* i. Par. Dist. xcvi. Cap. vii. *Satis evidenter.*)]

God alone among ye." Here M. Sander noteth, first, that he calleth them "Priests;" whereby he would prove they had power to offer external sacrifice: which is a simple reason; for then all Christian men and women, within [which in] the Scripture are called Priests, have the same power. Secondly, he confesseth they have "power to judge" the Emperor; for none can be greater than a Priest. In their challenge and spiritual government the Emperor meaneth; and not as the popish Church practiseth, to dispose [depose] the Emperor. Thirdly, that Priests "cannot be judged of men." If this be so, one Priest cannot be judged of another; and where is then the Pope's Supremacy? But he answereth, "If one Priest judge another, it is God's judgment, and not the judgment of men; because God hath set one Priest above another." O blockish answer! as though God hath not set one Prince above all his subjects. You see how popish Priests advance themselves to the honour of God, and withdraw their obedience from God's Lieutenants on earth. An undoubted note of Antichristians.

You will ask me then, what sense these words have, "You cannot be judged of men?" I answer, either they are meant, as Saint Paul speaketh, of the uprightness of his conscience in doing of his office, which is not subject to the judgment of men; or else Ruffinus, as he was a bold reporter, frameth the Emperor's words according to that estimation which he would have men to have of the Clergy: for it is certain by records of Constantinus' time, that he did judge Bishops, and took upon him as supreme governor in ecclesiastical causes. Master Sander confesseth he judged certain Priests, or ecclesiastical causes; but he did it, as Augustin sayeth, *Epist.* clxii.[2], "as one that would afterward ask pardon of the holy Bishops," at the importunity of the Donatists; and, as Optatus recordeth, he said: *De schis.* Lib. i.[3]: *Petitis a me,* &c.: "Ye ask of me judgment in the world, whereas I myself look for Christ's judgment." And Augustin reproveth the Donatists[4], that they would have "an earthly King" to be judge of their cause. Indeed, the importunity of the Donatists was wicked; who would so refer the matter to the Emperor, that without knowledge of ecclesiastical persons, who were only meet

2 [al. xliii. Cap. vii. §. 20. *Opp.* ii. 73.]
3 [Cap. xxiii. p. 22. ed. Antv. 1702.]
4 [*Epist.* xciii. Opp. ii. 178. ed. Ben.]

judges in respect of knowledge in that case, they would have the cause decided. But the Emperor, acknowledging his auctority, appointed judges ecclesiastical persons: first the Bishop of Rome, Melchiades, whom he commanded with other Bishops to hear the cause of Cæcilianus; as Eusebius, who lived in his time, writeth. Li. x. Ca. v.[1] And when the Donatists appealed from the Bishop's of Rome and his companions' judgment, he appointed other delegates, as Augustin also witnesseth. *Ep.* clxii.[2]

But, to leave this cause of the Donatists, Eusebius in his life, Libr. i.[3], sayeth of him: *Quoniam nonnulli variis locis inter se discrepabant, quasi communis quidem* [*quidam*] *Episcopus a Deo constitutus, Ministrorum Dei Synodos convocavit; nec dedignatus est adesse, et considere in illorum medio:* "Because some of them in divers places were at variance among themselves, he, as a certain general Bishop appointed of God, called together the Synods of the Ministers of God; and disdained not to be present, and to sit in the midst of them." And in Lib. iii.[4] he sheweth how he gathered the Universal Synod of Nice, "as it were leading forth the army of God to battle." To this Emperor did Athanasius the Great, Bishop of Alexandria, appeal from the Synod of Tyre, where he was injuriously handled; as both Socrates testifieth, Lib. i.[5], and the very Epistle of Constantine himself unto that Synod[6]; commanding all the Bishops to come unto his presence, and there to shew before him, (*quem sincerum esse Dei ministrum neque vos sane negabitis,* "whom you cannot deny to be a sincere minister of God,") how sincerely they had judged in that Council. Finally, in the end of the Epistle, he protesteth that he will execute his Supremacy in causes ecclesiastical: *Omni virtute conabor agere, quatenus quæ in lege Dei sunt, ea præcipue sine aliqua titubatione serventur. Quibus utique neque vituperatio, neque mala superstitio poterit implicari, dispersis utique, ac palam*

1 [p. 391. ed. Vales.] 2 [ut sup.]

3 [*De vita Const.* Lib. i. p. 169. Fulke has used the version by Musculus, Basil. 1549.]

4 [p. 189. "Proinde, quasi agmen Dei ad expeditionem ducturus, Synodum Œcumenicam collegit."]

5 [*Hist. Ecc.* L. i. Cap. xxxii. p. 290. ed. Musc.]

6 [Socrat. Lib. i. Cap. xxxiv. Fulke here quotes from the *Tripartite History,* L. iii. C. vii. Cassiodorii *Opp.* Tom. i. p. 223. edit. Bened. Venet. 1729.]

contritis, et penitus exterminatis sacratissimæ legis inimicis, qui sub schemate sancti nominis blasphemas [*blasphemias*] *varias ad* [*et*] *diversos* [*diversas*] *inijciant:* [*injiciunt:*] "I will endeavour with all my might to bring to pass, that those things that are in the law of God, those chiefly without any staggering may be observed. Which by no reproof or evil superstition can be entangled, when all the enemies of the most holy law, which under a shape of an holy name do cast out divers blasphemies unto sundry persons, are dispersed and openly trodden down, and utterly rooted out."

Let this suffice to shew what Supremacy Constantinus did exercise in causes ecclesiastical. Now Master Sander draweth us to see what honour he gave to the see of Rome.

First, he taketh it for "most certain" that Constantine was baptized by Silvester; which is an impudent lie and forged fable[7], as is manifest by Eusebius[8], who lived in his time and after him, who knew him familiarly, and affirmeth that he was baptized in his journey towards Jordan[9], where he had purposed to have been baptized if God had spared him life. But this manifest testimony of Eusebius Master Sander refuseth, because he was suspected for affection to the Arian heresy[10]. Beside that he was unjustly suspected, what reason is it to discredit his story, who wrote at such time as many thousands alive could disprove him, for any affection to that heresy, whereto the Baptism of Constantine pertained

[7] [But recorded as a truth in the Roman Breviary. (*In Festo S. Silvestri:* Par. Hiem. p. 258. Antverp. 1724.)]

[8] [*De vita Constantini*, Lib. iv. Cap. lxii.]

[9] [When he had come to the suburbs of Nicomedia.]

[10] [Baronius (Not. in *Martyrol. Rom.* die Jun. 21.) falsely declares that Eusebius persisted in favouring Arianism subsequently to the holding of the first Council of Nicæa, at which "errorem deposuit," according to Trithemius. (*De Scriptt. Eccles.* Cap. lvii.) In this imputation, as Crakanthorp remarks, (*Defence of Constantine*, p. 109. Lond. 1621.) the Cardinal "treads but in the steps of some of the worthy Fathers of their second Nicene Councell," whose indignation was excited by the unfriendliness of Eusebius to Image-worship. They "reject and anathematize" his writings, and all who should read them; (*Act.* v. pp. 80, 81. ed. Sirmond.) describing him as "a defender of the Arian heresy," and a Theopaschite: (*Act.* vi. p. 98.) forgetful, however, that the latter designation was singularly misapplied, inasmuch as the Theopaschite doctrine was not devised until about a century and a half after his death.]

nothing in the world? As for the stones and pillars of marble, in which any such matter is graven, bearing the name of his Baptistery[1], except Master Sander could prove that they were set up in his time, [they] are simple witnesses against the history of Eusebius, which lived in his time. Neither the forged Pontifical of Damasus[2], nor the writings of Beda, Ado, Marianus, Gregorius Turenensis, [Turonensis,] Zonarus, [Zonaras,] Nicephorus, late writers, following the fable of the Romish Church, are of any credit in respect of Eusebius, and the eldest writers of the ecclesiastical story[3], that agree with Eusebius that he was not baptized many years after Silvester was dead.

And concerning the Donation of Constantine[4], it is too

1 [We read in the Annals of Baronius (ad an. 324. §. xlii.) that within the Lateran palace "hactenus ejus visitur Baptisterium:" but Cardinal Bona confesses that this was named the Font of Constantine because that he erected it, and not on account of his having been baptized in it. (Vid. Papebrochii *Conatus Chronico-Histor.* p. 132. Bolland. *Præfatt. et Tractatt. prælim.* Tom. ii. Ant. 1749. Card. Polus, *De Bapt. Const.* fol. 63, b. Romæ, 1562.) Binius (*Concill.* i. i. 254-5.) has adduced what he terms a "testimonium non contemnendum" from the heathen writer Ammianus Marcellinus, who mentions "Constantinianum Lavacrum:" but this "Lavacrum salutare" was merely the *Thermæ*, or *Balneum*, which Constantine, following the example of other Emperors, had caused to be made. See Crakanthorp, ut sup. pp. 63—66.]

2 [Supra, note 4, pp. 98—9.]

3 [Socrat. Lib. i. Cap. xxxix. Sozom. L. ii. C. xxxiv. Theodor. i. xxxi. ed. Lat.]

4 [Gratiani *Decret.* Dist. xcvi. Cap. *Constantinus.* Cf. Flacii Illyrici *Refut. invect. Bruni contra Centur.* p. 45. Basil. 1566. James, *Corruption of the true Fathers*, p. 96. This much celebrated fiction is by Goldastus, (*Replicatio pro Imperio*, p. 167. Hanov. 1611.) and after him by Brown, (Præfat. in Gratii *Fascic.* p. xxv. Lond. 1690.) and Wharton, (Append. ad Cavei *Hist. Lit.* ii. 154. Oxon. 1743.) erroneously attributed to Joannes Diaconus, surnamed "Digitorum mutilus." (Conf. Fabric. *Bibl. med. et inf. Latin.* Vol. iv. p. 198. Hamb. 1735.) De Marca assigns the invention of this imaginary grant to the year 767, when the device may probably have been contrived by Joannes Subdiaconus, who was one of the Legates of Pope Paul I. (*De concord. Sac. et Imp.* Lib. iii. Cap. xii. pp. 169, 171. Paris. 1669.) The style, date, and purpose of this spurious Edict place it in harmony with the famous Isidorian forgeries. (Joan. Richardson *Prælectt. Eccles.* Vol. i. p. 369. Lond. 1726.) It is to be observed also that, strictly speaking,

absurd for any wise man to defend, which hath been so long before disproved by Laurentius Valla[5], no enemy of the Romish religion, although a discoverer of that fable. Again, his forsaking of the city of Rome, and building of Constantinople, is as great a fable: for although he beautified Byzantium, and made it an imperial city, as placed conveniently to keep the Oriental empire, yet he forsook not Rome, but still retained it as the chief see of his empire. So did the Emperors that followed him, until (after it was wasted by the barbarous nations,) they made less account of it. And therefore although Constans, the nephew of Heraclius[6], could not conveniently remove thither[7], yet he removed from thence what he thought good[8]. By which it appeareth he had authority in the city, by the providence of God, and not by chance: as M. Sander dreameth that he was prohibited by God's providence, in respect of the Pope's Supremacy, or else the world should be governed by chance.

But leaving Constantinus the father, we must come to Constantius his son, which was an Arian; of whom Athanasius

there are two supposed Donations of Constantine; the greater, and the less: the former recorded in the "Palea," or "Chaff," annexed to the genuine *Decree* of Gratian, in the place above referred to; the latter registered in the *Decretals*. (Sext. Decr. Lib. i. Tit. vi. Cap. xvii. *Fundamenta.*) By the smaller privilege the city of Rome alone was conferred upon the Pope: by the greater charter he received in addition the imperial palace, "and all the provinces, places, and cities of Italy, or the countries of the West." Vid. Joan. Naucleri *Chronograph.* Vol. ii. Gen. xi. pp. 503—4. Colon. 1579. *Conference betwene Rainoldes and Hart,* p. 402. Lond. 1584.]

5 [The manuscript of Valla's *Declamatio* is preserved in the Vatican library. (Montfaucon *Biblioth. Bibliothecar. MSS.* Tom. i. p. 119. n. 5314. Paris. 1739.) In opposition to him Bartholomæus Picernus de Monte arduo published the *Donatio Constantini* in a quarto tract, consisting of eight leaves, which he inscribed to Pope Julius II. An edition of Valla's treatise was dedicated to the succeeding Pope, Leo X., by Ulric de Hutten, in the year 1517. Both works appeared together under the title, "De Donatione Constantini, quid ueri habeat, eruditorum quorundam iudicium;" 4to; and the *Fasciculus* of Orthuinus Gratius contains a reprint of them. foll. lxii—lxxix. Colon. 1535.]

6 [Constans II. was the *grandson* of Heraclius. Fulke misinterpreted the word "*nepotis.*"

7 [Joan. Zonaræ *Annales*, Tom. ii. pp. 88—9. Paris. 1687.]

8 [Gibbon, iv. 403. ed. Milman.]

complaineth, that he had no reverence of the Bishop of Rome; *Ep. ad solit. vit. agen.*[1]; neither considering "that it was an Apostolic see, nor that Rome was the mother-city of the Roman empire." There were other Apostolic sees beside Rome; and the Christian world was larger than the Roman empire: therefore this maketh nothing for the singular prerogative of that see.

But the noble Emperors, Gratianus, Valentinianus, and Theodosius made a law, *lege* i. *Cod. de summ. Trinit.*, "that all their people should continue in that religion [in such a religion] as the religion which is used from S. Peter unto this day doth declare him to have delivered to the Romans; and which it is evident that Bishop Damasus doth follow, and Peter, Bishop of Alexandria, a man of Apostolic holiness." This law proveth that the Emperors had authority in ecclesiastical causes; and that they joined the Patriarch of Rome with the Patriarch of Alexandria, not because he of Alexandria agreed with him of Rome, but because they both agreed with Peter, and Peter with Christ.

From these Emperors he cometh to Bonifacius[2]; who, writing to the Emperor Honorius, and humbly desiring his aid to appease the tumults of his Church, useth these words: *Ecclesiæ meæ, cui Deus noster meum Sacerdotium, vobis res humanas regentibus, deputavit, cura constringit: ne causis ejus, quamvis adhuc corporis incommoditate detinear, propter conventus qui a Sacerdotibus universis et Clericis, et Christianæ plebis perturbationibus agitantur, apud aures Christianissimi Principis desim:* "The care of my Church, to which our God hath deputed my Priesthood, while you govern the affairs of men, doth bind me: that, although I am yet withholden by infirmity of body, I should not be wanting to the causes thereof, in the hearing of a most Christian Prince, by reason of the meetings that are held of all the Priests and the Clergy, with the perturbations of the Christian people." These words shew that the Emperor was supreme governor in causes ecclesiastical; for he writeth concerning the election of the Bishop. To whom the Emperor answereth, making a law against the ambitious labouring for succession; that if two Bishops should be chosen, they should be both

1 [*Hist. Arianor. ad Monachos:* Opp. i. i. 364. ed. Ben.]

2 [Pope Boniface I.]

banished out of the city. *Con.* To. i.[3] et *Dist.* xcvii.[4] I have set down the words at large, to shew the shameful falsification of M. Sander, who setteth them down absolutely thus: *Mihi Deus noster meum Sacerdotium, vobis res humanas regentibus, deputavit:* "Our God hath appointed my Priesthood to me; whereas you do govern worldly matters:" as though he had denied to the Emperor all government in ecclesiastical causes; when he flieth to his authority in a cause ecclesiastical, and doth not only acknowledge him to be a conserver of civil peace, as M. Sander would have it.

To Honorius he joineth Galla Placidia the Empress, in her Epistle to Theodosius, set before the Council of Chalcedon[5], affirming that Peter "ordained the primacy of the bishoply office in the see Apostolic." Thus wrote the Empress, or her secretary, and so it was taken in that time. The like saith Valentinianus, in his Epistle[6] to Theodosius his father[7], that "Antiquity gave the chiefty of priestly power to the Bishop of the city of Rome." And Martianus with Valentinian confess[8], that the Synod of Chalcedon "inquired of the faith by the authority of Leo, Bishop of the everlasting city of Rome." Add hereunto that the Council itself confesseth, *Act.* iii.[9], that Leo was over them "as the head over the members." All these prove indeed a primacy of the Bishop of Rome acknowledged in those days; but not such a primacy as is now claimed. For the same Council and Emperors decreed, that the see of Constantinople in the East should have the same authority that the see of Rome had in the West; the title of

3 [Crabbe *Concill.* T. i. p. 490. Colon. Agr. 1551.]

4 [Gratiani *Decret.* i. Par. D. xcvii. Cap. i.]

5 [Crabbe, Tom. i. p. 732.]

6 [Ib. p. 731.—"There is some doubt whether these Epistles are genuine." (Comber's *Roman Forgeries*, Part iii. p. 88. Lond. 1695.)]

7 [Valentinian III., Emperor of the West, was the son of Placidia, daughter of Theodosius the Great.]

8 [*Chalced. Concil.* Act. iii. Crabbe, i. 865. Fulke has erred in transcribing this passage: for the statement is, not that the faith was diligently investigated by the authority of Pope Leo; but that this Bishop of Rome sanctioned the establishment of the foundations of religion for "the holy city," (meaning the Church, according to Sanders, but more probably Constantinople,) as well as the grant to Bishop Flavian of "the palm of a glorious death."]

9 [Crabbe, i. 867.]

seniority only reserved to the Bishop of Rome: although the Bishop of Rome, Leo, by letters and his Legates in the Council, cried out against it as loud as they could; *Cont.* [*Conc.*] *Chal. Act.* xvi.; namely, Lucentius cried, *Sedes Apostolica*, &c., "The Apostolic see ought not to be abased in our presence[1]," &c.; but all the Synod and the judges continued in their Decree.

The saying of Justinian, *in Cod. de summ. Trinit.*, is examined and answered in the sixty-ninth Article of M. Sander's treatise Which is the true Church, before his book of Images: as also the sayings of the Bishop of Patara, of Eugenius Bishop of Carthage, and Gregory Bishop of Rome.

The report of the Council of Sinuessa[2] is too full of corruption and confusion to be credited for authentical authority. And yet it is plain that Marcellinus, the Bishop of Rome, was convicted by witnesses[3] to have committed

1 [Supra, note 5, p. 289.]

2 [The contemptible Acts of this fictitious Synod, said to have been held in the year 303, may be seen in Binius (*Concill.* i. i. 178—183.) and Crabbe. (i. 187—197.) They are continually cited as genuine by Romanists, (See Jewel's *Works*, iv. 464. ed. Jelf. Rainoldes and Hart, p. 655. Ussher's *Answer*, p. 13. Lond. 1631. Bp. Synge's *Rejoynder*, pp. 203—4. Dubl. 1632. Bzovii *Pontif. Rom.* pp. 122—3. Bellarm. *De Conc. auct.* Lib. ii. Cap. xvii. Bramhall, i. 255. Oxf. 1842.) and afford matter for perusal in the Breviary: (die xxvi. Aprilis.) but they are entirely rejected as counterfeit by Papebrochius, (*Conat.* apud Bolland. *Præfatt.* ii. 123.) Ant. Pagi, (*Crit. in Ann. Baron.* i. 333.) Launoi, (*Epistt.* pp. 131, 271. Cantab. 1689.) and Natalis Alexander. (*Hist. Eccles.* Tom. iii. 731. Paris. 1699.) Bellarmin was unable to allege in their favour any testimony anterior to that of Pope Nicholas I., who lived in the year 860. (*De Rom. Pont.* L. ii. C. xxvi. col. 817. Ingolst. 1601.)]

3 [These witnesses are styled in the Acts of this Council the "Libra Occidua," a name which has given rise to much discussion. It appears certain that this technical term was applied to them on account of their number, seventy-two, as the Roman Libra consisted of so many Solidi. From the word "Occidua," as distinguished from "Orientalis," it is plain that these Acts were invented after the division of the empire into East and West: and Valentinian I., who effected this partition of the provinces in the year 364, also made a change as to the number of Solidi which the Libra of gold was to contain; reducing the amount to seventy-two, from eighty-four, which had been the sum in the days of Constantine the Great. (Vid. Du Cange *Glossar.* in verb. Cf. Bingham, Book ii. Ch. xiv. §. xv.) Even if the term "Occidua"

idolatry[4] before he confessed the sin, and received sentence of condemnation and accursing of the Synod: howsoever that patch is thrust in after the Acts of the Council, *Prima sedes*, &c., "The first see is not judged of any[5];" which in every counterfeit decretal Epistle almost must have a place.

To prove that Phocas did not first make the see of Rome "Head of all Churches[6]," when the history is plain he did, M. Sander bringeth in these and such-like alleged before, which acknowledged a certain primacy of the see of Rome. And certain it is the Bishops of Rome before Phocas' time affected a great primacy, which of many was acknowledged; but yet never absolutely, never without controversy, until Phocas, for a great sum of money received of Boniface the third, strake the stroke, and made the Decree, for which in all popish writers he is highly praised: although in the Greek Church his Decree was not long observed. Touching the examples of Emperors and Princes of later times, although I could shew they have often resisted the Pope, yet I know many may be alleged that have submitted themselves to his Antichristian tyranny: which I will not stand to examine, because they can be no prejudice to the truth, approved by examples of the eldest age.

should signify "diminished," as Gothofred supposes, still the date of the Sinuessan Council is from the internal evidence of these Acts with equal clearness shewn to be imaginary; and Cardinal Baronius confesses that this single criticism demonstrates, "Acta illa Marcellini nequaquam his temporibus esse conscripta." (*Annall.* ad an. 302. §. xciv.)]

4 [The Pontifical (p. 13. Mogunt. 1602.) declares that S. Marcellinus sacrificed to Idols; but S. Augustin maintained his "innocence" against the Donatists. (*De unico Bapt. cont. Petil.* Cap. xvi.)]

5 [While the Canon Law directs that no mortal should presume to reprove the Pontiff's faults, "because that he who is to judge all must not be judged by any one," this ominous exception is subjoined: "nisi deprehendatur a fide devius." (*Dist.* xl. Cap. *Si Papa.*)]

6 ["Hic" [Bonifacius III.] "obtinuit apud Phocam Principem, ut sedes Apostolica beati Petri Apostoli Caput esset omnium Ecclesiarum." The Pontifical, from which these words are taken, is the authority for the concession of this noted privilege. It is commonly believed, but upon the questionable testimony of Baronius, (ad an. 606. §. ii.) and without the slightest ancient evidence, that the title of "Œcumenical Bishop" was conferred by the usurper Phocas upon Pope Boniface III. and his successors.]

As for the history of Lucius, King of Britain, that sent to Eleutherius for preachers, if it were true[1], it maketh nothing for the Supremacy of the Romish Bishop. I will therefore conclude this chapter with a saying of Socrates, *in Proœ.* Lib. v.[2], to shew what authority he judged the Emperors to have in ecclesiastical matters: *Et ipsos quidem* [*quoque*] *Imperatores hac historia continua complectimur; propterea quod ab illis, postquam Christiani esse cœperunt, res ecclesiasticæ pendent; et maximæ Synodi ex illorum sententia et congregatæ sunt et congregantur:* "And in this continual history we comprehend the Emperors themselves; because that upon them, since they began to be Christians, the matters of the Church depend; and the greatest Synods have been gathered and are gathered by their authority." The punishment he threateneth to them that forsake the Church of Rome shall one day fall upon them that take part with the Church of Rome, as in part it doth already.

THE SEVENTEENTH CHAPTER.

SANDER. *Sander.* Their doctrine, who teach the Bishop of Rome to be Antichrist himself, is confuted by the auctority of God's word, and by the consent of ancient Fathers. Why Antichrist is permitted to come.

FULKE. *Fulke.* After he hath shewed his opinion what manner a one Antichrist shall be, and alleged the cause of his coming out of S. Paul, 2 Thess. ii., "because men have not received the love of the truth, that they might be saved, God shall send them the working of error, that they may believe lying," &c., he stormeth out of measure against the Protestants, for that they can find no place to settle Antichrist in but in the see of Rome, so beautified and dignified by Christ, and all the primitive Church. But seeing Antichrist is appointed to sit in the temple of God, which is a higher place than S. Peter's chair, it is no marvel if Satan have thrust him into that see, which of old time was accounted the top and castle of all religion.

But let us see his reasons taken out of God's word, by

1 [But it is false. Supra, p. 128.]

2 [p. 365. Muscul. interp.]

which it is proved that the Pope cannot be Antichrist himself. The first is, because in S. Paul he is called ὁ ἄνθρωπος, &c., "the man of sin;" which signifieth one singular man, and not a number of men in succession: and this is affirmed to be the Greek article in this word man by Cyrillus. *In Joan.* Lib. i. Cap. iv.[3] But how frendly [fondly] Cyrillus was deceived you shall see by some examples even out of the New Testament. In S. Matthew, cap. xii. 35, you have ὁ ἀγαθὸς ἄνθρωπος, and καὶ ὁ πονηρὸς ἄνθρωπος, "A good man out of the good treasure of his heart," and "an evil man out of the evil treasure of his heart bringeth," &c., where no one singular man is meant. In S. Mark, cap. ii. verse 27, "The Sabbath was made" διὰ τὸν ἄνθρωπον, καὶ [οὐχ] ὁ ἄνθρωπος, "for man, and not man for the Sabbath." In S. Luke, cap. iv. verse 4, "Not with bread only," ὁ ἄνθρωπος, "a man shall live, but by every word of God." S. Paul, 2 Tim. iii. ver. 17, "That the man of God," ὁ τοῦ Θεοῦ ἄνθρωπος, "may be perfect, and prepared to every good work." These places, and an hundred more which might be brought, do prove how vain the argument is that is taken of the nature of the Greek article.

Neither is Hierom or any of the ancient writers to be heard, without authority of the Scripture, which supposed that Antichrist should be one man: although none of them directly affirmeth that he should be one man, as Christ was. Hierom, *in Dani.* Cap. vii.[4], saith, we must not think that Antichrist should be a Devil, "but one of the kind of men, in whom Satan should dwell." This proveth not that he should be a singular man; no more than the fourth beast, which signifieth the Roman empire, out of which he should rise, should be one singular Emperor. No more doth it prove that because Antiochus was a figure of him, he must be but one man. And as little that Ambrose, *in* 2 *Thess.* ii.[5], saith, Satan shall appear *in homine,* "in a man;" which may signify the kind of men, and not one singular person. Likewise Augustin[6], calling Antichrist "the Prince," and "last Antichrist," meaneth

[3] [fol. 11. Paris. 1508.]

[4] ["Ne eum putemus, juxta quorundam opinionem, vel Diabolum esse, vel Dæmonem; sed unum de hominibus, in quo totus Satanas habitaturus sit corporaliter." (*Opp.* Tom. v. p. 587. Basil. 1565.)]

[5] [See note 6, page 183.]

[6] [*De Civitate Dei,* Lib. xx. Cap. xix.]

no one person: for the words "Prince" and "last" may agree to a whole succession of men in one state, as well as the words "King" and "beast" to a whole succession of Emperors in Daniel. To conclude, there is not one whom he nameth that denieth Antichrist to be a whole succession of men, in one state of devilish government: and Irenæus thinketh it probable of the Roman kingdom. Lib. v.[1]

The second argument is, that Antichrist is called "the adversary;" and therefore is the greatest enemy of Christ, "denying Jesus Christ to be God and man, or to be our Mediator." I answer, the Pope doth so, denying the office of Christ; although with the Devils he confess in words Jesus to be "the Holy One of God," and to be "Christ the Son of God." Mark i. 24. Luke iv. 41. His Divinity the Pope denieth, by denying His only power in saving; His wisdom, in His word to be only sufficient; His goodness, in the virtue of His death to take away both pain and guilt of sin; which he arrogateth to himself by his blasphemous pardons. Christ's humanity he denieth by his Transubstantiation: His mediation, in which He is principally Christ, he denieth by so many means of salvation as he maketh beside Christ; *videlicet*, man's merits, ceremonies invented by man, pardons, a new Sacrifice of the Mass, &c.

The third argument is, that "Antichrist shall not come before the Roman empire be clean taken away;" for that which Saint Paul saith, "Ye know what withholdeth," &c. Although it be not necessary to expound this of the Roman empire, yet, following the old writers that so understood it, I say, the Roman empire was removed before Antichrist the Pope was throughly installed. For beside that the see of the empire was removed from Rome, the government itself was in a manner clean removed; the title of the Roman Emperor only remaining. At last another empire by the Pope was erected in Germany, whereof little beside a name remaineth at this day: the Pope claiming authority of both the swords; and he that is the Emperor in title, if he have no lands of his own inheritance, scarce equal with a Duke by dominion of his empire.

The fourth argument is, that "the deeds and doctrine of Antichrist against Christ must be open, and without all dissi-

[1] [Cap. xxx.]

mulation;" because Saint Paul maketh a difference between the mystery of iniquity, and the open shewing of Antichrist. I answer, they are open to all faithful Christians; although they be hid from such as be deceived by Antichrist. Here M. Sander answereth to that which he supposeth might be objected, that some Glosses of the Canon Law call the Pope God[2], or make him equal with Christ; yea, they call him God above all Gods: but he thinketh to avoid it by saying, they call him not God "by nature, but by office under Christ;" where they say he is equal with Christ. This blasphemy will not so easily be excused: neither is it to be thought that any man will ever call himself God by nature. But, to omit these flattering Glosses of the Canon Law, doth not the Pope exalt himself "above all that is called God, and worshipped" as God, when he commandeth to abstain from meats and marriage, whereof God hath created the one and instituted the other, as good and holy, for greater goodness and holiness than God created or instituted in them? Doth he not exalt himself above God the Redeemer, when he affirmeth His redemption to be either only from sins committed before Baptism, or only from the guilt of sin; whereas his popish pardons can absolve from both? Doth he not extol himself above God the Holy Ghost, when he taketh upon him to sanctify the creatures of the world otherwise than God hath sanctified them; to apply the merits of Christ otherwise than God's Holy Spirit worketh application by faith, &c.?

The fifth argument is, that "Antichrist should be received most specially of the Jews;" of which he bringeth the opinion of divers old writers: but because the Scripture saith no such thing, but contrary, that he shall sit in the Church of God, we deny the antecedent or proposition of this argument. But M. S. allegeth the saying of Christ, Joan. v.: "I came in My Father's name, and ye have not received Me: if another come in his own name, ye will receive him." This other man, saith M. S., is Antichrist; and so expounded by the ancient Fathers. I answer, they have no ground of this exposition: for Theudas the Egyptian, Cocabas, and such-like, deceived the Jews in their own name; yet none of them was this Antichrist.

[2] [Jewel's *Works*, Vol. ii. pp. 195—7. ed. Jelf. Calfhill, note 3, pp. 5—6. ed. Parker Soc.]

The sixth argument is, that Antichrist, according to the prophecy of Daniel, cap. vii., and the interpretation of Hierom, shall subdue three Kings; the Kings of Egypt, Africa, and Ethiopia: which seeing the Pope hath not done, he is not Antichrist. I answer, neither Hierom, nor any ecclesiastical writer whom he followeth, hath any direction out of the Scripture for this interpretation. Wherefore it is more like that the Emperor is the little horn; which, first diminishing, as it were, a third part of the strength of the fourth beast, at length began utterly to oppress and destroy it; I mean, the Commonwealth of Rome.

The seventh reason is: "Antichrist shall prevail in his reign but three years and an half; Dan. vii.; which time the Apocalypse calleth forty-two months." I answer, this time must not be limited by measure of man, but as God hath appointed it. Daniel nameth no years, but "a time, times, and half a time:" and Hierom, in his account of twelve hundred and ninety-three days, differeth from S. John, Apoc. xii. 6, who setteth them down twelve hundred and sixty days.

The eighth reason is, "that Helias shall come at the time of Antichrist; as Hippolytus, Augustin, Hierom, and Theodoret teach: who is not yet come, although the Pope have long flourished." I answer, the Scripture speaketh of no coming of Helias; but of Christ's two witnesses, which have never failed in the greatest heat of the popish tyranny. Apoc. xi.

The ninth reason is, that "Antichrist shall be of the tribe of Dan; by the opinion of Irenæus, Hippolytus, Theodoretus, and Gregory: whereas the Popes are of no such tribe." I answer, the Scripture hath not revealed any such matter: neither doth Irenæus[1] rest upon that opinion, but judgeth he may well be the King of the Roman empire; saying very wisely: *Certius ergo et sine periculo est sustinere adimpletionem prophetiæ, quam suspicari*, &c.: "Therefore it is more certain and without danger to tarry the fulfilling of the prophecy, than to surmise," &c. Again, if this opinion should be true, he should not rise out of the Roman empire; as all old writers have consented he must, according to the prophecy.

The tenth argument is, that "Antichrist shall not come before the latter end of the world; as Augustin and Theodo-

[1] [*Adv. Hæres.* L. v. C. xxx.]

retus judged." But Gregory, seeing the ambition of John of Constantinople, affirmed that the time of the revelation of Antichrist was even at hand; and that the same John was the forerunner of Antichrist, and Antichrist should shortly be revealed, and "an army of Priests" should wait upon him[2]. Now seeing he, whosoever took that which John refused, by Gregory's judgment should be Antichrist; and it is certain that Pope Boniface the third[3], soon after the death of Gregory and his successors, usurped not only that but more also; it is certain by Gregory's prophecy, that the Pope is Antichrist: who, being within the six hundred years, answereth to M. Sander's fond challenge. And although none within that compass had pointed out the see of Rome, yet the fulfilling of the prophecy in the latter times did sufficiently declare who it should be. And most of the ancient writers name Rome to be the see of Antichrist; although they could not foresee that the bishoprick of that see should degenerate into the tyranny of Antichrist.

M. Sander answereth, that Tertullian and Hierom call Rome Babylon, "because of the confusion of tongues of divers nations that haunted thither in time of the Emperors. And then Rome was full of idolatry, and did persecute the Saints; and namely more than thirty Bishops of Rome." The reason of tongues is very absurd, and not given by any of those writers. As for idolatry, and persecuting of Saints, although it might be said in time of Irenæus and Tertullian, yet could it not be said in the days of Hierom, Augustin,

[2] ["Rex superbiæ prope est; et, quod dici nefas est, Sacerdotum est præparatus exercitus." This remarkable sentence is found in an Epistle of S. Gregory the Great to John, Patriarch of Constantinople, who had usurped the title of "Universal Bishop." (*Epistt.* Lib. iv. xxxviii.) In the old Paris, Antwerp, and Roman editions, the reading is "Sacerdotum *exitus*," which is certainly corrupt. (See Dr. James's *Treatise*, Part ii. pp. 77—80. Lond. 1611. Bp. Jewel's *Works*, ii. 142. v. 458. vii. 174, 377. ed. Jelf.) The Benedictines have removed the error, which was probably occasioned by the MS. abbreviation "*exītus*." (Le Bas, *Life of Jewel*, p. 226, note. Lond. 1835.) Richerius informs us that the clause immediately following, viz. "Antichristum multos habiturum Sacerdotes iniqui sui mysterii cooperatores," "exstat in manuscriptis codicibus, et nihilominus ex omnibus novis editionibus abrasa est." (*Apologia pro Joanne Gersonio*, p. 202. Lugd. Bat. 1676.) Cf. Matth. Larroquani *Adversaria Sacra*, pp. 277—8. Ib. 1688.]

[3] [Supra, p. 365, note 6.]

Ambrose, Primasius, and a number that lived in time of the Christian Emperors. And whereas Hierom, *ad Algasiam*[1], expoundeth the name of blasphemy written in the forehead of the purple harlot to be "Rome everlasting," it agreeth very well unto the see of the Popedom; which they boast to be eternal, although the empire of Rome shall be clean taken away. For M. Sander himself liketh well the title given by Martianus and Valentinianus to Leo, whom they call "Bishop of the everlasting city of Rome." Cap. xvi.

But whereas Rome is the city builded upon seven hills, spoken of in the Apocalypse, cap. xvii., M. Sander counteth it a childish argument to prove the see of Antichrist to be there, for that "the city is now gone from the hills, and standeth in the plain of Campus Martius; and the Pope sitteth on the other side of the river, upon the hill Vatican, hard by Saint Peter's church; by whom he holdeth his chair, not at all deriving his power from the seven hills," &c. But if the Pope sit now in another Rome than Peter the Apostle sat, how will Master Sander persuade us that he sitteth in the chair of Peter? for that Rome where Peter sat was builded upon seven hills; and not gone down into the plain of Campus Martius, nor over the river. Beside this, it is plain, that although the people have removed their habitations from the hills, yet the Pope hath not: for on them be still to this day his churches, monasteries, and courts.

For on the Mount Cœlius be the monastery of Saint Gregory, the church of John and Paul, the hospital of our Saviour, the round church, the great minster of Lateran, in which are said to be the heads of the Apostles Peter and Paul, and the goodliest buildings in the world; where the Bishops of Rome dwelled until the time of Nicolas the second, which was almost eleven hundreth years after Christ.

The Mount Aventinus hath three monasteries; of Sabina, Bonifacius, and Alexius.

The Mount Exquilinus hath the church of Saint Peter himself, surnamed *Ad vincula.*

The Mount Viminalis hath the church of S. Laurence in Palisperna, [Panisperna[2],] and S. Potentiana.

[1] [*Opp.* Tom. iii. 173. ed. Erasm.]

[2] [Corrupted from "Perpernia." Vid. B. de Montfaucon *Diarium Italicum*, p. 203. Paris. 1702.]

The Mount Tarpeius, or Capitoline, hath an house of Friars Minors called *Ara Cœli:* and there did Boniface the ninth build a fair house of brick for keeping of courts.

The Mount Palatinus is a place called the Great Palace; and hath an old church of S. Nicholas, and of S. Andrew.

The Mount Quirinalis is not altogether void of habitation: to which appertaineth the church of S. Maria de Populo.

The city with seven hills is still the see of Antichrist; described by S. John at such time as those seven hills were most of all inhabited, and garnished with sumptuous buildings. But M. S., to darken the prophecy, saith, those "seven hills be the fulness of pride in secular Princes, to whom the Protestants commit the supreme government of the Church." I will not speak of this contumely that he bloweth out against Christian Princes; neither will I stand to prove that seven hills in that place are taken literally; which is an easy matter, because seven hills are the exposition of seven heads of the beast: but how will M. S., or all the Papists in the world, deny the city of Rome to be that Babylon and see of Antichrist, when the Angel in the last verse of the chapter saith, "And the woman which thou sawest is that great city, which hath dominion over the Kings of the earth?" which if any man say was any other city than Rome, all learning and learned men will cry out against him. The see being found, it is easy to find the person by S. Paul's description; and this note especially, that excludeth the heathen tyrants, "He shall sit in the temple of God:" which when we see to be fulfilled in the Pope, although none of the eldest Fathers could see it, because it was performed after their death, we nothing doubt to say and affirm still, that the Pope is that "Man of sin," and "Son of perdition," the adversary that lifteth up himself "above all that is called God;" and shall be destroyed "by the spirit of the Lord's mouth, and by the glory of His coming."

THE EIGHTEENTH CHAPTER.

Sander. Not the Pope of Rome, but the Protestants themselves are the members of Antichrist; by forsaking the Catholic Church, by setting up a new Church, and by teaching false doctrine against the SANDER.

Gospel of Jesus Christ. Heretics depart from the Catholic Church. Heretics, being once departed out of the Church, have new names. Why among the Catholics some are called Franciscans, Dominicans, &c. Heretics can never agree. The short reign of heretics. Heretics preach without commission. Heretics do prefer the temporal reign or sword before the spiritual. They are the members of Antichrist, who withstand the external and public Sacrifice of Christ's Church. Heretics deprive Christ of His glorious inheritance in many nations together. The intolerable pride of heretics, in making themselves only judges of the right sense of God's word. The Protestants teach the same doctrine which the old heretics did. The Protestants are the right members of Antichrist, in that they spoil God's Church of very many gifts and graces, and articles of the faith.

FULKE. *Fulke.* HE maketh eleven marks of an Antichristian. The first is: They "depart from the Church," as all heretics do. I answer, the Protestants have not departed from the Church of Christ, but are gone out of the Church of Antichrist, according as they are commanded by the Holy Ghost; Apoc. xviii. 4; and are returned to the Church of Christ, which by the Pope and the Devil was driven into the wilderness. Apoc. xxii. [xii.] 6.

But M. Sander would have the place named where they dwelt from whom the Pope departed; as though the place were material, when his departure from the doctrine of Christ is manifest. And Saint Paul prophesied of the great apostasy and departing from Christ which Antichrist should make, 2 Thess. ii., to himself and his own doctrine; as Irenæus doth expound it, Lib. v.[1], and Basi., *Ep.* lxxi.; which "all nations," peoples, and tongues should embrace. Apoc. xviii. 3. Therefore it were no marvel, if no place could be named altogether void of the infection of Antichrist; especially seeing the Church herself was driven into the desert, that is, out of the sight of men: yet there is no doubt, but God preserved His Church, though in small numbers, both in the East and in the West. And namely, one part of the Church of God was in Britain, both in Wales and Scotland, not subject to the Pope, nor acknowledging his auctority, at such time as Augustin the Monk came from Pope Gregory, and so continued long after the revelation of Antichrist. Bed. *Hist.* Lib. ii. Cap. ii. Lib. iii. Cap. xxv. And no doubt but the like was in many corners of the world.

[1] [Cap. xxviii.]

The second mark of an Antichristian he maketh to have "new names" after they be gone out of the Church; as Lutherans, Zwinglians, &c.; whereas they have none but Catholics. Yes, verily, the name of the popish Church and Papists is as ancient as the name of Luther and Lutherans, and more ancient too. M. Sander saith we give them these names of spite, eight or nine hundreth years since the Papacy began. The like I say of them, who call us Lutherans, &c., of mere malice, when we are nothing but Christians. Wherefore the trial must be in the doctrine which either sort profess, and not in names. The Christians of the Arians were called Homoousians, Athanasians, &c.: but the doctrine of the Catholic Christians, agreeing with the word of God, proved them to be no sectaries nor heretics. So doth our doctrine justify us; what names soever be devised against us.

But Master Sander would have us to shew a man, whose proper name was "Papa" or "Romanus;" as though many heretics were not called of their heresy, or place from whence they came, and not of proper names of men. Angelici, Apostolici, Barbarita, [Barbelitæ[2],] Cathari, Collyridiani, Encratitæ, Patripassiani, and a great number more were called of their heresy: Cataphryges, Pepuziani, and such-like were called of the place where they were. Wherefore the name of Papists and Romanists agreeth with the example of old heretics. As for the long tarrying, large spreading, and strange coming in of the popish heresy, [it] is therefore without example in all points like; because Antichrist is not a common petit heretic, but the greatest and most dangerous enemy that ever the Gospel had.

The names of Benedictines, Franciscans, &c., Master Sander would excuse, because these sects maintain no doctrine dissenting from the Pope, but all seek the perfection of the Gospel by divers ways; as though there were any other way but Jesus Christ. Saint Paul, 1 Cor. i., condemneth the holding of Peter, of Paul, of Apollo, when the doctrine was all one; and counteth them schismatics that so did. And the purer primitive Church condemned such apish imitators of the Apostles, in forsaking all things and possessing nothing,

[2] [A name given to the Gnostics. Vid. S. Epiphanii *Respons. ad Epist. Acacii et Pauli,* sig. i iij.; et Lib. i. *Adv. Hær.* Tom. ii. p. 85. ed. Petav.]

in abstaining from marriage, &c., for heretics; and called them "Apostolicos:" witness Epiphan. *Cont. Aposto. Hær.* lxi.[1]

The third mark of an Antichristian is "disagreement" among heretics. And here, not content to charge us with the disagreeing of Anabaptists from us, he amplifieth the dissension between Luther and Zwinglius about the presence of Christ's body in the Sacrament: for which contradiction he thinketh it must needs follow that one of them is an Antichrist.

I answer, every error stiffly maintained maketh not an heretic; except it be in an article of faith necessary to salvation. Cyprian, against the Bishops of Rome, Stephanus and Cornelius, held an error in Baptism as great as that same of Luther, dissenting from Zwinglius in the Supper of the Lord: yet is not Cyprian accounted for an heretic. Master Sander replieth, and sayeth, that Cyprian was not so "stubborn" that he would excommunicate them that held the contrary. Luther also and Zwinglius, although they could not be reconciled in opinions, yet agreed "to abstain from contention," at Marpurg, Anno Domini 1529. Sleid. Lib. vi.[2] Master Sander saith further, that in the contention of Cyprian and Stephanus the Catholic faith was not fully and universally received in any General Council. But he forgetteth that the Bishop of Rome was one party; whose judgment should have ended the strife, if his authority had been such then as he usurped most ambitiously afterward.

Now, whereas he defendeth the Papists for their unity, which he sayeth could not be without the Spirit of God, I answer, he might as well defend the doctrine of the Mahometists, where is greater unity than ever there was among the Papists: who, to omit an hundreth small contentions of the Schoolmen, are not yet agreed of the greatest question of all; whether the Pope be above the Council, or the Council above the Pope. For seeing some of the Papists make the Pope's determination to be the rule of truth, other make the Council, there is no unity among the Papists in truth, when they are not agreed what is the only rule of truth: whereas we all agree, that the word of God is the only rule of truth, whereby we would have all doctrine tried and examined.

The fourth mark of an Antichrist is "to reign but a short

[1] [*Opp.* i. 506.]

[2] [Joan. Sleidani *Commentt.* L. vi. p. 162. Francof. 1610.]

time." And here he would have us to mark how Luther's kingdom is come to an end; whose doctrine Melancthon hath changed, although Illyricus would defend it. What deep root the doctrine of God delivered by Luther hath taken, it is so well known that it cannot be dissembled. Neither hath Melancthon departed from him, except it were in his opinion of the Real Presence. Wherefore this is a great impudency, to triumph over the decay of Luther's doctrine; which daily increaseth, to the overthrow of the popish kingdom.

The fall of Hosiander, an heretic, no man either marvelleth or pitieth. The doctrine of Zwinglius and Œcolampadius of the Sacrament is the same that Calvin teacheth, as every wise man doth know: and their learned works shall live and be in honour when the Pope's Decretals and his Mass-books, &c., shall stop mustard-pots, and be put to viler uses.

Neither is Calvin's doctrine failed by our Oath of Supremacy: for Calvin, in the right sense of it, taught the same Supremacy of Christian Princes which we swear to acknowledge in our Sovereign. Neither doth Beza teach any otherwise of the descending of Christ into hell than Calvin did; nor otherwise expoundeth the place of the Psalm, cited in Acts the second, than Calvin doth; as all men that will read them both may see, notwithstanding the shameless cavil of M. Sander.

The long continuance of the popish kingdom is a small cause to brag of; when it, being found enemy to the kingdom of Christ, is now entered so far into destruction, out of which it shall never escape: although Master Sander saith it doth "flourish;" when it is banished out of so many regions, and daily decreaseth in every place: God's holy name be praised therefore.

The fifth mark of Antichrist, he sayeth, is "to preach without commission;" as Luther did, who was sent of none. I answer, in the state of the Church, so miserably deceived as it was in his time, God sendeth extraordinarily, immediately from Himself: as Helias, and Helizæus, and the Prophets were sent to the Jews and Israelites; which were not of the Priests and ordinary teachers. So Christ sent His Apostles and Evangelists: and so was Luther and such as he sent to repair the ruins of the Church. And yet the Papists have small advantage against the calling of Luther; seeing he was a

Doctor, authorized to preach in that Church where he first began: which, after he had reformed the abuses thereof, and restored true doctrine, in many points banished by the false doctrine of Antichrist, the same reformed Church hath ever since sent forth ordinary Pastors and teachers, and shall do to the end of the world.

The sixth mark of an Antichrist is, that heretics "prefer the temporal sword before the spiritual." And therefore Antichrist shall by force of arms compel men to a new faith: for "he shall come, as S. Paul sayeth, *in virtute,* that is to say, in power or strength." O impudent falsifier of the holy Scripture! doth not Saint Paul say that his coming shall be "according to the efficacy of Satan, in all power, and signs, and lying wonders, and in all deceitfulness of unrighteousness?" 2 Thess. ii.: by which is shewed seduction by false doctrine. But he shall maintain his kingdom by cruelty; as it is manifest in the Revelation, cap. xiii. and xvii, &c.

But M. Sander hath a great quarrel against the Bishop of Winchester[1], for saying in his book against Feckenham, that the civil Magistrates "may visit, correct, reform, and depose any Bishop in their own realms;" which is "directly to say, that the power of the King is higher and greater in God's Church than the power of a Bishop." And what inconvenience is this, in things pertaining to his office; seeing that the Bishop's power in his spiritual office of preaching, ministering, &c., is confessed to be above the King? Hereby we make "the body above the soul," saith M. Sander; "the temporal reign above the kingdom of heaven." Not a whit: no more than Salomon in deposing Abiathar[2]; and Christian Emperors in deposing proud Bishops of Rome. Only this we say, that M. Sander dissembleth: the cause must be just, for which the King should depose a Bishop or Pastor. For I think there is equal right in deposing of the greatest Bishop, and the poorest Priest from his benefice. This latter was always lawful by the common laws upon just cause. Now if the cause be just, it must be either manifest or doubtful. If it be manifest, as Abiathar's was, for murder, treason, adultery, &c., the King, observing the process of the law, as in all other men's causes, may proceed against a Bishop. If the cause be doubtful, it is either for life or doctrine. The trial of the

[1] [Robert Horne.] [2] [See note, p. 265.]

Bishop's life ought to be, as all other men's are, with due consideration of his accusers. The trial of doctrine is not in the King's knowledge ordinarily, but in the knowledge of the ecclesiastical state; who are judges of the doctrine by reason of their knowledge, and to depose him from his ministry by reason of their calling, if he be culpable: and the King hath power to exclude him from his place, and from his life also, if his offence deserve it.

But that in spiritual matters the King should rule the Bishops and Pastors otherwise than God's word would have them ruled, none of us did ever affirm: for that were tyranny, and not Christian government. And of such tyranny of Constantius, the Arian Emperor, doth Athanasius complain; *in Epist. ad sol. vit. agent.*[3]; and shew the judgment and answers of the Christian Bishops, Paulinus, Lucifer, Eusebius, Dionysius, Liberius, Hosius, unto him; when he would have enforced them to subscribe against Athanasius, for defending the eternal Divinity of our Saviour Christ. But yet the same Athanasius appealed himself to the godly Emperor Constantinus the Great; although in the end the Emperor, being carried away by multitude of false witnesses, as any mortal man may be, and deceived, as David was about Mephibosheth, gave wrong sentence against him. Socr. Lib. i. Ca. xxxiv.[4] And when the same Emperor, in his letters before, threatened to depose him if he were disobedient, he never repined, but acknowledged his auctority. *Si cognovero quod aliquos eorum qui Ecclesiæ student prohibueris, aut ab accessu Ecclesiæ excluseris, mittam e vestigio qui te meo jussu deponat, ac locum tuum transferat:* "If I shall know," saith the Emperor, "that thou wilt prohibit any of them that favour the Church, or exclude them from entering into the Church, I will send one immediately which shall depose thee by my commandment, and remove thy place." Socr. Li. i. Ca. xxvii.[5] Thus Athanasius, judging Constantius the heretical Prince for an Antichristian Image, in usurping auctority in matters of faith against the truth, obeyeth Constantinus, a defender of the truth, and seeketh aid of his auctority in ecclesiastical causes, according to the truth.

M. Sander, fearing we would object against him that

3 [Supra, p. 362.] 4 [Cap. xxxv. p. 291. ed. Lat.]
5 [Muscul. interp.]

Constantinus, Martianus, and other godly Emperors, used to sit in General Councils with the Bishops, replieth, that it was only "to keep peace;" whereas they did not only keep peace, but also prescribe and command the Bishops to proceed according to God's word, as Constantine did in the Nicene Council[1]: *Evangelici enim,* &c.: "The books of the Gospels and of the Apostles, and the oracles of the ancient Prophets, do plainly instruct us in the understanding of God. Therefore, setting all hateful discord aside, let us take out of the sayings of God's Spirit the explication of the questions." They did also publish the Decrees of the Councils by their auctority, like as they called the Councils together to make their Decrees.

But Ambrose saith, *Ep.* xxxii., [xiii.[2],] that even an heretical Emperor, coming to years of discretion, will be able to consider "what manner a [of] Bishop he is, who layeth the priestly right under the laymen's feet." By which, saith M. Sander, you may see what manner a [of] Bishop M. Horne and his fellows be, which give "the most proud and intolerable title of supreme head and governor to lay Princes." I answer, in giving this title they mean to take nothing from the right of the Clergy; and confess with Augustin, that there is no greater than a Priest in his office: although Moses, after the distinction, was no Priest, but a civil Magistrate; and in his calling above Aaron that was High Priest. And although M. Sander say "this is the divinity of England" only, to acknowledge the Prince to be chief governor, he sayeth most untruly: for all learned men, of all countries, do acknowledge the same in such sort as we do in England; and not as he in Flanders either dreameth or slandereth us to do. For we confess, with Valentinian the good Emperor, that the Prince must "submit his head" to his godly Pastor, in matters pertaining to his spiritual power. Theodor. Lib. iv. Cap. v.[3] And yet we allow the same Valentinian, writing to the Bishops of Asia and Phrygia: Theodor. Lib. iv. Cap. viii.: *Qui omnes*

[1] [The words alleged by Fulke are from Theodoret, Lib. i. Cap. vii., according to the version by Camerarius. Bellarmin endeavours to reply to this passage by saying: "Erat Constantinus magnus Imperator, sed non magnus Ecclesiæ Doctor." (*De verbo Dei non scripto,* Lib. iv. C. xi. col. 246.)]

[2] [*Opp.* T. v. c. 204.]

[3] [ed. Lat. interp. Camerar.]

noxios Dæmones student abigere precibus suis, &c.: "They, which study by their prayers to drive away all hurtful Devils, know to submit themselves to public offices, according to the laws: they speak not against the Emperor's power; but they keep the commandments of a sincere[4] and great Emperor, and the commandments of God, and are subject to our laws; but you are found disobedient."

Finally, we never meant to give the Prince by flattery auctority in such matters as belong to Bishops alone; neither would we have a confusion of the office of an Emperor and a Bishop. Wherefore neither the saying of Leontius to Constantius, nor of Eulogius to Valens, which were both heretics, and would enforce men to receive the heresy of Arius, doth any thing at all touch us, who limit the Supremacy of Princes within the compass of God's word, and Christian religion; against which neither Prince nor Priest hath any auctority to command.

The seventh mark of Antichrist is "the withstanding of the external and public Sacrifice of the Church;" by which he meaneth the Sacrifice of the Mass. Nay, rather, it is a setting up of a new altar, and Sacrifice propitiatory, against the only propitiatory Sacrifice of Christ's death once offered; by which one oblation "He hath made perfect for ever them that are sanctified." Heb. x. The auctor of this Sacrifice, which is the Pope, he is indeed Antichrist, the Son of perdition.

But Master Sander, for proof of the Sacrifice of the Mass, allegeth the prophecy of Malachi, cap. i., with sixteen fond comparisons of the defects of the Jews, and the perfection of the Gentiles; which he affirmeth to be "the uniform interpretation of the ancient Fathers; of whom no one denieth the body and blood of Christ to be here meant, albeit some of them expoundeth [expound] this prophecy of prayers and inward righteousness, which are always joined with the unbloody Sacrifice." I answer, no one of the ancient Fathers understandeth this prophecy of the Sacrifice of Christ's body and blood otherwise than of a Sacrifice of praise and thanksgiving: for proof whereof I must refer the reader to mine Answer to M. Heskins, Lib. i. Cap. xxxiii., xxxiv., xxxv., & xxxvi., where he shall find the places of the Doctors set down, which are by M. Sander in place only quoted.

4 ["sincerely keep the commandments."]

But one other strange reason of M. Sander to prove the Sacrament of the Lord's Supper to be a Sacrifice propitiatory I may not omit, because I remember not that I have read it before. "Every public and external fact, which is made by God's authority to put us in mind of that great Sacrifice once fulfilled on the Cross, must also be partaker of the nature of that Sacrifice whereof it is a remembrance. As, if the killing of a calf, which signified the death of Christ, was an external Sacrifice; how infinitely more shall the body and blood of Christ, being made of bread and wine, to signify His own death, be a public and external Sacrifice?"

This reason M. Sander maketh no small account of. But how beastly an absurdity his principle is you shall easily perceive, if you consider that Baptism is a public and external fact, made by God's authority to put us in mind of the death and bloodshedding of Christ: yet no man was ever so mad to say Baptism is a Sacrifice. Again, the calf that was killed was by God's appointment a Sacrifice of the only and singular Sacrifice of Christ's death, and not by virtue of the signification; for the Jews had other ceremonies than Sacrifices, which did signify the death of Christ: but the Lord's Supper is not by God's appointment a Sacrifice; therefore the signification cannot make it so.

The eighth mark of the false prophets of Antichrist is "to spoil Christ of His inheritance, which God gave Him in all nations;" as the Protestants do, which for eight or nine hundreth years cannot shew "any nation, town, or village, church, or chapel in the wide world, where they had public prayer." I answer, seeing the Spirit speaketh expressly of a general apostasy, and of the flying of the Church into the desert, it is no more derogation to the inheritance of Christ, that His Church among many nations was in persecution under Antichrist for seven or eight hundreth years, than that the same was in persecution under the heathen Emperors for three hundred years and more. For the nations were then the inheritance of Christ in as glorious wise as when the Church flourished in outward peace under the Christian Emperors. Yet was there towns and countries, not only in France, Italy, and Germany, but also in the east part of the world great nations, among which Christ had a visible Church, which were never subject to the Church of Rome. If M. S.

reply, that they held some errors which we deny, as Prayer for the dead, &c., I answer, holding the only foundation Jesus Christ, they might be true Christians, although they were infected with some such errors as these.

The ninth mark of Antichrist is "intolerable pride, to make himself judge of the sense of God's word, and of the text also." I allow this mark: and it agreeth to none that ever was so aptly as to the Pope; whom the Papists affirm that he cannot err in the sense of the Scripture; who affirm that he hath auctority to receive and reject what books of Scripture he will. But M. Sander saith this note agreeth to us; and that we make ourselves judges of the sense of God's word, and of the text. But we utterly deny that: for we make the Spirit of God in His word judge of the interpretation. No, saith M. Sander; and bringeth an example of these words, of S. Paul, "He that joineth his virgin in marriage doth well; and he that joineth her not doth better." Hereupon (saith he) we ground this doctrine, "Virginity is a better state, and more acceptable to God, than the state of marriage." This we grant in some respect, as the Apostle speaketh, but not simply. The question is of these words, "he doth better," what is meant thereby. M. Sander chargeth us to say, that S. Paul meaneth he doth better in the sight of the world: which is an impudent lie, and therefore all his foolish dialogism is a fighting with his own shadow. Beza expoundeth, he doth "better," that is, "more commodiously;" not in respect of the world, but in respect of godliness, for the reasons before alleged by S. Paul; and S. Paul himself is auctor of this interpretation, verse 35 of that seventh chapter 1 Cor., "This I say for your commodity," when he exhorteth to virginity.

And that his purpose was not absolutely and simply to prefer virginity above marriage, as a thing of itself more acceptable to God, it is plain by these words. First he saith, "Of virgins I have no commandment of the Lord:" but he hath a commandment to prefer those things that are most acceptable to the Lord. Secondly he saith, "I suppose this to be good for the present necessity:" by which words he doth imply, that it is not always and absolutely better; but at some times, and in some respects, for them that have the gift of continence, and for none other. So we hold virginity to be better than marriage, according to the meaning of the best ancient writers; whereof some were too great extollers of virginity, yet not like the Papists.

But M. Sander sayeth, the Protestants "make themselves judges not only of the meaning of God's word, but also of the books themselves. For they reject not only the books of Wisdom, Toby, and the Maccabees, with other such books, but also the Epistle of S. James." Nay, rather, the Pope is Antichrist, for receiving these books of Wisdom, Toby, Maccabees; which were never received of the Church of the Israelites, nor of the universal Church of Christ for Canonical Scripture, as I have often shewed. And as touching the Epistle of S. James, it is a shameless slander of him to say that the Protestants reject it. But we must hear his reason. First, Luther calleth it "a strawen Epistle[1]." So Luther called the Pope supreme head of the Church, and the Mass a Sacrifice propitiatory; if Protestants be charged to hold whatsoever Luther sometime held, and after repented. But the Confession of Zurich[2], with the consent of the Churches of Helvetia and Sabaudia, writeth thus of it: *Jacobus ille dixit,* &c.: that "James said that works do justify: not speaking against Saint Paul; otherwise he were to be rejected." Here, saith M. Sander, they think it possible "that S. James might be contrary to Saint Paul, and so his Epistle to be no holy Scripture." A wise collection, I promise you. S. Paul himself said, "If I myself, or an Angel from heaven, should preach any other Gospel than you have already received, let him be accursed:" *ergo,* S. Paul thought it was possible that himself or an Angel should be auctor of a new Gospel, and so his preaching should not be the Gospel. Who seeth not the madness of this consequence?

But S. James his Epistle (he saith) hath always been clearly admitted among true Catholics: and for witness hereof he quoteth most impudently Euseb., Lib. i. [ii.] Ca. xxiii., in which book and chapter Eusebius clearly affirmeth that it is a counterfeit Epistle[3]. I say not this to allow the judgment of Eusebius, but to shew the impudency of M. Sander. But

[1] [See Fulke's *Defence of the English translations of the Bible,* page 15. ed. Parker Soc.]

[2] [An. Dom. 1566.]

[3] [Perhaps only in the opinion of some. The word is "νοθεύεται."]

he saith we reject S. James "because he is contrary to our devilish doctrine of only faith." We teach only faith none otherwise than the Apostle teacheth; that a man is justified by faith, without works. We teach not that a man is justified by a dead faith, which is void of good works; but by a living faith, which "worketh by love." We say, with Saint James, "If a man say he have faith, and hath not works," his faith shall not "save him." For Abraham's faith, which was imputed to him for righteousness by God, was not without good works, as appeared by his obedience in offering his son: wherein God tried him, neither to know him, nor to justify him, whom he knew and justified before; but to shew his obedience, and to justify him before men. So it is true that S. James sayeth, "A man is justified of works, and not of faith only." For a solitary fruitless faith doth not justify before God: but a faith which is fruitful in good works is the only instrument to apprehend justification: and the works, as Augustin saith, "follow, and shew a justified man;" they go not before to justify. Thus our doctrine agreeth very well with the Epistle of S. James, and Saint Paul's doctrine: wherefore we have no need to reject the Epistle of Saint James, as contrary to our doctrine.

But the Protestants do not only "make themselves judges of the whole books, but also over the very letter" (saith he) "of Christ's Gospel; finding fault with the construction of the Evangelists; and bring the text itself in doubt." Example hereof he bringeth Beza[4], in his Annotations upon Luke xxii., of the words, "This cup is the new testament in My blood, which is shed for you." In which text, because the word "blood" in the Greek is the dative case, the other word that followeth is the nominative case. Beza supposeth that S. Luke useth a figure called *Solœcophanes,* which is "appearance of incongruity;" or else that the last word, "which is shed for you," might, by error of writers, being first set in the margent out of Matthew and Mark, be removed into the text. Hereupon M. Sander out of all order and measure raileth upon Beza, and upon all Protestants. But I pray you, good Sir, shall the only opinion of Beza, and that but a doubtful opinion, indict all the Protestants in the world of such high treason

4 [See Gregory Martin's *Discoverie of manifold Corruptions*, pp. 14, 260. Rhemes, 1582. Fulke's *Def. of Engl. transl.* pp. 132—139, 512. ed. Parker Soc.]

against the word of God? For what gaineth Beza by this interpretation? Forsooth, the Greek text is "contrary to his sacramentary heresy." For thus he should translate it: "This cup is the new testament in My blood; which cup is shed for you:" not the cup of gold or silver, (saith he,) but "the liquor in that cup;" which is not wine, because wine was not shed for us, but the blood of Christ. Why, then the sense is this: This blood in the cup which is shed for you is the new testament in My blood. What sense in the world can these words have? By which it is manifest that the words, "which is shed for you," cannot be referred to the cup, but to His blood. For the cup was the new testament in His blood, which was shed for us: which sense no man can deny, but he that will deny the manifest word of God. Neither doth the vulgar Latin translation give any other sense; although M. Sander is not ashamed to say it doth. The vulgar Latin text is this: *Hic est calix novum testamentum in sanguine Meo, qui pro vobis fundetur.* What grammarian in construing would refer *qui* to *calix*, and not rather to *sanguine?* Again, Erasmus translateth it even as Beza: *Hoc poculum novum testamentum per sanguinem Meum, qui pro vobis effunditur.*

Now touching the conjecture of Beza, that those words by error of the scrivener might be removed from the margent into the text, [it] is a thing that sometime hath happened, as most learned men agree, in the xxvii. of Matthew, where the name of Jeremy is placed in the text for that which is in Zachary[1]; and yet neither of the Prophets was named by the Evangelist, as in most ancient records it is testified[2]. The like hath been in the first of Mark; where the name of Esay is set in some Greek copies, and followed in your vulgar translation, for that which is cited out of Malachi; which name was not set down by the Evangelist, but added by some unskilful writer, and is reproved by other Greek copies.

But this place, you say, is not otherwise found in "any old

[1] ["It was a thing known among the Jews, that the four last chapters of the book of Zechary were written by Jeremy; as Mr. Mede has proved by many arguments." (Allix's *Judgment of the Jewish Church against Unitarians*, p. 15. Oxford, 1821.) See Mede's *Works*, pp. 786, 833—4. Lond. 1672.]

[2] [Vid. S. August. *De consensu Evangelistarum*, Lib. iii. Cap. vii.]

copy," as Beza confesseth. Then remaineth the second opinion; that S. Luke in this place useth *Solœcophanes,* which is "an appearance of incongruity, and yet no incongruity." Wherein I cannot marvel more at your malice, M. Sander, than at your ignorance, which put no difference between *Solœcismus* and *Solœcophanes;* but even as spitefully as unlearnedly you affirm that Beza should teach "that S. Luke wrote false Greek:" whereas *Solœcophanes* is a figure used of the most eloquent writers that ever took pen in hand; even Cicero, Demosthenes, Greek and Latin, profane and divine, and even of S. Luke himself in other places; whereof for examples I refer you to Budæus, upon the word *Solœcophanes.* The appearance of incongruity is, that it seemeth that τὸ ἐκχυνόμενον, which is the nominative case, should agree with τῷ αἵματι, which is the dative case: whereas indeed τὸ is used as a relative for ὃ, as it is often; and the verb ἔστι, which wanteth, is understood, as it is commonly in the Greek tongue; and so the translation must be: *Hoc poculum novum testamentum est in sanguine Meo, qui pro vobis effunditur,* or *effusus est.* So that this is nothing else but an impudent and unskilful quarrelling against Beza: whereas you Papists defend, against the manifest institution of the cup, and the practice of the primitive Church, the Communion in one kind, of bread only. *Con. Const.* Sess. xiii. xxi. [Can. iv.]

The tenth mark of an Antichristian is "to agree with the members of Antichrist," which are heretics. To agree with them in heresy is a point of Antichristianism, I confess: but not to agree with them in any thing; for every heresy affirmeth things that are true. But let us see in what points of heresy he chargeth us to agree with the old heretics.

First, "Eunomius said that no sin should hurt him, [a man,] if he were partaker of the faith which he taught." So the Protestants say of their faith. Yea, Sir; but their faith is not Eunomius' faith: and yet they say not that no sin shall hurt them, but no sin shall condemn them: and so say you Papists of your popish faith.

Secondly, Acesius, the Novatian Bishop, affirmed, that "mortal sins committed after Baptism might not be forgiven of the Priest, but of God alone." The Protestants deny the Priest to have any right to forgive sins. This is a loud lie, and false slander: for we hold that the Minister of God hath authority to forgive all sins that God will forgive, according to the power given to them, Joan. xx. But you Papists agree with the heretic in this point, that you deny the Priest to forgive all sins, according to the power given; but have your *Casus Episcopales et Papales*[1], by which you abridge the power given by Christ.

Thirdly, "The Messalians denied that Baptism doth pluck up the root of sins. The same is the opinion of the Protestants." The Protestants have none opinion common with the Messalians, who affirmed that our own merits and satisfaction, with prayers continual, were necessary for plucking up the root of sins; whereas we affirm that Baptism "saveth us," according to the Scripture, 1 Pet. iii. 21, by forgiveness of our sins, whereby even the root of sin is plucked up; although concupiscence remain after the act of Baptism, which you Papists also confess to remain, and to be the root of sin, although you grant it not to be sin. But we limit not the effect of Baptism to the time passed before the act of Baptism only, as you do, but extend it to our eternal salvation: "He that believeth and is baptized shall be saved." Mark xvi. 16. Therefore you Papists, both in this and in your continual lip-labour maintained in your abbeys, agree with the Messalians.

Fourthly, Aerius taught, "that we must not pray for the dead, nor keep the accustomed fastings, and that there is no difference between a Priest and a Bishop." The superstition of praying for the dead was justly reproved by Aerius: so was the fast of custom and decree, rather than of consideration. For the first that prayed for the dead were heretics, Montanists, as Tertullian and his sect. The first that made prescript laws of fasting was Montanus the heretic also, as Eusebius witnesseth. Lib. v. Cap. xviii. Of the third opinion was Hierom, *Evagrio*[2]; affirming that the distinction was made by men, and not by God.

Fifthly, "Jovinian judged virginity equal with marriage." So do the Protestants. I have shewed before how it is equal, and how it is superior.

Sixthly, S. Hierom reproveth Vigilantius of heresy, "for

[1] [These reserved Cases are commonly printed in tracts consisting of a few leaves. The title generally is, *Casus Papales et Episcopales*: sometimes the *Casus Abbatiales* are added.]

[2] [See before, p. 33, note 1.]

denying prayer to Saints, and giving honour to Reliques." For praying to Saints there is no mention in S. Hierom. The immoderate honouring of Reliques was justly reproved: and yet it was not then the one half of that it hath been since. Hieronym, although he rather rail than reason against Vigilantius, as Erasmus hath noted; yet he defendeth not the adoration or worshipping, but the reverent estimation of Reliques.

Seventhly, "The Arians would not believe the consubstantiality of the same, [the Son,] because that word was not written in the Scripture. So do the Protestants deny many things upon the like pretence." This is a mere slander: for we stand upon the sense of the Scripture, and not the words only.

Eighthly, Eusebius noteth it "for an heinous impiety in Novatus, that he was not consummate with Chrism, which the Protestants call greasing." Indeed, Cornelius Bishop of Rome reporteth, that Novatus was baptized in time of necessity, being very like to die: *Jacens in lecto, pro necessitate, perfusus sit: nec reliqua in eo quæ Baptismum subsequi solent solemniter adimpleta sunt; nec signaculo Chrismatis consummatus sit: unde nec Spiritum Sanctum unquam potuerit promereri:* "Lying in his bed, according to the necessity, he was baptized: neither were the other things that are wont to follow Baptism solemnly fulfilled; neither was he consummate with the seal of Chrism: whereby he could never obtain the Holy Ghost." First I say, this is noted as no impiety in Novatus, but as a defect of necessity. Secondly, that the Chrism which Cornelius speaketh of was either a seal of the extraordinary gifts of the Holy Ghost, which in some remained in the Church until that time; or else he magnifieth that ceremony intolerably, to deny the Holy Ghost to such as had it not; being none of the institution of Christ, and contrary to that the Papists themselves hold at this day.

Ninthly, "Lucius the Arian persecuted holy Monks. So do the Protestants." Nay, they punish none but filthy idle idolaters and hypocrites.

Tenthly, "The Montanists and Luciferians said there was a stews made of the Church." They said so falsely when the Church was chaste; but Esay said truly, "How is the faithful city become an whore!" when the Church of Israel was so indeed.

Eleventhly, "The Donatists said the Church was lost from all the world, and preserved only in Africa. So say the Protestants, that the Church was lost in all parts of the world, and raised up again in Germany." The Protestants say not so: for the Church hath been scattered over the face of the earth, since the first preaching of the Apostles unto this day. But the Papists say that the Church was lost out of all the world, and preserved only in a part of Europe; when, of all parts in the world, only a part of Europe, which is the least part of the world, was subject to the Church of Rome.

Twelfthly, "The Severians used the Law and the Prophets; but they perverted the sense of the Scriptures by a certain peculiar interpretation of their own. So do the Protestants." Nay, so do the Papists; that submit all understanding of the Scripture, be it never so plain, to the interpretation of their Pope and popish Church: as the Commandment of Images forbidden, and the cup to be received of all, do most manifestly declare.

Lastly, "It hath always been a trick of Jews and heretics to be still in hand with translating holy Scriptures; that by changing they may get some appearance of Scripture on their side; as Theodotion, Aquila, Symmachus. So do the Protestants now." Hieronym was no heretic; yet did he translate the Scriptures both into Latin and into the Dalmatian tongue. And the Papists have played the part of Antichristian heretics, to confirm the vulgar Latin translation; which is so manifestly corrupt and false, contrary to the truth of the Hebrew and Greek texts, upon pretence of avoiding uncertainty of translations; whereas there is none so bad as that.

I might here run through a great number of the old heresies, in which the Papists consent with the ancient heretics; the Valentinians, in their Cross; Montanists, in their Purgatory, and prescript fastings; Carpocratians, in their Images; the Hemerobaptists, in their Holy Water; the Ossens and Marcosians, in their Reliques, and strange tongue in prayers; the Heracleanites, in anointing them that are ready to die; the Caians, in praying to Angels; the Archontics, in their counterfeit monkery; the Marcionists, in extolling virginity and fasting, and in permitting women to baptize; the Encratists, in abstaining from flesh; the Apostolics, in their vow of continence; the Cyrians, [Collyridians,] in worshipping the Virgin Mary; the Pelagians, in their opinion of merits and freewill; the Eutychians, in denying the truth of Christ His body; the Anthro[po]morphites, in making Images of God; and many other, but that I have done it elsewhere more at large. But of these Epiphanius, Augustin, and others are witnesses.

The eleventh and last mark is, that Antichristians should go about "to make void and deny the supernatural graces which God hath given to His Church;" so that "the seal of Antichrist," by Hippolytus' judgment, should be *Nego*, "I deny." So do the Protestants, which deny five Sacraments of the Church, the Sacrifice of the Mass, &c.: and so maketh rehearsal of a great number of popish errors, which indeed we deny, because they be contrary to the truth of God's word. Among which he rehearseth some false and shameless slanders; as, that we "deny our sins to be taken away by the Lamb of God; saying they tarry still, but that they are not imputed." Indeed, "if we say we have no sin, we deceive ourselves, and the truth is not in us:" but we say all the sins that we have are taken away, when they are not laid to our charge.

Secondly, he chargeth us to teach, "that no justice is at all made in us by spreading charity in our hearts; whereas S. Paul saith, Rom. v., 'many shall be made just:' but they say only that justice shall be imputed." We say with Saint Paul, Rom. v., that "being justified by faith, we have peace with God:" rejoicing in hope, which doth not confound us in the midst of afflictions, "because the love of God is poured forth in our hearts:" I mean the love of God toward us, and not our love toward Him. We say likewise with Saint Paul, that "by the obedience of One," which is Christ, "many shall be made righteous." But how can we be made righteous by obedience of Christ, but that His obedience is imputed and made perfect unto us? O putid and absurd slanders!

He chargeth us thirdly, that we "deny Baptism to remit our sins:" which is false, except as Saint Peter denieth the work wrought to save us; 1 Pet. iii. verse 21: "Not the washing of the filth of the body, but the answer of a good conscience unto almighty God."

Fourthly, he chargeth us to deny "that Baptism is necessary to children which are born of Christian parents:" wherein he lieth most impudently; although we agree not with the Papists that the infants of Christians, excluded by necessity from Baptism, are damned. In which error although Augustin was, yet he is no more to be followed than in another error about the same infants, to whom both he and Pope Innocentius thought the Sacrament of the Lord's Supper as necessary as the Sacrament of Baptism; affirming that infants which have not received the Lord's Supper were damned: *Contra duas Episto. Pelag. ad Bonifac.* Lib. ii. Cap. iv.[1]: *Ecce, beatæ memoriæ Innocentius Papa sine Baptismo Christi et sine participatione corporis et sanguinis Christi vitam non habere parvulos dicit:* "Behold, Pope Innocent of blessed memory sayeth, that without the Baptism of Christ, and the participation of the body and blood of Christ, little children have no life."

To conclude, we deny nothing that they can prove to be true, but such matters as we prove by the only rule of truth to be false. But the Pope sheweth himself to be Antichrist, which denieth all the sovereignty of the office and prerogative of Christ.

He denieth that Christ is the only Head of His universal Church in heaven and in earth.

He denieth that Christ only is a Priest, according to the order of Melchisedech.

He denieth that Christ only is our Mediator, as well of intercession as of redemption.

He denieth that Christ's word is sufficient for our salvation.

He denieth that the Sacrifice of Christ His death is the only purgation of our sins.

He denieth that the merits of Christ are our only justification.

He denieth that God only is to be prayed unto.

He denieth the verity of Christ's body by his Transubstantiation.

[1] [Supra, pag. 41.]

Finally, he denieth all honour and glory to be due only to God by Jesus Christ: and therefore he is none other but even that detestable monster Antichrist, whom I beseech the Lord speedily to confound and abolish by the spirit of His mouth, which is His holy word, and by the brightness of His coming.
Amen.

God be praised.

INDEX.

Abdias, "a new-found old Doctor," 149, 172.

Abgarus, 53, 204.

Abiathar, whom Solomon deposed, or rather banished, not lawfully the High Priest, 265.

Acta Eruditorum, 33, 287.

Acta Sanctorum, 81, 355.

Ælfric, The Paschal Homily, 7, 20, 247 : Epistles, 20 : Ussher's mistake concerning his *Liber Canonum*, 22.

Aerius, 43, 67.

Aetius, the Anomœan, 43.

Agapetus I. (Pope) whether he first devised Processions, 184.

Agylæus (Henricus) omits a remarkable reference in the *Nomocanon* of Photius, 42.

Aidanus, 16, 26, 27.

Albertus Magnus, 167.

Alcuinus, at what time it is said that he composed the Caroline Books, 23, 154.

Alexander I. (Pope) first spurious Epistle, 81, 84 : Stapleton relies on it for the defence of Holy Water, 117.

Alexander (Natalis) rejects the fabulous Acts of the Synod of Sinuessa, 364.

"Algates," 183.

Allix (Peter, D.D.) 386.

Alteserra (Antonius Dadinus) 103.

Ambrosius (S.) his use of the term *Missa*, 81, 239 : year of his death, 81 : a Sermon *De Cruce*, by S. Maximus Taurinensis, ascribed to him, 154—5 : spurious Commentary on the Epistles of S. Paul, 183, 367 : his language concerning the Empress Helena, 202 : false testimony adduced as if from him at the second Council of Nicæa, 207 : questionable books *De Sacramentis*, 239 : a Sermon attributed both to him and S. Augustin, 284 : a Sermon ascribed to him, to S. Augustin, and to S. Maximus Taurinensis, 340 : undoubtedly not the author of the books *De vocatione Gentium*, 353.

—— *Officiorum libri*, 83.

—— *Concio de obitu Theod. Imp.*, 87, 202.

—— *De hort. ad Virg. Tractat.*, 92.

—— *In obitum Satyri*, 105.

—— *In S. Luc.*, 256, 304, 320—21.

—— *De Spiritu Sancto*, 256.

—— *De incarnat. Dom.*, 256, 310.

—— *Epistt.*, 266, 267, 380.

—— *In Psal.*, 284.

Ambrosius Camaldulensis, 110.

Amerbachius (Bruno) condemned as fictitious the Commentary on the Psalms attributed to S. Jerom, 208.

Ammianus Marcellinus, 360.

Anacletus (Pope), third spurious Epistle, what derivation it assigns for Cephas, 301.

Anastasius Bibliothecarius, whether the author of the Pontifical, 98—9.

Ancyra, Council of, permits the marriage of the Clergy, 96.

Angelici, the heretics, why so called, 41—2 : their doctrine condemned by the Council of Laodicea, 42.

Anthony (S.) 172.

Antiquity, the test of truth in matters of religion, 64, 175.

Apiarius, 70.

Appeals to Rome, 70—71, 308.

Aristotle, what called by Luther, 57.

Arnobius Afer, mistaken for Minucius Felix, 206 : confounded by Erasmus, Fulke, and others, with Arnobius Junior, 319.

Arnobius Junior, *Comment. in Psal.*, by whom and when first published, 319 : quoted, 319—20, 322, 347—8.

Arnoldus Carnotensis, treatises written by him, and attributed to S. Cyprian, 163, 238.

Article, sixth, of the Church of England, 221, 222.

"Assoiled," 48.

Athanasius (S.) 346, 347: appealed to Constantine, 358, 379: spurious *Quæstiones ad Antiochum*, 143, 177, 193, 206.
—— *De incarnatione Verbi Dei*, 198.
—— Fictitious *Liber de passione Imaginis Christi*, 200, 206.
—— *Hist. Arianor. ad Monachos*, 362, 379.

Augustin the Monk, miracles ascribed to him, 5, 76: defended by Bede with reference to the Monks of Bangor, 6, 186: though he and his companions carried a Cross, there is not (as Collier remarks, and Manning admits,) the least intimation given that they worshipped it, 17: how he and the ancient Ascetics differed from popish Monks, 17—18: received "codices plurimos" from S. Gregory the Great, 113.

Augustinus (S.) his opinion as to the necessity of administering the Communion to infants, 41, 392: his account of the Angelici, 42: condemned superstition at the tombs of Martyrs, 44: rejected the Canon cited about appeals to Rome, 70, 353: died out of communion with the Church of Rome, 71: spurious *Sermo* amongst those *de diversis*, 82: a work by S. Fulgentius, *De fide, ad Petrum Diaconum*, attributed to him, 86: Mendicants under the rule of, 103: fictitious addresses to Catechumens, 145: counterfeit *Tractatus contra quinque Hæreses*, 147: spurious *Sermo* xix. *de Sanctis*, 157: a Homily by S. Chrysostom, *De Cruce et Latrone*, erroneously assigned to him, 179—80: supposititious tract *De vera et falsa Pœnitentia*, 240: feigned *Hypog. contr. Pelag.*, 241: a Sermon attributed both to him and to S. Ambrose, 284: *Hom. de Pastoribus* wrongly rejected by Fulke, 291: his interpretation of the Rock, 294: a Sermon bearing his name, as well as that of S. Ambrose, and of S. Maximus Taurinensis, 340: maintained the innocence of Pope Marcellinus, 365.
—— *In Psalmos*, 31, 54, 92, 102, 111, 240, 245.

Augustinus (S.) *Epistolæ*, 36, 43, 62, 100, 111, 127, 133, 150, 242, 267, 294, 350, 351, 352—3, 357, 358.
—— *De Genesi ad literam*, 36.
—— *Cont. duas Ep. Pelag. ad Bon.*, 41, 392.
—— *De Hæresibus*, 42, 43, 147.
—— *De moribus Ecclesiæ Catholicæ*, 44, 99, 128.
—— *De unitate Ecclesiæ*, 50, 54, 230.
—— *De utilitate credendi*, 56, 67.
—— *Cont. Ep. Manich. quam voc. Fundam.*, 56, 241, 350—1.
—— *Contra Faustum*, 57, 88, 146, 182.
—— *Cont. Ep. Parmen.*, 62.
—— *De Civitate Dei*, 80, 85—6, 127, 150, 245, 367.
—— *Sermones de Scripturis*, 82, 317.
—— *Contra advers. Leg. et Proph.*, 86, 245.
—— *De Conjug. adult.*, 94.
—— *De cura pro mortuis*, 105.
—— *De consensu Evangelistarum*, 128, 234, 386.
—— *Contra Maximin. Arian.*, 130.
—— *De Doctrina Christiana*, 132, 221.
—— *De Trinitate*, 134.
—— *De vera Religione*, 149—50.
—— *Enchiridion ad Laurent.*, 150, 240—1.
—— *In S. Joannem*, 202, 294, 298.
—— *Contra Gaudent.*, 221.
—— *Contra Julianum*, 230.
—— *De Natura et Gratia*, 230.
—— *Cont. Cresconium*, 230.
—— *De Gratia Christi*, 230.
—— *De octo Dulcitii Quæstt.*, 241.
—— *Retractationes*, 287.
—— *De Agone Christiano*, 295.
—— *Serm.* lxxvi. *de verb. Evang. Matth.*, 298.
—— *De Bapt. contra Don.*, 313.
—— *Hom. de Pastoribus*, 291, 317.
—— *De unico Bapt. contra Petil.*, 365.

Aylmer (Bishop) his *Harborowe*, and Life by Strype, 37.

Babylon, mentioned in S. Peter's first Epistle, not Rome, 336—8: De Marca adopts Joseph Scaliger's conjecture, 336.

Bail (Louis) rejects the spurious inventory of Canonical books which Carranza ascribed to the Council of Florence, 222.

Balduinus (Franciscus) *Responsio ad Calvinum*, 73: his ingenuous acknowledgment of an interpolation in Optatus, 302: added the seventh book against Parmenian in small type, 323.

Ballerinius (Petrus et Hieronymus) 70.

Barlow (Bishop) *Brutum Fulmen*, 286, 290.

Baronius (Cardinal) 71, 328: fictitious Saint Synoris in his first edition of the Roman Martyrology, 44: maintains the genuineness of the spurious letter to Oceanus, attributed to S. Jerom, 97, 339: why he rejects a Sermon, ascribed to S. Chrysostom, *in adorationem venerab. Catenarum*, 110: his extraordinary proof of the antiquity of shaven crowns, 115: derived from Malmesbury an interpolated letter ascribed to Pope Sergius I., 119: disregards the counterfeit *Liber de passione Imaginis Christi*, which bears the name of S. Athanasius, 200: considered S. Jerom shamefully astray respecting the primacy of S. Peter, 292: approved of the irrational derivation of Cephas from κεφαλή, 302: vainly relied on the corrupted *Chronicon* of Eusebius, to prove that S. Peter was for twenty-five years at Rome, 337: refuses to admit the alleged antiquity of the Pseudo-Hegesippus, 339: endeavours to uphold the credibility of the Acts of Paul and Thecla, 339: adduces the valueless Acts of the Martyr Pontius, 355: his falsehood respecting the continuance of Eusebius's tendency to Arianism, 359: speaks of the preservation of the Font of Constantine, 360: his confession as to the imaginary Acts of the Synod of Sinuessa, 365: the authority for the common opinion as to the grant by Phocas to the Popes of the title of "Œcumenical Bishop," 365.

Barrow (Isaac, D. D.) calls S. Chrysostom "the Prince of interpreters," 285; and ascribes to him a counterfeit *Sermo in Pentecosten*, 286.

Bas (C. W. Le) *Life of Bishop Jewel*, 371.

Basil, Council of, a treatise annexed to its Acts, 294.

Basilius (S.) *Concio ad Adolesc.*, 134: questionable treatise *De Spiritu Sancto*, 239.

—— *Regulæ contractiores;* and Bellarmin's expression of uncertainty as to the author, 161.

—— *Hom. cont. Sabel.*, 177.

—— *Hom. in Barlaam Martyrem*, 199.

—— *Mor. Def.*, 239.

—— *Concio de Pœnit.*, 284.

—— *Advers. Eunom.*, 289.

—— *Epist.* lxxi., 374.

Basnage (Jacques) 101.

Bayle (Pierre) 37.

Beaven (James) 69, 340.

Becanus (Martinus) quotes as genuine a fictitious Catalogue of Canonical books, ascribed by Carranza to the Council of Florence, 222.

Becon (Thomas, S. T. P.) 38.

Beda (Ven.) his History translated by Stapleton, 5: refutes a charge against the Monk Augustin, 6, 186: variation in the numbering of chapters in his History, 9: his statement as to the relationship between S. Gregory the Great and Pope Felix III., 99: his journey to Rome a fiction, 119—20.

Bellarmin (Cardinal) rejects Gratian's corruption of a Milevitan Decree, 71: endeavours to discredit an Epistle of S. Gregory Nyssen, *De iis qui adeunt Hierosolyma*, 109: maintains the genuineness of the spurious treatise *Contra quinque Hæreses*, attributed to S. Augustin, 147: his doubt as to the author of the *Regulæ contractiores* ascribed to S. Basil, 161: adduces the fictitious *Liber de passione Imaginis Christi*, bearing the name of S. Athanasius, 200: cites as authentic a counterfeit Catalogue of Canonical books, assigned by Carranza to the Council of Florence, 222: quotes an interpolated passage in the Chronicle of Eusebius as proof that S. Peter continued for twenty-five years at Rome, 337: relies on the testimony of the Pseudo-Hegesippus, 339: alleges on two occasions the fa-

bulous Acts of the Sinuessan Council, 364: his opinion of the Emperor Constantine, 380.
Bergomensis. Vid. Forestus.
Berington (Joseph) 282.
Bernardus (S.) 321.
Beveregius (Episc.) *Pandectæ Canonum*, 50.
Beza (Theodorus) 73, 385—7.
Bibliothecæ Patrum, an instance of their following the instructions of the *Index Expurgatorius* of Rome, 236.
Biel (Gabriel) 22.
Bilson (Bishop) 283.
Bingham (Joseph) 82, 117, 183, 235, 238, 364.
Binius (Severinus) *Concilia*, 70, 71, 183, 288, 302, 364: his deceitfulness, or absurd mistake, concerning the Baptistery which bears the name of Constantine, 360.
"Bless," to, new signification of the word, 171—2.
Blondellus (David) *Pseudo-Isidorus et Turrianus vapulantes*, 71, 81, 160, 179, 236, 301.
Bollandus (Joannes). Vid. *Acta Sanctorum*, et Papebrochius (Daniel).
Bona (Cardinal) his statement relative to the Font of Constantine, 360.
Bonifacius I. (Papa) 362—3: his claim founded on a supposed Sardican Decree, 70—71, 308.
Bonifacius III. (Papa) what privilege it is said that he procured from Phocas for the Church of Rome, 72, 365: the nature of the evidence upon which it is believed that he obtained the title of "Œcumenical Bishop," 365. See 371.
Boxhornius (Henricus) *Harmonia Eucharistica*, 22.
Bramhall (Archbishop) mentions the fictitious Sinuessan Council, 364.
Brereley (John) 49, 57, 70, 71.
Brerewood (Edward) 328.
Breviarium Romanum, records as a fact the fable of the Baptism of Constantine by Pope Silvester, 359: contains matter taken from the imaginary Acts of the Synod of Sinuessa, 364.
Brown (Edwardus) his error respecting the feigned Donation of Constantine, 360.
Bruckeri *Hist. Crit. Philos.*, 101.
Bulkley (Edward) 74.
Bull (Bishop) mistaken as to a tract assigned to S. Hippolytus, 282.
Burchardus, 301.
Burhillus (Robertus, S. T. D.) 70.
Burton (Edward, D. D.) his remark concerning a supposed edition of Tertullian's works, 64: referred to about the Therapeutæ, 101.
Busæus (Joannes) 98.
Butler (Alban) 70.
Bzovius (Abrahamus) a remarkable addition made by him to a sentence cited from S. Cyprian, 322: adduces the fabulous Acts of the Council of Sinuessa, 364.

Caiani, the heretics, invoked Angels, 41, 86.
Caiaphas, not a Sadducee, 246, 326.
Calfhill (James, D.D.) 107: source of his error as to the date of the Synod of Elvira, 153.
Calvin (John) 33, 37, 38, 42, 58, 73, 90.
Camerarius (Joachimus) 380.
Cange (Car. Du Fresne, Dom. Du) 364.
Canones Apostolorum, 50, 95, 106, 222, 237.
Canones Pœnitentiales, 22.
Canute (King) Laws of, 22.
Cappellus (Marcus Antonius) 70.
Care (Henry) *Modest Enquiry whether St. Peter were ever at Rome*, 336.
Caroline Books, by whom and when composed, 23, 154, 188.
Carranza (Barthol.) *Summa Concill.*, 89, 151, 154, 184: fictitious Catalogue of Canonical books ascribed by him to the Council of Florence, 222.
Carthage, Council of, A.D. 256, S. Cyprian's memorable words at, 322.
—— second Council of, did not first use the term *Missa*, 81.
—— third Council of, one of its Canons corrupted, 89.
—— fourth Council of, what alb it speaks of, 113.
—— sixth Council of, condemned appeals to Rome, and checked the presumption of the Popes, 70, 71, 322—3, 353.

Casaubonus (Isaacus) *Exercitationes ad Annales Baronii*, 292.
Casaubonus (Mericus) 311.
Cassiodorius (Mag. Aurel.) *Historia Tripartita*, 64, 114, 116, 160, 346, 358.
—— *Exposit. in Psal.*, 144.
Casus reservati, 388.
Cave (Guil., S. T. D.) his unjust censure of Clichtoveus, 277: erred in rejecting the *Testimonia adversus Judæos*, by S. Gregory Nyssen, 295—6: to whom he attributes the books *De vocatione Gentium*, 353.
—— *Historia Literaria*, 147, 287.
—— *Discourse of ancient Church-Gov.*, 70.
Cecilius (Lucius) Le Nourri assigns to him a treatise commonly attributed to Lactantius, 336.
Centuriatores Magdeburgenses, 107,109, 255.
Ceolfrid (Abbas) Epistle to Naiton, King of the Picts, 8.
Cephas, supposed derivation from κεφαλή, 301—2.
Chalcedon, General Council of, its decision with regard to the Bishop of Rome, 288—9, 308, 327, 332, 363—4: why its twenty-eighth Canon was omitted by Dionysius Exiguus, 288: Gratian's shameless depravation of the text, and other corruptions noted, 288, 289, 364.
Chillingworth (William) 331.
Chrysostomus (S. Joannes) a phrase in one of his Sermons upon Lazarus gave rise to the formation of an imaginary Saint, 44: five spurious Homilies on Job ascribed to him, 110, 139, 189: fictitious Sermon *in adorat. venerabil. Catenarum*, 110: counterfeit *Oratio in principes Apostt. Petrum et Paulum*, 110: his silver Crosses, 120—1, 184: *Opus imperfectum in S. Matth.*, attributed to him, 137: spurious Homilies on the Gospel by S. Mark, 147: his first Sermon *De Cruce et Latrone* wrongly assigned to S. Augustin, 179—80: the Homilies *ex var. in S. Matth. locis* not authentic, 285—6: doubtful Homily upon S. Peter and Elias, 285: fictitious Sermon *De negatione Petri*, 285: the first counterfeit *Sermo in Pentecosten* alleged as genuine by Barrow, 286: an interpolation inserted by Possinus in the *Catena Græcorum Patrum*, 286.
—— *De Lazaro Conciones*, 44.
—— *De Pentecoste*, 67.
—— *Hom. in Ep. ad Rom.*, 110, 199.
—— *In Epist. ad Philem. Hom.*, 110.
—— *Hom. de Anna*, 111.
—— *In Epist. ad Ephes.*, 115.
—— *In Ep. ad Corinth.*, 168, 231.
—— *Demonst. ad Gentiles*, 181.
—— *Hom. in S. Joan.*, 198, 277.
—— *In Epistt. ad Thess.*, 231.
—— *De Sacerdotio*, 240, 317—18, 326.
—— *In S. Matth. Hom.*, 285, 298, 304.
—— *In Act. Hom.*, 286.
—— *In Ep. ad Gal.*, 286.
Ciampinus (Joannes) *Examen Libri Pontificalis*, 99.
Cicero, 150.
Claudius, Bishop of Turin, forbad the worship of the Cross, 208.
Clêmencet (Charles) *L'Art de vérifier les Dates*, 179: an error of his noted, 337.
Clemens Alexand., *Stromata*, 67.
Clemens Rom. (S.) spurious *Ep. ad Jacob. frat. Dom.*, 322.
—— fictitious third decretal letter, 81.
Clement VIII. (Pope) 21.
Clericus (Joannes) 50, 353.
Clichtoveus (Judocus) unjustly censured by Cave and many others, 277.
Climacus (S. Joannes) 287.
Coccius (Jodocus) *Thesaurus Catholicus*, 57, 85, 289.
Cocus (Robertus) *Censura quorundam scriptorum*, 70, 90, 110, 165, 200: mistaken about the Pontifical, 99.
Codex Canonum vetus, 107, 179.
Cœlestinus I. (Papa) alleged the famous Sardican Decree, 70—71, 308.
Coinualch (King) 119: deposed Bishop Wini, 16, 24.
Collier (Jeremy) his *Eccles. Hist. of Great Britain*, Book ii. Cent. vi., referred to. See Augustin the Monk.
Colomesius (Paulus) 338.
Comber (Thomas, D.D.) *Roman Forgeries*, 70, 289, 363.
Confession, Auricular, where anciently

used and abolished, 91: when absolutely instituted, 90.
Constance, Council of, its Decree relative to Communion in one kind, 31, 387: condemned Pope John XXIII., 269.
Constans II. (Emperor) not the nephew of Heraclius, 361.
Constantinople, when the name was first heard of, 339.
—— General Council of, an. 553, 308.
—— third Council of, condemned Pope Honorius I., 312.
—— Quinisext Council held at, 95: its seventy-third Canon referred to, and quoted, 151—2.
Constantinus Magnus (Imp.) the sign shewn to him exhibited the character of the name of Christ, 139—40, 148: his Labarum, 140: appealed to by S. Athanasius, 358, 379: fable of his Baptism by Pope Silvester, 359: his Font, 360: particulars concerning his Donation, 360—1: his admonition to the Bishops at the first Nicene Council, and Bellarmin's observation upon his words, 380.
Constantius (Emperor) 361—2, 379.
Cophti, or Copti, ("Sophi" is a title of the Emperor of Persia.) 328.
Cornarius (Janus) 100, 103, 286, 287.
Cornelius (Pope) second spurious Epistle, 71: false Epistle to Lupicinus, 81.
Cosin (Bishop) *Hist. of Transub.*, 21.
—— *Schol. Hist. of Canon of Script.*, 89, 221, 222.
Costerus (Franciscus) 338.
Crabbe (Petrus) *Concilia*, 15, 107, 179, 200, 243, 288, 294, 363, 364.
Crakanthorpius (Ricardus, S. T. D.) *Defensio Ecclesiæ Anglicanæ*, 110.
—— *Vigilius Dormitans*, 307.
—— *Defence of Constantine*, 359, 360.
Cranmer (Archbishop) 247.
Crinitus (Petrus) *De honesta Disciplina*, 159.
Crompton (William) 80, 240.
Cross, Invention of the, 190, 193—4.
Crucifix, how prayed to, 211.
Cyprianus (S.) language of the Roman Clergy in an Epistle to him, 159—60, 342: treatises composed by Arnoldus Carnotensis ascribed to him, 163, 238: depravation of the tract *De unitate Ecclesiæ*, 283, 290—91: his remarkable allusion to Stephen, Bishop of Rome, 322.
—— *De lapsis*, 83.
—— *De unitate Ecclesiæ*, 120, 283, 290—91, 315, 316, 331.
—— *Ad Demetrianum*, 138.
—— *Ad Pompeium*, 168.
—— *Ad Jubaianum*, 290, 329, 331.
—— *Ad Quintum*, 313.
—— *Ad Cornel.* Ep. lix., 253, 283, 330, 332, 341, 343—4.
—— *Epistt.*, 283, 333—4, 342—3, 345.
Cyrillus Alexand., (S.) *Contra Julianum*, 89, 112, 199.
—— *In S. Joan.*, 277, 278, 367.
—— Translation of his Commentary on S. John by Trapezuntius, with the addition by Clichtoveus, 277.
—— *De Trinitate*, 277—8, 297.

Dallæus (Joannes) *De vero usu Patrum*, 44.
—— *De lib. suppos. Dionys. et Ignat.*, 236.
—— *De Jejun. et Quadrages.*, 236.
Damascenus (S. Joannes) *De orthodoxa Fide*, 203.
—— *Historia SS. Barlaami et Josaphati*, supposititious, 287.
Damasus (Pope) not the author of the Pontifical, 98, 360: counterfeit Epistle to S. Jerom, 120.
Decretals, 361.
Denisonus (Joannes, S.T.D.) *De Confessionis Auricularis vanitate*, 90, 91.
Dioclesian (Emperor) 217—18.
Dionysius Areopagita, his "credit cracked" by Erasmus, 165: his writings not known for five hundred years after Christ, 235.
Dionysius Exiguus, 97, 107: his faithlessness with respect to a Canon of the Council of Chalcedon, 288.
Donne (John, D.D.) *Pseudo-Martyr*, 236.

Earconberct, King of Kent, commanded that all the Idols in his kingdom should be destroyed, and that the fast of forty days should be observed, 16, 24.

Ecgfrid (King) deposed Bishop Wilfrid, 17.
Eleutherius (Pope) 186 : fictitious Rescript to King Lucius, 128, 366.
Eliberis, Synod of, 126 : mistake made by Calfhill, and in one of the Homilies, as to its date, 153 : Canon against Images, 153—4 : forbad the lighting of candles in the day-time in cemeteries, 185.
Epiphanius (S.) reckons Invocation of Angels amongst the heresies of the Caiani, 41, 86 : speaks of the Angelici, 41 : mentions the superstition of the Valentinians with reference to the Cross, 139 : his famous letter to John, Patriarch of Jerusalem, 173—4: what he called the heresy of the Collyridians, 207 : spurious tract *De vitis Prophetarum*, 207.
—— *Panarium*, 41, 43, 44, 100, 103, 133, 287, 347, 375, 376.
—— *Ancoratus*, 286.
—— *Respons. ad Ep. Acacii et Pauli*, 375.
Erasmus (Desid.) 329 : distinguishes the true from the false Epistle to Demetrias, attributed to S. Jerom, 44 : his remark upon the spurious Epistle to Oceanus, 97 : his Life of S. Jerom expurgated, 103 : disbelieved the alleged antiquity of Dionysius the Areopagite, 165 : his Colloquies sentenced to extinction, 194 : his opinion as to the Commentary on the Psalms erroneously ascribed to S. Jerom, 208 : how he was treated on an important occasion by the Spanish Inquisitors, 290 : assigns the authorship of a Commentary on the Psalms, which he first published, to Arnobius Afer, instead of to Arnobius Junior, 319 : whom he supposed to have been the writer of the books *De vocatione Gentium*, 353.
—— *Adagia*, 299.
—— Life, by Jortin, 319.
Esdras, what books the name included, 222.
Essenes, not identical with the Therapeutæ, 101.
Eugenius IV. (Pope) 222.
Eulalius, Abp. of Carthage, 71.
Eusebius Pamph., his error with respect to the Therapeutæ, 101 : his authority for the statement about S. John's *petalum*, 113 : the Latin translation of his Chronicle corrupted, so as to make him bear witness of the invention of the Cross, 190 : his Chronicle falsified for the purpose of maintaining that Lent was instituted by Pope Telesphorus, and that Pope Pius I. commanded that the feast of Easter should be kept on Sunday, 236, 237 : strange interpolation in S. Jerom's version of his *Chronicon*, with regard to S. Peter's long-continued residence at Rome, 337 : did not persist in favouring Arianism after the holding of the first Nicene Council, 359 : why his writings were anathematized at the second Synod of Nicæa, 359.
—— *Hist. Eccles.*, 69, 105, 115, 149, 183, 189, 235, 238, 239, 263, 322, 355, 358, 384, 388.
—— *De vita Constantini*, 140, 148, 355, 358, 359.
Eustathius Sebastenus, supposed by some to have been the author of the *Regulæ contractiores* ascribed to S. Basil, 161.
Euthymius Zigabenus, 167, 278, 287.
Exuperius, Bishop of Toulouse, 115.
Eymericus (Nicolaus) *Directorium Inquisitorum*, 21.

Faber Stapulensis (Jacobus) 235, 237.
Fabianus (Papa) fiction of his having baptized the Roman Emperor Philip and his son, 355.
Fabricius (Joannes) *Historia Bibliothecæ Fabricianæ*, 18, 323.
Fabricius (Joannes Albertus) *Centifolium Lutheranum*, 18.
—— *Bibliotheca Ecclesiastica*, 81, 287, 323.
—— *Bibliotheca Græca*, 101, 110, 287.
—— *Biblioth. med. et inf. Latin.*, 103, 323, 360.
—— *Codex Apoc. Novi Test.*, 339.
—— *Vita*, per Reimarum, 101.
Fabrotus (Carolus Annibal) 99.
Fathers, appealed to by Bp. Jewel, 28, 58 : their books corrupted, 59 : counsel of Vincentius Lirinensis concerning them, 175.
Faucheur (Michel le) 115.

Felix III. (Pope) what relation to Pope Gregory the Great, 99.
Fell (Bishop) 290, 329.
Fisher (Bishop) his reply to Velenus, 336.
Fitzherbert (Thomas) 294, 295.
Flacius Illyricus (Matthias) *Catalogus Testium veritatis*, 232.
—— *Refut. invect. Bruni contra Centur.*, 360.
Fleury (L'Abbé) 81, 183.
Florence, Council of, spurious Catalogue of Canonical books ascribed to it by Carranza, 222.
Forestus, Bergomensis, (Jacobus Philippus) *Supplem. Chronic.*, 103.
Fox (John) 23, 37, 61, 74, 93, 209, 232, 247: an error of his noted, 98.
Frankfort, Council of, condemned the second Synod of Nicæa, 154.
Fulgentius Ruspensis (S.) his work *De fide, ad Petrum Diaconum*, ascribed to S. Augustin, 86.
Fulke (William, D.D.) 70, 168, 308, 384, 385.
Fuller (Thomas) *Church History of Britain*, 6, 9, 37.

Gage (Thomas) 22.
Galesinius (Petrus) source of his belief in the existence of the fabulous Saint Synoris, 44.
Galfridus Monumetensis, the character he gives of the Monk Augustin, 6, 186.
Gallandius (Andreas) 70.
Gangra, Synod of, 89.
Gavantus (Bartholomæus) 22.
Geddes (Michael) 70, 225.
Gelasius I. (Pope) 222, 339: date of his Decree, and Mabillon's opinion as to the author, 221.
"Gentility," 58, 60.
Geoffrey of Monmouth. See Galfridus.
Gerard, Abp. of York, 23, 94.
Gibbon (Edward) 98, 101, 361.
Gieseler (J. C. I.) *Text-book of Eccles. Hist.*, 33: his error with respect to the term *Missa*, 81.
Gildas, a passage contained in his Epistle generally misunderstood, 186.
"Girdeth at," 153.
Goldastus (Melch. Haim.) mistaken as to the author of the feigned Donation of Constantine, 360.
Gothofredus (Jacobus) his opinion respecting the Libra Occidua, 364—5.
Grabius (Joannes Ernestus, S.T.P.) *Prolegom. in edit. Alex. Septuag. Interp.*, 166.
—— *Spicilegium*, 338, 339.
Gratianus, *Decretum*, 33, 42, 81, 96, 97, 105, 107, 141, 179, 183, 184, 211, 221, 236, 237, 243, 244, 295, 323, 339, 356, 363, 365.
—— corrupted a Canon of the second Synod of Milevis, 71: falsified an Epistle of Pope Leo the Great, 82: his confession with regard to the celibacy of the Clergy, 96: supposititious sentence ascribed to S. Augustin respecting Purgatory, 240: his shameless depravation of a Canon of the Council of Chalcedon, 288: bears witness against the interpolations in a treatise by S. Cyprian, 291: puts forward an absurd derivation for Cephas, 301: exhibits the supposed Donation of Constantine, 360.
Gratius (Orthuinus) *Fasciculus rerum expetendarum ac fugiendarum*, 302, 360, 361.
Gregorius Nazianzenus (S.) *Ep. ad Cledonium*, 63.
—— *Orat. de Theologia*, 63.
—— *Or. in Julianum*, 84.
—— *In sanct. Pasch. Orat.*, 84.
—— *Orat. ad Arianos, et de seipso*, 114.
Gregorius Nyssenus (S.) his remarkable treatise concerning pilgrimages to Jerusalem, 109—10: his *Testimonia adversus Judæos* shewn to be genuine, 295—6.
Gregory I. (Pope) called the Emperor Mauritius his sovereign lord, 16: condemned the name of Universal Bishop, 49, 72, 258—9, 371: his memorable words with respect to the army of Priests prepared for Antichrist, 371.
—— *Epistt.*, 128.
—— *In Ezech. Hom.*, 314.
Gregory XI. (Pope) his condemnation of a tenet respecting the consecrated Host, 21.
Gregory XII. (Pope) 103.

Gretserus (Jacobus) 110: his hesitation with regard to Gorionides, 339.
Grindal (Archbishop) 41, 87, 164.
Guilelmus Malmesburiensis, *De gestis Pontificum Anglorum*, 22: his shameful depravation of a letter ascribed to Pope Sergius I., 119.
Guise (Duke of) 73, 74, 121.
Gunning (Bishop) speaks of two interpolations in the Chronicle of Eusebius, 236, 237.

Hagustalden, 11.
Haloander (Gregorius) 95.
Harding (Thomas, D. D.) 45, 113, 154.
Hart (John) *Conference* with Rainoldes, 283, 319, 361, 364.
Hegesippus, an account of the true and false, 338—9.
Helena (Empress) Invention of the Cross, 190, 193—4: language of S. Ambrose concerning her, 202.
Hentenius (Joannes) *Enarr. vet. Theol.*, 88.
Herebald, Abbot of Wye, account of his Baptism, 14.
Herod and Pilate, 77—8.
Hieronymus (S.) an account of his Epistle to Evangelus, 33: his genuine, and the spurious, Epistle to Demetrias, 44: fictitious letter to Oceanus, 97, 339: Epistles to Pope Damasus, two authentic, and one counterfeit, 120, 349: his correct testimony as to the form of the Samaritan *Thau*, 147: spurious Commentary on the Psalms, and the judgment of Erasmus and Amerbachius concerning it, 207—8: his evidence with respect to the Canonical books of Scripture, 221: how Baronius considered him shamefully astray, and Spondanus represents him as heretical, with reference to S. Peter's primacy, 292: strangely interpolated the *Chronicon* of Eusebius, relative to S. Peter's long continuance at Rome, 337: confessed that Pope Liberius was an Arian, 349.
—— *Super Esaiam*, 33, 78, 137.
—— *Ad Evangelum*, 33, 315, 388.
—— *Ad Demetriadem*, 44, 104.
—— *Comment. in S. Matth.*, 48, 150, 181, 285.
Hieronymus (S.) *Contra Luciferianos*, 63, 253.
—— *Ad Pammach. et Oceanum*, 63.
—— *Adversus Jovinianum*, 83, 97, 120, 285, 292, 332.
—— *In Eccles.*, 91.
—— *Ad Oceanum*, 97.
—— *In Aggeum*, 98.
—— *In Ep. ad Ephes.*, 98.
—— *Ad Paulinum*, 109.
—— *Ad Rusticum*, 115.
—— *Ad Damasum*, 120.
—— *Ad Pammach.*, 133.
—— *Apologia adversus Rufinum*, 181, 208.
—— *Ad Eustoch. Epitaph. Paulæ matris*, 181, 202, 224.
—— *Præfat. in Proverb.*, 221.
—— *Adversus Vigilantium*, 240.
—— *Ad Furiam*, 240.
—— *In Ep. ad Titum*, 315—16.
—— *De Viris illust.*, 323, 337, 338, 339, 349.
—— *In Daniel.*, 367, 370.
—— *Ad Algasiam*, 372.
Hilarius (S.) his testimony as to S. Peter, and the Rock of the Church, dreaded by Romanists, 289—90.
—— *De Trinitate*, 67, 283, 284, 289—90, 297.
—— *In S. Matth.*, 283, 297.
Hilarius Diaconus, 183.
Hippolytus (S.) spurious tract *De consummatione Mundi* attributed to him, and its authenticity maintained by Bishop Bull, 282.
—— *Passio Hippolyti*. Vid. Prudentius.
Holstenius (Lucas) observes that the Pontifical has been wrongly ascribed to Luitprandus, 99.
Homilies, Book of, error in as to the date of the Synod of Elvira, 153: name *Crinitus* corrupted into *Erinilus* therein, 159: Matrimony called a Sacrament in the Sermon *against Swearing*, 168.
Homily, The Paschal, 247: first and second editions, and imaginary reprint of it, 7: contains many passages taken from Ratramnus, 20.
Honorius I. (Pope) called the Emperor Heraclius his sovereign lord, 16: condemned by the sixth General Council, 312, 334.

Hooker (Richard) 237, 238.
Hopkins (William) his translation of the book of Ratramn, 20.
Hormisdas (Pope) the father of Pope Silverius, 98—9.
Horne (Bishop) 356, 378, 380.
Hosius (Cardinal) *De Hæresibus nostri temporis*, 4.
Hospinianus (Rodolphus) 103.
Hottingerus (Joannes Henricus) 296.
"Houseling," 11, 105.
Husenbeth (F. C.) attempts to avail himself of the seventh book against Parmenian, attributed to S. Optatus, 323.
Hutten (Ulricus de) published a treatise by Laurentius Valla against the Donation of Constantine, 361.

Ignatius (S.) his genuine and the interpolated Letters, 235.
—— *Epist. ad Smyrnæos*, 235.
—— Interp. Ep. *ad Philadelphenos*, 235: how the Vatican *Index* and the *Bibliothecæ Patrum* deal with a remarkable sentence herein, 236.
—— Spurious Epistle *ad Antiochenos*, 236.
—— Fictitious Epistle *ad Philippenses*, 237: adduced as authentic by Mr. Taylor, 236.
"Imps," 18.
Index Auctorum damnatæ memoriæ. Vid. Mascaregnas (F. M.).
Index Expurgatorius, 103, 194, 236, 290.
—— *Cathalogus librorum hæreticorum*. Vid. Mendham (Josephus).
Innocentius I. (Papa) 351—2: a tenet of his condemned by the Council of Trent, 41, 392: *Epist. ad Decentium* considered spurious, 90: Epistle to Victricius, ascribed to him, of what document the probable source, 179: Epistle to Exuperius, cited in his name by Gratian, 244: in what language addressed by one of the Synods of Carthage, 351.
Innocentius III. (Papa) *De sacro Altaris mysterio*, 21, 301: fourth Council of Lateran held under him, 90: his interpretation of the name Cephas, 301.
Ireland, why there was formerly pilgrimage into, 12: people of anciently called Scots, 16, 19.
Irenæus (S.) 245, 335, 340, 341, 368, 370, 374: rebuked Pope Victor, 69, 238, 308: reproved the Gnostics for having an Image of Christ, 127: speaks of the superstitious regard shewn for the Cross by the Valentinian heretics, 139: what he declares to have been the conduct of the Valentinians when confuted by the word of God, 219: his judgment as to the perspicuity of Scripture, 220: his testimony concerning the greatness and antiquity of the Church of Rome, 340—1.
Isidorus Hispalensis (S.) his account of the Angelici, 41—2: erred as to the origin of the name Cephas, 302.
Isidorus Mercator, 105, 107, 360.
Ittigius (Thomas) 70.
Ivo, *Decretum*, 81, 107, 222, 301, 323.

Jackson (Thomas, D.D.) 247.
Jacobson (Gulielmus, S.T.D.) *Patres Apostolici*, 189, 235.
James (Thomas, D.D.) 277, 283, 360, 371.
Jelf (R. W., D.D.) a note in his edition of Bp. Jewel's works referred to, 369.
Jerom (S.). Vid. Hieronymus.
Jerusalem, pilgrimages to, 108—9, 238.
Jewel (Bishop) 21, 22, 41, 45, 46, 48, 49, 70, 82, 89, 113, 149, 154, 236, 275, 281, 285, 289, 295, 296, 340, 356, 364, 369, 371.
—— his Challenge, 28, 58.
—— *Defence of the truth*, 45. See Advertisement.
—— Life, by Le Bas, 371.
Joan (Pope) the source of confusion in the numbering of the Popes named John, 269.
Joannes Cantator, "John the Chanter," introduced the Roman service into England, (A.D. 678.) 14.
Joannes Diaconus, "Digitorum mutilus," whether the author of the feigned Donation of Constantine, 360.
Joannes Sabaita, 287.
John (S.) what Polycrates declares that he wore, 113.
John, Patriarch of Antioch, 295.

John of Beverley (S.) 14, 25.
John XXIII. (Pope) condemned by the Council of Constance, 269, 334.
Johnson (John) 81.
Jonas Aurelianensis, 208.
Jortin (John, D.D.) *Life of Erasmus*, 319.
Josephus, does not state that Caiaphas was a Sadducee, 246, 326.
Josephus Ben-Gorion. Vid. Hegesippus.
Joverius (Franciscus) *Sanctiones Ecclesiasticæ*, 96, 113, 312, 322: his account of the variation in the numbering of the Popes named John, 269.
Jovinian, 43.
Julian, the Apostate, how he counterfeited religion, 116.
Julius I. (Pope) two spurious Epistles ascribed to him, 160.
Justellus (Christophorus) his edition of the *Nomocanon*, 42.
Justinianus (Imp.) *Constitutiones novellæ*, 95: words of his sixty-seventh Novel attributed to the first Synod of Orleans, 150: the same Decree referred to, 158—9, 185.
—— *Codex*, 362, 364.
Justinus Martyr (S.) his first Apology referred to respecting the sign of the Cross, 164, and the mingling of water with wine for the Lord's Supper, 237.
Juvenalis, 209.

Kirk (John) 282.
Kitchin (Bishop) his dexterity, 118.
Knox (John) 37, 121.
Kortholtus (Christianus) *Disquisitiones Anti-Baronianæ*, 44.

Labbe (Philippus) how he disposes of a Decree made by the Synod of Winchester, A.D. 1076, 23.
Lactantius, 142, 144: the verses ascribed to him, *De Passione Domini*, fictitious, 156, 206: treatise *De mortibus Persecutorum*, by him, or Lucius Cecilius, the source of an extraordinary error, 336—7.
Lælius Tiphernas, 110.
Lambardus (Gulielmus) *De priscis Anglorum Legibus libri*, 22.
Lanfrancus, his Decree in the Synod of Winchester, respecting sacerdotal celibacy, 23, 93.
Laodicea, Council of, circ. A.D. 366, a corruption in one of its Canons noted, 42: its Decree concerning the Canonical books, 89.
Larroquanus (Matthæus) 371.
Lateran, fourth Council of, private Confession instituted at, 90.
Latimer (Bp.) 29.
Laud (Archbishop) 71.
Launoius (Joannes) rejects the supposititious Acts of the Council of Sinuessa, 364.
—— Vid. Reiserus (Ant.)
Laurence, second Abp. of Canterbury, his acknowledgment of the British and Irish Clergy, 16, 26.
Laurence (S.) church of, "in Panisperna," 372.
Lent, not instituted by Pope Telesphorus, 236—7.
Leo I. (Pope) an Epistle of his corrupted by Gratian, 82: humbled by the Council of Chalcedon, 288—9, 308, 326—7, 332, 363—4: his statement as to the Rock of the Church shamefully perverted, 293—4: an emendation in one of his Epistles proposed by Quesnel, 319, who claims for him the composition of the books *De vocatione Gentium*, 353.
—— *Sermo de jejunio Pentecostes*, 182.
—— *Epist. ad Anastasium*, 259, 311.
—— *In ann. die Assump. Ser.* iii., 293.
—— *Epist. ad Episc. per prov. Vienn. const.*, 319.
Leo II. (Pope) confirmed the condemnation of Pope Honorius, 312.
Liberius (Pope) an Arian heretic, 334, 349.
"Libra Occidua," 364—5.
Lightfoot (John) 113, 246.
Lindsay (John) 118, 128, 265.
L'Isle (William) his second edition of the Paschal Homily, 7.
Lombardus (Petrus) condemned for his opinion as to the possibility of the consecrated Host being eaten by a beast, 21: cites the fictitious treatise *De vera et falsa Pœnitentia*, bearing S. Augustin's name, 240.

Long (Jacobus le) *Bibliotheca Sacra*, 166.

Longus a Coriolano (Franciscus) adopts Carranza's false Catalogue of Canonical books, ascribed to the Council of Florence, 222.

Lucius (King) 53 : imaginary Rescript addressed to him by Pope Eleutherius, 128, 366.

Luitprandus, not the author of the Pontifical, 99.

Luther (Martin) whether he acknowledged that his followers were worse than they had been when Papists, 18, 121 : published S. Jerom's Epistle to Evangelus, 33 : the name he gave to Aristotle, 57 : accused of rejecting books of Scripture, 130, 384.

Lycosthenes (Conradus) *De Prodigiis*, 148.

Lynde (Sir Humphrey) 236.

Mabillonius (Joannes) the year he fixed on as that of the death of S. Ambrose, 81 : his opinion as to the genuineness of the Gelasian Decree, 221 : refutes errors respecting the time when Hegesippus lived, 338.

Mæstræus (Martialis) 236.

Maitland (S.R., D.D.) *Puritan Thaumaturgy*, 76.

Manning (Robert) his admission relative to the Cross borne by the Monk Augustin, 17.

Marca (Petrus de) 71 : observes that the words of Paschasinus, the papal Legate at the Council of Chalcedon, have been vitiated, 288 : agrees with Scaliger in his opinion that the Babylon mentioned by S. Peter was not Rome, 336 : his conjecture with regard to the Donation of Constantine, 360.

Marcellinus (Pope) upon what evidence accused of having sacrificed to Idols, and by whom defended, 364—5.

Marcellus, Bp. of Apamea, how it is said that he effected the burning of Jupiter's temple, 116—17, 239.

Mar-Prelate (Martin) 37.

Martialis Lemovicensis, his counterfeit Epistles, 141—2, 177, 180.

Martiall (John) 107.

Martin (Gregory) 385.

Martyrologium Romanum, 287.

Mascaregnas (Ferd. Mart.) *Index Auctorum damnatæ memoriæ*, 302.

Mason (Francis) 118, 128 : his error with regard to the deposition, or banishment, of Abiathar, 265.

Matthæus Westmonasteriensis, *Flores Historiarum*, 23 : repeats the falsehood of Malmesbury concerning Beda's journey to Rome, 119—20.

Maximus Taurinensis (S.) his Sermon *De Cruce Domini* attributed to S. Ambrose, 154—5 : a Sermon ascribed to him, as well as to S. Augustin, and to S. Ambrose, 340.

Mede (Joseph) 386.

Melito, Letter to Onesimus, 222.

Mendham (Josephus) *Cathalogus librorum hæreticorum, de commiss. Tribunal. sanctiss. Inquisit. Venetiarum*, 302.

Mentz, Council of, an. 813, 183.

Merlinus (Jacobus) *Concilia*, 90, 105, 107.

Milevis, second Synod of, 351, 352 : how Gratian corrupted one of its Canons, 71.

Minucius Felix, his treatise *De Idolorum vanitate* attributed to Arnobius, 206.

Miræus (Aubertus) his error with reference to a tract erroneously ascribed to S. Hippolytus, 282.

Missa, the holy Communion, 7 : ancient use of the term, 81, 82.

Missale Romanum, alteration noted in the instructions prefixed to, 21.

Molinæus (Petrus). Vid. Moulin (Pierre du).

Monasteries, why first founded, 19, 25.

Monks, differences between ancient and modern, 17—18, 25.

Montfaucon (Bernardus de) *Diarium Italicum*, 110, 372 : his opinion of the counterfeit *Liber de passione Imaginis Christi*, attributed to S. Athanasius, 200.

—— *Bibliotheca Biblioth. MSS.*, 361.

Moreri (Louis) 74.

Morton (Bishop) *Catholike Appeale*, 49, 71.

—— *Of the Masse*, 82, 86.

—— *Grand Imposture of the (now) Church of Rome*, 70.

Moshemius (Joan. Laur.) *Instt. Hist. Eccles.*, 5, 225, 319.
—— *De rebus Christian. ante Const.*, 101.
—— Paulsen et Moshem. *Hist. Tartar. Eccl.*, 225—6.
Moulin (Pierre du) 71, 109, 347.
Musculus (Wolfgangus) 112, 115, 347, 358, 366, 379.

Nauclerus (Joannes) *Chronographia*, 361.
Neal (Daniel) 37—8.
Neander (Augustus) 101.
Neocæsarea, Synod of, one of its Canons altered, 96—7.
Nero (Emperor) supposed inscription to, (apud Gruterum,) 217: whether Simon Magus practised sorcery before him, 338—9.
Netter a Walden (Thomas). Vid. Waldensis.
Newman (J. H.) 81.
Nicæa, first Council of, 64, 153, 240: questionable Sardican Decree ascribed to, 70—71, 308, 353: allusion in one of its Decrees to the fifty-second Apostolic Canon, 106: an interpolation in the eighteenth Canon, 107: admonition of Constantine to the Bishops assembled at, 380.
Nicæa, second Council of, its Decrees rejected in England and France, 23: condemned by the Council of Frankfort, 154: fictitious *Liber de passione Imaginis Christi* alleged at, 200: false testimony adduced there, as if from S. Ambrose, 207: why this Synod anathematized the writings of Eusebius, 359.
Nicephorus Callistus, 115.
Nicholas I. (Pope) 364.
Nicholas II. (Pope) 372.
Nicolson (Archbishop) 20.
Nourri (Nicolas le) claims for Cecilius the well-known treatise *De mortibus Persecutorum*, 336.
Nowel (Alex., D.D.) 38, 58, 356.

Œcumenius, 88.
Oftfor (Bishop) consecrated at the command of Œdilred, 17, 24, 119.
Olearius (Jo. Gottfridus) *Biblioth. Scriptt. Eccles.*, 336.
Optatus (S.) 311, 331—2, 348—9, 357: an unfounded allusion to the origin of the name Cephas supposed to be an interpolation in his text, 302, which has been otherwise corrupted, 348—9: the *seventh* book *De schismate Donatistarum* referred to, though S. Optatus wrote but *six*, 323.
Origenes, *Hom. in Levit.*, 85.
—— *In Ep. ad Rom.*, 144.
—— *In Exod. Hom.*, 282.
—— *In S. Matth.*, 282—3, 298, 299—300.
Orleans, first Synod of, A.D. 511, a Canon attributed to it, containing words which belong to a Novel of Justinian, 150: called Litanies Rogations, 183.
Orosius (Paulus) asserts that Philip was the first Roman Emperor who was a Christian, 355.
Osuiu (King) ordered the Synod of Strenaeshale, 16.
Ottius (Joannes Henricus) *Examen perpetuum in Annales Baronii*, 44.
Otto Frisingensis, *Chronicon*, 226.
Oudinus (Casimirus) 98: his charge against Claud Morell, 109—10: mistaken concerning the *Testimonia adversus Judæos*, by S. Gregory Nyssen, 295—6: greatly astray as to the time when Gorionides existed, 338.

Pagi (Antoine) his conjecture as to the source of the fable that S. Peter was for twenty-five years at Rome, 336—7: rejects the counterfeit Acts of the Synod of Sinuessa, 364.
Pagi (François) *Breviar. gest. Pontiff. Rom.*, 337.
Pagitt (Ephraim) *Christianography*, 328.
Palmer (William) *Jurisdiction of Brit. Episc. vindicated*, 118.
—— *Treatise on the Church*, 324.
Papebrochius (Daniel) his opinion as to the date of the death of S. Ambrose, 81: retains a word in the Life of Pope Silverius, which Platina had unfairly omitted, 99: records the testimony of Cardinal Bona relative to the Font of Constantine, 360: rejects the fictitious Sinuessan Council, 364.

Paphnutius, 240.

Parker (Archbishop) patronised the publication of the Saxon Homily, 7, 247, and parts of two Epistles of Ælfric, 20: his two editions of the *Flores Historiarum* of Matthew of Westminster, 119: how addressed by Sanders, 215—16: advised to revolt to the popish Church, 247.

Paul (S.) *Acts of Paul and Thecla*, 339.

Paul I. (Pope) 360.

Paulinus, Bishop of Nola, 158.

Paulsen (Hermannus Christianus). Vid. Moshemius (Jo. Laur.).

Pearson (Bishop) his opinion as to the author of the Pontifical, 98: when he believed that Hegesippus flourished, 338.

Pelagius, S. Augustin attributes to him an Epistle found amongst S. Jerom's works, 44.

Petavius (Dionysius) referred to concerning the *Stationes* of the primitive Church, 183: his description of the counterfeit tract *De vitis Prophetarum* ascribed to S. Epiphanius, 207.

Peter (S.) whether he wrote his first Epistle from Rome, and continued there for five-and-twenty years, 336—8.

Peterborough, Saxon History of, 23.

Philippus, the Roman Emperor, by some considered to have been a Christian: fiction as to his Baptism, 355.

Phillpotts (Bishop) source of an extract from the Canon Law adduced by him with reference to Purgatory, 240.

Philo, his account of the Therapeutæ, 101.

Phocas, what privilege it is said that he granted to the Church of Rome, 72: the authority for this statement, 365: upon whose testimony it is commonly believed that he conferred upon the Popes the title of "Œcumenical Bishop," 365. See 371.

Photius, his remark respecting the Angelites; and how Agylæus has omitted a reference in his *Nomocanon*, 42.

—— *Bibliotheca*, 101.

Picernus de Monte arduo (Bartholomæus) published the feigned Donation of Constantine, 361.

Picus (Joannes) 282.

Pilate and Herod, 77—8.

Pilkington (Bishop) 3.

Pin (L. E. Du) 71, 296, 302, 323.

Pius I. (Pope) third spurious Epistle, 81: supposititious Ordinance relative to the feast of Easter; and the Chronicle of Eusebius corrupted to maintain the falsehood, 237.

Pius II. (Pope). Vid. Sylvius (Æneas).

Pius V. (Pope) Missal sanctioned by, 21.

Placcius (Vincentius) *Theatrum Anon. et Pseudon.*, 103.

Platina (B.) omits an important word in his Life of Pope Silverius, 99.

Plinius Sec. (C.) 339.

Polanus (Amandus) 291.

Polus (Cardinalis) *De Baptismo Constantini*, 360.

Polycarpus (S.) 335: refusal of his remains to those who wished for them, 188.

Polycrates, 69, 238: his mention of S. John's *petalum*, 113.

Pontificalis Liber, bears witness that some Bishops of Rome were the children of Priests, and one Pope the son of another, 98: an account of this important record, 98—9: referred to concerning the Baptism of Constantine, 360: declares that S. Marcellinus was an idolater, 365.

Pontius, the Martyr, worthless Acts of, 355.

Poole (G. A.) 331.

Pope, called God, 247, 369.

Pope (R. T. P.) 86.

Popes, false Epistles attributed to, 59, 281.

Popes, the sons of Priests, 98.

Possinus (Petrus) shameful interpolation noted in his *Catena Græcorum Patrum*, 286.

Prester John, 225—6.

Priorius (Philippus) 302.

Probianus, 161.

Processions, 182—189.

Prosperus (S.) 288: whether Bishop of Rhegium, 353: not the author of the books *De vocatione omnium Gentium*, 353.

Prudentius, *Peristeph.* Passio Hippolyti, 346.
Psellus, 287.

Quesnellus (Paschasius) 71, 319: maintains that S. Leo was the author of the books *De vocatione Gentium,* 353.
Quintinus (Joannes) 95.
Quiroga (Cardinal) his Expurgatory Index, 103.

Rabanus Maurus, his explanation of the word "Statio," 183.
Raderus (Matthæus) 287.
Rainoldus (Joannes, S.T.D.) his error about the Pontifical, 99.
—— *Conference* with Hart, 283, 319, 361, 364.
Rastell (John) 45.
Ratramnus, many passages from his book *De Corpore et Sanguine Domini* found translated in the Paschal Homily, 20.
Raynaudus (Theophilus) *Erotemata de malis ac bonis libris,* 86, 200, 287.
—— *Heptas Præsulum,* 86, 340.
Record, Church Missionary, 60.
Reiserus (Antonius) *Launoii Anti-Bellarminus,* 44, 71.
Richardson (Joannes) 360.
Richerius (Edmundus) *Hist. Concill. Gen.,* 70.
—— *Apologia pro Joanne Gersonio,* 371.
Ridley (Bishop) mentions as absurd the papistical derivation of Cephas from κεφαλή, 301.
Rigaltius (Nicolaus) 113, 339.
Rivetus (Andreas) 296.
Rogerius de Hoveden, *Annales,* 23.
Rome, the city built upon seven hills, 372—3.
Routh (Martinus Josephus, S. T. D.) *Reliquiæ Sacræ,* 338.
Rufinus, 239: words added in his abridgment of a Nicene Canon, 107: a passage in his History misapplied in the Canon Law to prove that the Pope is God, and above human judgment, 356.
Ruinart (Theodoricus) *Acta Martyrum sincera,* 189.

Sacrilege, 114.
Sanders (Nicholas, D.D.) 215.
Sardica, Council of, A.D. 347, remarks on the famous Decree attributed to it, respecting appeals to Rome, 70—71. See pages 308, 353.
Savilius (Henricus, Eq. Aur.) 22.
Scaliger (Josephus) maintained the identity of the Essenes and Therapeutæ, 101: points out interpolations in the Chronicle of Eusebius, 236, 237, 337: his conjecture as to the Babylon mentioned by S. Peter in his first Epistle, 336: his opinion concerning Gorionides, 338.
Schedel (Hartmann) *Chronicon Chronicorum,* 103.
Schmidius (Jo. Andr.) 339.
"Scholies," ancient Greek, 87, 88.
"Scots," the ancient Irish, 16, 19.
Scultetus (Abrahamus) 295.
Senwalch (King). Vid. Coinualch.
Septuagint, principal editions of the, 166.
Serarius (Nicolaus) his idea as to the meaning of the name Cephas, 301.
Sergeant (John) *Anti-Mortonus,* 70.
Sergius I. (Pope) the fable respecting his interview with Beda, 119—20.
Shacklock (Richard) *The Hatchet of Heresies,* 4.
"Shore," 288.
"Shore up," 144.
Sighard, a Monk, made King, 18, 24.
Silverius (Pope) the son of Pope Hormisdas, 98—9.
Silvester I. (Pope) feigned story of his having baptized Constantine, 359.
Simeon Dunelmensis, *De Regibus Anglorum,* 23.
Simon Magus, fables concerning his sorcery, 338—9.
Sinuessa, an account of the fictitious Synod of, 364—5.
Siphanus (Laurentius) 296.
Siricius (Papa) the fourth Epistle attributed to him whence probably derived, 179, 243: the text of S. Optatus which contains his name corrupted, 348—9.
Sirmondus (Jacobus) *Concilia Generalia,* 90, 288, 289, 359.
Sixtus Senensis, mistaken in ascribing five Homilies on Job to S. Chrysostom, 110: misled by Carranza with

respect to a Catalogue of Canonical books, untruly assigned to the Council of Florence, 222.
Sleidanus (Joannes) 376.
Smyrna, Epistle of the Church of, 188—9.
Soames (Henry) 20, 23, 225, 319.
Socrates Scholasticus, 115, 116, 121, 153, 160, 184, 240, 347, 358, 360, 366, 379.
Solomon, by a civil sentence, banished Abiathar from Jerusalem, 265.
Sonwalch (King). Vid. Coinualch.
"Sophi," a title of the Emperor of Persia, 328.
Sozomenus (Hermias) 91, 112, 184, 346, 347, 360.
Spanhemius (Ezech.) 89, 199.
Spanhemius (Fridericus) 98.
Spelmannus (D. Henricus) *Concilia*, 23.
—— *De non temerandis Ecclesiis*, 114.
Spina (Alphonsus de) *Fortalitium Fidei*, 5.
Spondanus (Henricus) how he altered a sentence in Baronius, and in effect represents S. Jerom as an heretic, 292.
Staphylus (Fridericus) the validity of his reference to a tract by Luther questioned, 18: an apostate, 58: Stapleton's translation of his *Apologia*, 76—7.
Stapleton (Thomas) *A Return of untruths*, 3: his translation of Bede's History, 5, 45: indebted to Staphylus for a charge against Luther's followers, 18: allusion to his name Thomas, 51, 53, 59: his admonition about Church goods, 114.
Stations, what they were in ancient times, 183, 238.
Stellartius (Prosperus) *De Coronis et Tonsuris*, 115.
Stephanus I. (Papa) S. Cyprian's remarkable words in allusion to his conduct, 322.
Stephanus V. (Papa) 141.
Stevenson (Joseph) the first to discover the source of the fiction concerning Beda's journey to Rome, 119—20.
Stillingfleet (Bp.) corrected a common error with respect to a passage in the Epistle of Gildas, 186.
Strenaeshalch, Synod holden at, 16.
Struvius (Burc. Gott.) *Dissertatio de doctis Impostoribus*, 338.
Strype (John) 37, 45.
Succession, Apostolic, 67, 74.
Suicerus (Joannes Casparus) 235.
Surius (Laurentius) *Vitæ Sanctorum*, 355: his version of the Apology of Staphylus, 77.
Sylvius (Æneas) rejected the papistical etymology of the name Cephas: his subsequent Retractations: his Commentaries prohibited; and his works in general to be read with caution, 302.
—— *Comm. de gestis Basil. Conc.*, 302.
—— *Germania*, 302.
Synagogue, erred, 45—47.
Synge (Bishop) *Rejoynder to the Iesuite's Reply*, 364.

Tassin (René-Prosper) *Hist. Lit. de la Congrég. de S. Maur*, 101, 238.
Taylor (Bishop) 44.
Taylor (Isaac) cites as authentic a counterfeit Epistle ascribed to S. Ignatius, 236.
Telesphorus (Pope) a fictitious Decree attributed to him; and the Chronicle of Eusebius corrupted to maintain the false supposition of his having instituted the Lent-fast, 236—7.
Tertullianus, *Advers. Hermog.*, 64.
—— *De præscript. Hæreticorum*, 75, 238, 281—2, 336.
—— *Apologeticus*, 234.
—— *De Baptismo*, 339.
—— his Montanistic treatises: *De Monogamia*, 113: *Cont. Marcion.*, 131, 147: *De Pudicitia*, 136, 282, 291: *De Jejuniis*, 183, 238.
Thau, the letter, in the book of Ezekiel, 138, 147.
Thecla: *Acts of Paul and Thecla*, 339.
Theodoretus, *Historia Ecclesiastica*, 44, 64, 239, 360, 380—1.
—— *Theophiles*, 64.
—— *Comment. in Cantica Canticorum*, of uncertain authenticity, 287.
—— Epistles to Dioscorus and Pope Leo, said by Crakanthorp to have been forged, 307.
—— *In Ep. ad Tim.*, 309.
Theodorus (Pope) his father a Bishop, 98.
Theodosius II. (Emperor) Decree made by him and Valentinian III., con-

cerning figures of the Cross engraven or painted on the ground, 159.
Theophylactus, 138, 278.
Therapeutæ, mistakes concerning them, 101.
Thorndicius (Herbertus) 70.
Tillemont (L.-S. Le Nain de) 70, 183, 338, 353.
Tillet (Jean du) in what year he published the Caroline Books, 23.
Todd (J. H., D.D.) speaks of a fictitious tract ascribed to S. Hippolytus, 282.
Tours, second Synod of, meaning of one of its Decrees, 150—1.
—— third Synod of, Canon concerning the translation of Homilies, 15.
Trent, Council of, anathematizes all who should hold an opinion maintained by S. Augustin, and Pope Innocent I., 41: its Decree concerning the Canonical books of Scripture, 222: not a lawful General Council, 231.
Trithemius (Joannes) his testimony as to the abandonment of Arian tendencies by Eusebius, 359.
Turrianus (Franciscus) *Advers. Magdeburg. Cent.*, 301.
Twysdenus (Rogerus, Eq. Aur.) *Hist. Angl. Scriptores decem*, 23.

Urban VIII. (Pope) 21.
Ussher (Archbishop) 70, 87, 116, 236, 241, 319, 364: remarked the identity of passages which occur in the Paschal Homily, and in the book of Ratramn, 20: his error respecting the *Liber Canonum* of Ælfric, 22: misapplied words in the Epistle of Gildas, 186: when he published the genuine and the interpolated Ignatian Epistles, 235.

Valentinian I. (Emperor) his division of the empire, and law as to the Libra, 364.
Valentinian III. (Emperor) Decree issued by him and Theodosius II., with respect to figures of the Cross made on the ground, 159: not the son of Theodosius the Great, 363.
Valentinians, heretics. See Irenæus (S.).
Valesius (Henricus) 101.
Valla (Laurentius) his famous *Declamatio* against the Donation of Constantine, 361.
Van de Velde (Joannes Franciscus) 61.
"Vawmure," 30.
Vedelius (Nicolaus) *De Cathedra Petri*, 336.
Velenus (Ulricus) his treatise intended to prove that S. Peter never was at Rome, 336.
Vergilius (Polydorus) a work of his expurgated, 103.
Veronica (S.) 204.
Victor I., Bp. of Rome, reproved by S. Irenæus, 69, 238, 308.
Vigilantius, 44, 67, 188.
Vilfrid (Bishop). See Wilfrid.
Villegaignon (Nicholas Durand de) 61.
Vincentius Lirinensis, recommends recourse to the most ancient writers, 175: states that Philip, the Roman Emperor, was a Christian, 355.
Vini (Bishop). See Wini.
Vossius (Gerardus Joannes) mistaken about the Pontifical, 99: his perplexity concerning Gorionides, 338: for whom he claims the authorship of the books *De vocatione Gentium*, 353.
—— *De Histor. Lat.*, 99, 338.
—— *De Histor. Græc.*, 338.
—— *Hist. Pelag.*, 319.
Vossius (Isaacus) when he published the genuine Epistles of S. Ignatius, 235: manuscripts of his corrupted as to the name of the Pseudo-Hegesippus, 338.

Wæchtler (Christfrid) 33.
Waldensis (Thomas) *Doctrinale antiquitatum Fidei*, 22.
Waltonus (Episc.) 166.
Water, Holy, defended by a counterfeit Epistle of Pope Alexander I., 117.
Waterland (Daniel, D.D.) 86.
Whartonus (Henricus) mistaken as to the author of the supposed Donation of Constantine, 360.
—— *Dissertatio de duobus Ælfricis*, 20.
—— *Auctarium ad Usserii Historiam dogmaticam*, 22.
—— *Treatise of the Celibacy of the Clergy*, 23.
Whelocus (Abrahamus) 22.
Whitby (Daniel, D.D.) 41.

Wicelius (Georgius) 98.

Wilfrid (Bp.) deposed by King Ecgfrid, 17; and also by King Aldfrid, 24: consecrated Oftfor at the command of Œdilred, 17, 24.

Wilkins (David, S.T.P.) *Concilia*, 22.

Willet (Andrew, D.D.) *Synopsis Papismi*, 122.

Winchester, Synod of, an. 1076, 23, 93.

Wini (Bishop) deposed by King Coinualch, and afterwards through simony made Bp. of London, 16, 24.

Wolsey (Cardinal) suppressed monasteries, 122.

Zacagnius (Laur. Alexand.) *Collectanea Monumentorum:* vindicates S. Gregory Nyssen's claim to the authorship of the *Testimonia adversus Judæos*, 295—6.

Zapata (Cardinal) his *Index librorum prohib. et expurg.*, 103, 194.

Zonaras (Joannes) *Comment. in Canones Concill.*, 95.

—— *Annales*, 361.

Zosimus (Pope) his conduct in the case of Apiarius, 70—71, 308.

Zurich, Confession of, 384.

Zurich Letters, 22.

www.ingramcontent.com/pod-product-compliance
Lightning Source LLC
LaVergne TN
LVHW020519100826
845148LV00010B/1290
* 9 7 8 1 6 0 6 0 8 4 2 5 0 *